HOW TO CREATE
THE GARDEN YOU WANT

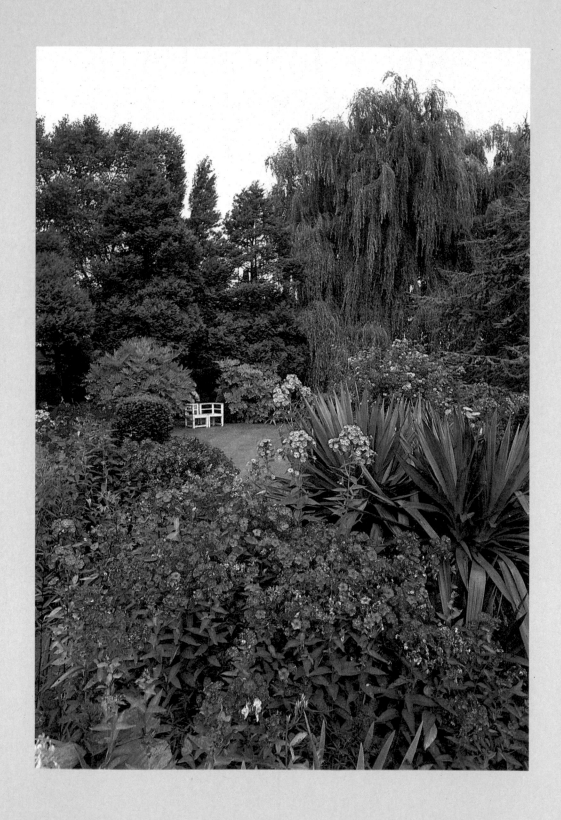

How To Create
The Garden
You Want

CONSULTANT EDITOR:
ARTHUR HELLYER M.B.E.

CHARTWELL
BOOKS, INC.

A QED BOOK

Published by Chartwell Books Inc
A Division of Book Sales Inc
110 Enterprise Avenue, Secaucus,
New Jersey 07094

ISBN 0-89009-793-3

This book was designed and produced by
QED Publishing Ltd
32 Kingly Court
London W1

This book was designed and produced by
QED Publishing Limited
32 Kingly Court, London W1

Coordinating Editor: Geoff Rogers
Senior Editor: Jim Miles
Copy Editor: Mike Darton
Design: Patrick Burton, David Papworth
Editorial Director: Christopher Fagg
Art Director: Alastair Campbell

Typeset in Great Britain by QV Typesetting Limited
Printed and bound in Italy by Poligrafici Calderara S.p.a.
Origination by Hong Kong Graphic Arts Services Centre

Contributors
Richard Gorer
Arthur Hellyer
Peter McHoy
Jim Mather
Yvonne Rees
Alan Toogood
Jack Wilson

Photographs
Gillian Becket
Eric Crichton
Daansmit
Bob Gibbons Photography
Richard and Sally Greenhill
Jerry Harpur
Neill Holmes
Arthur Hellyer
Ian Howes
Patrick Johns
Tom Leighton
National Vegetable Research Station
Photobank
The Plant Photo Library (Susan Roth)
Harry Smith Photography Collection
Photos Horticultural (Michael Warren)
Dennis Woodland

Illustrations
Norman Bancroft-Hunt
Sally Launder
David Papworth
John Woodcock

CONTENTS

PLANTS FOR SPECIAL PURPOSES

COLOR IN THE GARDEN

TREES AND SHRUBS

THE HEALTHY GARDEN

INTRODUCTION

Garden design is a branch of art that is specially suitable for amateurs. It is a notable fact that many of the world's most admired gardens were planned by their owners with little or no advice from professional designers. Part of the explanation is that, unlike buildings, most gardens are in a constant process of change as plants grow too large, or prove unsuitable, for the purpose they were chosen for. As a result, successful garden-making usually demands varying degrees of change and adjustment over a period of years, and this is of course true even of professionally-designed gardens which may require considerable planting alterations as they develop.

Garden planning and design

Professional garden designers invariably prepare accurate plans in order to show their clients what is proposed and to guide the workforce in construction and planting. For a garden that is to be made and planted by the owner-designer such detailed plans are unnecessary — after all, it is far easier to do much of the planning on the ground with sticks, string or powdered lime trickled out of a bag to mark the suggested outlines of paths, lawns, beds, borders and so on. It may indeed save some time and crystallize ideas if a rough sketch plan is prepared before marking out the ground, but such a preliminary sketch is entirely flexible and may be considerably modified as the plan is transferred to actuality. That a plan like this must in any case be regarded as totally tentative, subject to alteration, is inevitable in that without considerable experience of planning it is difficult to relate the areas shown on a sheet of paper with the actual areas on the ground, and in that garden designing is a three-dimensional art whereas plans are only two-dimensional. A perspective sketch gives a three-dimensional effect but is much more difficult to draw. Out on the ground, with the aid of canes to indicate key features such as trees, arches, pergolas or buildings, it is much easier to visualize what the garden is really going to look like as it matures and to ensure that there will be enough tall objects to give the composition height and solidity, to screen parts that need to be hidden and give privacy.

In all but the smallest gardens it is usually wise for a plan not to allow the whole area to be seen at once but to unfold progressively as it is explored. The best preparation for garden-making is to look at as many mature gardens as possible, picking up one idea here, another there, until the whole design begins to shape itself in the mind. This can then be sketched out on paper and finally transferred to the ground. Perhaps only at that stage will it be possible to view the garden properly from different angles, from each creating a mental picture of what the effects will be once the constructional features have been made and the plants have grown up. Even after all this foresight it is probable that adjustments will seem necessary as garden-making proceeds, and maybe years later, when the plants are at last making their full contribution to the scene, still more alterations will appear necessary.

Formal and informal gardens

Gardens may be roughly classified as formal or informal: the formal based mainly on regular, geometric patterns, the informal on much more flowing and irregular shapes. The extreme example of informality is the "natural" or "wild" garden which superficially seems to owe little to any art of the designer although in fact it probably depends greatly for its effect on the skill with which it has been put together and kept in balance by pruning, thinning and replanting. Regrettably, nature left to herself nearly always finishes up by producing a wilderness of weeds and tangled growth.

In practice there is no reason for formal and informal designs not to be combined. A very common, and usually effective, formula is to plan the area close to the house formally and break into increasing informality the farther away from this starting point. In tiny gardens, however, there may well be room for only one style, usually formal, its shape and architectural features chosen to match the building it accompanies.

Specialist gardens

There is one type of gardening that is hardly ever mentioned in books, and is anathema to professional garden designers, and that is specialization in some particular group of plants. Rose lovers, for example, devote most of their gardens to roses irrespective of what this does to the design; alpine plant enthusiasts make raised beds with unmortared retaining walls, or grow their choicest plants in frames; lovers of dwarf conifers plant mini-pinetums; and those who love full-scale trees (and have the space to grow them) make arboretums. These are all perfectly sensible ways of making gardens if that is what the owners require — but the results owe little to the rules of aesthetics.

The garden environment

Choice of plants is regulated by soil, temperature, rainfall and availability of light. Soils may be rich or poor, light or heavy, acid or alkaline, and plants have individual preferences for combinations. Fortunately, most of these characteristics are not too difficult to alter. Soils that are poor can be fed with manures and fertilizers. Those that are too light and porous can be improved by manuring and by forking in moisture-holding materials such as peat, leaf mold, decayed garden refuse, spent hop manure and other bulky organic materials. It may seem a little odd that these same dressings should also improve heavy soils, but they do — partly because they are spongy and help to keep soil open, and also because as they decompose they produce humus, which has a great effect on the texture of soil, improving it by binding tiny particles into larger granules with bigger air spaces between them.

Lime improves soil texture in a similar way, but it can also introduce new problems; some plants object to it, and only grow satisfactorily in soils that are acid and contain no free lime. Other plants prefer alkaline soil, and for these lime can do no harm, providing a simple and safe way of reducing soil acidity. It is, however, more difficult to make alkaline soils acid, although prolonged manuring and the use of sulphate of ammonia as a fertilizer eventually achieves this effect over a period of years.

Another way of catering for plants that do not like the soil-type of the garden is to make special beds for them filled with the soil-type that does suit their needs. All the same, beds of acid soil on an alkaline site need to be raised above the natural ground level, or alkaline water is likely to seep into them.

Temperatures may be either too high or too low for the needs of the plants desired in the garden. There are some plants that survive in very cold places and in the wild may be covered with snow in winter; they may suffer when transferred to even slightly warmer places that have little or no snow in winter. Another potential problem is that plants that are quite safe if they remain dormant throughout the cold season may be at risk if set in a place where winter temperatures vary a lot, for then they may start to grow too soon and the tender young growth may be killed by frost. At the other extreme, gardens in the tropics or sub-tropics may encourage plants to go on growing all year when by nature they should have a resting period; this can be just as fatal to success as too much cold.

Gardeners are often heard to talk of "hardy" and "tender" plants as if there were some hard and fast divisions between them — it is not so. There is a huge range of variability, from plants that begin to suffer when the temperature falls below 15°C (59°F) to those that are unlikely to be damaged until the temperature falls to -18°C (0°F) or even lower.

Many plant encyclopedias divide countries, or even continents, into zones of hardiness, giving the plants zone numbers to indicate where they can survive. The system can be very helpful — but there can of course be great differences in temperature within a single zone, and sometimes even within a garden, so it is always wise to get local advice about exactly what does grow, or to observe in the locality what is thriving in other gardens.

Rainfall can vary tremendously, from the minimal amount of the great deserts to the constant wetness of the rainforests. Plants that have adapted themselves to dry conditions can be killed if planted in wet places and vice versa. Fortunately, one can again usually do something about this, watering plants that require more moisture than the district normally supplies, or protecting in some way those that would otherwise be too wet. Such protection is usually most necessary in winter for the many plants that then suffer from a combination of wet and cold for which they are not adapted.

Finally, there is the light factor. Some plants need a great deal of light to make them flower, others are scorched by too much direct sunlight and much prefer to be in the shade. Books and nursery catalogues usually give reliable advice on these matters. One point they may overlook, however, is that many plants with yellow or yellow-variegated leaves only develop their full color when exposed to fairly strong light: in the shade the color may be dull or lacking.

Evergreen or deciduous?

All plants with foliage can be classified as either evergreen or deciduous. These terms are usually applied to trees and shrubs, but there are also some herbaceous (soft-stemmed) plants that retain their leaves in winter, kniphofias and some irises for example, and many that grow in winter and die down in summer.

There is a tendency for beginners to suppose that evergreens must be superior to deciduous plants in terms of garden decoration, but this is not so. Each class has its uses, and part of the charm of a well-planted garden can be the constant change of foliage colors, mainly in the deciduous trees and shrubs, and the emergence in winter of entirely new patterns of branch and leaf. A garden filled entirely with evergreens can seem heavy and depressing, and the lack of change can become boring.

Trees and shrubs

Trees and the larger shrubs, whether evergreen or deciduous, play an important role in giving height to the overall garden composition. One well-placed tree may become a vital focal point in a vista or, in large gardens, groups of trees may perform a similar function. Landscape gardens depend mainly on trees for their shape and for the contrast between light and shade, open spaces and solid masses, on which all composition is based. The great English landscape gardens of the eighteenth century were made entirely with trees, grass, water and occasional buildings (which might be classical or romantic, Roman temples, gothic ruins or oriental pavilions, according to the taste of the designer and the fashion of the period).

Trees vary in shape, branch pattern and density. Some are wide-spreading, others tall; the overall shape may be rounded, billowy, weeping, conical or columnar. Some trees produce mutations, or sports, that are different in shape from the norm. In the wild these would not be perpetuated but gardeners may see value in them and maintain them by vegetative propagation.

Weeping and columnar (fastigiate) forms have been particularly welcome. The golden weeping willow is a tree of uncertain origin, in which the secondary branches are completely pendulous and the young bark yellow. The common silver birch is called *Betula pendula* because the ends of its branches hang downwards — this is exaggerated in such varieties as 'Dalecarlica', 'Tristis' and 'Youngii'. There are weeping forms of both green-leaved and purple-leaved beech, a beautiful weeping form of the spring cherry, *Prunus subhirtella* 'Pendula Rosea', and many more grown in gardens for their pendulous habit.

At the opposite extreme are forms that hold all their branches erect. The most famous of these is the Lombardy poplar, a fastigiate sport of the black poplar which has transformed the landscape of parts of France and Italy but is not a good garden tree because of its wide-spreading thirsty roots. There are many other columnar trees that are far more suitable, particularly among the evergreen cypresses and also less well known trees such as the Dawyck beech and the cypress oak (*Quercus robur* 'Fastigata'). The Irish yew and the golden-leaved variety named 'Standishii' are both columnar sports of the common yew; the Irish juniper is a narrowly erect form of the common juniper; and *Prunus* 'Amanogawa' is a Japanese flowering cherry so narrowly erect that it is sometimes called the flagpole cherry.

These narrow trees can be used as eye-catchers, especially — and valuably — in small gardens because they take up little space. As a contrast with these strong vertical lines, the garden designer may use wide-spreading, even horizontally-branched shrubs such as the two forms of yew known as 'Dovastoniana' and "Dovastonii Aurea", the first dark green, the second green and gold. Equally impressive, horizontally, are the wide forms of juniper such as *Juniperus X media* "Pfitzerana" and *J. sabina tamariscifolia*, and the horizontally-branched cherry laurels (*Prunus laurocerasus*) such as "Shipkaensis" and "Zabeliana".

Herbaceous perennials

Trees and shrubs are more or less permanent occupants of the garden. They provide the firm "skeleton" of plant design around or within which less permanent plants can be displayed. These are classified as herbaceous perennials, bulbs (which are really herbaceous perennials that have a special kind of food and moisture storage organ but are always listed separately), biennials and monocarpic plants, and annuals. The longevity of herbaceous perennials varies greatly, from quite short-term plants such as lupins and perennial verbascums to very long-lived plants such as goldenrod (*Solidago*) and Michaelmas daisies (*Aster*). All get larger and larger with age and tend to starve themselves out. In gardens it is wise to lift most of them every three or four years, split them up into smaller pieces if that is possible (it is not for plants such as lupins and verbascums which make a single solid crown or tap root), and replant after digging and feeding the soil. Exceptions are peonies, eryngiums, hellebores and a few others which dislike disturbance and are best left alone until there is clear indication that they are deteriorating.

Because of their semi-permanence, these herbaceous perennials are the second-rank plants in the garden designer's stock. They make their full effect more rapidly than trees and shrubs and so can be used to fill in while the latter are growing but not yet occupying the full space allocated to them. They are also useful to maintain a continuity of color and to provide a greater diversity of foliage shapes and colors. They can also be moved and rearranged readily when faults in the original planting are revealed.

Annuals and biennials

At the bottom of the time-scale come annuals and biennials, ephemeral plants which are nevertheless extremely useful for temporary displays, to fill gaps which occur through losses, or because the more permanent plants are not yet fully grown. True annuals live for one year only and, when they have flowered and ripened their seed, they die and decay. Their flowering season is often quite brief but spectacular. The hardy kinds can be sown where they are to flower, the half-hardies raised in some protected place and planted out when there is little further risk of frost.

Biennials resemble annuals in dying after flowering and ripening their seed but they require two years to complete the cycle. Note, however, that they must be resown every year to maintain a continuity of flower. Monocarpics die after flowering and seeding but take an indefinite number of years to complete this cycle. In the main they are plants to be grown for their own interest or beauty, not to fit into a general pattern of display because it is uncertain when they will bloom.

Many plants that are actually perennial are grown as annuals or biennials because this is the simplest and most satisfactory way to treat them. This is true of antirrhinums, *Begonia semperflorens* and *Salvia splendens*, which in temperate climates are generally grown as annuals, and of wallflowers, double daisies *(Bellis)* and Brompton or East Lothian stocks *(Matthiola)* which are grown as biennials. It is becoming true of other plants including zonal pelargoniums (zonal-leaved geraniums) and penstemons, which used to be renewed from cuttings but are increasingly being raised from seed in places where it is too cold in winter for them to survive outdoors. This is due in part to the increase in cost of fuel to heat greenhouses or frames, in part to the great improvement of seed varieties. Such plants as these, used temporarily for display and then destroyed or over-wintered in a protected place, are usually referred to as "bedding plants".

Plants growing in the wild segregate themselves into species which are fairly uniform in character. They have adapted to the particular environment in which they live and any departures from this norm that are not positively useful tend to drop out after a generation or so. If gardeners decide that these variations suit their purpose they can perpetuate them either by increasing them by vegetative means — cuttings, layers, divisions or grafts — or by growing them in isolation from others of their kind in the hope that, when fertilized with their own pollen, they will reproduce the desirable features for which they have been selected. There have been great improvements in producing such true-breeding varieties and, in particular, in developing hybrids which, in their first generation, breed extremely true to type. In seed catalogues these are distinguished as F_1 hybrids (first filial hybrids). Seed of these is always much more expensive than that of ordinary varieties, and the extra cost can perhaps only be justified if it is really necessary to have plants that are very uniform in habit and flower color.

Climbers

One type of plant which has not yet been mentioned (because it spans several of the groupings already discussed) comprises the climbers. These may be woody or herbaceous, perennial or annual. Climbers also differ widely in the manner in which they climb. The simplest, such as the climbing roses, are thrusters which push quite stiff but long stems through the branches of trees and shrubs and hang on with their thorns. Next in simplicity of means are the twiners, such as honeysuckles and wisteria, which wind themselves around any firm object they meet, whether it be the trunk of a tree or the laths in a trellis.

More sophisticated are the tendril climbers, such as sweet peas, which are annuals, or vines, which are perennials. These have slender, spiralling appendages which wind around any suitably slender object, be it twig or netting, wire or trellis. Clematis uses a similar method but it is the leaf stalks that do the twining.

Lastly, there are the self-clingers which, either with aerial roots (ivy and climbing hydrangea) or with little adhesive pads (*Parthenocissus tricuspidata*, the Boston ivy), cling to any firm object, even a smooth vertical wall.

Climbers are of great value to the garden designer because they enable walls, fences and other solid objects to be clothed, pergolas and arches covered, and otherwise uninteresting trees made to burst out in cascades of beautiful bloom or decorative foliage. They may be thought of as fulfilling much the same purpose as the wallpapers and drapes used by interior decorators, and in fact, there is a great deal of similarity between the use of many plants in gardens, especially those chosen for their flower color or leaf shape, and the use of fabrics and paints indoors. Both garden makers and interior decorators are trying to make harmonies or striking color schemes, and each must maintain a satisfactory balance of scale and a pleasing disposition of objects. It is no accident that some of the most successful garden makers have also been distinguished interior decorators.

Here, then, is the cast which the garden maker can dispose according to inclination. It numbers many thousands of varieties and it is small wonder that the plant population of most gardens is in constant change as owners experiment with one thing and another to see if it is an improvement or just for the pleasure of enjoying something different. It is the design of the garden and the architectural features it contains — buildings, walls, terraces, pergolas, statues, fountains and so forth — plus trees and shrubs that give the garden a more or and decorations of a house, which are subject to easy regarded as embellishment, rather like the furnishings and decorations of a house, which is subject to easy change according to the whim of its owner.

Cost and maintenance

Finally there are two matters to be considered which have nothing to do with aesthetics but everything to do with economics and mechanics. How much will it cost, and how much energy will it take to maintain the garden once it has been made? Here we meet the old paradox: gardens that cost a lot to make are often the easiest and cheapest to run. Paving costs more than grass, and architectural features are usually more expensive than plants, but neither requires much maintenance. When it comes to the plants themselves, trees and shrubs generally cost more than herbaceous perennials and annuals, but are usually easier and cheaper to look after. Bedding plants and bulbs can be fairly costly and time-consuming, although a good deal depends on the way in which they are grown. Daffodils or crocuses naturalized in grass can be left alone for years, but tulips and hyacinths in beds may need to be lifted and replanted every year, especially if used to maintain color for a long time in a sequence of flowers.

Science and technology have lightened many gardening tasks. Herbicides take the backache out of weeding, and light electric or gasoline-engined lawn-mowers make short work of lawn mowing. In large gardens, ride-on mowers or garden tractors can save a great deal of time and labor. But machines themselves require maintenance, and repairs can be expensive.

So, to sum up, if you are short of money and of time or strength, go easy on lawns, herbaceous borders and bedding out and concentrate instead on a few well-chosen trees and shrubs and ground covered with paving or gravel or maybe a mixture of the two. Plants can be grown in gravel if there is soil not far below, and gravel beds, or even complete gravel gardens, are becoming increasingly popular as a means of saving time and labor.

Difficult sites
Suggestions on those problems that confront most gardeners, such as shaded areas under large trees and unsightly sheds.

The healthy garden
Basic advice on general care and hygiene in the garden plus information on the prevention, recognition and treatment of pests and diseases. Propagation techniques to keep your garden stocked with new plants.

Trees and shrubs
Suggestions on using the form and color of a wide range of trees and shrubs.

Backdrops and boundaries
Advice on deciding on garden screens whether they are walls, hedges or fences. Information on construction, cultivation and maintenance.

Plants for special purposes
Ideas on choosing plants to achieve a specific effect or perform a particular function.

Color in the garden
The ground rules of effective color planning with tables to help you to select a color scheme for your garden.

Garden features
Advice and suggestions on a wide range of garden architecture and patio areas.

BACKDROPS
&
BOUNDARIES

Hedges can provide distinctive features as well as effective boundaries. Yew grows so densely that it can be trimmed into arches (**right**) to echo the formal style of this garden pool.

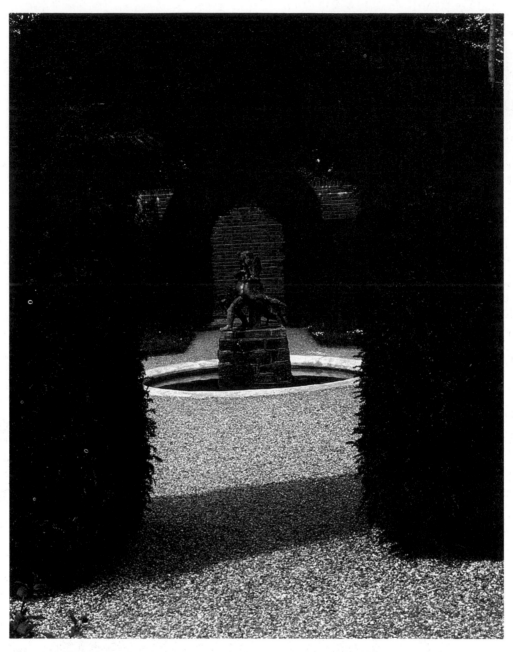

Most of us seek that sense of privacy, even if it is sometimes illusory, which a boundary fence or hedge gives us. It marks our plot out from the others, and forms a framework for the garden. You do not have to be a recluse to want privacy or to define your boundary.

Walls, fences and hedges do more than mark out our territory, however. To a large extent they are the setting, the backdrop, or the stage in which we set our plants. They are part of good garden design.

There are, of course, times when a visible barrier is *not* the right answer. If the view from your home is a stunning one, the last thing that you'll want to do is block it out. Even so, you'll probably want to keep animals either in or out of your garden, and to have some physical mark of your territory. If you are ambitious, and the site is suitable, you could even make a

modest ha-ha; but there are other boundary markers, such as a post-and-chain, which can be small and unobtrusive. Even plastic-coated wire mesh with low-growing shrubs in front can be effective. Whatever the size and shape of your garden, there are good ways and there are bad ways of marking what is, after all, its external skeleton.

Since hedges and screens are a backcloth for many of your plants, and an integral part of many well-designed gardens, it is a mistake to think of them only as boundary markers. *Internal* hedges, or walls, play an important role that should not be overlooked.

A screen, whether it is a hedge, a wall, or a fence, also benefits the plants. It can provide shelter and possibly even a microclimate within the garden — but some provide shelter more efficiently than others.

Deciding what you want

You will need to take into account both the *function* of the "fence" and the *appearance*. Ignore either consideration and you may well regret the decision.

If you are disabled or infirm, or simply do not like the aspect of hard physical work in gardening, then the required amount of initial effort and of later maintenance may also affect your decision.

The pros and cons of the major alternatives are set out below, but do not overlook the less obvious benefits: a hedge requires a lot more maintenance than a wall, but it is better at filtering the wind without causing turbulence, and it is more likely to encourage wildlife. There are also drawbacks to hedges that may not be obvious at first; if you want to use a hedge or living screen as an attractive background for your borders, you will also have to cope with the fact that it will impoverish the soil for the other plants near by.

Walls

Few gardeners would doubt their competence to plant a hedge; yet for those with neither the muscle-power nor the confidence that comes with DIY jobs well done, the prospect of building a wall can seem daunting. It is not difficult if you take it in logical steps and easy stages and if you have not done a job like this before, it can give you a tremendous sense of satisfaction when it is finished.

The advantages of a wall are its robustness and lack of maintenance. If it is high enough it may also make a satisfactory background for many wall-trained plants, from fan-trained fruit to decorative wall shrubs. A brick or solid block wall is also more peep-proof than most wooden fences of the same height. A brick or concrete wall does not have to be unimaginative; there are many permutations of materials and patterns that you can try.

The disadvantages are mainly two-fold: cost and effort. This applies mainly to brick, and to a lesser extent to concrete blocks. All materials, even in natural dry stone walling, have to be laid on a firm base, which generally means proper concrete foundations.

In addition to the cost of the bricks or blocks there will be the expense of concrete (and possibly hardcore) and mortar. This can add quite substantially to the total outlay — especially if you decide to hire a concrete-mixer too.

Laying a wall can be hard physical work, and should not be rushed.

A solid wall can cause a lot of wind turbulence; this is much less of a problem with pierced blocks (often called screen blocks, although they do not offer a screen of privacy).

Garden walls create turbulence on their leeward side (**above right**); hedges "filter" the wind to shelter plants effectively.

Picket fencing, ranch style fencing and elegantly trimmed hedges harmonize in this American garden (**right**).

Fences

Fences are generally cheaper than brick or concrete, and much more "instant" than a hedge. New, they can also look quite attractive; but difficulties come with age. Then they begin to look jaded, and gaps and cracks all too frequently precede different types of rot and the structure's eventual collapse. Quality can be as variable as the design — and there is a bewildering range to choose from.

Advantages include instant cover or privacy at less cost (and probably time) than a brick or concrete wall.

Disadvantages include the fact that if you want your fence to last, you will have to apply a preservative every second year, and even then a fence is likely to succumb long before a wall. Many are not peep-proof (although this may not matter).

Hedges

Hedges are hard to beat for sheer variety of shape, color and form. Some are evergreen, some deciduous, some have flowers, a few have the bonus of berries, many with much more interesting shape and form than the useful but overworked privet. A hedge can range in height from 30cm (1ft) or so (such as the dwarf box *Buxus suffruticosa*, and dwarf

lavenders) to screens more than 4.5m (15ft) high (such as *X Cupressocyparis leylandii*).

Advantages: sheer variety, and the ability to provide the *changing* interest associated with living plants, are always attractions. Low cost is another. (If you can take cuttings, and have the patience, a hedge may cost you nothing.) Even if you have to buy plants, it still almost certainly works out cheaper than a fence or a wall.

Disadvantages: revolve around the additional problems of growing other plants close to the hedge, and the effort of keeping a hedge trimmed.

Do not be afraid to mix

The danger of looking at the options in turn in isolation is that you may miss the possibility of good combinations that might give you the best of all worlds.

On these and the following pages there are examples in pictures of fences on walls, hedges with fences, and hedges with walls. The results can be aesthetically pleasing; alternatively, in such a combination the attractions of one may offset the shortcomings of the other. Or you could perhaps improve things by "grafting on" a different type of background to one that is already there.

Walls

Traditionally walls are made from brick. They can in fact be quite decorative, but you may feel that a plain brick boundary wall is a little old-fashioned and boring.

A vast expanse of brickwork does look overpowering, unless you relieve it with suitable plants, or combine it with other materials — perhaps flints if you live in the right area, or pierced concrete blocks.

Remember that brickwork can be painted, which can be very effective in a courtyard style of garden.

If you simply do not like brick, you could use one of the many types of concrete walling blocks available. If multicolored walls appeal, plenty of manufacturers produce blocks that should keep you happy. And if you decide on something more 'natural', such as imitation natural stone, again there are plenty of suitable products.

For a fairly low wall, you could actually use natural stone, although you should make sure you have a suitable source of supply locally before you set your heart on this, or the expense may become prohibitive. Transportation costs could also be high.

The desired height of your wall should affect any decision about materials. Natural stone would look out of place in a wall about 2m (6½ft) high, whereas concrete blocks, perhaps a combination of pierced and solid, could look perfectly acceptable. A combination of brick and pierced concrete blocks may look even better. If you want privacy, the pierced blocks can go high in the wall; if that is not so important, they might perhaps look more decorative in the center surrounded by brickwork.

Cost, of course, has to be taken into account. The higher the wall, the more important finance becomes. A wall 1.2m (4ft) high needs four times the number of bricks than one 60cm (2ft) high — not twice as many — because it has to be of "full brick" instead of "half-brick" (in other words, you need a double thickness of bricks to provide the strength). If the wall is long, you also need strengthening piers. It will pay you to calculate the costs of the alternatives carefully before committing yourself.

Ideas for the use of various materials are given on the following pages, but to help you appreciate the pros and cons of some of the materials that you may be choosing from, the main options are summarized below:

Staggered concrete blocks provide an interesting "texture", but call for skill and precision in laying (**6**). Concrete blocks are simple to lay, and they are available in various colors and textures (**7**).

Clay bricks

Most bricks are made from clay, but there are concrete bricks (as opposed to blocks) too. Their uses in the garden are similar, but generally the coloring and feel of clay bricks are more sympathetic to all but the most formal gardens.

You are more likely to be able to blend the garden structures and walls in with your home using a clay brick — although it might be quite difficult to get an exact match if you do not know the name of the brick used for your home. And even if you do, that particular brick might not be suitable for garden walls. The bricks used in home construction are, after all, only exposed on one side; a garden wall is open to being wet and frozen from both sides and, unless it is frost-resistant the surface will begin to flake and crumble or crack.

You must be prepared to shop around for the right brick. Brick prices can vary considerably, especially when you take delivery into account.

Concrete blocks

It is important to distinguish between solid concrete blocks that resemble either bricks or stone, and pierced concrete blocks, which are very different in application as well as appearance.

There are many manufacturers of concrete walling blocks, some distributing only in a local area. Each one usually offers a range of sizes and finishes. Of the concrete blocks they produce, some make no pretence to be

A brick wall can be made more interesting by working in a few coloured bricks to form a design (**4**). Oblique bricks call for a lot of difficult cutting, and special tools. Strictly for the ambitious (**5**).

anything but what they are (albeit with a pleasant finish); others are so well disguised that at a distance they can be difficult to tell from natural stone. Imitation stone blocks often come in different sizes so that they may be used to give a "random" effect.

For pure visual appeal, there is a lot to be said for choosing either a really good reconstituted stone finish or blocks that are brazenly concrete (perhaps using some colored finish). The least pleasing effect is "stone" that is clearly fake.

As with bricks, you must allow for the cost of foundations and mortar when calculating cost. Again, transportation can sometimes also be a substantial additional charge.

Natural stone and brick combine well (**3**), though stones as large as these can be difficult to work with. Flints are smaller and easier.

Set the stones in a stiff mortar mix as the brickwork is built up, packing them closely.

7

6

5

Basket weave brickwork (**1**) looks pretty, but it has aligning vertical joints that need wire mesh reinforcement. Running bond, usually used for a single thickness wall, here is used double (**2**).

Random "stone" blocks topped by pierced (screen) blocks look good for patios as well as boundaries (**8**). Ordinary concrete blocks can be rendered and then painted to make a distinctive surround for screen blocks (**9**).

Pierced (screen) concrete blocks

This includes all forms of decorative blocks, including circular and other molds as well as the much more common rectangular type with various patterns within the rectangle.

Although often used as part of a boundary wall (perhaps in combination with brick) and occasionally for the whole wall, the rather symmetrical, almost austere appearance of a whole wall of pierced blocks is best reserved for patios and internal areas, where they usually suit the more formal style.

Area for area, pierced block walling generally works out cheaper than solid concrete blocks, and because pierced blocks are usually quite large, less mortar is required, and you have the advantage of seeing quite rapid progress as you lay them.

Pierced (screen) blocks are popular for patio walls, but can make an attractive boundary between properties too (**10**).

Pierced blocks can be useful for relieving a solid brick wall (**11**). A single row may be enough.

Concrete blocks and stone walls

Random natural stone is usually used for low informal walls, but if you have the patience and are prepared to spend some time and effort on the job, it can be used to create a more formal type of wall. One like this must be mortared for strength and stability, and needs to be of ample thickness.

Although there are many makes, and lots of variations in pattern, and even in size, there are basically three types of concrete walling that you might want to consider for your garden: screen (pierced block) walling, block walling, and imitation stone walling. They all have a place in the garden, and they can be mixed, but generally it is best not to mix all three or your garden will begin to look rather like a display area for walling materials.

Whichever one you choose, much the same advice on buying and building applies, with the main exception to the general rule arising in reference to building a screen block wall.

Screen block walls

Screen (pierced) walls are popular because they act as a barrier and as a wind filter, without casting the shade that is part of the penalty you pay for a solid wall or fence.

If you want something that looks more substantial, you could build the screen blocks either centrally into the wall, or along the top of the wall. If you are combining brick and concrete blocks, check the sizes carefully — the block dimensions occasionally vary from one manufacturer to another, and you could find that one or other dimension of the blocks does not match with the brickwork's.

Construction

There is a fundamental difference between the way that screen blocks are laid, and the way that other blocks and bricks are laid. Because screen blocks are all the same size (there are no 'half-blocks', and because of the pierced center design it is silly to try to cut a block), you cannot *bond* them in the same way as bricks. Bonding (staggering so that there is an overlap) gives a wall strength, and reduces the risk of splitting or collapse under strain or impact.

For that reason 'ties' must be embedded in the mortar across the joints. (Pieces of old wire netting will do, although you can buy proper ties from a builders' supplier. Pilasters, upright pillars, are also of crucial importance. Some manufacturers offer pilasters of different thicknesses (and therefore strength), such as those of 30cm (12in) or 20cm (8in) diameter; the larger the diameter, generally the greater the stability. The need for such strength should be considered, for example, if the pillars are to support say a car-port roof. If there is no specific need for strength, the normal pilasters should be adequate.

Ideally, all pilasters should be reinforced if the wall is more than three blocks high, and certainly if it is over 1.2m (4ft). Angle-iron or something similar should be pushed down inside the hollow center of the pilaster. It can be

Aubretia and other plants find a convenient home on this brick and tile wall (**left**). Many rockery plants grow splendidly on garden walls; the warm dry conditions created during the summer months suit them perfectly. Flowering plants effectively soften the edges of such 'inanimate' boundaries.

mortared into position as you gradually build up the wall.

You will have to be particularly accurate and careful in laying the blocks. Because the blocks are so regular and have a fine finish, irregularities in laying, and poor joints, will be very visible in the finished wall.

A mortar mix of 1 part masonry cement to 5 or 6 parts soft sand is suitable for bonding. This ordinary mix may look rather gray against a brilliant white block, however, in which case you could use 1 part cement, 1 part lime, and 5 or 6 parts sand to give a whiter finish. Alternatively, you could use the ordinary mortar for the basic bonding and then point between the blocks with white or coloured mortar.

Concrete blocks

Concrete blocks are laid in a similar way to bricks; much the same principles apply. Some blocks are made in different sizes, however, so that the builder can simulate the type of effect obtained with natural stone. But before purchasing, calculations should ensure that at least some dimensions are compatible — perhaps depths, with mortar joints, of 5cm (2in), 10cm (4in) and 15cm (6in) — so that

overall alignment can still be maintained. Plan the pattern carefully beforehand. It is probably better to start with a wall of more regular bricks or blocks first.

Natural stone

Do not set your heart on natural stone unless you either live near a local source of supply, or are prepared to pay a substantial premium for having the real thing instead of a concrete imitation. To see what is available, try calling stone suppliers listed in your classified telephone directory.

Dressed stone may be available, in which case you can lay it normally, but you are more likely to be able to get 'random stone'.

Random stone walls should never be tall — 90cm (3ft) is high enough. They have to be fairly wide for their height, to make them stable.

The wall should taper slightly toward the top on both sides. Use large stones for the bottom layers, smaller ones towards the top. Use some larger ones as 'tie stones' placed *across* the wall.

With skill you may be able to make a dry stone wall (without mortar), but for your first attempt it is probably best to mortar the stones together.

Brick walls

Bricklaying is not difficult, and a low garden wall — or better still, a small raised bed within the garden — is a good job with which to start.

Although the common stretcher bond (each brick overlapping the ones below by half its length) is practical and easy to lay, do not think that brick walls all have to be the same. There need be nothing dull or boring about brick.

Before you start on the more decorative finishes, however, it is a good idea to become proficient at simple bricklaying. There is almost certain to be some small project that you could tackle first — maybe to create a small raised bed (even a raised pond), or perhaps a brick barbecue.

You should soon gain the confidence to tackle more ambitious projects...such as a boundary wall. Low boundary walls are not difficult, but walls higher than about 45cm (18in) should be full-brick (two rows wide), and for some bonds you may have to cut quite a number of bricks to size. As boundary walls are usually long, strengthening piers must be introduced every 2.4m (8ft) or so on a single thickness brick wall. On a thicker long wall you may also need to provide expansion joints, in which case it is worth reading a book on bricklaying first.

Flemish bond is decorative but is not considered as strong as English bond. You will have to be prepared to cut some bricks for this pattern.

Honeycomb brickwork is usually built by omitting alternative bricks on alternative courses. This shows a variation with deeper holes.

This bonding pattern has a basket-weave effect, but the horizontal courses give it more strength than a normal basket weave bond.

English bond, with alternating colors of 'headers' and 'stretchers'. A large expanse can be brightened by using two different bricks to create a pattern.

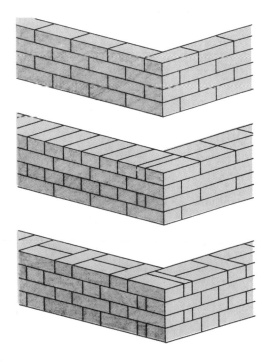

Stretcher bond (**top**) is simple to lay, and there is no need to cut bricks — the one to choose for a single thickness ('half-brick') wall. English bond (**centre**) is easy to lay, strong, and a good choice for double-thickness ('full-brick') wall. You will need to cut bricks to synchronize the bonding pattern. Flemish bond (**above**) can look particularly decorative.

Choosing the right brick

This really is important. Many of the bricks sold by builders' suppliers are unsuitable, and surprisingly frequently their staff do not appreciate the various technical qualities of the bricks that they sell. Unless you are an expert in bricks, there is certainly no way that you will be able to tell whether a brick is suitable simply by looking at it.

You should use a *frost-resistant* brick. Check with the manufacturer or someone who really knows, if you are in any doubt. Some bricks that are perfectly suitable for a house wall may start to flake and crumble if used for a garden wall.

Most of us think first of clay bricks, but there are bricks made from other materials, such as calcium silicate (which are more regular and 'clinical' in appearance, and generally of a pale colour). Again you need to check whether they are suitable for a garden wall.

All this may sound rather confusing, but it does not mean that you should just give up any aesthetic considerations which, after all, may be one of the most significant reasons for choosing brick.

A rough finish and muted colors can look right for a farmhouse; a brighter, more 'finished', perhaps redder, brick could be more in keeping with a formal modern setting, for example.

Preparing the ground

Do not be tempted to skimp on the foundations. The width of the foundation should be about three times the width of the wall, but for a low wall — for example, of 60cm (2ft) — this can be reduced to say twice the width.

For a wall only a single brick or block wide (known as a 'half brick' wall), 13cm (5in) of hardcore and 15cm (6in) of concrete would be adequate; but for a 'full brick' wall (two bricks side by side), increase the concrete by about 8cm (3in). Use 1 part cement to 5 parts combined aggregate.

Step by step

Prepare the trench for the foundation, and consolidate the hardcore before filling with concrete. Tamp the concrete to compact it, then leave for about a week to allow it to harden. The surface of the finished foundation should be several inches below ground level.

The first course, below ground level, will need a strong mortar mix of 1 part masonry cement to 3 parts sharp sand. For subsequent layers, use the normal mortar mix of 1 part masonry cement to 4 or 5 parts soft sand. Use a suspended cord line to lay the bricks to.

Build up the corners several bricks high, then fill in between them (some useful bonding patterns are illustrated below). To lay a brick, place a 'sausage' of mortar in the centre of the brick or block, and roll it back with the trowel to make a fairly smooth layer about 12mm (½in) thick. When laying it up to a brick on the same level, place two small slices of mortar on the end first.

Press the brick in place, and use the handle of the trowel to tap it level. Use the trowel to remove any surplus mortar from the joints.

Fences

A fence is by far the quickest way to screen your garden or mark your boundary. It is obviously more 'instant' than a hedge — which may take several years to grow to the height that you require — and quicker than a brick or block wall to erect.

Wooden fences

Although most fences are close-board or something similar (because these offer privacy), there are many other options well worth considering.

Most fences provide more than merely a screen for people: they offer protection to plants in exposed places and even a framework for suitable climbers (if you provide the necessary additional support).

For complete privacy, a close-boarded fence is the answer. Interwoven fencing is a good screen from a distance, but not peep-proof at close quarters.

Posts

A fence is only as strong as its supports. A solid fence offers a lot of wind resistance and requires stronger posts than an open fence. Sizes generally vary between 50mm x 75mm (2in x 2½in) and 100mm x 150mm (4in x 6in). You should also allow sufficient depth in the ground; as a guide, a low fence intended to rise 60cm (2ft) above ground needs at least 30cm

(1ft) below ground. For a fence 1.8m (6ft) high, there should be at least 75cm (2ft 6in) of post below ground.

The fence manufacturer should advise on the size of posts required — if in doubt, though, err on the large side even if it means paying a bit more.

All timber posts should be treated with a preservative, preferably pressure or vacuum impregnated by the fencing supplier. If you cut the timber for any reason, this is likely to expose untreated timber in the center; overcome this by soaking the cut end in a preservative.

Concrete posts solve the problem of rot, but not everyone likes the appearance. In the right setting, however, they can be perfectly acceptable. Most are cast with grooves to take a fencing panel, and this does make erection a little easier.

A less common option is a metal post — again with grooves in to take a fence panel.

You must be careful to order the right type and number of concrete or metal posts — for, as opposed to working with wooden posts, you need to specify what is required in the way of corners, and ends, together with the number of intermediate posts (because of the position of slots for the panels).

Chain-link and other wire fences

The posts at each end of a wire, chain link or chestnut paling fence need struts to take the strain when the wire is pulled tight.

Metal post supports

If you do not like the idea of digging or boring holes, and perhaps mixing concrete to pack back into them, you could use a metal fixing post instead. There are several kinds, varying in sophistication, but the principle in all is the same.

The metal stake is driven into the ground using a sledge-hammer or club hammer (there is an attachment available to protect the top of the post support while you drive it in).

The advantages of metal supports are that they demand less effort than digging and filling holes, and you do not have to buy, carry, and mix concrete. The posts can be smaller (although the saving on the post does not in itself pay for the cost of the post holder), and do not rot in the ground.

The disadvantages are that you must make sure the post fits, and it is not always easy to drive them in absolutely straight (which is vital). In some circumstances you may find they look obtrusive, even though only a small section is visible at the base of the post.

Concrete panels

The panels are slotted into the grooves in the concrete posts. Do not do this until the concrete anchoring the posts has set firmly.

The panels sometimes seen around commercial premises are undisguised concrete and hardly attractive. There are finishes available, however, that you might find acceptable as a surround to a patio. Although one

---

Erecting a wooden fence

1 Start by marking the line of the intended fence with string stretched between two stakes, and lay the posts in approximately the right positions. Remember that the distance between the center of one post and the next is not the length of the fencing panel, but the panel plus post.

2 Make the first hole. You can dig this out with a spade, but a post-hole borer should make easier work of it.

3 Pack bricks or rubble around the base to hold the post upright, and check for plumb in both directions, using a long spirit-level. Once you are confident that it is true, pack more rubble round the base to firm it, and check verticals again.

4 Lay the first panel on the ground butted up to the post as a guide to the correct positioning of the next post. Make the next hole.

5 Insert the second post as the first, but also check that the two are the same height by using a string stretched taut at the final

height, or by using a spirit-level on a board spanning the two.

If the fence has rails that have to be jointed to the post, fit the rails into the first post before you position the second (an extra pair of hands really is essential).

6 Fix the panel into position with galvanized nails or screws. You may find it easier to use brackets to fix the panels. It is in fact more convenient to fix these to the posts before you erect them.

7 Always use a line stretched between the ends at the height of the top of the fence, to ensure that the height is even.

8 Try to ensure that the main part of a timber fence does not come into contact with soil. Either use a gravel board (which you can replace more easily if it rots), or rest the fence on a layer of bricks or blocks.

9 Finally, firm the posts again, double-checking that they are vertical. Small posts can be firmed with rammed earth and rubble, but it is generally better to concrete in posts with more than about 90cm (3ft)

above ground. If you are setting the posts in concrete, nail temporary struts to keep the post in position until it sets (wait for a few days before removing them).

Warning: **do not attempt to erect tall or solid fences on a windy day, or if strong winds are forecast.**

Fences made with concrete panels (**above**) can provide a durable boundary but may have a rather 'industrial' appearance. Choose panels with a more attractive finish than just plain concrete, a simulated brick or a 'shiplap' pattern for example. Make sure that the posts are correctly aligned before sliding the panels one by one into the preformed grooves.

side has the traditional finish and the usual concrete strip appearance, the other (ideally 'inside') side has an imitation brick finish. The effect is one of a white brick wall, but you can paint it with any good quality exterior grade emulsion paint to make a potentially exciting backdrop for your plants.

Concrete comes in other disguises too — as simulated stone walls, or in an overlapping 'shiplap' pattern for instance.

A word of warning about erecting a concrete fence: the posts must align *exactly*, or you will find it difficult, if not impossible, to slide the inflexible panels into the grooves that should — but do not — correspond.

Wire mesh

Probably not taken seriously enough as a form of fence, the various wire mesh fences available are not serious contenders for a front garden boundary. Yet they have potential as useful dividers between back gardens where you want a fairly open outlook and are not bothered about privacy. They are also useful where the garden borders open countryside, many of them being inconspicuous, especially when shrubs are planted against them.

A wire fence, especially chain-link, can be both strong and cheap. It is also easy to erect (see below), but the job must be done properly if disappointment is not to follow. It is imperative that wire fences be properly strained and kept taut.

Galvanized wire should last for 10 years or more; plastic-coated wire should have an even longer life, and also looks better.

Erecting a chain-link fence

Chain-link is quick and easy to put up, but time and care must be taken to erect the posts properly. Posts bought directly from the fence manufacturer are likely to be made of angle iron, although some makes of fencing are also designed to be fixed to wooden or concrete posts. Some steel supports are plastic-coated. Screwed eye-bolts can be used to tension the line wires between concrete or timber posts; also needed are stretcher bars and winding brackets as well as strainer bars. If you are in doubt about the necessary bits and pieces, ask the dealer's advice.

1   Start by marking out the line of the fence with string, then inserting the posts into levelled ground. The holes for angle-iron supports should be about 45cm (18in) square and 60cm (2ft) deep for a fence of about 1.2m (4ft) height; increase the depth to about 75cm (2ft 6in) for taller fences. Straining stay holes can be smaller — about 45cm (18in) by 30cm (1ft), and 45cm (18in) deep. Intermediate posts should not be more than 3m (10ft) apart.

Ideally, the posts should be concreted into position. Make sure that the straining bars are positioned on the right side to take the strain.

2   Once the posts are fixed firmly, unroll the line wire and strain it between the posts. For a fence of 1.2m (4ft) or less, two wires will be sufficient, but for more than this height use a third wire. The wires are fixed to the winders bolted to the angle-iron at end and corner posts. It is threaded through suitable holes in the intermediate posts.

3   Unroll the fence against the first post, and pass a stretcher bar through the last row of meshes, bolting this to the post.

4   Unwind the roll, keeping it as taut as you can, and use wire or string to fix it temporarily to the line wires. Fasten the mesh to each intermediate and straining post in turn, maintaining tension. Wherever there is a change of direction, use a stretcher bar to bolt the chain link to the post.

Finally, fix the fence to the line wires with tying wire. Ideally, it should be fixed to the top wire every 15cm (6in), but intervals of 45cm (18in) should be adequate along the bottom and middle wires.

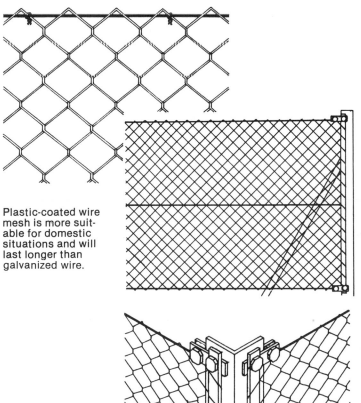

Tension the top line between the posts and attach the chain-link mesh with twists of tying wire at 15cm (6in) intervals (**left**).

Plastic-coated wire mesh is more suitable for domestic situations and will last longer than galvanized wire.

For fences higher than 1.2m (4ft) use three wires to stabilize the mesh between the posts (**left**). Attach the mesh to the middle and bottom wires about every 45cm (18in). Brace the end posts with angled struts, ideally concreted into the ground in the same way as the end, corner and intermediate posts.

Where the fence changes direction pass stretcher bars through the last row of meshes and bolt these to the metal posts (**left**).

Some alternatives

If the prospect of the more conventional fencing panels seems boring, or does not fit in with the tone of your garden, and you do not want a wall, there are plenty of other possibilities. Many of them have attractive-sounding names — palisade (or picket), ranch-style, and wattle, for instance — and each can take on an important role in the right setting.

If privacy is not the first consideration, do not overlook trellis panels. This kind of fence or screen is very useful *within* the garden: covered with climbing plants it can become an invaluable and atmospheric element of the garden. A combination of close-board fencing with a trellis top can give you the best of both worlds.

Ranch-type fencing looks attractive as a boundary to a generally open-plan garden.

Hazel wattle fences or osier hurdles have a very rural look, and can be just right in a coun-try garden. They are very useful for protecting newly-planted or early-flowering shrubs, and for partitioning off or screening a section of the garden. On the other hand, they can soon begin to look the worse for wear.

No matter how attractive a particular fence seems in isolation, however, you must consider the practicalities and decide whether it will actually do the job you have in mind. A post-and-rail fence might be useful for keeping horses in, but it certainly does not keep dogs and other small animals out. Palisade or picket fencing might be chosen because it looks superb when it is newly painted white, but if you are unwilling to paint it regularly to keep it looking that way, maybe you should think again (or choose a PVC version). If it is a windbreak you want, then neither of these would do, but a wattle fence would.

Always try to match visual appeal with practical function.

Ranch fencing

Although ranch fencing has much in common with post-and-rail fencing — horizontal bars fixed between posts — it is much more decorative, especially if it is painted white (or is made from white PVC).

There are many kinds; you can make it yourself or buy kits. The horizontal planks are usually about 10-15cm (4-6in) wide and 2.5cm (1in) thick. Typically about 10cm (4in) is left between the boards. Most makes are designed to fix to PVC posts, but some can be screwed into timber posts or bolted to concrete posts.

The gap between boards means that the garden is still fairly exposed, but you can opt for a version to which you can fix boards on the opposite side, facing the gaps, to give a louvered effect.

A white finish is impressive — until it becomes dirty. If you are not prepared to paint the timber regularly to keep it looking good,

White ranch fencing creates an "open-look" boundary to this cottage garden (**left**). Such fencing blends well with garden plants, particularly small shrubs. For a clean look keep it freshly painted in white, or buy white PVC fencing kits for a maintenance-free finish.

There are several alternatives to conventional fencing panels that you can use to create various boundary styles (**right**). Wattle provides an effective screen and a natural background for garden plants. Bamboo or reed screens also look suitably "organic" and are ideal for highlighting small areas. Be sure to replace these regularly. Post-and-rail and ranch fencing both create a sense of spaciousness and look particularly good with garden shrubs planted close by. Chestnut paling provides a low-cost boundary useful while hedges mature. Trellis panels are available in many styles and are ideal as supports for ornamental climbing plants.

Wattle

Bamboo screen

Post-and-rail

Ranch fencing

Chestnut paling

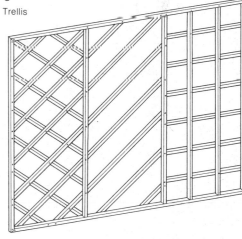

Trellis

quickly erected, and so has its uses. It is probably most worth thinking about if you want to make your garden reasonably animal-proof while a new hedge is becoming established. By the time the hedge has grown sufficiently, the paling fence may well have become rather untidy and ugly — but it will have served its purpose.

A trellis
The sort of trellis panels intended purely as a support for climbing plants should not be considered for a fence. (Most of the diamond-pattern trellises are plant supports rather than fences.)

Much more suitable for use as a boundary, but really better as a screen or support within the garden, are the trellis panels made about the same size as normal fencing panels. In the right place, perhaps dividing off a section of the garden, they mark territory without isolating it — and are ideal if you want to grow a multitude of climbing plants.

Erect trellis panels exactly as you would ordinary fencing panels.

Wattle hurdles
Wattle hurdles are ideal for screening the compost heap or an oil tank. They are not unattractive at any time, and during the summer moreover they make a natural-looking background for most garden plants.

You could also use them in combination with a hedge, perhaps to afford protection and privacy while the hedge is becoming established.

Wattle hurdles are generally supported by stakes driven into the ground; there is no need to undertake the high cost of quality fencing posts.

Their main disadvantage is their relatively short life — perhaps five to ten years. The supporting stakes are likely to rot first, so it is worthwhile checking these every year to see whether replacing them could extend the overall life of the fence.

Bamboo or reed screens
These are also useful for providing a screen or backdrop *within* the garden, but they are not widely available, nor are they particularly durable. You may, therefore, prefer to use them for small areas of screening. You need to provide stout posts (in relation to the diameter of the canes), which can spoil the effect, and to be prepared to replace the screen every four years or so. However, in the right setting, perhaps as part of a "Japanese" garden, this kind of fence can be ideal.

Post-and-rail
This type is useful for a paddock, convenient for a very large garden — but totally unsuitable for a small one.

Assuming that there is no compulsion to make your garden animal-proof, scale is the important consideration. If you have rolling

either choose PVC, or instead of painting it keep it treated with a wood preservative (you can choose one to change the color if you want).

Ranch fencing can look good, but you can easily have too much of it in a small garden. For real impact it is probably best used to surround a small area, rather than as a boundary fence for the whole garden.

Chestnut paling
This type of fencing is certainly not an attractive permanent feature, but it is cheap and

countryside at the end of your garden, post-and-rail can act as a boundary with the minimum interruption between you, your garden, and the countryside.

Post-and-rail makes an adequate background for shrubs. The shrubs do not have to make a continuous screen; once the timber has mellowed, the rails that show between the shrubs do not look obtrusive.

If the fence is close to a sitting-out area, or near the house, it is in fact a good idea to plant shrubs close to it so that the garden looks somewhat less like a cattle pen.

Garden walls come 'alive' (**top** and **above**) when covered in climbing plants.

Planting near a wall

The ground near walls and fences is often much drier than the rest of the garden. This means the plants there have to be watered more often than the rest of the garden, and ·it also means careful planting.

Make the hole about 30cm (1ft) away from the wall. (If you want the plant to go up the fence or wall, you can train it toward it, using a sloping cane if necessary.)

Always incorporate plenty of moisture-holding material, such as peat, well-rotted compost, or manure.

After planting, water well and then mulch the moist ground with damp peat, pulverized bark or compost.

Making them more beautiful

No matter how tasteful or how well constructed boundary walls and fences are, their appearance can usually be improved by plants.

Low walls and fences of 1.2m (4ft) or less in height do not really call for intensive planting; in any case, climbers are clearly unsuitable for a wall or fence of that height. It is best to make a feature of such a wall or fence rather than try to hide it. (In fact, if you feel that you have to hide a low fence or wall, the chances are you have made the wrong choice in the first place.)

Of course, a previous owner may have committed the error of putting it up, leaving you with a decision either to pull it down and start again, or to make the best of what is there. If you feel that it has to be improved, try to use shrubs, particularly evergreens, to soften the overall effect. Alternatively, low walls can be extended in height with either closeboard or trellis panels, allowing you more privacy, and more scope for planting climbers and wall shrubs.

Climbers and wall shrubs (**right**) add elegance to any garden wall. Choose from the wide range of flowering plants and striking foliage shrubs available.

The sort of plants that you can use to liven up an unexciting fence or wall are:
- climbers;
- all shrubs;
- ordinary shrubs, particularly evergreens; or
- 'architectural' plants.

Climbers

Climbers are generally not the easy solution that they may seem at first thought. Most of them are far suitable more for climbing a house wall or up a specially prepared trellis or other support. Virginia creeper (*Parthenocissus quinquefolia*) and Boston ivy (*Parthenocissus tricuspidata*) can cover a building superbly but are not for garden walls and fences; sweet peas and morning glories (*Ipomoea rubro-caerulea*, syn *I. violacea*) are among the most attractive annual climbers, but neither makes a good screen, nor can they fend for themselves without a suitable support.

There are, however, a few plants that do climb and clothe without much help and with no need to erect netting or trellis for them to grow up. Some ivies are among the most useful, but there are other plants equally so,

Wisteria

Hedera   *Clematis montana*

Fatsia japonica

28

Pyracantha

Elaeagnus pungens
'Maculata'

such as *Polygonum baldschuanicum* and various loniceras (honeysuckles).

Ivies are particularly useful because they are evergreen, and there are many variations in leaf color and shape. Two large-leaved varieties of outstanding merit are the Persian ivy *Hedera colchica* 'Dentata Variegata', and the Canary Island ivy *H. canariensis* 'Glorie de Marengo', also called 'Variegata'. Both these variegated ivies look interesting all the year round, although the Canary Island ivy may look the worse for wear in very cold areas.

The ordinary *H. helix* varieties are also suitable, although these tend to look better on walls than on fences. There are dozens of varieties from which to choose.

Another evergreen to consider is the Japanese honeysuckle *Lonicera japonica* 'Aureoreticulata', which has golden reticulation on bright green leaves. It tends to lose leaves in a severe winter.

Deciduous climbers are obviously less desirable, assuming the object is to cover the fence or wall, but there are also some useful plants in this category.

The mile-a-minute, or Russian, vine *(Polygonum baldschuanicum)* is a rampant plant that covers a large area quickly, and crowns the fence or wall with foaming masses of small creamy flowers in late summer and through autumn. Not a particularly pretty plant, it is fine though if you want quick cover.

For a really pretty flowering climber, it is difficult to beat clematis. Some initial support is required, such as netting or a trellis, but then species such as *C. montana* simply romp along the fence. The species is white, but the pink variety 'Rubens' is justifiably more popular.

If you are prepared to use a trellis of some kind, the various large-flowered hybrids can make a spectacular show. One of the most popular, 'Nelly Moser', actually does best on a shady fence (its color is stronger out of sunlight): a useful bonus.

Wisterias must rank among the most desirable of all climbers and wall shrubs, but only a large, tall wall can do them justice. If your wall is suitable, and you have the patience to wait for a few years to see it at its full glory, a wisteria can be very rewarding.

For an annual climber that covers a fence quickly, try the Japanese hop, *Humulus japonicus*. The variety 'Variegatus' is particularly decorative.

There are many other climbers that you could try, including honeysuckle.

The pink-and-white blooms of *Clematis* 'Nelly Moser' (**above left**) flourish on a garden wall. Climbing plants create a 'vertical' aspect to the garden (**right**).

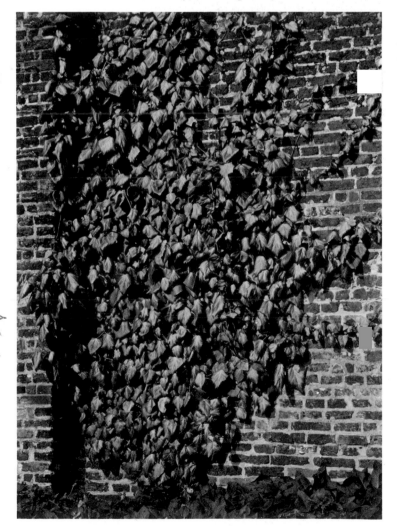

Wall shrubs

Although most wall shrubs grow equally well in the open, they usually have some feature or 'habit' that makes them especially suitable for growing against a structure such as a wall. Some, for example, have become known as wall shrubs because they are not particularly hardy and tend to grow better with the protection offered by a wall.

Pyracanthas come high on the list of desirable plants because, apart from summer foliage (and some small white flowers), there is the bonus of autumn and winter berries.

'Ordinary' shrubs

There are so many good shrubs that it is always difficult to single out a few. But the shortlist can be confined to plants that are:

- evergreen;
- able to grow well against a fence or wall;
- widely available; and that
- make a good screen/provide good cover.

High on the list must be the variegated hollies *Elaeagnus pungens* 'Maculata', and *Viburnum tinus*. Many conifers provide year-round cover and interest, of course, but their shape tends to be more upright and less bushy than those mentioned.

'Architectural' plants

You do not have to have a densely planted area to offset the boredom of a long wall or fence. Often, one or two really striking plants can enliven the scene and act as focal points.

A large clump of phormium, a single yucca, or a large castor oil plant (*Fatsia japonica*) may be all that is needed.

A large-leafed ivy, Dentata variegata | softens the outline and colour of its wall.

Living screens

For sheer impact, there is no substitute for the living boundary or screen formed by a hedge, even though it needs regular maintenance.

Apart from the regular trimming or pruning that is necessary with all hedges, there is one other big drawback: waiting for results.

Yet despite the extra work involved, a hedge is much preferred by many gardeners, for, besides marking the boundary, a hedge can, by illusion, extend it; it can blur the boundary even while defining it.

Often treated as a background against which to set other plants, a hedge can also be something beautiful in its own right. There are some spectacular flowering hedges to consider, and certainly many more pleasing evergreens than privet. Many of the most useful hedging plants are described on the following pages.

Big is not necessarily best

Because it is natural to want to see results quickly, there is the temptation to buy tall hedging plants. Resist it. They often take several seasons to become established and to start growing again, and frequently they lack the dense base that can be achieved by planting small and clipping early.

Small plants are cheaper, as well as better, in the long run.

To speed your hedge along, it is better to put money and effort into preparing the ground well.

Deciding what you want

It is worth being quite clear what you want from your hedge — a screen, something to keep animals in or out, a barrier to muffle sound from a busy road, or a decorative feature that contributes its own quota of beauty to the garden. The possible requirements are numerous.

The Table below includes all the plants described on the subsequent pages. It should enable you to find a hedge that suits your needs, whether you want a formal evergreen screen or an informal flowering hedge.

Planting distances differ according to whether you require a screen or a hedge. Distances between plants for a screen are

Name	Evergreen/deciduous	Recommended height	Formal/informal
Berberis darwinii	evergreen	1.2 – 1.8m (4 – 6ft)	formal/informal
Berberis x stenophylla	evergreen	1.8m (6ft)	informal
Berberis thunbergii	deciduous	0.4 – 1.8m[1] (1½ – 6ft)[1]	formal/informal
Buxus sempervirens	evergreen	0.3 – 1.2m[1] (1 – 4ft)[1]	formal
Carpinus betulus	deciduous[2]	1.5 – 2.4m (5 – 8ft)	formal
Chamaecyparis lawsoniana	evergreen (conifer)	1.5 – 2.4m (5 – 8ft)	formal
Cotoneaster lacteus	evergreen	1.8 – 2.4m (6 – 8ft)	informal
Crataegus monogyna	deciduous	1.5 – 2.4m (5 – 8ft)	formal
X Cupressocyparis leylandii	evergreen (conifer)	3 – 4.5m (10 – 15ft)	formal
Cupressus macrocarpa	evergreen (conifer)	2.4 – 5m (8 – 10ft)	formal
Elaeagnus x ebbingei	evergreen	1.2 – 1.8m (4 – 6ft)	formal
Euonymus japonicus	evergreen	1.5 – 1.8m (5 – 6ft)	formal
Fagus sylvatica	deciduous[2]	1.5 – 2.4m (5 – 8ft)	formal
'Flamboyant'	deciduous	2.4 – 3m (8 – 10ft)	formal
Forsythia	deciduous	1.2 – 1.8m (4 – 6ft)	informal
Griselinia littoralis	evergreen	1.5 – 2.1m (5 – 7ft)	formal
Ilex aquifolium	evergreen	1.5 – 1.8m (5 – 6ft)	formal
Lavandula spica	evergreen	0.3 – 1.2m[1] (1 – 4ft)[1]	informal
Ligustrum ovalifolium	semi-evergreen	1.2 – 1.8m (4 – 6ft)	formal
Lonicera nitida	evergreen	0.6 – 1.2m (2 – 4ft)	formal
Potentilla	deciduous	1 – 1.2m (3 – 4ft)	formal/informal
Prunus cerasifera 'Nigra'	deciduous	1.5 – 2.4m (5 – 8ft)	formal/informal
Prunus x cistena	deciduous	1.2 – 1.5m (4 – 5ft)	informal
Prunus laurocerasus	evergreen	1.5 – 1.8m (5 – 6ft)	formal
Rosa	deciduous	1 – 1.8m (3 – 6ft)	informal
Rosmarinus	evergreen	1.2 – 1.5m (4 – 5ft)	informal
Spiraea x arguta	deciduous	1.2 – 1.5m (4 – 5ft)	informal
Taxus baccata	evergreen	0.9 – 1.8m (3 – 6ft)	formal
Thuya plicata	evergreen (conifer)	1.5 – 2.4m (5 – 8ft)	formal

[1] Depends on variety
[2] Old leaves remain throughout winter

greater, for the plants themselves are to become bigger; close spacing keeps the plants more compact for a low hedge. Recommended spacings for each plant are given on the appropriate page. Also in the Table, the likely number of necessary cuts in a year will help you to decide whether a particular hedge is too labor-intensive for you.

What is a hedging plant?
Some of the plants grown as hedges could reach 9m (30ft) or more if grown as individual plants. Others could make specimen shrubs if grown in isolation. What makes them into a hedge is the close spacing (which restricts their growth and modifies their habit), coupled with clipping and pruning.

The dramatic difference between a beech tree and a beech hedge should be sufficient to demonstrate how even a seemingly unpromising plant can be tamed and trained into a first-class hedge. Do not rule a plant out simply because you do not normally associate it with your idea of a traditional hedge. On the other hand, be cautious with plants that you do not know will work; not every plant responds.

Living screens can be grown in almost any shape, size and color (**below**). Many potentially very tall conifers can be kept in check to create dense attractive hedges. Color and fragrance are provided by such plants as lavender and roses. For a long flowering season choose a potentilla or for a spring 'blaze' forsythia is hard to beat.

X *Cupressocyparis leylandii*

Chamaecyparis lawsoniana

Lavandula spica

Euonymus japonicus

Forsythia

Potentilla

Floribunda rose

Main features	Cuts/year
foliage/flowers	one
flowers	one
foliage	one/two
foliage	one/two
foliage	one
foliage	one
foliage/berries	one
foliage	one/two
foliage	one
foliage	one
foliage	one
foliage	one
foliage	one
foliage	one
flowers	one
foliage	one
foliage	one
foliage/flowers	one
foliage	six
foliage	six
flowers	one
foliage	one
foliage	one
foliage	one
flowers	one
foliage/flowers	one
flowers	one
foliage	one
foliage	one

Coniferous hedges

All the conifers generally used as a hedge or screen are evergreen. . . or evergold, blue, or gray. After all, conifers need not be drab or monotonous.

One conifer in particular can give the others a bad name — mainly because it has merits which make it so popular that it is frequently planted when others would actually be more suitable. The Leyland cypress (*X Cupressocyparis leylandii*) possesses the distinction of being one of the fastest-growing evergreens. It can grow a meter (3ft) a year, and provides a good screen in two or three seasons. In consequence it can obscure many of the choicer types that are planted where speed and height are not the most important attributes, and is over-planted in some areas.

Generally, most conifers need little clipping; in any case, they are not difficult to cut. Once the top has been removed, upward growth should be slowed.

The plants

Chamaecyparis lawsoniana: Lawson cypress
Useful as a tall screen or as a windbreak, even in an exposed position.

If you find conifers confusing, as many do, the *chamaecyparis* are the ones with flat sprays and small cones, *cupressus* (also used for hedging) has round sprays and large cones. The Lawson cypress is the *chamaecyparis* most often used for hedges — but there are over 80 varieties! Some are dwarfs for the rock garden, others can form huge trees (so it is important to buy the right ones).

Although there are lots of good hedging varieties, some of the best are:

'Allumii': Blue-gray; grows about 30cm (1ft) a year; use to form a screen of about 2.4m (8ft).

'Fletcheri': Blue-gray; slow-growing; for a hedge about 1.5m (5ft).

'Pembury Blue': Silvery-blue; forms a hedge or screen about 1.5-2.4m (5-8ft) high.

'Green Hedger': Rich green; for a hedge or screen about 1.5-2.4m (5-8ft).

Trim once a year, in late summer. **Plant** 60cm (2ft) apart.

X Cupressocyparis leylandii: Leyland cypress
Popular because of its fast growth, it can put on about 1m (3ft) in a year. Such a growth rate is a useful attribute in the early years, but unfortunately it is difficult to convince the plant when it is time to stop. Even if you remove the growing point to restrict upward growth after it has reached sufficient height, annual trimming is still required to keep it to size.

There is a form with pale yellow new growth, 'Castlewellan', that is less vigorous than the green form, and is best planted 60cm (2ft) apart.

It will easily make a screen 3-4.5m (10-15ft) high, or form a windbreak of 4.5-7.5m (15-25ft) with wider spacing.

Trim once a year, in late summer. **Plant** 75cm (2½ft) apart for a hedge.

Cupressus macrocarpa: Montery cypress
Another fast-growing conifer, and particularly useful as a shelter belt in coastal areas, as a screen of 2.4-3m (8-10ft), or as a taller windbreak if planted farther apart. The densely-packed foliage is bright green.

For a golden screen, the variety 'Goldcrest' is one of the best, although it prefers an open, light position to intensify the coloring. It forms a nice screen of about 3m (10ft), or taller if extra height is required.
Trim twice a year, in spring and late summer.
Plant 60cm (2ft) apart.

Taxus baccata: Yew
Undoubtedly one of the finest hedging plants, but seldom planted nowadays because of its reputation for slow growth. It does not grow as rapidly as most hedges, but it is not as slow as many people believe. (And bear in mind that slow growth means less clipping!) It does well on alkaline (chalky) soil, but tolerates most others too, although good drainage is important; it even tolerates heavy shade.

There are many varieties, but the ordinary species makes a fine hedge. For a golden form, try 'Elegantissima': its young leaves are an attractive yellow.

Yew suits a hedge about 90-180cm (3-6ft) high.

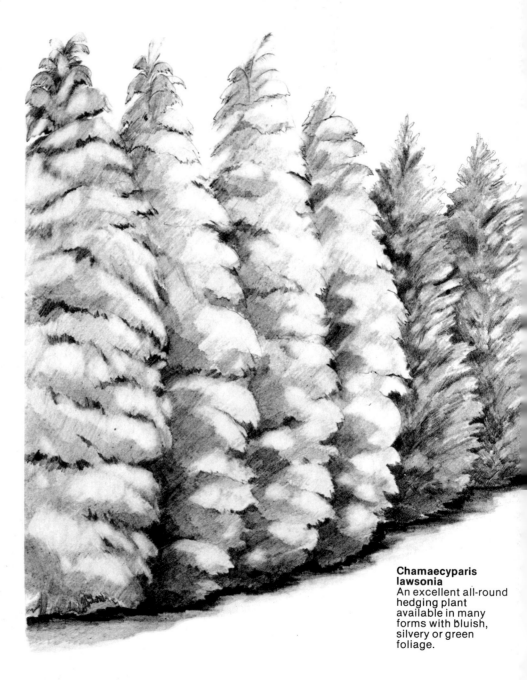

Chamaecyparis lawsonia
An excellent all-round hedging plant available in many forms with bluish, silvery or green foliage.

Trim in late summer. **Plant** 45-60cm (1½-2ft) apart.

Thuja plicata: Western red cedar
One of the finest hedging plants, especially in the variety 'Atrovirens', although other varieties can be used too. (Be careful that you do not buy a dwarf variety — some can take 30 years to grow about 1.2m/4ft!) 'Atrovirens' has bright green foliage and grows rapidly. The leaves have a fruity odor when crushed. **Trim** once a year, in late summer. Use pruners rather than shears, so that the natural shape of the plant — which is bushy yet upright — is not spoiled. **Plant** 60cm (2ft) apart.

Most hedging conifers will grow into exceedingly tall trees if they are left untrimmed. Be sure to cut out the central growing point (**right**) when the hedge reaches the desired height.

Cupressus macrocarpa
Ideal for providing a tall windbreak near the sea; the dense green foliage tolerates salt-laden air. The cultivar 'Goldcrest' is a more adaptable hedging plant than the type species.

X **Cupressocyparis leylandii**
Famed for its rapid growth rate, this popular hedging conifer can easily get out of hand. Be sure to cut out the growing point when the plant reaches the desired height. Annual trimming will create a neat hedge.

Taxus baccata
An excellent dense-growing hedging conifer that can be intricately trimmed and shaped to create arches, narrow hedges and all forms of topiary. It will tolerate chalk soil.

Thuja plicata
The foliage of this useful hedging plant is aromatic when crushed. Excellent for providing a medium-dense screen on almost any type of soil. The foliage resembles that of *Chamaecyparis*.

Broadleaved evergreens

Not everyone likes conifers, and no one at all would want too many of them in a small garden. If an evergreen hedge is still required, however, there are many excellent plants.

Although evergreen hedges have the merit of color and interest all the year round, remember alternatively that deciduous hedges have a charm of their own when they come into leaf again each spring. If there is space for several hedges in your garden, it may be worth trying to incorporate both deciduous and evergreen plants for the best of both worlds.

Evergreens are particularly useful as boundary hedges, and especially where the garden fronts a road. The "permanent" covering of leaves helps to filter noise as well as wind, and of course acts as a visual screen if desired.

The plants
Berberis darwinii: Darwin's barberry
See flowering hedges (page 39). A small-leaved evergreen with the bonus of bold orange-yellow flowers in mid- or late spring. Can be clipped as a formal hedge, but this could affect flowering and a less formal hedge is more likely to give the best display of flowers.
Trim once a year, after flowering. **Plant** 60cm (2ft) apart.

Berberis X stenophylla
See flowering hedges (page 39). The arching sprays of yellow flowers are at their best in late spring and early summer, but this evergreen will make an impenetrable hedge useful the year round. Makes a nice informal hedge of about 2.1-2.4m (7-8ft).
Prune after flowering. **Plant** 60cm (2ft) apart.

Buxus sempervirens: Box
One of the classic hedging plants, traditionally used for edging beds and borders. There are, however, many varieties, so make sure that you choose one of those most suited to hedging.

The one used for a low edging of about 30-45cm (1ft-1½ft) is "Suffruticosa". If you want a taller hedge of about 90-120cm (3-4ft), try "Handsworthensis".
Trim in mid- to late summer; it can also be cut back hard in mid-spring if you are careful.
Plant small varieties about 15cm (6in) apart, the tall ones about 45cm (1½ft) apart.

Cotoneaster lacteus
An evergreen with the bonus of a crop of long-lasting berries. The small leathery olive-green leaves act as a foil for the small milky-white flowers in late spring or early summer. These are succeeded by scarlet berries, which unfortunately the birds also appreciate.

It is best treated as an informal hedge, and it can reach about 2.4m (8ft).
Trim in summer, simply pruning off long shoots. **Plant** 60cm (2ft) apart.

Elaeagnus X ebbingei
A hardy, fast-growing shrub with pewter-colored leaves, silvery beneath, useful for creating a shelter belt in a coastal garden. It forms a nice hedge 1.2-1.8m (4-6ft) high.
Trim once a year, in spring or late summer. **Plant** 60cm (2ft) apart.

Euonymus japonicus: Evergreen spindle
One of the best evergreens for coastal areas. It also thrives in sun or shade, and is not unhappy in a city atmosphere.

There are variegated varieties, but the plain green probably makes the best hedge, and can make a substantial hedge, ideally 1.5-1.8m (5-6ft) high.
Trim once a year, in spring. **Plant** 45cm (1½ft) apart.

Griselinia littoralis
A highly desirable plant that always looks fresh; sadly, it is not completely hardy, and really is only suitable as a hedging plant in coastal areas, preferably in districts where the winters are mild.

The apple-green, leathery leaves tolerate salt-laden winds. The plant also grows well on chalky soil, but is unlikely to be happy on clayey soil.

It is best seen as a hedge about 1.5-2.1m (5-7ft) high.
Trim once a year, in early summer. **Plant** 60cm (2ft) apart.

Ilex aquifolium: Holly
Holly has a reputation for being a good 'sound filter'; exactly how it compares with other evergreens in this respect, however, it is difficult to be sure, but there can be no doubt that holly does make a superb and impenetrable hedge — given time.

Regarding a holly hedge, there are two points to bear in mind: if you want berries, you must plant both male and female plants; and if you want to prevent if from looking dull when there are no berries, you must plant a few variegated varieties in among the green ones.

Holly thrives in most soils — but avoid poorly-drained land, and do not plant in a draughty position (between two buildings, for instance).

It responds to clipping to form a hedge about 1.5m (5ft) tall, but can grow higher if allowed to.
Trim once a year, in late summer. **Plant** 45-60cm (1½ft-2ft) apart.

Ligustrum: Privet
The privet needs no introduction. Most books apologize for including it because it is so widely planted and yet in many ways a far from ideal hedging plant; it needs considerable trim-

ming, and is visually dull rather than attractive.

Do not dismiss the privet, however. The ordinary green privet is a tough plant, and may thrive in drafty spots (between buildings for example) in town and city gardens, where many other plants would fail. It thus forms a useful hedge for a difficult position.

The oval-leaf privet (*L. ovalifolium*) is the plant usually used for hedging. Although practically evergreen, it loses most of its leaves in cold areas.

The golden and variegated privets are really much more desirable plants, and deserve a place in any garden. They still need regular clipping during the season, however, so they may be best used for a small run of hedge,

A mature hedge of *Cotoneaster lacteus* (**left**) acts as a superb foil for a mixed flowering border. The dark evergreen foliage is adorned with white spring flowers and abundant red berries in autumn.

perhaps as an internal divider within the garden. *L. ovalifolium* 'Aureum' makes a good golden hedge, although again it may lose its leaves by the end of winter.

Both green and golden forms are suitable for a hedge 1.2-1.8m (4-6ft) high.
Trim monthly from mid-spring to late summer. **Plant** 30cm (1ft) apart.

Lonicera nitida: Shrubby honeysuckle
Not a beautiful hedge, but neat and easily clipped to a formal shape. There are several forms, 'Fertilis' being the best for a hedge because it has a more upright habit and is a strong grower. For a golden form, try 'Baggesen's Gold' (which tends to turn more green in the autumn).

It is suitable for a formal hedge 60-120cm (2-4ft) high.
Trim monthly from mid-spring to late summer. **Plant** 30cm (1ft) apart.

Prunus laurocerasus: Common laurel
A widely used evergreen, its large, glossy foliage makes it a useful plant for a screen or shelter belt, forming an impressive hedge of about 1.5-1.8m (5-6ft).
Prune in mid- or late summer, using pruning shears. **Plant** 60cm (2ft) apart.

Prunus lusitanica: Portugal laurel
The large, dark glossy leaves of this plant, less coarse and gross than those of the common laurel, form a thick and effective hedge.

It is particularly hardy, tolerates chalk better than the common laurel, and does not object to shade.

It is especially good as a hedge of about 1.5-1.8m (5-6ft).
Prune in mid- or late summer, using pruning shears. **Plant** 60cm (2ft) apart.

Rosmarinus: Rosemary
See flowering hedges (page 39). A useful plant for an informal hedge, being evergreen (actually grayish-green, white beneath), and flowering freely in late spring. The flowers on the best variety for a hedge — 'Miss Jessop's Variety' — are light mauve.
Prune only lightly, immediately after flowering. **Plant** 60cm (2ft) apart.

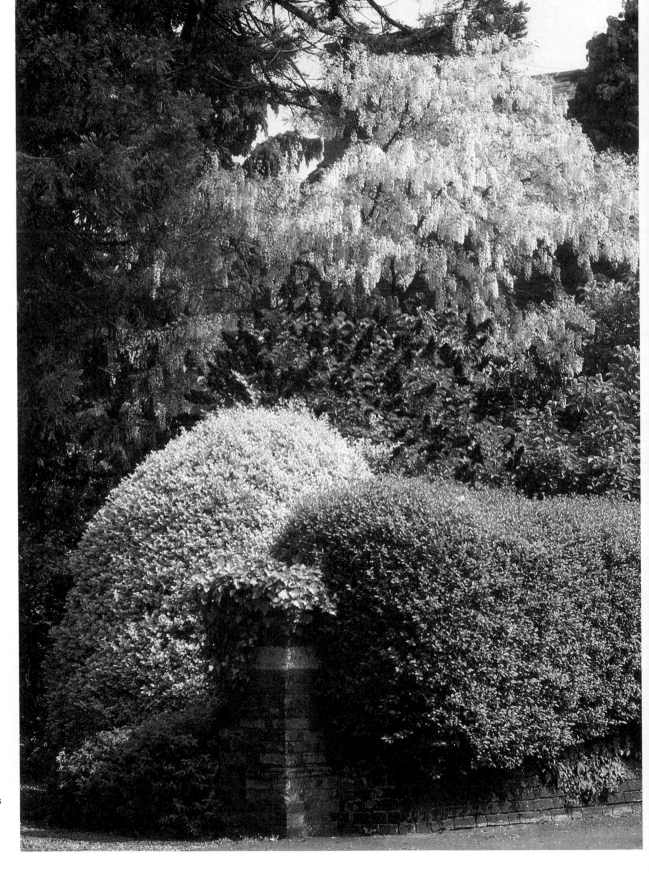

Privet (*Ligustrum ovalifolium*) is one of the most commonly grown of hedges. It can remain evergreen in mild areas but loses most of its leaves in cold regions. The yellow form 'Aureum' provides a refreshing contrast to the mid-green of the type species. This garden corner (**right**) features the green and yellow forms of privet, backed by *Syringa* and *Laburnum*.

Deciduous foliage hedges

Deciduous hedges need not be dull, nor necessarily useless in winter — many types still form an impenetrable barrier, and do not cease to serve their prime functions of marking a boundary or acting as a barrier or filter. Few of them, though, actually provide a good screen in winter (beech and hornbeams are the exceptions), but there is the thrill of fresh new leaves each spring. A hedge that has just come into full leaf again often has a freshness about it that is lacking in many other hedges. And of course it is usually the deciduous hedges that are the most spectacular in flower.

The plants

Berberis thunbergii: Barberry
Berberis can make a very fine hedge; some, such as *B. darwinii* and *B. X stenophylla*, are evergreen and have attractive flowers. There is also a very good deciduous species that makes up for winter bareness with a summer display of rich purple-red — *B. thunbergii* 'Atropurpurea'.

The foliage deepens to a vivid red in autumn, when there is usually a bonus of red berries; primarily, though, it should be grown for its foliage.

There are in fact three varieties of *B. thunbergii* that are particularly useful as hedging plants. 'Atropurpurea' makes a hedge of about 1.2-1.8m (4-6ft), 'Atropurpurea Nana' is a dwarf variety and is suitable for a hedge about 45-60cm (18in-2ft) tal!. Less common is 'Erecta', which has narrow, upright growth and is suitable for a narrow hedge of about 60-120cm (2-4ft).

Trim the plants in winter. For a formal hedge, you can trim lightly again in midsummer. It can also be cut back hard in early spring, although this should not be necessary every year. **Plant** 'Atropurpurea Nana' 38cm (15in) apart, 'Erecta' at 75cm (1½ft), and 'Atropurpurea' every 60cm (2ft).

Carpinus betulus: Hornbeam
Similar to the beech in appearance and qualities, but more suitable for heavy, wet soils, the hornbeam also tolerates an exposed site. Like those of the beech, the brown dead leaves usually hang on throughout winter.

It makes a medium to tall hedge, best about 1.5-2.4m (5-8ft) tall.
Trim in winter or later summer. **Plant** 45cm (1½ft) apart.

Crataegus monogyna: Hawthorn; Quickthorn
Although more often thought of as a 'country' hedge than a 'town' hedge, the hawthorn looks good anywhere. It is, however, most useful where a large, thick, dense hedge is required. An established hedge is thick and impenetrable even in winter.

It is best for a medium to large hedge of 1.5-2.4m (5-8ft).
Trim in summer; it can also be cut back hard in winter if necessary. **Plant** 30cm (1ft) apart.

Beech (**below left**) can be shaped into 'architectural' garden hedges. Its fresh green spring growth replaces the brown wrinkled leaves that have persisted through winter.

Hornbeam (**above**) is similar to beech but more tolerant of heavy soils. Alternating green- and purple-leaved prunus plants creates a striking effect (**below**).

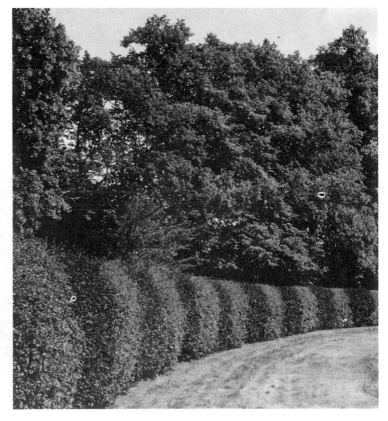

Fagus sylvatica: Beech

Although technically deciduous, the beech could almost be grouped with the evergreens. Its old leaves can be induced to hang on until the luster that they had while young). If there brown does not detract from their usefulness as a winter screen.

It tolerates chalky soil — but avoid heavy, wet soils, in which the similar hornbeam, *Carpinus betulus,* can be used instead.

The common green beech is the one most generally planted, but a hedge of copper beech can also be attractive (although less so as the leaves age during the season, gradually losing the luster that they had while young). If there is a large enough run of hedge to be able to make it work, you could mix the two for more impact.

Either makes a medium to tall hedge about 1.5-2.4m (5-8ft), but can grow much taller — one very old hedge exists which is over 30m (100ft) high!

Trim in late summer so that the leaves hang late. **Plant** 45cm (1½ft) apart.

Flamboyant

This is not one plant, but the name given to a planting combination. Two plants of the purple-leaved *Prunus cerasifera* 'Pissardii' followed by one plant of a green form of Myrobalan plum *(P. cerasifera).* For a long run of hedge, it is more effective if the contributory blocks of each plant are larger — say, four purple to two green, or even six purple to three green.

It is best as a large hedge, up to 3m (10ft) high.

Prune hard in May, restricting annual growth to 45-60cm (1½-2ft) to keep the hedge bushy and compact. **Plant** 60cm (2ft) apart.

Deciduous hedges (**right**) change refreshingly with the seasons. Their spring growth is a 'tonic' to the garden as it emerges from winter's drabness. Many varieties, such as *Berberis thunbergii* 'Atropurpurea', have purple foliage to provide a striking background to a herbaceous border.

Prunus X cistena: Purple-leaf sand cherry

This is often known as Crimson Dwarf. It makes a good low or medium hedge, that has the bonus of small white single flowers in spring, although it is grown primarily for its foliage. This is rich crimson, with bright red tips to those on young shoots. It looks especially fine as a boundary to a green lawn or beds of pink or white roses, and makes a hedge of 1.2-1.5m (4-5ft); it is best, however, to restrict growth to about 15cm (6in) a year.

Trim after flowering. **Plant** 60cm (2ft) apart.

Crataegus monogyna
Where a sturdy impenetrable hedge up to 2.4m (8ft) is required this spiny shrub/small tree can be recommended. Spring flowers and autumn fruits are an added bonus.

Prunus cerasifera 'Nigra'

This plant is often listed as *P.* 'Pissardii Nigra', and may be sold as a hedging plant under the name Blaze.

Although the plant has small pink flowers in early spring, when bloom is always welcome, it is best regarded as a foliage hedge. The dark purple — almost black — leaves make it a bold hedge during the summer months.

Trim in mid-spring, after flowering. **Plant** 60cm (2ft) apart.

Berberis thunbergii
The compact growth and range of green- and purple-leaved cultivars recommend this shrub for a wide variety of hedging purposes. Up to 1.2m (4ft) high.

Prunus cerasifera
The green- and purple-leaved forms of this ornamental plum can provide superb foliage hedges up to 3m (10ft) high.

Fagus sylvatica
Beech hedges are widely grown for their exuberant spring growth and their easily trimmed growth pattern. Purple-leaved forms are available. Up to 2.4m (8ft) as a hedge.

The vigorous upright growth of the rose 'Queen Elizabeth' (**below**) makes it ideal as a flowering hedge up to 1.5m (5ft) in height. A floribunda rose of the hybrid-tea type, it bears large, pale pink slightly scented blooms amid dark green foliage. Be sure to allow sufficient space for this rose to develop.

Flowering hedges

There is often a temptation to regard flowering hedges as second-rate hedges in other respects. They can, in fact, be useful and practical boundary hedges too — *Berberis darwinii* and potentillas are examples.

It has to be admitted, however, that most flowering hedges are decorative rather than impenetrable barriers — but you may not want a hedge that has to be able to keep out everything from animals to children. Sometimes boundary hedges can be informal, whereas internal hedges are often ideal candidates for flowering shrubs.

Do not dismiss the idea of a low flowering hedge for a small front garden, especially if most of the surrounding gardens are open-plan. To have a tall formal hedge in this situation could look incongruous.

The plants

Berberis darwinii: Darwin's barberry
A small-leaved evergreen with the bonus of bold orange-yellow flowers in mid- or late spring.

It can be clipped as a formal hedge, but doing so can affect flowering, and a less formal hedge is thus more likely to give the best display of flowers.
Trim once a year, after flowering. **Plant** 60cm (2ft) apart.

Berberis X stenophylla
The arching sprays of yellow flowers are at their best in late spring and early summer, but this evergreen makes an impenetrable hedge useful all the year round.

It makes a nice informal hedge of about 2.1-2.4m (7-8ft).
Prune after flowering. **Plant** 60cm (2ft) apart.

Forsythia: Golden bell bush
Not an ideal hedge on its own, it can be very effective planted behind a low wall to overcome the drawback of sparse growth at the base. It can also make a bright divide between properties with an open-plan layout. Although not neat or particularly attractive for the rest of the year, a good forsythia hedge is such a splendid sight in spring that it is well worth considering. Properly pruned, it creates a sheet of vibrant yellow.

It makes a hedge about 1.2-1.8m (4-6ft) high.
Prune to shape immediately after flowering, but do not cut back harder than necessary; it may need further *light* shaping in late summer, just to remove straggly branches.
Plant 60cm (2ft) apart.

Lavandula: Lavender
Potentially a really nice dwarf hedge of about 30-90cm (1-3ft) high, according to species and variety. Superb in flower, its gray foliage is interesting the rest of the year. Lavender also has a long flowering season — from mid-summer to mid-autumn — and of course there is the very substantial bonus of its fragrance.

As if this were not enough, it is also evergreen (actually silvery-gray), tolerates coastal areas, and grows in most soils that are well drained. It does, however, need a sunny position to do well.

The only problem is that old plants can become rather straggly and woody unless trimmed carefully and methodically. But you

Light mauve flowers adorn the silver-gray aromatic foliage of *Rosmarinus officinalis* (**right**) in spring and may appear on and off until autumn. Rosemary makes an excellent informal hedge up to 1.5m (5ft) tall.

can replant the hedge from cuttings when eventually it is decisively past its best.

Lavender looks nice as a background to a blue or gray border, or as a boundary for a rose garden. It also associates well with stonework.

For a really low hedge, choose *L. spica* 'Nana Munstead Dwarf', which makes a hedge about 45-60cm (1½-2ft) tall, or 'Hidcote', a deep blue variety that makes a hedge about 30-60cm (1-2ft) high.

For a taller lavender hedge, the ordinary species *(L. spica)* can grow to about 1-1.2m (3-4ft).
Trim all varieties in mid-autumn, once flowering has finished. **Plant** the species about 45cm (1½ft) apart, the dwarf varieties about 30cm (1ft) apart.

Potentilla

If you are confused by labels in the nursery, it is the shrubby potentilla that is of course used for hedges, and not the herbaceous type. There are quite a few kinds to choose from, mainly varieties and hybrids of *P. dahurica* and *P. fruticosa*, but they all make a 'soft'-looking hedge of about 1-1.2m (3-4ft). *P. fruticosa* 'Jackman's Variety' is particularly nice as a hedge: it has sage-green leaves and dense clusters of brilliant yellow flowers.

Prune in spring, not cutting into old wood more than necessary. **Plant** 60cm (2ft) apart.

Rose

Roses are popular garden plants but seldom used for hedging, probably because most roses are far from pretty in winter, and look very sparse after they have been pruned. Yet a suitable species or variety can look superb in flower.

The answer to the problem lies in the careful choice of plant, and the minimum of pruning, other than cutting out dead wood and light shaping.

For an impenetrable hedge, choose a rose such as *R. xanthina* 'Canary Bird'. Most of the *R. rugosa* varieties are also suitable. 'Canary Bird' looks glorious when clothed with its large single, deep yellow flowers in early summer.

The vigorous floribunda (hybrid-tea type cluster-flowered) 'Queen Elizabeth', with its shapely, and sweetly scented pink flowers, also makes a good divider, having an upright habit. The trouble with this variety is that it is usually full of flowers at the top, but naked below.

'Queen Elizabeth' and 'Canary Bird' easily make a hedge 1.5-1.8m (5-6ft) high, *R. rugosa*

The bright yellow flowers of *Potentilla fruticosa* (**left**) are carried amid the delicate finely divided foliage from spring until autumn. Excellent for an informal boundary.

Fragrance is an added bonus in a hedge formed of rose 'Penelope' (**above**). The shell-pink flowers appear in early summer and again in autumn. Up to 1.8m (6ft) tall.

is best at about 1.2-1.5m (4-5ft).
Prune in late winter or early spring. **Plant** about 90cm (3ft) apart.

Rosmarinus: Rosemary
A useful plant for an informal hedge, being evergreen (actually grayish-green), white beneath), and flowering freely in late spring. The flowers on the best variety for a hedge — 'Miss Jessop's Variety' — are light mauve.

This variety has an upright habit, and makes a hedge about 1.2-1.5m (4-5ft) high.
Prune only lightly, immediately after flowering. **Plant** 60cm (2ft) apart.

Spiraea X arguta: Bridal wreath
As an internal hedge, or as a boundary marker, this *spiraea* makes an informal hedge that looks wonderful in late spring. It is free-flowering, and the arching sprays of small

white flowers seem to cascade from the plant like a fountain.
It makes an informal hedge of about 1.2-1.5m (4-5ft).
Prune immediately after flowering, but as it will not make a formal clipped hedge, do not cut back too drastically. **Plant** 45-60cm (1½-2ft) apart.

For color and variety choose from among the many flowering hedges available (**below**). Most are adaptable as far as soil and position are concerned and will reward routine attention with a refreshing seasonal display of bloom.

Berberis x stenophylla
Golden yellow flowers appear in spring on the elegant arching branches. Up to 2.4m (8ft) high.

Spiraea x arguta
Abundant white blooms are borne in spring on slender stems. It should not be severely pruned but can be lightly trimmed to create a flowering informal hedge up to 1.5m (5ft) high.

Potentilla fruticosa
Several cultivars can be used to create soft hedges up to 1.2m (4ft) tall. Flower color ranges from yellow through orange to red.

Rosa rugosa
This species of rose grows into a sturdy bush that forms an excellent flowering hedge about 1.5m (5ft) high. Several named varieties are available.

Lavandula spica
The type species can provide a fragrant informal hedge up to 1.2m (4ft) tall. Various dwarf varieties are available for more restricted areas.

Forsythia intermedia
Bright with vivid yellow spring flowers, forsythia provides a colorful if short-lived floral display. The cultivar 'Spectabilis' is commonly available and can form a hedge up to 1.8m (6ft) tall.

Plants to grow by a hedge

Hedges make a fine backdrop for many plants, but unfortunately they also cause problems for plants close to them. There is a potential shade problem, the ground near the base is always very dry because the soil is largely protected from driving rain, and the soil is also likely to be impoverished.

Whatever is planted close to a hedge has to compete for light, moisture and food.

As a very rough guide, anything that you plant within a distance of half of the height of the hedge is likely to suffer unless you choose particularly tolerant plants. So a 1.8m (6ft) hedge could cause problems for a distance of about 90cm (3ft). If the hedge backs a large border, you probably need a path at the back anyway in order to be able to trim the hedge, and in these circumstances a 1.2m (4ft) hedge is likely to cause fewest problems.

The main difficulty arises with narrow beds between lawn and hedge. It is those borders narrow enough to be reached over to trim the hedge that are the most difficult in which to grow plants.

Nature has adapted plants to grow in even the most adverse spots, however, and some of the possible candidates are listed below. But because most of them are fairly tough does not mean that you can neglect them — they do need special care while they are becoming established.

Always water the plants regularly and thoroughly until they are established. Even if they tolerate dry soil normally, give them an extra chance to start with.

Be prepared to feed the plants, at least perennials, for the first year. Foliar feeding has the advantage of feeding the plants without encouraging the hedge to compete.

Because the plants likely to succeed near hedge range from shrubs to annuals, they have here been grouped under type. But do not be afraid to mix them — there is no harm in mixing shrubs and herbaceous perennials, nor annuals with perennials. Often, however, it is best to keep to one or two plants in a small bed for real impact.

Bergenia cordifoia (**above**) is excellent for spring colour in the shade of a hedge.

The plants: Herbaceous perennials

Ajuga reptans: Bugle Excellent as a ground cover plant. There are several good varieties, all of them suitable. Most of these ground-hugging plants have attractive colored and variegated leaves. They have the considerable merit of being evergreen. Small spikes of blue flowers appear in late spring and early summer, but its main use is as a foliage ground cover.

Anemone X hybrida: Japanese anemone Useful if you want a late-flowering herbaceous plant. The usually white or pink flowers (it depends on variety) are carried on stems about 60-90cm (2-3ft) tall in late summer to mid-autumn.

Bergenia Another useful evergreen ground cover, but with striking flowers in spring. The large, round leaves often take on a reddish-purple hue in winter. Most varieties have pink flowers; the height seldom rises to more than 30cm (1ft).

Epimedium perralderianum Although almost evergreen, the leaves usually look the worse for wear by the end of winter. The bronze-yellow flowers in mid-to late spring are not particularly conspicuous, but it is a useful if slow-growing plant. The height is of about 30cm (1ft).

Euphorbia: Spurge There are many different spurges, but *E. robbiae* is one of the most suitable for this situation. Its habit is always interesting, with rosettes of dark green leaves, over which yellowish-green flowers are carried in early to mid-summer. Its height is of about 45cm (1½ ft). *E. wulfenii* is also a possible candidate, but is a much bolder plant, reaching 1.2m (4ft).

Lamium maculatum
Another low-growing carpeting plant. There are several varieties, with either pink or white flowers in mid-spring to early summer. It is grown mainly as a foliage plant, however; the leaves are usually marbled or splashed with white.

Liriope muscari
An established clump of this distinctive plant is always interesting when in flower in late summer to mid autumn. Its foliage is evergreen and rush-like, with blue spires of flowers resembling a grape hyacinth. Its height is of about 30cm (1ft).

Polygonatum X hybridum: Solomon's seal
Frequently sold as *P. multiflorum*, but useful whatever its name. The greenish-white bell flowers hang down from arching stems in late spring and early summer. The height is of about 75cm (2½ ft).

Pulmonaria
Can be used as a ground cover, or as isolated 'clumps' — either way, a desirable plant. There are several species and varieties available, generally with spotted or mottled leaves, and with pink, violet, and blue flowers in mid to late spring.

Shrubs
Aucuba japonica
Only suitable near a large hedge, otherwise probably too big.

Berberis
Dwarf kinds can be used, or larger ones if the hedge is substantial in size.

Cotoneaster
A diverse family, some species of which make small trees, others ground-hugging carpeters. For planting in a small bed near a hedge, a dwarf kind such as *C. dammeri* or *C. salicifolius* 'Repens' is probably best. Both these are evergreen.

Danae racemosa: Alexandrian laurel
Not a spectacular plant, but a useful evergreen with glossy green leaves and orange berries, appreciated most in winter.

Hedera: Ivy
Ivies are very versatile. In addition to the uses described elsewhere in this book, they make a fine ground cover for difficult sites.

Hypericum calycinum: Rose of Sharon
A tough plant that completely takes over its bed in time. The evergreen leaves give year-round cover (although they can look tatty in winter and may drop), but it is worth growing just for its vibrant display of large yellow flowers from early summer to early autumn. Height: 30-45cm (1-1½ ft).

Mahonia aquifolium: Holly-leafed berberis
An evergreen shrub growing 60-120cm (2-4ft). Its leaves take on red and purple tints in winter.

43

Planting and training

Planting a hedge

Every hedge is intended on planting to remain in place for a long time, so there is only one chance to prepare the ground properly. It is easy to be tempted to short cuts, but thorough preparation helps the hedge to become established more rapidly.

Prepare the ground in advance by digging two spits deep (a spit is the depth of a spade blade), and incorporate as much well-rotted manure or compost as can be spared. Level the ground and rake in a general fertilizer at about 140g per sq m (4oz per sq yd) before planting.

Excavate holes at the spacing recommended for the hedge, large enough to take the rootball, and for the roots to be spread out if the plants are bare-root.

Always firm the soil around the plants, and water thoroughly.

Container-grown trees can be planted at any time, provided the ground is not frozen or waterlogged, but bare-rooted and balled plants are generally best planted from mid-autumn to early spring. Mid- to late autumn is a good time for deciduous hedges, but evergreens are better planted in spring — mid- to late spring is satisfactory — so that they are not exposed to water loss from the leaves before the soil has warmed up enough for the roots to grow and take up more moisture.

There should be no need to stake your hedge, but if the site is very exposed it is a good idea to provide a temporary screen or fence. If this is too much for the horticultural budget, stretch strings or wires between stakes to support the intervening plants.

After planting

Water your hedge if the weather is dry, at least until it is established — especially if you want your hedge to grow quickly while it is young. Soak the ground thoroughly rather than sprinkling the surface, even if it means doing so less often.

Feed it with a foliar feed regularly for the first year. This may seem an extravagance for a hedge — it is certainly not essential — but even if you never feed it again, it is worth a little extra effort to get the hedge moving as quickly as possible.

Prune early. Shaping and forming your hedge can begin as soon as you have planted it. Cut back straggly stems, and even upward growth if you want a row of even plants. (The only exceptions are plants, such as tall conifers, that you want to grow up as a *high* screen.)

Tall windbreaks and screens

For a tall windbreak or screen, some of the plants listed on pages 30 and 31 are suitable, but you must plant them further apart. Bear in mind that such tall screens are really suitable only for a fairly large garden.

Shaping the hedge

The terms 'pruning' and 'trimming' can mean much the same thing, but pruning implies a more careful and individual selection of the shoots to be cut than trimming with hand shears or electric hedgetrimmers.

Always shape your hedge carefully, and use pruners for large-leaved plants such as laurels. (If you use shears on these, the mutilated leaves are conspicuous and ugly, especially as they die.)

An *informal* hedge is not clipped or pruned to a neat, regular shape. A *formal* hedge is clipped to produce 'flat' surfaces.

Although most formal hedges are rectangular in cross-section, like a wall, it is better to taper the sides, narrowing them toward the top. The lower part then receives more light, and the wedge shape offers the best form of wind protection without causing too much turbulence.

After planting (or in spring if planted earlier), cut back all growths to half or two-thirds of their length. Remove any straggly shoots.

An informal hedge needs little more formative pruning, but at the end of the first summer a formal hedge should be pruned or trimmed again to form the outline shape of the hedge. It is a good idea to make two wooden frames to the desired shape and size of the hedge (obviously not its final size) and stretch strings between these, so that you have a clear idea of the shape to prune to.

Topiary, the art of pruning and shaping hedging plants into sculptural features to decorate the garden, has been a traditional pursuit for centuries. Early training may involve the use of wire to hold growing stems in the required shapes. With expert trimming and meticulous attention to detail, fantastic shapes can be achieved with plants such as privet and yew. These privet peacocks (**right**) perch atop crisply clipped blocks formed from the same plant.

Pachysandra terminalis Eventually forms good evergreen ground cover, about 30cm (1ft) high. The white-splashed 'Variegata' is much more attractive than the green form against a dark hedge.

Vinca: Periwinkle Both *V. minor* and the larger *V. major* are worth growing if there are no restrictions to their spreading habit. Neither grows much more than 30cm (1ft) high, and there are variegated forms that are more striking against a dark background.

Balsam *(Impatiens balsamina)* has colorful flower spikes and most varieties range between 30-45cm (1-1½ft). Even more spectacular are the more popular kind of *impatiens*, the Busy Lizzies. There are many varieties, usually little more than 15cm (6in) in height, most of which provide a bold splash of color for the summer.

Both these *impatiens* are half-hardy.

Shaping hedges for decorative effect is not a pursuit reserved solely for stately homes. These elegant shapes (**left**) herald the entrance to a modest house.

Yew hedging is ideal for precise trimming. These smooth shapes (**left**) create a striking feature in this Victorian garden.

DIFFICULT
SITES

Very dry sunny banks

Anyone who has explored the hillsides in Mediterranean countries must be aware that many plants flourish in hot, dry, arid conditions. A very dry sunny bank in the garden may, in the spring and summer, present very similar conditions. So why not try turning it into a little bit of Mediterranean hillside? It is easy if the right plants are chosen.

Sun and soils

A bank that receives sun for much of the day can become extremely hot in spring and summer. The sun rapidly dries out the soil, so that plants at times have minimal moisture. The rate at which the soil dries out depends also on the type. If it is a heavy clay, for instance, it will take longer to dry out than a sandy or gravelly soil and the sun bakes it hard on the surface. Sandy and gravelly soils cannot hold onto large amounts of moisture — rain rapidly drains through them to the lower levels, out of reach of plants' roots. So shortage of moisture can be very severe on a sunny bank with sandy or gravelly soils.

Dry sunny banks can be used to grow a wide variety of plants that thrive in arid conditions (**below**)

Spartium junceum in fragrant bloom (**above**)

For autumn color try the bulb *Nerine bowdenii* (**top**) The unusual flowers of *Phlomis fruticosa* (**above**)

PLANTS FOR A DRY SUNNY BANK
Botanical Name
SHRUBS
Artemisia arborescens
Cistus
Colutea arborescens
Cytisus X beanii
Cytisus X kewensis
Genista hispanica
Genista lydia
Helichrysum angustifolium
Helianthemum
Lavandula officinalis
Perovskia atriplicifolia
Phlomis fruticosa
Phygelius capensis
Potentilla fruticosa
Rosmarinus officinalis
Salvia officinalis 'Purpurascens'
Santolina chamaecyparissus
Spartium junceum
Ulex europaeus 'Plenus'
Yucca filamentosa
PERENNIALS
Acaena microphylla
Acanthus spinosus
Anthemis cupaniana
Echinops ritro
Eryngium
Euphorbia myrsinites
Potentilla 'Gibson's Scarlet' and 'William Rollinson'
Sedum
Sempervivum
Thymus serpyllum cultivars
Verbascum hybrids
Zauschneria californica
BULBS
Allium
Crocus
Nerine bowdenii
Tulipa tarda

The paper-thin petals of *Cistus albidus* sparkle in the sunshine (**right**)

Common Name	Height	Spread	Color	Season of interest	Notes
Wormwood	1m (3.3ft)	1m (3.3ft)	Yellow	Summer	Feathery silvery leaves
Rock rose	0.6–2m (2–6.5ft)	0.6–2m (2–6.5ft)	Red, pink, purple, white	Summer	Evergreen
Bladder senna	2.4m (8ft)	2.4m (8ft)	Yellow	Summer/Autumn	Balloon-like seed pods
Broom	45cm (18in)	90cm (3ft)	Yellow	Spring	–
Broom	45cm (18in)	1.2m (4ft)	Pale Yellow	Spring	–
Spanish gorse	60cm (2ft)	2m (6.5ft)	Yellow	Summer	Very spiny
Broom	60cm (2ft)	1.8m (6ft)	Yelow	Spring	–
Curry plant	60cm (2ft)	60cm (2ft)	Yellow	Summer	Gray leaves
Rock rose	15cm (6in)	60cm (2ft)	Wide range	Summer	–
Lavender	90cm (3ft)	90cm (3ft)	Gray-blue	Summer	Gray leaves
–	1.2m (4ft)	90cm (3ft)	Violet-blue	Summer	Gray leaves
Jerusalem sage	1m (3.3ft)	60cm (2ft)	Yellow	Summer	Gray wooly leaves
–	90cm (3ft)	60cm (2ft)	Scarlet	Summer	Evergreen
Shrubby cinquefoil	0.6–1.2m (2–4ft)	0.6–1.2m (2–4ft)	Yellow, orange, red, pink, white	Summer	–
Rosemary	2m (6.5ft)	2m (6.5ft)	Mauve	Spring/Summer	Evergreen
Purple-leaf sage	30cm (12in)	60cm (2ft)	Purple leaves	–	–
Cotton lavender	60cm (2ft)	60cm (2ft)	Yellow	Summer	Wooly silvery leaves
Spanish broom	2.4m (8ft)	2.4m (8ft)	Yellow	Summer	Green stems
Double gorse	2m (6.5ft)	2m (6.5ft)	Yellow	Spring	Very spiny
Adam's needle	60cm (2ft)	90cm (3ft)	Cream	Summer	Sword-like leaves
New Zealand burr	50cm (2in)	45cm (18in)	Crimson	Summer	Bronze leaves
Bear's breeches	1.2m (4ft)	60cm (2ft)	White and purple	Summer	Deeply cut spiny leaves
–	15cm (6in)	30cm (12in)	White	Summer	Gray scented leaves
Globe thistle	90cm (3ft)	60cm (2ft)	Steel blue	Summer	Gray-green leaves
–	0.6–1.2m (2–4ft)	45–60cm (18–24in)	Blue	Summer	Leaves often spiny
Spurge	15cm (6in)	30cm (12in)	Sulphur yellow	Spring	Blue-gray leaves
Cinquefoil	45cm (18in)	45cm (18in)	Rod and orange respectively	Summer	–
Stonecrops	Prostrate to 45cm (18in)	15–45cm (6–18in)	lYellow, pink, red or white	Summer	Fleshy leaves
House-leeks	Prostrate	15–30cm (6–12in)	White, yellow, pink or red	Summer	Fleshy leaves in rosettes, often red, pink or purple
Thyme	Prostrate	60cm (24in)	Pink, red or white	Summer	Aromatic leaves
Mullein	1.2m (4ft)	60cm (2ft)	Mainly yellow or pink	Summer	Large wooly leaves
Californian fuchsia	45cm (18in)	45cm (18in)	Bright red	Summer	Gray wooly leaves
Ornamental onions	30cm (12in) to 1.2m (4ft)	30–45cm (12–18in)	Pink, red or yellow	Summer	Plant bulbs in groups
–	10–15cm (4–6in)	10–15cm (4–6in)	Mainly yellow, orange blue or purple	Spring	Plant bulbs in groups
–	60cm (24in)	About 15cm (6in)	Pink	Autumn	Plant bulbs in groups
Tulip	15cm (6in)	10cm (4in)	White and yellow	Spring	Plant bulbs in groups

How plants cope

There are many plants that actually revel in these seemingly arid conditions, and a fair selection may be found in the accompanying table. But how is it that some plants succeed in these hot dry conditions, whereas others simply shrivel up and die?

The answer is that many plants have to become specially adapted to arid conditions: in many parts of the world, plants thrive on hot, dry, rocky hillsides with virtually no soil, or they can be found in semi-deserts where very little rain falls.

Some of these plants have very deep roots which can tap supplies of moisture many feet below the surface. Others have fleshy or swollen roots and stems, also leaves, which store water towards periods of drought. Many plants from hot climates have wooly or waxy leaves. The wool, hair or waxy coating prevents the leaves from rapidly losing moisture during hot weather.

To help the plants along

In the garden there is never any need to give the plants a difficult time — it is possible to help them grow and really flourish by preparing the soil well for them before planting.

To ensure that the soil does not dry out too rapidly, plenty of organic matter can be dug in: well-rotted manure, garden compost, peat, spent hops, mushroom compost or shredded bark. This acts as a sponge and helps to retain moisture, so is particularly important if the soil is sandy or gravelly.

Dig a dry sunny bank to at least the depth of a spade before planting, and place a layer of organic matter in each trench. If the bottom of the trenches seems very hard and compacted, break it up with a fork, to the depth of the fork's own tines if possible, so that the roots of plants are able to grow deeply in search of moisture.

Also try to mix organic matter into the surface of the soil. Before planting it is a good idea to prick into the surface of the soil a general-purpose fertilizer.

To make a feature as interesting as possible, and to imitate a natural rocky hillside, consider using a few specimen rocks. A few pieces of well-shaped natural rock, their bases partly sunk in the soil, should do the trick and also provide a cool root run for some of the plants. Some of those recommended in the table can be effectively grown over a rock, such as *Cytisus*, helianthemums, *Acaena*, sempervivums and thymes.

Planting tips

Plants put out new roots and become established more quickly if the planting-hole is well prepared. Mix some moist peat into the bottom of the hole, and also into the soil removed, before returning it around the roots. Make sure the roots — or the ball of soil around the roots — are moist before planting.

Looking after the plants

Try not to leave plants to their own devices once they are planted — a little care and attention will encourage them to grow that much better.

Water them thoroughly if the soil is dry after planting. Then, during the first season after planting, apply water whenever the soil starts to dry out. It is best to water plants on a bank with a garden sprinkler attached to a hosepipe to give a gentle rain-like effect. The water is then less likely to run off, as would be the case with a watering can or hosepipe.

To prevent soil from being washed down a bank during periods of heavy rain, to help prevent rapid drying out of the soil in hot weather, and to create a pleasing natural appearance, consider covering the soil after planting with a layer of shingle or stone chippings, both of which are available from the larger nurseries. A layer 2.5-5cm (1-2in) deep is sufficient. This also helps to prevent weed growth.

An annual feed in the spring, with a fertilizer such as blood, fishmeal and bone, ensures that the plants do not have a starved appearance.

Wet and flooded areas

Gardeners with very wet soil that may become waterlogged or hold surface water in the winter, could be forgiven for giving up gardening in despair. Yet a most attractive garden could be created in such conditions by choosing moisture-loving plants.

It may not, of course, be the entire garden that is affected — maybe just an area at the foot of a slope, for example, where water drains down from a higher level.

Generally it is the heavier types of soil that commonly lie wet — like clay. If you live in a low-lying peaty area (marsh country, for example), then you also may have very wet soil.

The royal fern (*Osmunda regalis*) develops into a fine specimen plant in moist conditions (**above**). Here the delicate pale green fronds take on the hues of autumn.
The lovely blotched blooms of monkey flower (*Mimulus luteus*) dazzle the eye all summer long (**left**).
The stunning white flower spathes of *Zantedeschia aethiopica* 'Crowborough' (**far left**).
The spathes of *Lysichitum americanum*, a brilliant yellow (**left**).
A wide variety of moisture-loving plants (**below**), including the plumes of *Aruncus* and *Astilbe*, the upright spikes of *Lobelia*, the broad leaves of *Hosta*.

PLANTS FOR WET AND FLOO

Botanical Name

TREES AND SHRUBS

Acer negundo

Alnus cordata

Alnus glutinosa

Alnus incana

Betula pendula

Betula nigra

Cornus alba varieties

Cornus stolonifera 'Flaviramea'

Rhamnus frangula

Salix alba 'Chermesina'

Salix alba 'Vitellina'

Sambucus nigra 'Albovariegata'/'Aurea'/ 'Purpurea'

Sambucus racemosa 'Plumosa Aurea'

Taxodium distichum

PERENNIALS

Astilbe X arendsii cultivars

Filipendula ulmaria

Gunnera manicata

Ligularia

Lysichitum americanum

Mimulus guttatus/luteus

Osmunda regalis

Zantedeschia aethiopica

The right way to start

It pays to improve soil before attempting to plant anything. Drainage of surplus water needs to be effected, and the soil should be 'opened up' as much as possible to allow air to penetrate to the roots of the plants. In bad cases of waterlogging there is very little air in the soil, a situation that can result in the death of plants, even those which are moisture-lovers.

Soil preparation involves deep digging — to two depths of the spade (known as double digging). This ensures that the lower soil (the subsoil) — which may be hard and compacted, preventing surplus water from draining down to the lower levels of soil well away from plant roots — is well broken up.

During digging, work in plenty of grit or coarse sand, which has the effect of keeping the soil open and therefore well drained and aerated. Mix it well into the subsoil and into the top layer. There may be no need to prepare the entire garden in this way — only the beds and borders, and certainly any area in which it is intended to lay a lawn.

Take care with planting

Planting-holes on wet sites need to be prepared especially well so that plants have every chance to become established quickly. Make each planting-hole sufficiently large to take the roots of the plant without cramping them. Before inserting the plant, dig the bottom of the hole to the depth of a fork and make sure it is well broken up. Mix into the bottom a liberal quantity of peat, or one of the proprietary planting mixtures available from nurseries.

The soil removed should be replaced around the plant, but first thoroughly mix into it plenty of peat or planting mixture which makes it easier for the plants to quickly root into the surrounding soil.

Aftercare of plants

Lavish care and attention on your plants to ensure good growth. Feeding is important on wet soils because plant foods can be washed down into the lower levels of soil, out of reach of the roots. (This is known as leaching.) Carry out a regular feeding program in the spring and summer, when plants are growing. Use a general-purpose fertilizer or blood, fishmeal and bone.

Wet gardens often have problems with slugs and snails; these creatures love damp conditions. Use slug pellets.

Common Name	Height	Spread	Color	Season of interest	Notes
Box elder	6m (20ft)	4.5m (15ft)	–	Summer	'Variegatum' has white and green foliage
Italian alder	12m+ (39ft+)	–	–	Spring/Summer	Spring catkins
Common alder	9m+ (30ft+)	–	–	Spring/Summer	Spring catkins
Gray alder	12m+ (39ft+)	–	–	Spring/Summer	Spring catkins
Silver birch	10m+ (33ft+)	–	Yellow autumn foliage. White peeling bark	Summer/Autumn	–
River birch	10m+ (33ft+)	–	Pinkish-white bark	Summer	–
Shrubby dogwood	2.4m (8ft)	2.4m (8ft)	Red stems	Winter	'Sibirica' has red stems in winter. 'Elegantissima' and 'Spaethii' have variegated foliage
Shrubby dogwood	2.4m (8ft)	2.4m (8ft)	Yellow stems	Winter	–
Alder buckthorn	2.4m (8ft)	2m (6.5ft)	Yellow autumn foliage	Autumn	Red fruits
Scarlet willow	10m+ (33ft+)	–	Orange-scarlet shoots	Winter	Usually cut back for winter shoots
Golden weeping willow	15m+ (49ft+)	–	Yellow shoots	Winter	Usually cut back for winter shoots
Elder/Golden elder	2.4–3.6m (8–12ft)	2.4–3.6m (8–12ft)	Cream and white/yellow/purple foliage	Summer	–
Golden cut-leaf elder	2.4–3.6m (8–12ft)	2.4–3.6m (8–12ft)	Golden foliage	Summer	–
Swamp cypress	10m (33ft)	4.5m (15ft)	Green/bronze	Spring/Autumn	Fresh green spring growth. Foliage turns bronze in autumn. Deciduous conifer. Red-brown bark
–	0.6–1m (2–3.3ft)	45–60cm (18–24in)	Shades of red and pink, plus white	Summer	
Meadow sweet	1m (3.3ft)	60cm (2ft)	Creamy white	Summer	Fragrant flowers. The cultivar 'Aurea' has golden foliage and is only 30–45cm (12–18in) high
–	3m+ (10ft)	3m+ (10ft)	Foliage	Summer	Massive rhubarb-like leaves. 'Bottlebrush' flowerheads
–	1.2m (4ft)	60cm (2ft)	Yellow, orange	Late summer	Daisy-like flowers. Large leaves, up to 30cm (12in) across
False American skunk cabbage	90cm (3ft)	1.8m (6ft)	Yellow	Spring	Arum-like flowers with green spadix
Monkey flower	45cm (18in)	45cm (18in)	Yellow with red spots and plain yellow	Summer	–
Royal fern	1.2m (4ft)	1.2m (4ft)	Pale green fronds	Summer	'Purpurascens' has purple-copper foliage
Arum lily	1m (3.3ft)	1m (3.3ft)	White	Spring/Summer	Cultivar 'Crowborough' is hardier than the type species

Shady areas under large trees

Too often there is nothing but bare soil under large trees, because of the shade they create, commonly despite the attempts the owners have made without success to grow plants there. Yet if the right plants are chosen, the area under the canopy of branches can actually be made most attractive: it is an ideal opportunity to create a 'woodland garden', in fact.

Consider the soil

The choice of plants depends on soil conditions under the trees. Very often the soil is dry because a large tree takes up large quantities of water from the soil. Shade with dry soil is the most difficult combination for plants — nevertheless, there are subjects that can be grown successfully.

On the other hand, the soil beneath a large tree may conversely be moist — often the case where the soil is heavy or clayey and is able to hold more than enough water for the tree. Shade with moist soil is a much easier combination, and indeed there are many choice woodland-type plants that can be grown.

Preparing for planting

If the soil is dry, really thorough preparation is essential before planting. It is a case of adding as much organic matter as possible to act as a 'sponge' and help retain soil moisture. Dig in to a spade's depth anything readily available: well-rotted farmyard manure, garden compost, peat, spent hops, mushroom compost, pulverized or shredded bark, and so forth. Work into the surface a general-purpose fertilizer a few days before planting.

If the soil is moist, there is not such a great need for organic matter; nevertheless, it is advisable to add something — for example, peat, pulverized bark or leaf-mold.

When planting in dry soil, the plants need all the help they can get to become established: add to each planting-hole a proprietary planting mixture, which is peat enriched with fertilizer. This can also be used when planting in moist soils if there is some reason to think that the soil is on the poor side.

Aftercare of plants

In dry conditions, plants should be well watered in and then watered heavily whenever the soil starts to dry out. Aim to keep the soil moist throughout the growing seasons. It is best to use a garden sprinkler, for large amounts of water are required — it needs to penetrate the soil to a depth of at least 15cm (6in).

Regular feeding is necessary under large trees, for they take a great deal of plant food out of the soil. A topdressing of general-purpose fertilizer in the spring, and another in summer, are needed each year.

It is particularly important with dry soil to cover the surface with bulky organic matter — a mulch. Spread a layer 5-7.5cm (2-3in) deep between and around plants. Use any of the materials already recommended for digging in. Even in moister conditions a mulch is beneficial, for it also helps to keep the roots of the plants cool, and prevents the growth of annual weeds.

Choice of plants

In the accompanying table there are listed shrubs, perennials and bulbs suitable for shade and dry or moist soil conditions.

The 'Excelsior' foxgloves (*Digitalis purpurea*) (**top**) are excellent for planting in dappled shade. The graceful flowers of *Cyclamen hederi-folium* (**above**), in pink, mauve and white, bring welcome splashes of color to woodland shade during late summer and early autumn.

PLANTS FOR SHADE UNDER L.
Botanical Name
FOR DRY SOIL
SHRUBS
Aucuba japonica
Hedera colchica
Ilex aquifolium 'J.C. van Tol'
Ruscus aculeatus
Skimmia japonica
Vinca minor
PERENNIALS
Ajuga reptans
Alchemilla mollis
Bergenia cordifolia
Digitalis 'Excelsior' strain
Epimedium
Geranium macrorrhizum
Iris foetidissima
Lamium maculatum
Liriope muscari
Pachysandra terminalis
Pulmonaria saccharata
Symphytum grandiflorum
Waldsteinia ternata
BULBS
Cyclamen hederifolium (*neapolitanum*)
Endymion nonscriptus

Bluebells, here *Endymion hispanicus* (**left**), are classically associated with lightly shaded woodlands.

These lovely flowers of *Bergenia cordifolia* (**above**) are borne in spring above attractive rounded leaves. Ideal for dry shade.

All these plants (**right**) will grow quite happily in the shade of trees, some preferring damper soil conditions than others. Be sure to grow a decorative variety of ivy and not the common one, which is invasive.

Common Name	Height	Spread	Color	Foliage	Season of interest	Notes
Spotted laurel	2.4m (8ft)	2.4m (8ft)	Green	Evergreen, mottled yellow	Spring	Choose the cultivars 'Crotonoides' and 'Maculata'
Persian ivy	Prostrate	Indefinite	–	Evergreen, large, green	–	Grow as ground cover. 'Dentata Variegata' has cream and green leaves
Holly	2m (6.5ft)	1.2m (4ft)	–	Evergreen, almost spineless	Autumn/Winter	Heavy crops of red berries
Butcher's broom	60cm (2ft)	60cm (2ft)	Green	Evergreen, spiny	Spring	Large red berries are produced
–	1m (3ft)	1.2m (4ft)	Cream	Evergreen	Spring	Produces red berries – grow both male and female plants to ensure berries
Periwinkle	10cm (4in)	1m (3ft)	White, purple or blue	Evergreen	Spring/Summer	Many cultivars available
Bugle	10cm (4in)	30cm (12in)	Blue	Evergreen, purple or variegated in cultivars	Summer	Excellent ground cover
Lady's mantle	30cm (12in)	45cm (18in)	Yellow-green	Light green	Summer	–
Pig squeak	30cm (12in)	45cm (18in)	Deep pink	Evergreen, large, leathery	Spring	Many other species and cultivars – all worth growing
Foxglove	1.5m (5ft)	45cm (18in)	Pink, purple, cream, white	–	Summer	Raise from seeds
Barrenwort	15-30cm (6-12in)	30cm (12in)	White, yellow, pink, orange	Often tinted in spring and autumn	Spring/Summer	Good ground cover, many species
Crane's bill	30cm (12in)	45cm (18in)	Magenta-pink	Aromatic	Summer	Also a white cultivar, 'Alba'
Stinking gladwyn iris	45cm (18in)	45cm (18in)	Pale purple	Evergreen, rank smell when bruised	Summer	Scarlet seeds in autumn
Dead nettle	20cm (8in)	45cm (18in)	Pink or white	Evergreen	Spring	Several cultivars available
–	30cm (12in)	30cm (12in)	Mauve	Evergreen, grassy	Autumn	–
–	30cm (12in)	45cm (18in)	Whitish	Evergreen	Spring	Good ground cover
Lungwort	30cm (12in)	30cm (12in)	Pink and blue	Silver–spotted	Spring	Several other species with blue flowers
Comfrey	20cm (8in)	45cm (18in)	White	Rough, hairy	Spring	Good ground cover – rapid spreader
–	7.5cm (3in)	30cm (12in)	Yellow	Lobed	Summer	Good carpeter
–	10cm (4in)	15cm (6in)	Pink	Marbled silver	Autumn	–
Bluebell	30cm (12in)	30cm (12in)	Blue	–	Spring	Plant in bold drifts

The green-and-white variegated leaves of *Hosta crispula* (**far left**) make a bold splash of color. Hostas are highly suitable for moist shady situations. The magnificent spring flowers of *Rhododendron yakushimanum* (**left**) open pure white from pink buds amid the glossy evergreen foliage. A lovely dwarf shrub ideal for partial shade.

Daffodils are often planted in the shade of trees (**above**). Most varieties flower in the spring before deciduous trees are in full leaf.

Primulas and a *Hosta crispula* thrive together in this shady spot (**right**), producing an attractive combination of bright color in the flowers and bold markings in the foliage.

Botanical name	Common name	Height	Spread	Color	Foliage
FOR MOIST SOIL					
SHRUBS					
Fatsia japonica	–	2.4–3.6m (8ft–12ft)	2.4–3.6m (8ft–12ft)	White	Evergreen, large, hand-shaped
Hamamelis mollis	Chinese witch hazel	2.4m (8ft)	2.4m (8ft)	Yellow	Autumn tints
Hydrangea macrophylla Hortensia and Lacecap cultivars	–	To 1.8m (6ft)	To 1.8m (6ft)	Blue, pink, red or white	–
Pernettya mucronata	–	90cm (3ft)	90cm (3ft)	White	Evergreen
Rhododendron 'Elizabeth'	–	60cm (2ft)	1m (3.3ft)	Scarlet	Evergreen
mucronulatum	–	2.4m (8ft)	1.2m (4ft)	Rose-purple	Deciduous
scintillans	–	60cm (2ft)	60cm (2ft)	Blue	Evergreen
yakushimanum	–	60cm (2ft)	1m (3.3ft)	White	Evergreen
PERENNIALS					
Convallaria majalis	Lily-of-the-valley	15cm (6in)	30cm (12in)	White	–
Helleborus orientalis	Lenten rose	45–60cm (18–24in)	60cm (24in)	Pink, crimson, purple, white	Evergreen
Hosta	Plantain lily	30–60cm (12–24in)	30–90cm (12–36in)	White or lilac	Large, many shades of green, also variegated
Primula japonica	Japanese primrose	60cm (24in)	30cm (12in)	Magenta-red	–
Primula denticulata	Drumstick primrose	30cm (12in)	30cm (12in)	Lilac to purple	–
Viola cornuta	Violet	15cm (6in)	15cm (6in)	Lavender, blue, purple, white	–
BULBS					
Eranthis hyemalis	Winter aconite	10cm (4in)	10cm (4in)	Yellow	–
Galanthus nivalis	Snowdrop	15cm (6in)	7.5cm (3in)	White	–
Lilium tigrinum	Tiger lily	1–1.8m (3.3–6ft)	15cm (6in)	Orange-red	–
Lilium 'Enchantment'	Lily	60cm (24in)	15cm (6in)	Orange	–
Narcissus	Narcissus, Daffodils	30–45cm (12–18in)	15cm (6in)	Yellow, white, orange	–

Cheiranthus cheiri 'Fair Lady Mixed' (**above**) flourishes in chalky soils.

Early summer sees the appearance of *Viburnum opulus* 'Sterile' (**below**).

Thin chalky soils

It is easy to tell visually whether you have a chalky soil — when the surface dries out it appears whitish or grayish. Also, there may be lumps of chalk in it, as well as flints.

Often there is only a shallow layer of topsoil, overlying solid chalk. Drainage of water in these conditions is generally very rapid and the topsoil therefore dries out quickly, so there may be problems with drought in the spring and summer.

There are, however, many plants that can be grown. Observe what is growing in the local countryside, for instance. You may well find dogwoods, junipers, yews, viburnums, field maple, hazel, beech, whitebeam and wild clematis.

Season of interest	Notes
Autumn	–
Winter	Needs acid soil
Summer	Blue flowers on acid soils, pink on alkaline
Spring	Pink or red berries if male and female plants grown together. Must have acid soil
Spring	Must have acid soil
Winter	Must have acid soil
Spring	Must have acid soil
Spring	Must have acid soil
Spring	Sweetly scented blooms
–	
Summer	Many species and cultivars available
Summer	One of the candelabra primulas
Spring	Flowers in globe-shaped heads
Spring/Summer	–
Winter/Spring	Plant in bold groups
Winter/Spring	Plant in bold groups
Summer	Plant in bold groups
Summer	Plant in bold groups
Spring	Plant in bold groups

Preparing the soil and planting

Chalky soils are said to be alkaline, as opposed to acid. Acidity and alkalinity are measured on the pH scale. To test your soil to see if it is acid or alkaline, use one of the simple soil-testing kits available from nurseries; instructions are supplied. If a reading shows a pH of 6.5 or below (the neutral point on the pH scale is 7) then you have an acidic soil. If it is in the region of pH 8 or above then it is alkaline.

Although to encourage good growth it is generally necessary to prepare the soil well before planting, it is impossible to add enough bulky organic matter to thin chalky soils, for it rapidly disappears.

Plants must also be fed regularly in the spring and summer as plant foods are also quickly lost. Many plants suffer from a shortage of nitrogen (one of the most important

Garden pinks, such as *Dianthus* "London Lovely" (**left**), thrive on chalky soils.

PLANTS FOR THIN CHALKY SOILS

Botanical Name	Common Name	Height	Spread	Color	Season of interest
TREES AND SHRUBS					
Acer campestre	Field maple	6m (20ft)	3m (10ft)	Yellow leaves in Autumn	Autumn
Berberis	Barberry	Up to 2.4m (8ft) depending on variety	Up to 2.4m (8ft)	Yellow or orange flowers. Purple, red or black berries. Red, yellow or purple leaves	Spring/Autumn
Buddleia davidii	Butterfly bush	2.4m (8ft)	2.4m (8ft)	Blue, purple, red, mauve, white	Summer
Carpinus betulus	Hornbeam	30m (100ft) as mature tree	–	–	Summer
Cornus alba varieties	Shrubby dogwood	2.4m (8ft)	2.4m (8ft)	Red stems	Winter
Corylus avellana	Hazel	3m (10ft)	3m (10ft)		Spring/Summer
Fagus sylvatica	Beech	30m+ (100ft+)	–	–	Summer/Autumn
Juniperus	Juniper	Dwarf shrubs to large specimens	Prostrate forms available	Blue, blue-green, blue-gray, gray-green, yellow, golden	Year round
Sorbus aria	Whitebeam	6m+ (20ft+)	4.5m (15ft)	Leaves grayish white beneath. Autumn tints	Spring to Autumn
Taxus	Yew	Dwarf shrubs to large specimens	–	Green or gold foliage	Year round
Viburnum opulus	Guelder rose	4.5m (15ft)	4.5m (15ft)	White flowers. Red berries	Summer/Autumn
Viburnum o. 'Compactum'	Guelder rose	2m (6.5ft)	2m (6.5ft)	White flowers. Red berries	Summer/Autumn
Viburnum o. 'Sterile'	Snowball bush	3m (10ft)	3m (10ft)	White snowball-like flowers	Summer
PERENNIALS					
Anemone X hybrida	Japanese anemones	1m (3.3ft)	60cm (24in)	White, pink	Summer/Autumn
Centranthus ruber	Valerian	60cm (24in)	60cm (24in)	Red, deep pink	Summer
Cheiranthus	Wallflower	23–60cm (9–24in)	–	Many colors available	Spring
Clematis heracleifolia/ integrifolia	Herbaceous clematis	1m (3.3ft)/60cm (2ft)	1m (3.3ft)/60cm (2ft)	Purple blue/deep blue	Summer
Dianthus	Border carnations; Pinks; Sweet William	60–90cm (2–3ft)	–	Many colors available	Summer
Gypsophila paniculata 'Bristol Fairy'	Baby's breath	90cm (3ft)	90cm (3ft)	White	Summer
Sanguisorba canadensis	Burnet	2m (6ft)	30cm (12in)	Greenish white	Autumn
Sanguisorba obtusa	Burnet	1.2m (4ft)	30cm (12in)	Blue-gray leaves, pink flowers	Late summer

plant foods) on chalky soils, so it pays to use a fertilizer with a high proportion of this element, to ensure steady growth.

Planting technique should include mulching the soil with bulky organic matter like well-rotted manure, garden compost, peat, leafmold, spent hops, or shredded bark, all of which help to improve the humus content of the soil and conserve moisture during dry weather. A layer 5-7.5cm (2-3in) deep is ideal. Regular watering is necessary in dry weather to keep plants growing well.

Some plants for chalky soils

A wide range of plants can be grown, provided that they are well cared for. The exceptions are lime-hating plants, which must have acid soils — examples are rhododendrons and azaleas, camellias and many heathers. If these are grown on chalk, their leaves turn yellow, the plants become stunted and they may die.

The table features some of the best-known plants that really thrive in chalky conditions.

White flowers smother *Gypsophila paniculata* (**right**) in summer. Other chalk-loving plants include sweet Williams (**above far right**) and pinks (**below far right**).

Notes
Wide choice of evergreen and deciduous varieties available for all purposes
Fragrant
Gray fluted bark. Use as hedging in small gardens
"Sibirica" has red stems in winter. "Elegantissima" and "Spaethii" have variegated foliage
Spring catkins. "Aurora" has yellow leaves. "Contorta" has twisted stems
Use for hedging. "Purpurea" has purple foliage.
Evergreen conifers
"Decaisneana" and "Lutescens" are desirable cultivars
Evergreen conifers. *T. baccata* good for hedging
Rich autumn tints
Flowers and fruits freely
No berries
—
"Albus" has white flowers
Raise new plants from seeds in spring
Climbing forms also thrive on chalk soils
Fragrant flowers
—
Bottlebrush flowers
Bottlebrush flowers

Carpinus betulus

Sanguisorba canadensis

Centranthus ruber

Sanguisorba obtusa

Dianthus

Fagus sylvatica

Anemone

Juniperus
A formal arrangement featuring plants that thrive on thin chalky soils.

Gypsophila paniculata

Berberis x stenophylla

Viburnum opulus

Clematis heracleifolia

Berberis

Narrow flower beds

In many gardens there are straight narrow borders, perhaps running along a boundary or beside a garden path or drive. This is not the ideal design for a garden; these days the aim is for more informal beds and borders. If you are genuinely stuck with a narrow strip of soil, however, there are ways of creating pleasing effects by the careful choice of plants.

For practical purposes let us consider borders only 30-60cm (1-2ft) wide: it is this sort of width that causes problems. There is not much room to group plants as well as one would like and, of course, very large plants must be excluded altogether.

If it is possible to modify the border slightly so that it has a gently undulating edge, then a more interesting feature is created.

Bright with late spring flowers, *Iberis sempervirens* (**right**) spills between two rockery stones. This hardy evergreen perennial will grow strongly in poor soils and revels in sun.

These late winter flowers of *Scilla tubergeniana* (**right**) are of the palest blue. The bulb can be inter-planted with snowdrops and winter aconites for a colorful winter display.

The abundant flowers of *Phlox subulata* (**top**) appear in spring on spreading mats of foliage that will look in scale with the narrowest of borders. Grow this charming plant in the brightest sunshine.

Also suitable for a dry sunny corner is this *Sedum spathuli-folium* 'Cappa Blanca' (**above**). The rosettes of tough gray leaves form dense hummocks that are crowned with bright yellow flowers from late spring until early summer. Plant in a well-draining soil.

Consider the path

Very often a lawn comes right up to the edge of a border. When the border is very narrow, however, this is not a particularly good idea, because it is visually better to allow some plants to trail over its edge to 'soften' it. If plants are allowed to overhang the lawn, though, it not only makes mowing difficult but results in the death of the grass beneath them.

One alternative is to have a path between the lawn and the border. The path can follow the line of the border, whether it is straight or curved. Plants can then trail happily over the edge of the border without causing any problems.

There are several materials that can be used to construct the path. For instance, there is available a wide range of concrete paving slabs, both colored and in natural stone colors. Square or oblong slabs look best in a formal garden. Natural stone crazy paving is the ideal choice for an informal garden; another popular alternative is a brick path. A gravel path also looks good in a formal or informal setting, using pea shingle, obtainable from builders' material stores. It should be about 5cm (2in) deep and can, if desired, be retained by small curbing stones. Do not allow gravel to spread on to the lawn; it can damage mower blades.

A popular material for paths is shredded or pulverized bark, which gives a soft well-drained surface.

Another idea is to allow the lawn to butt hard up against the border, but to have an in-termediary, intermittent path of stepping stones. Some plants can then be allowed to grow partly over some of the stones. Hex-agonal paving slabs are ideal for this purpose. The stones should be carefully sunk slightly below the level of the lawn, so that a mower can run over them easily, without damage.

- Clematis
- Hedera
- Stachys lanata
- Erigeron
- Miniature roses
- Iberis sempervirens
- Kniphofia galpinii
- Juniperus
- Dianthus
- Phormium tenax
- Spiraea x bumalda 'Anthony Waterer'

The pretty lavender-blue flowers of hardy *Tradescantia* (**above**) are carried above the strap-shaped leaves from early summer until early autumn. An excellent plant for narrow borders in sun or dappled shade.

A typical narrow border (**left**), hemmed in on one side by a wall and confined on the other by a path. Fortunately, there are many plants and shrubs that can cope with these restrictions and turn a seemingly unusable strip into a flourishing display of color and form.

For spring color (**below**) plant a narrow border with polyanthus (*Primula vulgaris*). These compact plants produce flowers in a wide range of colors, all with yellow centers. Grow in fertile soil in sun or partial shade.

Choosing plants

In wide borders, plants are normally planted in bold groups, perhaps three to five of each variety. Even in a narrow border you should aim for this method of display. It does mean restricting the number of different kinds of plants, but the overall effect is better than if too many kinds of plants are used and grown as single specimens, resulting in a 'spotty' effect which is more distracting than pleasing.

In the main, plants for a narrow border must be dwarf and compact, for obvious reasons. But one or two larger plants should be used to create some variation in height; a few examples have been included in the table. Consider also habits of growth, and aim for pleasing contrasts. For instance, some upright plants could be included among low-growing prostrate kinds, perhaps some with grassy foliage, or sword-like leaves, like the phormiums. The tall, slim *Juniperus* 'Skyrocket' contrasts well with low growers.

If the border is backed by a wall or fence, make use of it for climbing plants. Some can be trained comparatively flat against the support, taking up little horizontal space, such as ornamental ivies, Virginia creeper, *Cotoneaster horizontalis*, clematis, winter jasmine and climbing roses.

The accompanying table of plants indicates the conditions they prefer — sunny with well-drained soil, or shady with moister soil — in case the border combines the two extremes.

Alyssum
Scilla
Raoulia
Sempervivum
Iberis sempervirens
Bellis
Muscari
Stachys lanata
Crocus
Iberis sempervirens
Stachys lanata

Primula 'Wanda'

PLANTS FOR VERY NARROW BORDERS

Botanical name	Common name	Height	Spread
SHRUBS			
Berberis candidula	Barberry	60cm (24in)	60cm (24in)
Calluna vulgaris	Heather	15–60cm (6–24in)	15–60cm (6–24in)
Erica	Heaths and heathers	15–30cm (6–12in)	30–45cm (12–18in)
Fuchsia 'Tom Thumb'	–	30cm (12in)	30cm (12in)
Hebe elliptica 'Variegata'	Shrubby veronica	30cm (12in)	60cm (24in)
Juniperus 'Skyrocket'	Juniper	6m (20ft)	Very slim
Juniperus communis 'Compressa'	Juniper	45cm (18in)	15cm (6in)
Phormium tenax 'Thumbelina'	New Zealand flax	30cm (12in)	30cm (12in)
Rosa	Miniature roses	Average 30cm (12in)	Average 30cm (12in)
Spiraea X bumalda 'Anthony Waterer'	–	60cm (24in)	60cm (24in)
PERENNIALS			
Alyssum saxatile	–	22cm (9in)	45cm (18in)
Armeria maritima	Thrift	15cm (6in)	30cm (12in)
Aster (dwarf)	Michaelmas daisies	30cm (12in)	30cm (12in)
Ceratostigma plumbaginoides	–	30cm (12in)	45cm (18in)
Dianthus	Carnations; Pinks	15–45cm (6–18in)	15–45cm (6–18in)
Erigeron	Fleabane	45cm (18in)	45cm (18in)
Euphorbia 'Fireglow'	Spurge	60cm (24in)	45cm (18in)
Festuca glauca	Fescue (grass)	15cm (6in)	30cm (12in)
Iberis sempervirens	Perennial candytuft	22cm (9in)	45cm (18in)
Kniphofia galpinii	Red-hot poker	45cm (18in)	45cm (18in)
Phlox subulata	Moss phlox	15cm (6in)	45cm (18in)
Primula 'Wanda'	Coloured primrose	10cm (4in)	15cm (6in)
Stachys lanata 'Silver Carpet'	Lamb's ears	10cm (4in)	30cm (12in)
Tradescantia	Spiderwort	45cm (18in)	45cm (18in)
BULBS AND TEMPORARY PLANTS			
Alyssum	Annual alyssum	10cm (4in)	15cm (6in)
Begonia semperflorens	Wax begonia	15cm (6in)	15cm (6in)
Bellis	Double daisy	15cm (6in)	15cm (6in)
Chionodoxa	Glory of the snow	15cm (6in)	Plant bulbs in groups
Crocus	–	15cm (6in)	Plant bulbs in groups
Myosotis	Forget-me-not	15cm (6in)	15cm (6in)
Muscari	Grape hyacinth	15cm (6in)	Plant bulbs in groups
Nemesia	–	30cm (12in)	Grow in a bold group for effect
Pelargonium peltatum	Ivy-leaved geranium	20cm (8in)	45cm (18in)
Primula	Polyanthus	15cm (6in)	15cm (6in)
Scilla	–	10–15cm (4–6in)	Plant bulbs in groups

Even narrower areas

In some gardens there are even narrower areas than those considered so far. For instance, a narrow strip may be found between a path and the wall of a house — where the concrete does not quite meet up with the wall. Even here, faced with possibly only a 15cm (6in) wide gap, you can make good use of it with plants.

Firstly, dig out the soil to a depth of about 30cm (1ft); in a gap like this it is probably not of very good quality and may well contain a lot of builders' rubble. Then break up the lower soil, which may be hard and compacted, thus allowing excess water to drain away easily. Next fill the hole with good-quality topsoil, or with pot-ting compost. Make the soil or compost moderately firm.

The strip is now ready for planting, and of course in this situation you should choose really low-growing or mat-forming plants. Here, many alpines or rock plants come into their own, especially if the site is reasonably sunny.

The houseleeks or sempervivums are a

Flower color	Season of interest	Preferred conditions Sunny/well drained	Shady/moist soil
Yellow	Spring	√	√
Pink, red, purple or white	Summer/Autumn	√	
Pink, red, purple or white	Summer/Autumn/Winter	√	
Violet and carmine	Summer	√	√
Violet	Summer	√	
–	–	√	√
–	–	√	√
–	–	√	
Many colors	Summer	√	
Light crimson	Summer	√	
Golden-yellow	Spring	√	
Pink or red	Spring	√	
Blue, mauve, pink, red	Autumn	√	
Blue	Summer/Autumn	√	
Pink, red, white	Summer	√	
Blue, pink, mauve, etc	Summer	√	
Red-orange	Summer	√	
Gray-blue	Summer	√	
White	Spring	√	
Orange-yellow	Autumn	√	
Blue, pink or red	Spring	√	
Claret, purple	Spring		√
Gray foliage	–	√	
Blue, purple or white	Summer	√	√
White, pink, purple or red	Summer	√	
Pink, red, white	Summer	√	√
Pink, white	Spring	√	
Blue	Spring	√	
Yellow, blue, purple, white	Spring	√	
Blue	Spring	√	√
Blue	Spring	√	√
Many colors	Summer	√	
Pink, red or white	Summer	√	
Many colors	Spring		√
Blue	Spring	√	√

To liven up the spaces in a concrete driveway grow robust prostrate plants such as thyme and houseleeks (**above**).

commendable choice. They are neat, hummock-forming plants, producing their leaves in tight rosettes, and are rather succulent; the leaves may be green, or green and red/purple. Some cultivars are completely red or purple. The common houseleek is *Sempervivum tectorum* with green and maroon leaves. A particularly attractive species is *S. arachnoideum*, the cobweb houseleek, with green leaves, flushed red, and 'woven' together with hairs, resembling a cobweb.

The sedums are also succulent plants. Some are very low growing, forming neat mats. There are many species, such as *Sedum album*, with white flowers; *S. spathulifolium* 'Cappa Blanca', purplish foliage covered with grayish-white 'bloom'; *S. acre*, which bears a profusion of yellow flowers; and *S. spurium*, with heads of deep pink flowers.

The ground-hugging raoulias from New Zealand and Australia are also ideal for this situation. Popular ones are *Raoulia australis*, with minute silvery leaves; *R. hookeri*, with slightly larger silver leaves; and *R. tenuicaulis*, which forms green moss-like growth.

The middle of the drive

In some gardens a concrete driveway has a strip of soil down its center, a popular method of drive construction many years ago in which, no doubt, the object was to save concrete.

Something has to be done with the strip — if it is just left it simply becomes a weed patch. Admittedly, weeds can be treated with a 'path weedkiller', but the result is not very pleasing to look at.

Instead, excavate it, drain it and prepare it as described for the strip between the house and path, and then plant some suitably mat-forming, spreading plants, preferably those that do not mind being walked on occasionally. Ideal for this are the thymes, some of which are really prostrate and, what is more, when trodden on give off a delightful aromatic fragrance.

Well worth growing are *Thymus lanuginosus*, with wooly gray leaves; *T. serpyllum* 'Albus', with white flowers; *T. serpyllum* 'Annie Hall', with pale pink flowers; and *T. serpyllum* 'Coccineus', with red flowers. *T.* 'Doone Valley' has deep green foliage marked with gold, and mauve flowers.

Cover the soil with pea shingle to create a smooth finish. Alternatively, use stone chippings. Both can be obtained from nurseries, and a layer of about 2.5cm (1in) deep is sufficient. Incidentally, a similar covering would also look attractive in the narrow strip between path and house, and would help to keep down the weeds.

Small concrete backyards

A small concrete back yard, devoid of plant life, is certainly a depressing sight, yet it can be turned into a most delightful patio garden.

'Patio' is a Spanish word meaning the inner courtyard of a house, where the house is built in the form of a square, enclosing an open space. In hot climates the patio garden often has a pool and perhaps a fountain, and plants are grown either in soil beds or in ornamental containers. The idea is to create a cool shady place — a refuge from the heat of the day.

You can turn a small concrete back yard into a similar haven of tranquillity. And if it is surrounded by a brick wall or a fence, then so much the better, for it will then be a very private little world.

Many city or suburban houses have nothing more than a yard at the back, yet many have been turned into the most delightful patio gardens.

Varying the surface

A very simple and practical idea for making an area of nothing but concrete more interesting is to have some areas of gravel. This immediately provides a pleasing contrast in textures. The same advice applies if the back yard is covered with concrete paving slabs.

There are two ways of creating such gravel areas. The simplest is to lay gravel directly on the concrete; a layer of about 2.5-5cm (1-2in) deep is sufficient. The material to use is pea shingle, which is readily available from builders' stores and some nurseries.

The gravel must be retained in some way or it will not stay in its allotted place. This is easily achieved with the aid of small concrete curbing or edging stones, or with a single layer of ornamental walling bricks. These ideally should be cemented in place.

If the gravel is placed directly onto concrete, you will have to find containers in which to grow plants on it. If, however, you wish to grow plants in soil beds topped with gravel, you will have to break up and lift some of the concrete, then dig out the soil to a depth of about 30cm (1ft), and replace it with good topsoil or with potting compost. Before refilling, though, break up the bottom of the hole to the depth of a fork, for the subsoil is bound to be compacted. This helps surplus water to drain away and ensures that plants can easily root into the lower soil.

Plants for gravel areas

Particularly suitable plants for these gravel areas, whether they are grown directly in soil or in ornamental containers and tubs, are those with bold or dramatic foliage that give an exotic atmosphere, imitating the patio gardens of the Mediterranean.

Phormiums or New Zealand flax have the

most dramatic leaves of all: they are sword-shaped and held erect. And what is more, the foliage is evergreen. They need a sunny situation, although they do not mind partial shade. Some of the modern cultivars have very colorful foliage. Try the following: *Phormium cookianum* 'Tricolor', leaves striped green, white and red, height: 90cm (3ft); also *P. tenax* cultivars: 'Bronze Baby', deep bronze leaves, 60cm (2ft) high; 'Purpureum', purplish leaves, height: 2m (6½ft); 'Sundowner', cream-pink and greyish-purple, height: 90cm (3ft); 'Thumbelina', purple-bronze, 30cm (1ft) high; 'Yellow Wave', golden-yellow and green, height: 75cm (30in); 'Dazzler', deep red, similar height; and 'Variegatum', cream and green, 2m (6½ft) in height.

The *yuccas* have stiff sword-like evergreen leaves and also need a sunny situation. They are generally grown as single specimens rather than in groups. There are several to choose from, such as *Yucca filamentosa*, whose leaf edges have curly threads, height: about 60cm (2ft); *Y. filamentosa* 'Variegata', with green and cream striped leaves; *Y. flaccida* 'Ivory', noted for its creamy white flowers, height: about 60cm (2ft); and *Y. gloriosa*, popularly known as Adam's needle, which forms a trunk-like stem topped with spine-tipped leaves, and produces creamy white flowers, height: up to 2m (6½ft).

The *hostas* or plantain lilies are dwarf herb-

Clematis

Tagetes patula

Flagstones, a narrow border, climbing wall plants and a wide variety of planted containers transform this small back yard (**above left**) into a haven of color and interest. Ablaze with the bright blooms of pelargoniums and petunias, this back yard (**left**) also features the cooler contrasts of sempervivums and herbs. Lack of space should never cramp your gardening ambitions. Here a compact yard (**below left**), viewed from the house, features an ornamental pond, a luxuriant planting of choice foliage and flowering subjects and a classical statue as a focal point.

Gazania hybrid

aceous plants with large, bold leaves, which come in various shades of green, also bluish gray and variegated cream, white and green. There are many cultivars; choose any which appeal. They have lily-like flowers in summer, generally lilac or white. The plantain lilies are particularly useful for shady parts of the garden, for they like moist soil. They look particularly fine growing at the edge of a pool.

Rodgersias are also grown mainly for their attractive foliage, which is bold and hand-shaped. They can be grown in sun or partial shade, and prefer reasonably moist conditions — so keep them well watered. A popular cultivar is *Rodgersia pinnata* 'Superba', with bronzy purple leaves. Height: about 90cm (3ft).

The ornamental grasses associate well with many plants, particularly plants with bold foliage like the *hostas* and *rodgersias*. There are many grasses to choose from. All of the following are perennial in habit and appreciate a sunny spot: *Helictotrichon sempervirens*, blue-gray foliage, 45cm (18in); *Cortaderia selloana* 'Gold

Crazy paving (**above**) enhances an informal planting. A sword-like phormium (**top right**) in a patio corner. *Rodgersia pinnata* 'Superba' (**above right**).

Band', leaves striped yellow and green, 75cm (30in); *C. selloana* 'Sunningdale Silver', variety of pampas grass, with creamy white plumes of flowers, 2m (6½ft); *Festuca glauca*, blue-gray foliage, 30cm (12in); *Holcus mollis* 'Variegatus', green and silver variegated, 30cm (12in); *Miscanthus sinensis* 'Zebrinus', the zebra grass, whose leaves are banded with gold, 2m (6½ft); and *Phalaris arundinacea* 'Picta', popularly called Gardener's garters, a vigorously spreading grass with green and white striped leaves, height: 60cm (2ft).

Prostrate or low-growing junipers are useful for contrasting with spiky or grassy leaves. There are many to choose from, such as *Juniperus horizontalis* 'Bar Harbor', completely prostrate with gray-green foliage; *J. X media* 'Old Gold', height and spread about 90cm (3ft); and *J. sabina tamariscifolia*, a flat-topped bush with deep green foliage, 30 cm (12in) high, and a spread of about 1.2m (4ft). They like sun or partial shade.

The evergreen shrub *Fatsia japonica* has large, bold, hand-shaped leaves and makes a specimen about 2.4m (8ft) in height and spread. White flowers are produced in autumn. It is a good shrub for shade, but takes full sun.

In areas where the climate is perhaps a little milder, you could try the Chusan palm *Trachycarpus fortunei*, which has large fan-shaped leaves on a thick trunk. It is slow growing but eventually makes a specimen well over 2m (6.5ft) in height, and the leaves have a similar spread. Sun is needed, plus a spot sheltered from wind.

There are all kinds of hardy ferns that can be planted in cool shady spots, including around the edge of a pool where the soil is moist.

Rodgersia pinnata

Garrya elliptica

Hedera

Hosta

Fatsia japonica

Yucca

Agave

Cordyline australis

Pelargonium

The illustration (**left**) shows how an unpromising walled area can be brightened up with a blend of tough shade-tolerant foliage subjects and colorful flowering plants.

A new dimension

To add another dimension, consider a pool. Such an attraction is very easy to put in these days, using one of the small prefabricated pools obtainable from nurseries or water-garden specialists, made from rigid fiberglass or plastic. A formal square or rectangular pool is more suitable for a patio than an informal shape. Moreover, to avoid your having to dig a hole in the concrete, the pool could be raised — simply by placing it on the concrete and building up the sides with bricks or ornamental walling blocks. The variation in height adds life to an otherwise flat area.

Water also provides the patio garden with another texture, reflecting the sky and plants, and creating further interest. Miniature waterlilies are available for small pools, and around the edge, in the shallow water, marginal aquatics like marsh marigold and perhaps a water iris could be planted. Include some submerged oxygenating plants or 'water weeds', and introduce some fish. For best results, choose a sunny place for the pool.

Make best use of vertical space

If the yard is surrounded by a wall or fence, these will make ideal supports for climbing plants which can be trained to horizontal wires or to trellis panels fixed to the wall or fence.

There are many climbers and wall shrubs to choose from, even for shady aspects, such as winter jasmine, *Jasminum nudiflorum*, with yellow flowers; ornamental ivies with green or variegated foliage; Virginia creeper; and *Garrya elliptica*, which has greenish catkins in winter.

For sunny walls and fences choose from the wide range of clematis, climbing and rambling roses (these two subjects look good together and can be allowed to intertwine); honeysuckles; and summer jasmine, *Jasminum officinale*, with white scented blooms.

Bold splashes of color in stylish containers (**above**) create a superb miniature garden. Here pelargoniums, *Impatiens*, begonias and fuchsias predominate. Screens and trellis work (**left and far left**) form a striking background to patio plants. A cramped town back yard may seem an unpromising site but here (**below left**) a small patio is engulfed by a 'jungle' of foliage and flowering plants.

Containers for plants

A look around a good garden centre reveals a wide range of ornamental containers, in all shapes, sizes and materials.

Very popular are terracotta pots and vases, as well as modern concrete tubs. Traditional wooden tubs are also attractive. Classical urns are very much in keeping with a patio garden. In order to fill every available inch of space, make use also of window boxes and hanging baskets.

For a large container for planting, consider constructing a floor box. This structure is essentially a raised bed and may be built directly on concrete or paving from timber, railway sleepers, bricks, walling blocks, or similar building materials.

All containers must have drainage holes in the base. Before adding compost, place a layer of drainage material in the bottom, such as pebbles, stones or broken clay flower pots. Top this layer with coarse peat, and then fill up to within a couple of centimeters (roughly an inch) of the top with a proprietary potting compost. A large raised bed should be filled with good quality topsoil, which will probably have to be brought in.

Colorful plants for containers

It is not only permanent plants, recommended earlier, that can be used in containers, but also temporary subjects to give color in spring and summer — the spring and summer bedding plants.

For summer color in shade, try *Begonia semperflorens* (wax begonia), fuchsias, *Impatiens* (busy lizzie), and the annual *Mimulus* (monkey flowers).

For summer color in sunny parts of the garden there is a very wide choice indeed: pelargoniums (geraniums), petunias, French and African marigolds, *Nicotiana*, tuberous begonias, *Verbena, Lobelia*, Gazanias, Livingstone daisies, *Heliotrope* and ageratums.

Spring bedding plants suitable for shade include polyanthus, forget-me-nots and colored primroses. For sun, plant bulbs such as tulips and hyacinths, and plants such as double daisies and wallflowers.

For a hot sunny spot, try some succulent plants in pots outdoors for the summer, such as the century plant *(Agave)* and *Cordyline australis*, (the cabbage palm), but remember these have to be taken indoors in early autumn in temperate climates.

Hard-wear areas

Some parts of the garden receive very hard wear. Consequently, they never really look attractive — more often than not they are an eyesore To improve this situation it is generally a case of re-thinking in terms of more resilient surfaces and tougher plants.

The main problem areas commonly center on parts of a lawn — or even the whole lawn if it is small — especially the areas used for sitting on or as playing areas for children. The grass simply becomes worn away.

Play areas themselves often look very shabby, perhaps down to nothing more than bare earth where the grass has completely died out. In wet weather, such areas often become mud patches. Plants around a play area may look rather untidy; they do not readily make new growth after being damaged or trodden on.

Areas around the house doors are obviously used a great deal, and again may resemble a children's play area. Other vulnerable parts of a garden are borders or beds beside drives and paths.

But there is really no need to put up with shabby areas. Choose the right kinds of plants, the appropriate surfacing materials — and hard-wear areas can be considerably improved and in time even look attractive, yet *still* be used just as much. After all, a garden is meant to be used as well as to be decorative.

Hard-wear lawns

The lawn is without doubt the most vulnerable part of a garden, used more than any other for sitting and playing. Consequently, bare patches quickly appear as the surface becomes very compacted, and muddy patches develop in wet weather. Tiny lawns, the norm in modern pocket-handkerchief gardens, come off worse than larger grass areas because use is concentrated in one area. With a large lawn, the area actually in use can at least be moved around before damage occurs, to give the worn grass a chance to recover.

A lawn that is to be subject to hard wear should be made by sowing a grass seed mixture which produces a resilient turf. These mixtures contain a high proportion of

ryegrass; a typical composition is: three parts perennial ryegrass (*Lolium perenne*), a broad-leaved grass which grows in tufts; four parts chewings fescue *(Festuca rubra commutata)*, which is a tufted drought-resistant grass with thin leaves that produces a fine appearance; two parts crested dog's-tail *(Cynosurus cristatus)*, which grows in broad-leaved tufts and is also drought-resistant; and one part rough-stalked meadow grass *(Poa trivialis)*, a broad-leaved grass that spreads by runners above the ground. Many mixes, such as Sprinter, contain dwarf ryegrass which produces a less tufty-looking lawn.

On no account use a grass seed mix formulated for a luxury lawn. These mixtures contain very fine grasses, such as browntop

The variegated leaves of *Euonymus fortunei* 'Silver Queen' (**left**) are usefully tough.

Resilient ground cover is provided by *Cotoneaster dammeri* (**above**).

Rhus typhina

Buddleia davidii

Mahonia aquifolium

Phalaris arundinacea 'Picta'

Cortaderia selloana

Prunus laurocerasus

Pyracantha

Lamium galeobdolon

bent *(Agrostis tenuis)* and chewings fescue, which do not stand up to hard wear. Chewings fescue is used in utility mixes mainly to improve the appearance of a lawn — to give a 'thick pile'.

It is also possible to have special grass seed mixtures made up that contain clover. Most people would consider this to be a weed, but a lawn with a high proportion of clover is nevertheless very hard wearing and, as a bonus, stays green during drought conditions. It is also possible to have an entirely clover lawn. For clover mixtures or pure clover, contact a specialist lawn grass seed dealer. Clover can be mown just like an ordinary lawn to give a fairly smooth surface. Alternatively, it can be allowed to grow fairly tall and flower before it is cut.

Gravel areas

A very tiny lawn is not a practical proposition if the area is to be used a great deal. One alternative is to consider laying gravel. Admittedly, the surface is not as soft as grass but it can look neat at all times, especially if perhaps some containers are grouped on it, filled with colorful plants.

A gravel area is easily constructed. First, make sure the area is as level as possible before setting garden curbing stones around the edges to contain the gravel, ideally bedded in cement. Next, sprinkle dry cement all over the soil — a layer about 12mm (½in) deep will be sufficient. Fork this into the top 5-7.5cm (2-3in) of soil, mixing it well in. Do this preferably when the soil is moist but not wet. Then firm the soil really well, ideally by using a heavy garden roller. Eventually the cement hardens and binds the soil together, giving a very hard surface. Subsequently, cover the area with gravel — pea shingle from a local builders' material supplier — to a depth of about 5cm (2in).

If any weeds grow through the gravel, spray them with a proprietary path weedkiller. It is also a good idea to rake the gravel about once a week to keep it looking neat and level. Apart from that, no maintenance is needed.

Sitting-out areas

Within a larger lawn that is used for sitting, why not consider constructing a special sitting-out area — a hard surface for a table and chairs? It can certainly be more comfortable — no longer does your chair sink into the lawn, nor does your table rock crazily, endangering

Hypericum calycinum (**above**) is an outstanding ground cover plant for hard-wear areas. Once established, it forms a dense growth of evergreen leaves that are smothered in showy yellow flowers throughout the summer.

For an exceptionally robust and rewarding shrub it is hard to beat the low-growing *Prunus laurocerasus* 'Otto Luyken' (**below**). The attractive white flower spikes are borne above the glossy evergreen foliage in spring.

things upon it. You will also be able to sit out when the grass is very wet.

Mark out an area of suitable size — it could be formal (square or oblong) in a formal garden, or perhaps an irregular shape in a more informal garden. Some superb paving materials are available today, as a visit to a nursery reveals. Paving slabs come in all shapes, sizes and colors; an alternative is natural-stone paving, particularly in a cottage garden. Paving should be laid on a foundation consisting of about 15cm (6in) of well-rammed hardcore, topped with a thin layer of sand. Lay paving slabs preferably on mortar, and leave a 6mm (¼in) gap between them. The gaps should later be grouted with cement and sand to prevent weeds from growing through.

Play areas

Small children need somewhere to play, and it is a good idea to allocate one specific part of the garden for this purpose, where they can dig

TOUGH PLANTS FOR HARD WEAR AREAS

Botanical name	Common name	Height
SHRUBS		
Berberis X stenophylla	Barberry	2.4m (8ft)
Buddleia davidii	Butterfly bush	2.4m (8ft)
Cornus alba	Shrubby dogwood	2.4m (8ft)
Cotoneaster horizontalis	–	60cm (2ft)
Cotoneaster species	–	60cm-3.6m (2-12ft)
Elaeagnus X ebbingei	–	3m (10ft)
Euonymus fortunei	–	Prostrate or low growing
Hedera colchica	Persian ivy	Prostrate
Hedera colchica 'Dentata Variegata'	Variegated Persian ivy	Prostrate
Hypericum calycinum	St John's wort	30cm (12in)
Kerria japonica 'Pleniflora'	Jew's mallow	2.4m (8ft)
Leycesteria formosa	–	2m (6.5ft)
Lonicera pileata	Shrubby honeysuckle	60cm (2ft)
Mahonia aquifolium	Oregon grape	1.5m (5ft)
Prunus laurocerasus 'Otto Luyken' and 'Schipkaensis'	Dwarf cherry laurels	60cm (2ft)
Pyracantha	Firethorn	3.6m (12ft)
Rhus typhina	Stag's horn sumach	3.6m (12ft)
Ribes sanguineum	Flowering currant	2.4m (8ft)
Symphoricarpos albus	Snowberry	1.8m (6ft)
PERENNIALS		
Cortaderia selloana	Pampas grass	2.4m (8ft)
Elymus arenarius	Lyme grass	60cm (2ft)
Lamiastrum galeobdolon 'Variegatum'	Yellow archangel	30cm (12in)
Phalaris arundinacea 'Picta'	Gardener's garters grass	60cm (2ft)

holes, make a 'camp', and have a swing, slide and climbing frame. This should also, to some extent, act as a protective measure for the rest of the garden, keeping it looking good, most of its plants safe from tiny feet and garden toys.

Furthermore, if ever you are talked into buying a tent, put it up in the play area and *not* on the lawn; if a tent is erected on the lawn even for only a few days, the grass beneath turns yellow, and takes some time to recover.

A play area needs a suitable surface, certainly not grass or soil, or it will end up as a mud patch. One good idea is to surface it with pulverized or shredded bark, which gives a very soft, well-drained surface and can be laid directly onto well-firmed soil. A depth of about 5-7.5cm (2-3in) is sufficient. If children fall over on this they do not hurt themselves and, what is more, they keep clean.

Plant life need not be entirely absent from a play area — indeed, some groups of suitable shrubs not only make it look more attractive

but may also possibly be appreciated by youngsters as they play amid them. The play area could also be surrounded (or partly surrounded) by shrubs, not only as a partial screen, but so that children know exactly which is their part of the garden.

Of course such shrubs must be really tough, and ought also to be quick-growing. Some of them could be flowering shrubs — but avoid prickly or thorny kinds. Particularly recommended are *Buddleia davidii* cultivars, shrubby dogwoods with colored stems, and *Kerria japonica* 'Pleniflora'. Also avoid any shrubs which produce berries in case small children might be tempted to eat them (although the berries of most garden shrubs are not poisonous).

Smartening up access areas
Other hard-wear areas are those around the house doors, around gates, and borders or beds alongside drives and paths. For these

areas, which are likely to be walked on occasionally, if not regularly, one suggestion is to clothe the soil with really tough ground-cover plants: there are some that can put up with the occasional heavy foot.

Plant ground-cover plants in bold groups or drifts, setting the plants fairly close together so that they quickly close up and provide dense cover. Most of the ground-cover plants recommended here can be planted approximately 30-45cm (12-18in) apart in every direction.

Before planting, however, it pays to prepare the soil well by digging in plenty of well-rotted manure or garden compost, and pricking in some sterilized bonemeal or a general fertilizer. Feed and water the plants well and they will grow vigorously.

Suitable tough ground-cover plants include *Cotoneaster horizontalis, Euonymus fortunei* cultivars, *Hedera colchica, Hypericum calycinum, Lonicera pileata* and *Lamiastrum galeobdolon* 'Variegatum'.

Spread	Color	Season of interest	Shade tolerance	Notes
3.6m (12ft)	Golden yellow	Spring	√	Evergreen, prickly
2.4m (8ft)	Blue, purple, red, mauve, white	Summer		Deciduous, fragrant flowers
2.4m (8ft)	White	Summer	√	Red stems, deciduous. Several cultivars available
2–2.4m (6–8ft)	White	Summer	√	Red berries in autumn. Deciduous. Ideal for ground cover
Variable	White	Summer	√	Many species and cultivars, all with colorful autumn berries
3m (10ft)	White	Autumn	√	Evergreen, silvery gray leaves
Variable	–		√	Ground cover. Evergreen. Many cultivars have variegated leaves
Variable	–	–	√	Dark green evergreen leaves, large and heart-shaped. Ground cover plant
Variable	–	–	√	Cream and green variegated leaves. Ground cover
Variable	Yellow	Summer	√	Evergreen ground cover, very vigorous
2m (6ft)	Yellow	Spring		Deciduous, forms thickets of growth
2m (6.5ft)	White and claret	Summer	√	Deciduous, produces purplish berries in autumn
1.2cm (4ft)	Greenish	Spring	√	Ground cover shrub, semi-evergreen, bright green foliage
2m (6.5ft)	Yellow	Spring	√	Glossy, deep green evergreen, spiny foliage. Blue-black berries
1m (3.3ft)	White	Summer	√	Evergreen leaves. Good ground cover
3.6m (12ft)	White	Summer	√	Grown for red, orange or yellow autumn berries, evergreen, spiny
3.6m (12ft)	Pale red	Summer		Good autumn leaf color. Crimson berries
2.4m (8ft)	Red, crimson or pink	Spring		Deciduous, black autumn berries
1.8m (6ft)	Pink	Summer	√	Grown for its large white berries. Choose one of the cultivars
2m (6.5ft)	Silvery plumes	Summer/Autumn		Arching, grassy evergreen leaves. 'Sunningdale Silver' is a good cultivar
Indefinite	Gray-blue	Summer		A vigorous grass with gray-blue foliage. Needs plenty of space to spread
Indefinite	Yellow	Summer	√	Excellent ground cover. Very vigorous. Evergreen leaves splashed with silver
Indefinite	Greenish	Summer		Very vigorous and spreading grass with white and green striped leaves. Makes good ground cover

Problems with lawns

No matter how well a lawn is maintained invariably at some time or another bare patches appear where the grass dies out.

Many factors cause bare patches; once the cause is known, we can start to effect a cure. One of the main and most obvious causes of bare patches is excessive use. Using a lawn when it is very wet can result in muddy patches which stifle the grass and result in it dying. Worm-casts flattened by feet or by mower may also result in mud patches.

Lawn weeds, such as dandelions, plantains, clover, moss and pearlwort can smother grass and cause it to die. But killing these weeds with lawn weedkillers may additionally cause bare patches of soil.

Incorrect mowing commonly results in bare patches. If the mower blades are set too low the machine 'scalps' raised areas or humps. Alternatively, if the lawn is mown very closely in drought conditions the grass may die (although it may recover later when conditions are more moist).

Poor drainage, so that the surface of a lawn remains saturated after rain, can eventually lead to poor growth.

And finally shade can be a problem — especially under large trees. A combination of heavy shade, which results in weak grass growth, and very dry conditions, may cause grass to die, after which the area may become infested with moss.

If the lawn becomes very thin over most of its surface, the reason might again be compaction of the soil — in other words, a very hard surface caused by constant and heavy use.

Relieving compaction

To relieve a compacted surface and prevent it from recurring, spike the lawn regularly: it may be necessary during the spring or summer, depending on whether or not the soil quickly becomes hard on the surface, but it is essential during the autumn.

The usual method of spiking is to insert a garden fork 10-15cm (4-6in) deep all over the lawn, at 15cm (6in) intervals. This sounds laborious, and indeed it is, so with a large lawn it is better to hire a mechanical spiker.

Spiking also helps to improve drainage — so you may be killing two birds with one stone. If the lawn is very badly drained it is advisable to use a hollow-tine fork for spiking. This tool is specially designed for the job, and is inserted in the same way as an ordinary fork except that it takes out cores of soil. The holes must be kept open, so it is the usual practice to brush a topdressing into them, consisting perhaps of a mixture of finely sifted loam or good topsoil and coarse sand — an ideal mixture where the soil is heavy clay. Spread a layer over the lawn and brush it in with a besom broom. The best time for hollow-tine spiking/topdressing is in the early autumn.

Correct mowing

During drought conditions, try not to mow a lawn — unless of course the grass is growing vigorously following artificial watering. Always make sure the grass is cut to the correct height: a utility lawn should be cut to a height of 30mm (1¼in) in spring, autumn, and during dry periods, and down to 25mm (1in) in summer. A luxury lawn with fine-leaved grasses, however, can be cut to 20mm (¾in) in spring, autumn, and during dry periods, and down to 10mm (½in) in summer.

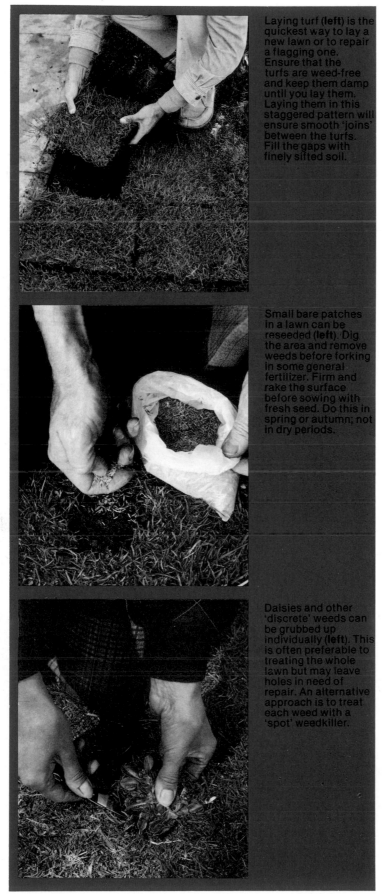

Laying turf **(left)** is the quickest way to lay a new lawn or to repair a flagging one. Ensure that the turfs are weed-free and keep them damp until you lay them. Laying them in this staggered pattern will ensure smooth 'joins' between the turfs. Fill the gaps with finely sifted soil.

Small bare patches in a lawn can be reseeded **(left)**. Dig the area and remove weeds before forking in some general fertilizer. Firm and rake the surface before sowing with fresh seed. Do this in spring or autumn; not in dry periods.

Daisies and other 'discrete' weeds can be grubbed up individually **(left)**. This is often preferable to treating the whole lawn but may leave holes in need of repair. An alternative approach is to treat each weed with a 'spot' weedkiller.

Lawns can make or break a garden. A superb lawn like striped velvet **(above)** is a dream most gardeners aspire to. A discolored moss-ridden 'grassy patch' **(left)** is often the sad reality. Converting one to the other demands the techniques described on these pages.

Controlling weeds and worms

Weeds are easily controlled with modern lawn weedkillers, normally used in the spring when the lawn — and weeds — are growing actively. A lawn moss killer provides moss control: again in spring, when the moss is dead and black, rake it out with a wire-tine lawn rake. Rake really vigorously to remove dead grass and other debris with it. It is possible to buy (or hire) a 'lawn scarifier' for raking large lawns.

If worms are a problem in the lawn, they can be controlled by applying a proprietary worm-killer in the spring or autumn. Brush off worm casts with a besom before mowing.

Grass under trees

One of the most difficult problems in keeping a lawn is caused by trees overshadowing the lawn, subjecting particular areas to heavy shade and dry conditions. For the best results, dig in plenty of organic matter specifically near to trees before sowing; garden compost, peat, spent hops or mushroom compost are all excellent, and help to retain moisture. Then sow with a grass-seed mixture specially formulated for shady conditions — one such is available in most nurseries. Water the area regularly, and heavily in dry periods.

Keeping the grass growing

There is no doubt that regularly feeding the lawn, watering it in dry weather, and carrying out maintenance tasks such as spiking, raking and weed control, all encourage vigorous, strong growth. The lawn is then less likely to become thin or bare.

Sowing bare patches

But before taking measures to prevent future bare patches from occurring, it is obviously necessary to make good existing bald patches by sowing grass seeds or by turfing. Before sowing, dig the bare patch with a fork, about 15cm (6in) deep, and remove any weeds, and any roots as well. Then prick in a little general-purpose or lawn fertilizer. Firm the soil well by systematically treading down with your heels. Rake it down to a fine level surface with an iron rake. Sow the grass seed at a rate of 42gm per m² (1½oz per sq yd), and lightly rake it into the surface. The best time to sow grass seed is in spring or early autumn.

Turfing bare patches

Remove any dead grass and square up the bald area. Prepare the soil as described above. It may be necessary to remove some of the soil to allow for the depth of the turf, for it will come with up to 2.5cm (1in) of soil. Set the turf in place and lightly firm down by patting with the back of a spade. Fill any gaps with finely sifted soil, brushing it well in. Keep it well watered in dry periods. The best time to re-turf is in early autumn.

Sloping sites

A sloping garden can certainly look more attractive than a perfectly flat site — but is not without its problems.

For instance, drainage of water from the soil can be too effective; moreover, if the soil is of a type to be naturally well drained — such as sand or gravel — then the garden may be very dry indeed. This is further accentuated if the site also faces the sun for much of the day.

Water of course drains to the bottom of any slope. If it cannot then escape — it may be blocked by the house if the garden slopes down to the house — then the ground is inevitably very wet and boggy. Such a damp spot can also

become a frost pocket as cold air additionally drains down to the bottom and builds up. It is obviously not an appropriate site for a greenhouse, or for growing fruit trees.

If the garden slopes very steeply, there may well be the need to create some flatter areas. This can be achieved by terracing — either all or part of the garden, depending on the size of the plot — which involves building retaining walls and levelling the land between them.

Of course, conversely, there are advantages in a sloping site. If it faces the sun for much of the day, the soil warms up and dries out quickly in the spring, so that an early start can be made with sowing vegetables and flowers. And it is ideal for the building of a rock garden, which always looks far more natural when not built on a completely flat site.

Dealing with a wet patch

If constructing terraces is too strenuous a means of dealing with a damp spot at the bottom of a slope, there are two other ways of approaching the problem. At the outset a line of clay land drain pipes (or the newer perforated plastic land drainage piping) could be laid across the plot from one side of the garden to the other at the bottom of the slope. The pipes should slope gently to a soakaway.

Alternatively, good use could be made of the wet area for growing bog and moisture-loving plants. A rock garden could perhaps be built just above it, and a natural looking pool and bog garden created in the wet area.

Creating level areas

Terracing creates a very pleasing feature in a

Informal steps in a rock garden setting form a natural link between levels on a sloping site.

garden. On a very steep site, however, some level terraces may actually be necessary in order to grow plants easily.

The type of terracing should suit the style of the house and garden. Near a modern house, for instance, the retaining walls for the terraces should be built of modern materials, such as concrete walling blocks, or perhaps of bricks that match those of the house.

On the other hand, next to a farmhouse, for example, more natural materials such as logs or tree sections are probably much more suitable. In some areas, such as New England, it may be appropriate to build dry-stone walls using local natural stone. The stones of such walls are not cemented together, although soil pockets can be made between some of them in which to grow trailing rock plants.

If they can be obtained, timber railway sleepers could be used to form the terraces; they can look good whether in a modern or old-style garden. Really, terraces are no more than a series of very wide 'steps', but the width of each step is determined by the gradient. On a very steep slope the retaining walls have to be much closer together than on a more gently sloping site.

Make a start with the terracing by moving soil around to form the outlines of the terraces — but before you start forming the terraces themselves, the topsoil should be removed and stacked in some convenient spot, so that it is not mixed up with the subsoil. After the terraces have been constructed the topsoil can then be replaced.

Brick, concrete or stone walls should be built on a solid foundation — a 15cm (6in) layer of well-rammed hardcore, topped with about 10cm (4in) of concrete that must be perfectly level across the width of the plot. Such horizontal flatness can be achieved by inserting a line of wooden pegs, and ensuring that the tops are parallel by means of a spirit-level and straight-edge board.

Make sure that any wall built with bricks, concrete walling blocks or stone, cemented together, does not block the natural flow of water through the soil, or wet areas will build up behind the walls. To prevent this, leave gaps at intervals between bricks or blocks or, better still, insert plastic tubes. Water can then pass freely through each wall. If still in doubt about drainage, then behind each wall fill in with rubble or stones, to about 30cm (12in) below the final soil level.

Remember that retaining walls should not be completely vertical, but should tilt back slightly into the slope to compensate for the weight of soil behind them. This applies especially to dry-stone walls.

A mountainscape
Basically, building a rock garden on a sloping site again involves constructing a set of terraces with level soil between them — but in this case, large and small pieces of natural rock are used, the idea being to simulate natural rock outcrops. Use the local rock of the area — if your garden is in a limy or chalky area, use limestone rock, which is whitish; if your garden is in a sandy area, then it is likely that honey-colored sandstone is the natural rock. The accompanying drawing shows how a rock garden should be built, but before you start construction, study some examples in gardens open to the public.

The flat-topped flowerheads of *Achillea* cascade around the base of a fine specimen of *Corylopsis pauciflora* (**below**). This sunny sloping garden has low walls and clearly defined terraced areas.

Public gardens provide ideas for coping with difficult sites such as steeply sloping gardens. This bold rockery (**right**), planted with dwarf conifers and bulbs, features a series of interconnecting rock pools.

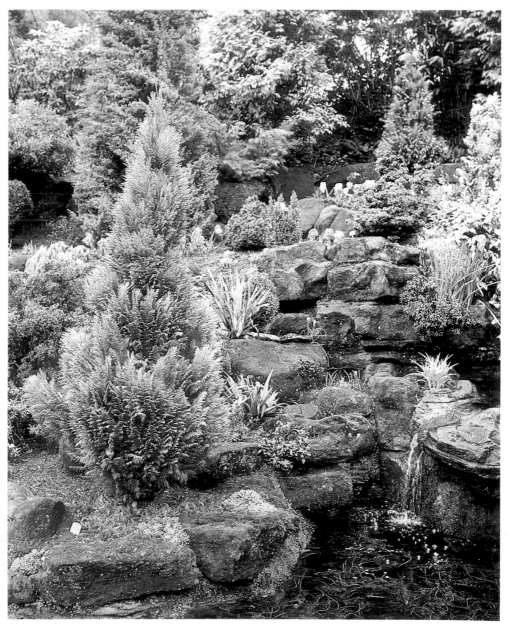

Plants for polluted areas

Gardeners living in towns, cities and industrialized areas are only too well aware of the pollution problem — fumes not only from traffic, but also from smoky factories. Smoke and fumes can have an adverse effect on many plants. Not only are the leaves (and greenhouse glass, too) quickly covered with a film of grime which makes them look unsightly and also impairs their functions, but the growth of the plants may be severely retarded.

In recent times it has become apparent that pollution even affects the rain: in particular areas it is contaminated with chemicals and is popularly known as acid rain. At highest risk from acid rain are cities, towns and industrialized zones — but of course it falls even in country areas. It not only pollutes the soil, making it less suitable for plant growth, but also directly affects the plants themselves. Symptoms include a marked lack of vigor; sudden leaf drop; yellow or brown spots on the upper leaf surfaces; and browning around the leaf edges.

Choosing suitable plants
Fortunately there is a good range of plants that can be grown successfully in gardens subject to town and industrial pollution. A range is described in the accompanying table. In general, deciduous plants (which drop their leaves in autumn) are a better choice than evergreens, because they produce fresh new leaves each spring. However, some evergreens can be successfully grown. Herbaceous plants and bulbs are a good choice, too, for the same reason. Rather surprisingly perhaps, many alpine or rock-garden plants also succeed. It is also worthwhile growing temporary spring and summer bedding plants.

Other plants found to thrive in gardens subject to pollution include laurels, hydrangeas, ivies, *Euonymus*, buddleias, mahonias, *Hamamelis* and Virginia creeper (in addition to those described in the table); all are listed and described in other sections of this book.

Plants to avoid, because they have been found to suffer badly, include beech hedges, many conifers, dahlias, chrysanthemums, lupins, and the summer bedding plants petunias and asters.

How to care for plants
Obviously the plants that can be grown need care and attention if they are to give of their best. To keep the leaves as free as possible from grime you should spray them regularly with water, preferably using a hosepipe with a spray nozzle on the end. If the leaves are functioning properly, growth in general will be much improved.

Watering the soil regularly in dry weather also helps, as does regular feeding in the spring and summer. As well as a topdressing of dry fertilizer in the spring, give plants an additional boost by feeding with liquid fertilizer in spring and summer. Foliar feeding is also to be recommended: spray a special foliar fertilizer onto the leaves in the summer.

If plants are subject to salt spray from the roads in winter, then again spray them with clean water, whether or not they still have leaves.

Mulching the soil with peat, leaf-mold, garden compost, pulverized bark, mushroom compost or spent hops can also help to minimize the effect of pollution on soil and plants.

The glass in the greenhouse or garden frame should be rinsed off regularly, using greenhouse glass cleaner, to remove the film of grime which reduces light transmission and results in weak or spindly growth of plants. It is particularly important to keep the glass clean in winter, when light levels are low.

POLLUTION-TOLERANT PLANTS

Botanical name	Common name	Height	Spread
TREES			
Acer campestre	Field maple	6m (20ft)	3m (10ft)
Acer negundo	Box elder	6m (20ft)	4.5m (15ft)
Carpinus betulus	Hornbeam	30m (100ft) as mature tree	
Crataegus oxyacantha	Ornamental thorn	4.5–6m (15–20ft)	4.5–5.5m (15–18ft)
Gleditsia triacanthos 'Sunburst'	Honey locust	6m (20ft)	4.5m (15ft)
Laburnum X watereri 'Vossii'	Golden Rain tree	4.5m (15ft)	3.6m (12ft)
Malus	Ornamental crab	Small trees – depends on species/cultivar	
Prunus 'Amanogawa'	Ornamental cherry	6m (20ft)	2m (6.5ft)
Prunus 'Kanzan'	Ornamental cherry	7.6m (25ft)	6m (20ft)
Robinia pseudoacacia 'Frisia'	False acacia	6m (20ft)	4.5m (15ft)
Sorbus aucuparia	Mountain ash	4.5–7.6m (15–25ft)	2.4–3.6m (8–12ft)
SHRUBS			
Berberis thunbergii	Barberry	1.2m (4ft)	2m (6ft)
Cornus sanguinea	Common dogwood	2.4m (8ft)	2.4m (8ft)
Cotinus coggygria	Smoke bush	2.4m (8ft)	2.4m (8ft)
Erica carnea (herbacea)	Winter-flowering heather	15–30cm (6–12in)	45–60cm (18–24in)
Fatsia japonica	–	2.4–3.6m (8–12ft)	2.4–3.6m (8–12ft)
Forsythia X intermedia 'Lynwood'	–	2.4m (8ft)	2.4m (8ft)
Hebe	Shrubby veronica	Prostrate to 1.8m (6ft)	
Ilex aquifolium 'J.C. van Tol'	Holly	2m (6.5ft)	1.2m (4ft)
Ligustrum ovalifolium	Oval-leaf privet	–	–
Magnolia X soulangeana	–	3.6m (12ft)	3.6m (12ft)
Philadelphus	Mock orange	1.2–2.4m (4–8ft)	1.2–2.4m (4–8ft)
Pyracantha	Firethorn	3.6m (12ft)	3.6m (12ft)
Rosa	Rose	Very variable	
Syringa vulgaris	Lilac	3.6m (12ft)	3.6m (12ft)
Viburnum opulus 'Sterile'	Snowball bush	3m (10ft)	3m (10ft)

A roof garden flourishes high above the city streets (**left**). A magnificent *Magnolia X soulangiana* (**below**) blooms in the polluted air of a city.

The double white fragrant blooms of *Crataegus oxyacantha* 'Plena' (**right**) herald the onset of summer. All forms are extremely tolerant of grimy air.

Plants for seashore gardens

Gardeners living by the sea have a different set of problems from those living inland, and one of the most significant — and potentially troublesome — differences is of course the ubiquitous salt spray. It has the effect of severely scorching the leaves of plants, even some considerable distance from the sea.

Cold, drying winds — common in most coastal areas — can also result in scorched foliage. Furthermore, strong winds directly off the sea can cause trees and shrubs to become stunted and deformed; they grow away from the wind, taking up a leaning position.

Very near the sea the soil has a generally high salt content, not liked by many plants. Plants that now grow naturally in maritime habitats have evolved in adaptation to saline conditions over millions of years. In such locations, the soil may well also be very light and sandy, inclined to blow away when dry unless stabilized by dense plant growth.

But although there are considerable problems, there are additionally several points in favor of gardening near the sea. For instance, there is a reduced risk of plant damage through spring frosts. Coastal areas are usually milder than inland areas, and it is therefore possible to grow quite tender plants there; even subtropical plants can be grown in some temperate coastal regions.

Improving the soil

The next major task is to improve the soil as much as possible. If it is very light and sandy, it needs plenty of bulky organic matter dug in: well-rotted farmyard manure, garden compost, mushroom compost or spent hops are all excellent.

One of the best ways of overcoming soil erosion is by planting closely and using plenty of ground-cover plants so that no areas of soil are exposed. The roots then stabilize the soil. In the early days of planting when soil is exposed, mulch it with organic matter (any of the materials mentioned above): a layer about 5-7.5cm (2-3in) deep is ideal.

Plants typical of seashore gardens

Despite the problems, there are many plants which thrive in coastal gardens; in fact, they are too numerous to list them all. The table features a range of plants typical of seashore gardens. All are guaranteed to thrive, given the necessary wind protection.

Wind protection

The first priority when taking over a garden by the sea is to ensure that wind protection is provided, if none exists already, by installing windbreaks around the boundaries, particularly on the side facing the sea. In the long term, natural windbreaks are best, using suitable

Color	Foliage	Season of interest	Notes
–	Deciduous, autumn tints	Autumn	–
–	Deciduous	Summer	Cultivar 'Variegatum' has white and green leaves
–	Deciduous	Summer	Used for hedging
White, scarlet, red, pink	Deciduous	Spring	Several attractive cultivars available
–	Deciduous, yellow	–	Thornless, unlike the species
Yellow	Deciduous	Spring	Leaves, twigs and seeds are poisonous
White or pink	Deciduous, often good autumn tints	Spring	Many of the cultivars produce colorful autumn fruits
Pink	Deciduous	Spring	Very slim habit
Pink	Deciduous	Spring	Very popular cultivar
–	Deciduous,	Spring/Summer	–
White	Deciduous, autumn tints	Spring	Orange-red berries in autumn
Pale yellow	Deciduous, good autumn color		Scarlet berries. 'Atropurpurea' has purple foliage
–	Deciduous, purple in autumn	–	Stems flushed with red
Purplish	Deciduous, good autumn color		Purple-leaved cultivars available
Pink, red, carmine white	Evergreen	Winter	Can be grown in chalky soils
White	Evergreen, large	Autumn	Good for shaded areas
Yellow	Deciduous	Spring	Broad petals
Blue, purple, red, pink, white	Evergreen	Summer/Autumn	Many species and cultivars
–	Evergreen, almost spineless	Autumn/Winter	Heavy crops of red berries
–	Evergreen	–	Grown as a hedge. 'Aureum' has golden leaves
White, flushed purple	Deciduous	Spring	Can be wall trained
White	Deciduous	Summer	Sweetly scented flowers
White	Evergreen	Summer	Red, orange or yellow berries
Many colors	Deciduous	Summer	Wide range of hybrids and species
Many colors	Deciduous	Spring	Many cultivars available
White	Deciduous, yellow in autumn	Summer	–

The daisy-like flowers of *Senecio laxifolius* (**top**) held above gray-green foliage.

These clouds of white flowers adorn *Crambe cordifolia* each summer (**above**).

trees and shrubs. For the first line of defense use any of the trees in the accompanying table distinguished by the letters WB (suitable for boundary windbreaks).

As a second line of defense immediately behind the line of trees, use dense bushy shrubs — again indicated in the table by the letters WB.

It will take some years for windbreaks to become effective, however; in the early years, even the windbreak plants need protection, which can be effected by erecting artificial windbreaks. The best material to use is proprietary windbreak netting, small-mesh plastic netting which has the effect of filtering the wind and slowing it down. Do not use solid materials — such as fencing panels or walls — for windbreaks; these only cause any wind to rush over the top and swirl down violently on the other side, resulting in a great deal of damage to plants.

Make the artificial windbreak as high as possible, at least 2.5m (8ft). The netting should be supported on stout timber posts and horizontal wires, and should remain in place until the windbreak trees and shrubs are definitely established and themselves becoming effective. Moreover, once it has served this purpose, the netting can always be useful for protecting other young plants in the garden.

PLANTS FOR SEASHORE GARDENS

Botanical name	Common name
Note: Plants indicated WB are suitable for forming windbreaks	
TREES	
Acer pseudoplatanus (WB)	Sycamore
Crataegus monogyna (WB)	Hawthorn
Pinus radiata (WB)	Monterey pine
Pinus nigra austriaca (WB)	Austrian pine
Quercus ilex (WB)	Holm oak; Evergreen oak
Salix alba (WB)	White willow
Sorbus aria (WB)	Whitebeam
SHRUBS	
Atriplex halimus (WB)	Tree purslane
Cordyline australis	Cabbage palm
Escallonia	–
Griselinia littoralis	–
Hebe	Shrubby veronica
Hippophae rhamnoides (WB)	Sea buckthorn
Olearia X haastii (WB)	Daisy bush
Pittosporum tenuifolium	–
Senecio laxifolius	–
Tamarix pentandra (WB)	Tamarisk
Tamarix tetrandra (WB)	Tamarisk
PERENNIALS AND TEMPORARY PLANTS	
Armeria maritima	Thrift
Crambe cordifolia	–
Elymus arenarius	Lyme grass
Erigeron	Fleabane
Eryngium alpinum	–
Eryngium maritimum	Sea holly
Gazania X hybrida	Blanket flower
Limonium latifolium	Sea lavender
Mesembryanthemum criniflorum	Livingstone daisy

The seashore garden can play host to a wide range of plants that flourish in the fresh and usually milder conditions near the coast. The great enemy is the wind, and a screening hedge may be needed (**below**).

Sorbus

Griselina hedge

Thrift

Mesembryanthemum

Eryngium bou

Erige

Escallonia

Olearia

Thrift

Mesembryanthemum

Tamarix

Height	Spread	Color	Foliage	Season of interest	Notes
10m+ (33ft+)	4.5m (15ft)	Greenish	Bright green, deciduous	Spring	Leaves color in autumn
7.6m (25ft)	4.5m (15ft)	White	Deciduous	Spring	Crimson autumn berries
15m (50ft)	6m (20ft)	–	Evergreen, bright green needles	Year round	–
10m (33ft)	6m (20ft)	–	Evergreen, dark green needles	Year round	–
6m (20ft)	4.5m (15ft)	–	Evergreen, dark green	Year round	Best for use in mild coastal areas
9m (30ft)	6m (20ft)	–	Deciduous, gray-green	Summer	–
6m+ (20ft+)	4.5m (15ft)	Cream	Deciduous, silver-gray	Spring to Autumn	Scarlet autumn berries, autumn tints
3m (10ft)	1.8m (6ft)	–	Deciduous, silver-gray	Summer	–
6m (20ft)	2.4m (8ft)	Creamy white	Evergreen, strap-shaped	Year round	For mild coastal areas
2–3.6m (6.5–12ft)	2–3.6m (6.5–12ft)	Pink, red, white	Evergreen	Summer	Many cultivars available
4.5m (15ft)	3m (10ft)	–	Evergreen, yellow-green	–	For mild coastal areas
Prostrate to 1.8m (6ft)		Blue, purple, red, pink, white	Evergreen	Summer/Autumn	Best in mild areas, many cultivars
3m (10ft)	3m (10ft)	Yellow	Deciduous, silvery	Spring	Orange berries if male and female plants grown
2m (6ft)	2.4m (8ft)	White	Evergreen, white below	Summer	Many other olearias also suitable. Fragrant flowers
4.5m (15ft)	2.4m (8ft)	Purple	Evergreen, pale green	Spring	Best for mild areas
1.2m (4ft)	1.2m (4ft)	Yellow	Evergreen, white-felted	Summer	–
3.6m (12ft)	3.6m (12ft)	Pink	Decidous	Summer	–
4.5m (15ft)	4.5m (15ft)	Pink	Deciduous	Spring	–
15–30cm (6–12in)	30cm (12in)	Pink	Evergreen	Spring/Summer	Red, deep pink and white cultivars
2m (6ft)	1.2m (4ft)	White	Large fleshy leaves	Summer	Attractive foliage
60cm (24in)	Indefinite	Gray-blue	Grassy, grey-blue	Summer	Vigorous spreading grass, ideal for stabilizing soils, e.g. on banks
45cm (18in)	45cm (18in)	Blue, pink	–	Summer	Many cultivars
60cm (24in)	60cm (24in)	Steel blue	Green-blue	Summer	–
45cm (18in)	45cm (18in)	Metallic blue	Silver-green	summer	–
23cm (9in)	30cm (12in)	Orange, yellow and red tones	Green and grey	Summer	Tender summer-bedding plant
60cm (24in)	45cm (18in)	Blue	–	Summer	–
15cm (6in)	15cm (6in)	Many colors	Succulent	Summer	Tender summer-bedding plant

monium latifolium

Eryngium maritimum

Gazania

sembryanthemum

Midsummer sees the brightly banded blooms of *Gazania x hybrida* 'Ministar' (**far right**). The gazanias flower until the first frosts, which are usually late reaching temperate coastal areas.
The purple-blue flowers of *Erigeron macranthus* (**right**) are borne on tough erect stems that will withstand a seashore breeze.
These dazzling blooms of *Mesembryanthemum criniflorum* form a carpet of color in mid-to-late summer (**far right**). Native to South Africa, these Livingstone daisies thrive in temperate coastal gardens.

Difficult weeds

What is a weed? A practical definition is 'a plant growing where it is not wanted'. In this context garden plants as well as wild plants are included. But, from the gardener's point of view, a weed is a wild plant — a member of the native flora — which is growing among, and competing with, cultivated garden plants. Weeds compete with our garden plants for food, water and light, and they can seriously reduce growth and cropping if not controlled.

There are two groups of weeds — annuals and perennials. Members of the first group are short-lived plants, completing their life cycle from seed germination to seed production within one year. Once they have set seeds they die.

Examples are chickweed, groundsel, shepherd's purse, and bittercress. Generally they are easily controlled: by hand weeding, hoeing while the seedlings are tiny, mulching with organic matter or black mulching polythene, or by applying a weedkiller like paraquat and diquat. They can even be prevented from germinating, by applying to weed-free soil among garden plants what is known as a 'soil-acting' weedkiller, such as *simazine*. This will keep the soil free from annual weeds for many months, provided the film of chemical on the soil surface is not broken by cultivating.

Perennial weeds are not so easy to eradicate, although with modern weedkillers this is not the problem it used to be. Perennial weeds live for a number of years and can become permanently established if not controlled. Examples are ground elder, bindweed, couch grass, mare's tail, docks, dandelions, creeping thistle, buttercups, bracken and brambles or wild blackberries.

It is these more difficult weeds that we are considering here. The main reason they are more difficult to eradicate than annual weeds is that many of them are deep rooting, like docks and dandelions. Mare's tail is the extreme example, for it sends roots several feet into the soil. Some weeds, like ground elder, bindweed and couch grass, spread by means of rhizomes or underground stems.

If the roots or rhizomes of perennial weeds are left in the ground during digging they will send up new growth from them. Even little pieces of root or rhizome left in the soil are capable of producing new plants.

Many perennial weeds in the past have proved somewhat resistant to weedkillers, but formulas are changing, and with the range of weedkillers introduced in recent years even the most resistant perennial weeds can now be effectively controlled.

Digging them out
The time-honored practice of digging out perennial weeds still holds good; but it is time-

Convolvulus arvense
(Field bindweed)
Type: Perennial; spreads by rhizomes; creeping stems
Control: MCPA + dicamba, glyphosate

Equisetum arvense
(Mare's tail, horsetail)
Type: Perennial; very deep rooting
Control: Difficult, glyphosate

Veronica chamaedrys
(Germander speedwell)
Type: Perennial; lawn weed; forms dense mats
Control: MCPA + dicamba + ionoxyl, ionoxyl + mecoprop

Achillea millefolium
(Yarrow)
Type: Perennial; lawn weed; spreading mats
Control: 2, 4-D + mecoprop or fenoprop

Taraxacum officinale
(Dandelion)
Type: Perennial; deep tap root
Control: In lawns 2, 4-D + mecoprop or fenoprop; elsewhere glyphosate

Rumex obtusifolius
(Broad dock)
Type: Perennial; deep tap root
Control: Glyphosate, dichlorbenil

Sagina procumbens
(Pearlwort)
Type: Perennial; lawn weed; moss-like mats
Control: Ioxynil + mecoprop

Aegopodium podagraria
(Ground elder)
Type: Perennial; spreads by rhizomes; common in shade
Control: Glyphosate, dichlobenil

Tussilago farfara
(Coltsfoot)
Type: Perennial; very deep rooted; often on clay soil
Control: Can be difficult, glyphosate, dichlobenil

Pteridium aquilinum
(Bracken)
Type: Perennial; strong spreading rootstock; mainly on acid soils
Control: Difficult, 2, 4-D + 2, 4, 5-T

Polygonum aviculare
(Knotgrass)
Type: Annual; mat former
Control: Paraquat, simazine, propachlor

Cardamine hirsuta
(Hairy bittercress)
Type: Annual; rapidly spreads by seeds
Control: Paraquat, simazine, propachlor

Ranunculus repens
(Creeping buttercup)
Type: Perennial; spreads by runners; moist places
Control: Glyphosate, dichlobenil

consuming, and, as mentioned earlier, every piece of root or rhizome must be removed. It is of course sensible to remove any perennial weeds while digging.

Roots and rhizomes must not be put on the compost heap, or they will continue growing; it is better to dispose of them by burning or, if facilities exist, dumping them on a local refuse tip.

Using weedkillers

The most effective method of controlling perennial weeds is to use one of the modern weedkillers. If the garden, or part of a garden, is badly infected, then the first priority should be to completely eradicate weeds before planting or cropping. This may mean leaving the ground fallow for a complete growing season while weed control is being undertaken.

Weedkillers are best used when weeds are in full growth. Weedkillers containing the chemical *glyphosate* will kill most perennial weeds. If couch grass is the problem, then use a weedkiller containing *alloxydim sodium*.

For tough woody perennials like brambles and bracken, use a brushwood killer, containing the chemicals 2,4-D and 2,4,5-T.

If perennial weeds are growing among established plants, such as shrubs, fruit trees and bushes, and perennial-border plants, you can still use *glyphosate* and *alloxydim sodium*.

Obviously you have to be especially careful when using weedkillers among established plants, but they are safe if used as directed by the makers. If there are only a few perennial weeds among plants then carry out 'spot treatment' — that is, treatment of individual weeds with a weedkiller. The old method was to apply the weedkiller with an old paint brush, but today there are available proprietary 'spot weeders', usually containing *glyphosate*. Basically they consist of a cannister of weedkiller which feeds an applicator, usually a sponge-rubber pad. The tool has a long handle, and you simply dab each weed to cover it with the chemical — very easy and safe, with no risk of splashing nearby plants with weedkiller.

A 'spot weeder' is of course extremely useful for controlling weeds in difficult places, such as on a rock garden where weeds may be growing between rocks and are impossible to dig out. It can also be used for weeds growing at the base of hedges.

Weeds in paths

Perennial weeds can grow almost anywhere, and it is not unusual for them to grow through cracks in paving or concrete, or through gravel paths and drives. There are proprietary weedkillers available especially for use on paths or drives. Most contain several chemicals to control annual as well as perennial weeds, such as *paraquat*, *diquat*, *simazine* and *aminotriazole*.

Before using any weedkiller, read the manufacturer's instructions on use thoroughly and follow them to the letter.

Bryonia dioica
(White bryony)
Type: Perennial; climber; often in hedges
Control: Glyphosate, dichlobenil

Hedera helix
(Ivy)
Type: Perennial; climbing or trailing; problem in hedges
Control: 2, 4-D + 2, 4, 5,-T

Plantago lanceolata
(Ribwort plantain)
Type: Perennial; lawn weed
Control: 2, 4-D + mecoprop or fenoprop

Rorippa sylvestris
(Creeping yellow cress)
Type: Perennial; creeping stems, very deep rooting
Control: Very difficult, glyphosate

Poa annua
(Annual meadowgrass)
Type: Annual; lawns and cultivated ground; seeds freely
Control: In lawns regular mowing; elsewhere paraquat, simazine, propachlor

Urtica dioica
(Stinging nettle)
Type: Perennial; generally found on rich soil
Control: MCPA + dicamba, dichlobenil, glyphosate

Plantago major
(Great plantain)
Type: Perennial; lawn weed; deep tap root
Control: 2, 4-D + mecoprop or fenoprop

Rumex acetosa
(Common sorrel)
Type: Perennial; lawns and cultivated ground
Control: In lawns 2, 4-D + mecoprop or fenoprop; elsewhere glyphosate

Oxalis corniculata

Type: Perennial; spreads by bulbous rhizomes
Control: Difficult, glyphosate, dichlobenil

Bellis perennis
(Daisy)
Type: Perennial; lawn weed; seeds freely
Control: 2, 4-D + mecoprop or fenoprop

Cirsium arvense
(Creeping thistle)
Type: Perennial; spreads by creeping stems
Control: MCP + dicamba, glyphosate

Agropyron repens
(Couch grass)
Type: Perennial; vigorous rhizomes
Control: Alloxydim sodium, dalapon

Rubus fruticosus
(Bramble)
Type: Perennial; clambering stems, often found in hedges
Control: 2, 4-D + 2, 4, 5-T

Trifolium repens
(White clover)
Type: Perennial; lawn weed, mat-forming
Control: Can be difficult, 2, 4-D + mecoprop

GARDEN
FEATURES

Planning your garden

The secret of a successful garden is to plan it carefully before beginning to build or to plant. Every site has its limitations — maybe size, shape, soil or orientation — which have to be taken into account in order to get the best results.

Begin by making a scaled plan of the garden on graph paper, marking in accurately any existing large features such as sheds, trees, mature shrubs, paths and patios, and working out their orientation: whether they face north, south, east or west, thus also showing which areas receive most sunshine.

Now make a detailed list of what you and your family want from the garden, remembering to think at least a few years ahead to when your needs may possibly have changed. (If you have very small children, for example, it is safer not to include any pond or water features in your plan. A sunken sand-pit included in the original design can easily be converted into a pool when the children are older.)

Decide how much of the garden should be devoted to sitting and sunbathing in, to having room to eat and to entertain friends, and possibly to having a permanent built-in barbecue. Do you want an area for growing vegetables or soft fruit? Have you always yearned after herbaceous borders and beds of bright annuals? Must you leave space for pets or the storage of bikes and large outdoor toys? If there is no room for a full-scale tennis court, perhaps it would be possible to fit in a net for badminton or a small *boules* pitch.

When your list is complete, place the items in order of importance, remembering that some features require far more time and effort to maintain than others. Try not to be over-ambitious: avoid leaving yourself more mowing, digging or sowing than you can face once the initial enthusiasm has worn off.

Calculate how much space is needed to accommodate each feature, making a note of any that can double up: a playhouse makes a good bike shed, for example, or a putting green a fine lawn; make a paper cut-out to the same scale as your plan for each one, and move them around on the plan to see how they fit together. Try not to be influenced too much by existing features that seem not to fit into the scheme of things; remember, many can be moved or disguised later.

A shed or an ugly view at the end of the garden can be hidden behind screening, a trellis, pergolas or hedges, planted with quick-growing climbers such as *Polygonum baldschuanicum*, wisteria and ivy, or sweet-scented flowering climbers for spring and summer such as roses, honeysuckles and clematis.

Paths and paving can be moved from one area to another without too much upheaval, and even established shrubs and small trees can often be safely transplanted if tackled at the right time of year and moved with plenty of soil around their roots.

Many patio and seating areas are for convenience sited close to the house, which is fine if it happens to receive plenty of sun. If, however, your house partly shades the garden, you would do better to create a special area at the other end of the garden, with adequate paved access to prevent wet feet after showers. The inconvenience of carrying food, drinks and seating across the garden is generally far outweighed by the advantages of a sunny site. On the other hand, children's play areas should be positioned near the house where they can be more easily supervised.

When planning features in the garden, take note of its overall shape. Whether the garden is long, wide or small, it is possible to adjust the basic contents to create the optical illusion of planning and space. A long, thin plot can be broken up across its width with staggered beds or hedging, or the eye distracted by trees or large shrubs planted along the sides. Vistas can be created in short, wide gardens by directing the eye along its length to a focal point at the end of the garden: a fountain or statue, an urn, perhaps, or a specimen shrub.

In a small or awkwardly shaped garden consider a change of levels using terracing, steps and raised beds to create immediate, ground-level interest which prevents the eye straying too far afield. Alternatively, beds in the center — rather than along the sides — always offer the opportunity to walk around in several directions rather than simply up and down.

It is important to make a garden genuinely interesting. However small the plot, try not to let it all be seen at once. Create hidden areas using steps, hedges and sunken gardens, and make sure there is some focal point to catch the attention. Large areas can be broken up using paving or a similar change of material. And in every garden, there should be a good variety of plants chosen for their leaf-shape, color and habit, with some variation in height from ground cover to trees, trellis and pergolas.

Make sure also that there is something interesting to look at all year round by planting a strong background of evergreens and berried shrubs for autumn and winter, bulbs for spring, and a few favorite summer flowering perennials in case the annuals are late. Plants should be chosen with care and placed according to their own preferences; a shade-loving plant can hardly flourish in full sunlight, nor can an ericaceous species thrive in a chalky soil. Test the soil in the garden in several places, using a pH meter or test kit, before choosing the plants; selected specimens can of course be grown under controlled conditions, using plastic sheeting or tubs.

Plants are best placed in groups (rather than dotted around singly), each clump complementing or contrasting with the next for impact. A variety of shapes, colors and heights stimulates the eye. The best features should be sited to make the most of them, allowing surrounding plants to provide a frame that sets them off. Never forget the obvious rule: tall plants to the back, short to the fore.

Variety of shape, height and color can be used to add interest to the garden and create perspective. Here the eye is drawn to a fine urn against a background of tall hedging by a clever arrangement of staggered flower beds and a framework of different shrubs and trees.

The seating area should always be positioned where it receives maximum sunshine, with adequate paths to keep feet dry if it is not near the house. Roses, clematis, ivy and other climbing plants entwined round a trellis create a pleasant outlook and help break up the length of the garden.

Clipped hedges in staggered breaks add an air of mystery and the illusion of width to a long garden. Choose warm-colored varieties with gold or dark green leaves, and space them farther apart near the house, using closer-planted, paler shades in the distance for extra feeling of depth.

Containers

Pots and tubs are an excellent way to brighten a plain expanse of concrete or paving on patio or terrace, and are flexible enough to be planted for year-round interest with small evergreen shrubs and plants, spring bulbs and summer annuals.

There is available a wide range of plain and decorated containers, from wood, metal and concrete to stone, fiberglass, plastic and terra-cotta scaled-up versions of ordinary flower pots. Earthenware strawberry-pots with holes (and possibly cups) up the sides are ideal for alpine plants and bulbs as well as strawberries; urns and pedestal vases are particularly suited to framing steps and archways.

Do not be afraid to mix different styles of container: arrange them in groups, and try to vary heights and shapes for interest — some planted with a single tree or shrub, others containing a mixture of varying foliage and flowering plants. Take special care when securely fixing window or balustrade boxes; floor-standing containers should be raised on bricks or wood blocks to aid drainage.

When finally satisfied with the arrangement, fill each container with a good level of crocks or stones before topping up with a quality potting mixture. If a container does not already have holes at the bottom, it may be worthwhile drilling them yourself to improve drainage.

Container-grown plants need more attention than your garden planted varieties. In such restricted space, weed seedlings should be pulled out the instant you spot them; as soon as the plants themselves grow too big or begin to die down, they too should be pulled out and replaced. Spring bulbs which have finished flowering should be lifted and stored until the next season. The soil is of course prone to drying out, so keep it well watered during the summer and feed it regularly while plants, of colors, shapes and textures. Small may need watering in winter too.

Choice of plants is crucial in such a limited space: aim at a good balance of tall and trailing plants, of colours, shapes and textures. Small shrubs, trees and evergreens are useful for providing a permanent background to other plants — almost any slow-growing or dwarf species can be grown in a tub. If the situation is shady and the soil lime-free, you can grow camellias and rhododendrons, or a selection of the wide-ranging heather family: varieties of *Erica carnea (herbacea)* for winter and early spring flowering, bell heather *(Erica cinerea)* and ling *(Calluna vulgaris)* for summer.

Hollies and oleanders make good tub plants with a fine variety of foliage or flowers. For a more formal look, consider the clipped shapes of box *(Buxus)*, bay *(Laurus nobilis)* or yew *(Taxus)*. Other shrubs worth considering are prickly barberry *(Berberis)*, blue-flowered *Caryopteris*, bush or standard fuchsias, the slow-growing dwarf conifers, sweet-scented *Skimmia japonica*, and spiky lavender.

Seasonal plants should be chosen with equal care to create the most impact. Silver and green trailing foliage is the perfect foil for other plants and helps 'soften' the edges of containers: try silver senecio, lobelia, tiny green creeping Jenny *(Lysimachia)*, or one of the variegated ivies.

Summer annuals are wonderful for creating a riot of color for very little cost, and it is worthwhile giving thought to which combinations work best. White alyssum and marguerites set off most colors well but tend to disappear against a white wall or container. Combine with the blues of lobelias, campanulas or violas against red brick and save the brilliant scarlets of geraniums *(Pelargonium)*, cinerarias and salvias to team with golden marigolds, calceolarias and marigolds *(Tagetes)*.

For spring set off miniature tulips and narcissi with forget-me-nots, saxifrage, candytuft and wallflowers; and for autumn keep the show going with dwarf dahlias and chrysanthemums, ornamental peppers and winter cherry *(Solanum)*.

Floor-standing containers must have good drainage. Check that window boxes are securely fixed with metal clips **(left)**.

Contrasting foliage and flowering plants provide a fine display of shapes and colors in large single containers. Lobelia, alyssum, trailing fuchsia and ivy are all useful creeping plants to 'soften' the edges of your tubs and boxes. Marigolds, petunias and pelargoniums are traditional for bright summer color. Add a couple of dwarf conifers for a change of height, and don't forget to plant some spring bulbs for an early show of blooms.

Plant containers are available in a wide range of shapes and sizes, from ornate stone urns and wooden Versailles baskets to more simple plastic or concrete tubs and boxes. Make the most of the fancier and more expensive styles by planting with a single specimen plant, such as a bushy purple hydrangea or a shaped bay tree; use plainer, cheaper containers for arranging in pairs or groups on the patio. Tub shrubs and small trees need a fair amount of space, so they may have to be planted singly, and their tubs interspersed with boxes of lower-growing plants and flowers. Evergreen varieties are ideal for providing a background to more sensational plants

and for keeping the arrangement looking good throughout the winter. Dwarf conifers are particularly useful in that they are slow-growing and available in a range of colors, from the bluish gray *Chamaecyparis* 'Columnaris' to the deep green *C. l.* 'Ellwoodii' and the golden leaved *C. l.* 'Minima Aurea'. Barberry (Berberis) can be both deciduous and evergreen, with glossy red or green leaves and golden flowers sometimes followed by red, black or blue currant-like fruits. Eucalyptus is valuable for its silver leaves. Mixed plant containers can include a selection of variegated foliage such as ivies, euonymous and herbs like thyme and

marjoram to set off the green leaves of spring bulbs and summer annuals. Aim for a good variety of blooms, from tiny trailing white and yellow alyssum or blue lobelia to the vivid mauves and pinks of petunia. Experiment with the arrangements of containers before filling with soil and plants.

Gravel **(left)** forms an ideal patio surface, here decorated with planted containers. The clean lines of modern french doors **(left)** are softened by a crazy paving patio and colorful tubs.

A sheltered seating area **(above)** can be created anywhere in the garden by surrounding a paved area with evergreens to provide protection from winds and drafts. A selection of conifers, hollies, rhododendrons, *Fatsia japonica* and *Choisya ternata* are hardy enough to make good informal screening; a well-clipped hedge of privet, box, or other evergreen hedging looks more formal. A few matching paving slabs extending across the lawn from the seating area link it to the rest of the garden and keep feet dry.

Paving slabs mixed with brick **(above)**, a mellow effect for informal patios.

Plain bricks **(below)** laid end-to-end weather into subtle variations of color.

Varying the gaps between plain paving slabs **(above)** adds interest and variety.

Bricks or blocks laid on sand in a herringbone pattern **(below)** for a patio.

A crazy-paving effect in pastel shades **(above)**, in different sizes and styles.

Square gray tiles **(below)** give a discreet, traditional feel to a patio.

PATIOS: PAVING

Patios are no longer extravagantly paved terraces overlooking acres of garden nor limited to wealthy land-owners. Today even the most modest garden can aspire to a small area, easy to maintain and relatively dry underfoot, in which a few chairs can be placed in the sun, and meals eaten right after being cooked on a small outdoor barbecue.

A patio can be as large or as small as you wish, depending, for example, on how many you want it to seat and whether you need room for a built-in barbecue, pool, or other integrated feature. It is important, however, to position it where it receives maximum sunshine — even at some distance from the house — for a cold, drafty patio will be poorly used.

Cold winds can be screened using a trellis, hedges of privet, box or other evergreens, or with an informal planting of evergreen shrubs such as conifers, hollies or rhododendrons.

Paving materials depend on personal preference and finances. Gravel is the cheapest and probably the easiest to install: simply level the site and firm the soil before spreading with a 2.5cm (1in) layer of washed pea shingle. Because gravel offers excellent drainage, log slices can be bedded in it (to add interest and a change of texture) without becoming damp and slimy underneath.

Paving slabs are most people's idea of a conventional patio surface; they are readily available both in 100 per cent natural stone and in a reconstituted form which works out considerably cheaper. Variety of shape and color — from gray and sand to pastel pinks — provides unlimited scope for pattern and design, but simplicity is a good guideline: anything too elaborate may ruin the overall effect. A simple pattern of different sizes, or even a slight variation in the spacing between conventional slabs, can turn out just right.

Bricks are quite expensive new, but second-hand they can work out much cheaper and look more mellow too, laid end-to-end for a conventional design, or herringbone fashion if you are looking for something more elaborate. They also look very effective combined with paving slabs; try leaving some of the spaces empty for planting sweet-scented herbs, shrubs or even a small tree.

If you fancy the old traditional cobbled surface, concrete or granite cobbles are available singly or in blocks to make installation easier.

Slabs and bricks need to be laid on an 8cm (3¼in) bed of sand spread over firmed and levelled soil. Use a straight edge or spirit level to make sure the surface is flat but sloped slightly to allow the rain to run away easily, away from the house if it is near by. Grout the slabs or bricks with a dry mortar mix, taking care not to get any on the surface of the paving — it's very difficult to remove later. If mortar does get onto the paving slabs or bricks,

remove it immediately with dry sand and a good stiff broom.

You could experiment with several types of paving within the patio area. As an alternative to the bricks and paving stone combination mentioned previously, you could divide the patio into large, distinct areas of gravel, pebbles or cobbled surface and create a paving slab surround. In this way, other features could be integrated with a similar border: a formal pool with a few fish and a fountain, or an area for plants perhaps.

If your patio is well sheltered yet catches plenty of sun, it may get very hot. In any case, some form of shade is a good idea for more comfortable eating and reading, using maybe a tree to fend off the sun at its hottest or one of those large umbrellas which fit into a picnic table. Prettiest is a pergola construction that can be intertwined with a quick-growing vine, such as *Vitis coignetiae* (the glory vine), or with other climbers.

The patio (**below**) is shaded by a pergola entwined with a hardy vine, and features a variety of paving effects. Log slices have been set in gravel for good drainage and surrounded by a more formal path of conventional paving slabs. Also enclosed by the paving is a small formal pool and fountain and an interesting scree garden using stone chippings.

Patios: terraces

An elegant raised terrace can be simple or elaborate, traditional — with formal paving and a stone balustrade — or use the natural warmth of wood to create a smart, timber decked surface. Whatever you choose, you can follow the theme through with steps constructed from matching brick, stone or timber and provide shelter from winds and drafts with stone or timber screening and hardy evergreen shrubs and climbers.

The traditional terrace has a dominant formal pattern of paving in stone or brick with shallow steps and ornate urns flanking an elegant stone balustrade. Elements of these can be bought in pre-cast sections and constructed on site quite easily. Plant containers should be carefully chosen to match the style of this type of terrace: highly decorated urns and tubs or smart Versailles baskets.

If you prefer a warmer, more informal look, timber decking is easy to make and maintain; second-hand wood costs a lot less than stone or brick. Any rough-textured splinter-free timber (such as old railway sleepers or split oak) is ideal; simply cut it to shape and treat with a suitable wood preservative before laying in your chosen pattern or design. To help it last longer, first lay a bed of sand over a polyethylene sheet punched with holes; water can then drain through it although damp is prevented from coming up from below. Alternatively, support the deck on wooden joists to allow air to flow freely underneath.

Timber can be laid in a variety of designs: straight, on the diagonal, or in square sections at right angles. It is advisable to work out your design on paper in order to calculate how much wood you need. Pot plants are essential to add height and interest, either planted in spaces

left in the decking or arranged in simple tubs and boxes, and sheltered using matching timber or bamboo screens. The deck surface should be brushed regularly with a wire brush to keep the surface rough and moss-free, or it becomes slippery.

Timber deck terraces (**above**) are inexpensive and easy to make, using second-hand planking rubbed smooth and treated with a good wood preservative.

The combination of a rock garden and terrace (**above**) is a particularly effective design feature. The neat form of the terrace contrasts with the random nature of the rockery. The inclusion of a fountain and statues in a small terraced garden (**right**) adds an element of tranquil formality. Many different styles of fountains are widely available to create a variety of effects in the garden.

Steps

Steps are not as difficult to install as they may seem at first, provided that you take care when making your initial calculations. After you have decided on the materials to use, estimate from their dimensions the number of steps needed, dividing the slope as evenly as possible. Bear in mind that steep steps are not suitable for young children or elderly people in the household. Any step more than 30cm (1ft) high is generally uncomfortable for most people to negotiate. Treads should be slightly sloped to the front or side to prevent puddles from forming after rain.

Steps can be constructed from a variety of materials and laid in different ways to create varying effects: brick (**above left**), paving slabs with brick risers (**above**), or simple wooden steps (**left**) are only a few of the options. Curved steps (**right**) look elegant.

This traditional terrace (above) features a formal design using paving slabs inlaid with bricks. The balustrade, which can be bought in sections and constructed on site, is flanked by a pair of steps down to the garden and a couple of handsome urns. Timber decking (left) arranged in sections laid at right-angles for a pleasing design. There is no reason for the patio to be square or rectangular: the random paving (right), has been laid in a circular design framed by shrubs.

The bright blooms of annuals blend well with garden steps (above). When planting near steps ensure that overhanging leaves do not become a hazard.

There are many ways in which steps can be constructed; shown here in profile are brick steps with paving risers (top left), simple wooden steps made using old railway timbers (center left), paving steps with brick risers (bottom left), and logs held in place with wooden stakes (right) to create both steep and shallow steps depending on how many logs are used. Take care not to make them too steep, especially if they are to be used by young children, the elderly or the handicapped.

Patios: eating areas

They say food tastes even better outdoors, and it is hard to beat the pleasure of eating in an area set aside in the garden for impromptu or planned meals, paved to keep feet clean and dry, providing some sort of shelter from the midday sun, and possibly lit by outdoor spotlights for after-dark entertaining.

If you enjoy barbecues you may like to build one into your eating area or, if you are very keen, to construct a separate, paved barbecue unit, raised with tubs of edible herbs for cooking or sunken with handy seats round the grill. You might add to this surfaces for food preparation and storage for fuels and utensils.

Garden furniture, which you can buy or make yourself, falls roughly into three groups: stone, hardwood and cast metal, which can be left out all year with minimum maintenance; plastic and plastic-coated chairs and tables, which should collapse or fold easily for storage at the end of summer; and upholstered chairs and cushions, which need to be brought indoors every evening.

Wooden picnic tables with integral bench seats, wood-slatted seats, and tables are all fairly inexpensive to buy (or relatively easy to construct) and so ideal for family meals. They simply need an annual re-varnish or oiling, depending on the type of wood, and should last for years. Alternatively, build seating units with concrete bases in right-angled, circular or hexagonal shapes and top them with removable wooden slatted tops that can be stored indoors over winter. Sections can be topped with concrete to provide casual table tops, or left empty to accommodate evergreen shrubs or small trees. The easiest of all seating is sawn log sections, which should be treated with a good wood preservative before being placed around an informal table top or barbecue.

Table tops can be made of a variety of materials; the main points are that they should be weather-proof and the base strong enough to take the weight of them. Concrete, brick and ceramic tiles need sturdy support but are tough enough to survive most weather conditions, provided that the bricks are of engineering quality and the tiles are frost-proof. Wood is more lightweight and can be stained and varnished, or primed and gloss painted, in bright colors. Be sure always to use yacht varnish for exterior surfaces: ordinary polyurethane tends to crack and blister in prolonged sunlight.

Sturdiest of the ready-made furniture is that of re-constituted stone, or cast aluminum in imitation of ornate Victorian cast iron. Both can be left out in all weathers and need very little maintenance. (Rub down and repaint the metal furniture when it begins to peel.) Hardwood seats and benches also need very little care. Teak and iroko can be cleaned with white spirit and a good scrub with soap and water once a year, followed by an application of teak oil. Beech and elm should be rubbed down with fine sandpaper and treated with linseed oil.

Tubular steel and plastic-coated chairs and tables are tough enough to be left out all summer, and have usually been treated to prevent cracking and color-fading in strong sunlight. Most are self-stacking or fold away for easy storage, and simply need wiping down; any metal parts then need oiling before use next season.

Although some people prefer their patio area to be quite a sun-trap (as is ideal for lounging and tanning), diners may nevertheless welcome a little shade when the sun is at its hottest. Many of the pre-cast metal and plastic molded tables include a center hole for fixing a large parasol umbrella, which can be purchased in a wide range of colors and designs. For a more natural effect but still only

You can build your own semi-permanent seating area **(top)** by installing concrete benches and fitting them with removable wooden slatted tops. The wooden slatted seats and table **(above)** collapse for storage.

Seats and tables for outdoor meals are available in a wide range of materials and styles. The wooden picnic table **(above)** is ideal for family meals but not very comfortable over long periods.

The stone table and bench **(right)** are sturdy enough to be left out in all weathers.

A simple timber open style roof over this patio (**above**) supports a creeper that provides welcome shade at midday. For protection against a summer shower an awning of canvas can be drawn across the beams.

A conventional paved patio with built-in circular planting areas for a variety of flowering shrubs can be protected from the midday sun by bamboo screening (**above**). A mixed paving and brick surface is shaded by a wooden framework supporting lengths of canvas (**below**).

a temporary method of shading the table, consider installing over the patio area a pergola with a vigorous vine grown to smother it and soften its shape. A split bamboo screen can be pulled over the top of the pergola to provide extra shade when needed. To keep off the occasional summer shower as well, build a simple wooden frame and stretch colored lengths of deckchair canvas over it.

Eating outdoors leads to *al fresco* cooking. If you are new to barbecuing, start by buying a small purpose-made metal grill — very simple, yet big enough for one or two — or build your own small barbecue using concrete blocks to a height of about 90cm (3ft) and a metal bootscraper. As you become more proficient and keener, progress to a larger bought model, with legs and wheeled platform, hoods, wind screens, spits and skewers, or expand your home-built model to include a food preparation area, seating units and a proper roof for shelter, channelled at one end to help the smoke escape.

Even the smallest bought or home-made model can be improved with a canopy and chimney made of sheet metal to improve ventilation; a simple palisade of logs can also screen the barbecue from drafts. If you prefer not to improvise a barbecue out of bits and pieces, you might buy a do-it-yourself barbecue kit which includes grill and brackets, and sometimes spit and skewers too.

A hexagonal paved eating area is lit by outdoor spotlights for a convivial evening's entertaining. Matching seating unit with solid section for dishes is concrete-based with a wood slatted top and space in the center for a bushy evergreen. Sawn off logs among the tubs of annuals provide extra seats all around.

If you enjoy barbecuing, you might like to consider making this special sunken barbecue area in a corner of the garden (**below**). The concrete barbecue is set in the center of a circular paved area with a low wall all the way around to provide ample seating. A small step is sufficient for easy access to the sunken area.

A permanent built-in barbecue can be a modest affair, using simple concrete blocks, a metal boot-scraper and a sheet of metal for the fire (**left**), or a complete unit for preparing, cooking and eating under a roof channelled across one end to encourage the smoke to escape (**far left**). Even the most humble barbecue can be fitted with a sheet metal canopy and chimney, whereas a simple bought unit can be protected from drafts by a palisade of upright logs (**above**).

Purchased barbecue units are available in a wide range of shapes and sizes, from the tiny hibachi (**above**) — ideal for one or two — to larger cooking grills with their own stand and shield (**below**).

Pergolas

Intended primarily to show climbing plants at their best, a pergola adds height and width to a garden, and is useful for screening a paved sitting and eating area from neighbors and strong sunshine. Pergolas can be simple or elaborate, and need not be expensive to build if second-hand materials such as bricks and timber are used. A wooden structure is particularly good for softening the effect of paved areas of hard stone and tile, especially those smothered in flowers and foliage.

A limited range of pergolas is available in kit form — but they are quite simple to build yourself, using a variety of building materials which should be sound and stable enough to withstand wear and stress. Any metal parts should be checked and treated for rust and corrosion regularly; timber should be given an initial treatment of wood preservative, remembering to use one that is non-poisonous to plants.

The simplest construction is a plain wooden framework using 10 x 5cm (4 x 2in) sawn timber and comprising a series of uprights joined in pairs to form a tunnel of arches, linked across the top with cross-pieces. For variation, the uprights can be replaced by metal poles or the cross-pieces cantilevered out over the side of the structure for added interest.

Peeled larch poles make a very effective rustic pergola and simply need notching and fixing together to create a sturdy, good-looking structure which blends in well with most garden settings. Alternatively, build your cross-piece framework using 15 x 5cm (6 x 2in) sawn boards supported by masonry pillars and tall chimney-pots. The mellow terracotta colors of the brick and earthenware look particularly good in mature gardens.

If the position of the pergola seems too windy or drafty, it can be wholly or partially screened using bamboo, lattice fencing, vertical timber boarding, ornamental concrete screening blocks or timber louvers.

The pergola (right) is a mixture of poles and timber: plain metal poles form the uprights, and ordinary recycled timber is used above it as the horizontal framework.
Climbing plants can be grown to smother the frame by planting in tubs with a layer of pebbles on top to keep the roots cool.

Pergolas can be constructed many ways from a wide variety of materials to suit the individual budget and garden. Here, chimneypots on brick or stone piers (top) provide the uprights, with planks slotted together to form a grid framework along the top. A rambling red rose is the perfect foil for the mellow terracotta of the bricks and pots. The simple wooden frame over a formal paved area (center) has been planted with wisteria and clematis for color and scent; the more rustic construction (right) is made using stripped larch poles smothered in honeysuckle.

A simple wrought iron gazebo planted with clematis and rambling roses (**below**) forms a superb feature in the garden.

Gazebos

Gazebos serve very much the same function as pergolas in that they are like open summerhouses in which you can sit and enjoy the rest of the garden, and where climbing plants can be trained to cover the structure. Commercial models are usually made of metal and ornately decorated, but you can make your own simple gazebo, using wood and wrought iron railings.

Plants for both pergolas and gazebos must like plenty of sun on their leaves and flowers but prefer their roots in the shade. Protect the roots in summer by covering the base of each stem with damp pebbles or a mulch. The choice of climbers naturally depends on their position and the local climate, but there are many that can provide scented blooms as well as foliage: wisteria, clematis, roses, jasmine, passion flower, honeysuckle and potato vine *(Solanum crispum)*. Quick climbers are the glory vine *(Vitis coignetiae)*, the Persian ivy *(Hedera colchica)* and the climbing hydrangea *(Hydrangea petiolaris)*.

A simple gazebo can be easily made using timber and wrought iron in the way that is shown (**right**); this one has been planted with ivy to soften its shape. The purchased model below is more elaborate, constructed in metal throughout and placed over a circular paved area.

Summerhouses

A simple wooden summerhouse with open doorway makes a pleasant place to sit and contemplate the view of the garden. This one has been positioned overlooking a tranquil stretch of water and has a conical timbered roof which gives it a slightly Oriental flavor.

If there is room for one in your garden, a summerhouse is a marvellous combination of sheltered seating area and useful store for chairs, tables and other garden paraphernalia. Its primary purpose is generally to provide somewhere to sit and enjoy the sun, out of the wind and sheltered from the occasional shower, so your main concern must be to position it so that it obtains the maximum sunshine. In exposed situations, screening can be provided using shrubs, hedging or evergreens, bamboo screens or timber fencing, all of which help to 'soften' the lines of the building.

Ideally, a summerhouse should also face a pleasant view — a stretch of water is ideal, especially if it is possible to position the structure on the edge, or even raised on stilts over the water. If it is elegant enough, alternatively, the summerhouse can be used as the focal point within the main plan of the garden.

There is a wide range of sizes and styles available, either to buy ready-made or to build yourself. The basic type consists of a simple roofed structure which, depending on how exposed its position is, can have glazed or open sides. The standard summerhouse, however, is a timber-built building big enough to store sunloungers, chairs, and maybe a fold-away patio table, with folding or double doors that open out to enable you to sit out, or just inside, depending on the weather. Some styles feature an additional verandah with half-timbered sides, which extends the seating area into the garden and provides some extra internal protection from drafts.

When choosing a summerhouse, be careful to select both size and style appropriate to your requirements and the garden's appearance.

In front of your summerhouse it is a good idea to build some sort of paved area to provide a dry, stable surface for tables and chairs when the weather is especially fine. This might be constructed of concrete paving slabs, brick or crazy paving (according to taste) — but a timber decked area, raised on joists, always looks particularly good beside a wood-built building. Judicious planting of evergreens and tubs of bright annuals help to soften any hard edges and to blend the area into the garden.

Of course, if you are blessed with a house that faces more or less due south, a lean-to sunroom extension makes an excellent part-conservatory part-summerhouse, that you don't even have to go out of the house to use. With either folding or patio doors, the room can be opened out on to a paved area in summer for sitting out.

An ornamental hexagonal greenhouse makes a very elegant summerhouse if you are short of space or want to make a feature of it. Offering all-year-round shelter, specially made blinds are available to screen the glass from hot sun in summer.

The pavilion-type summerhouse (**above left**) often features folding doors and a matching veranda, which can be extended with concrete paving.

A wooden summerhouse (**above right**), more simply styled and positioned to open directly onto a matching timber-decked patio area.

A simple shelter (**above left**) is perfect for enjoying the sunshine. A lean-to sunroom extension (**left**) makes an excellent part-conservatory part-summerhouse.

This octagonal greenhouse has been boxed in with conifers for privacy and doubles as an all-year-round shelter. Blinds are available to screen the glass in very hot weather.

Greenhouses

A greenhouse offers the keen gardener freedom from the restrictions of climate and soil, so that almost any plant can be grown or propagated from seeds or cuttings.

Basically, the greenhouse is a wooden or aluminum frame infilled with glass panels to catch maximum light and warmth; it should also have its own controllable system of heating, screening and ventilation.

A lean-to is ideal for gardens with restricted space or where the garden side of the house faces maximum sunshine; painting the wall white reflects and can amplify the light and warmth. A free-standing structure, alternatively, can be positioned anywhere in the garden of course, but should be placed to receive maximum light and sunshine and so provide more scope and better results.

The traditional greenhouse has an apex roof and glass half-way or right down to the ground. Newer designs are smart enough themselves to constitute garden features, and to be allowed therefore to remain visible and distinct from the rest of the garden. Some are made up of small hexagonal shapes fitted together to create a honeycomb complex or a futuristic geodesic shape which, although not very economical on space inside, looks suitably presentable in the right setting. The Victorian-style conservatories now produced by a few companies are expensive but create a wonderful environment for growing plants like palms and ferns among colonial-style chairs and tables.

A glasshouse naturally attracts and stores heat during the day when the sun is shining,

The standard, ornate conservatory is perfect for Victorian-style plants.

but cools quite considerably at night. There are various forms of internal heating available with which to control the temperature and help to ensure the success of your plants, particularly the tender varieties.

Paraffin (kerosene) heaters are the cheapest to buy — although they can be expensive to run and the fumes are damaging to some plants. Oil-fuelled heating can be very effective, using a system of heated pipes, but again is expensive to run. Electricity is clean and has the advantage of being thermostatically controlled. But probably the most economical form of heating is a portable natural gas stove.

Control of the temperature and humidity within the greenhouse is essential if plants are not to suffer from scorching or shrivelling. Some models come complete with vents that open thermostatically according to the temperature of the air inside; with manually-operated forms of heat control, however, it is advisable in summer to open vents first thing in the morning and close them again about an hour before sunset.

The glass panes can be shaded against too much heat in summer by spraying with limewash or a proprietary shading compound in late spring or early summer, and washing off in early to mid-autumn. Alternatively, the panes can be fitted with blinds that can be lowered as and when needed.

Sheds

Sheds are useful for storing garden equipment in and, if large enough, for providing a bench area suitable for propagating cuttings and sowing seeds. If there is room in the garden for a fairly large structure, the building can also double as a workshop or hobby-room, containing possibly a workbench, table and tools.

Sheds are usually constructed of concrete or timber, and have either an apex or a pent (single sloping) roof. Wood generally blends better with the rest of the garden, but needs a coat of preservative every year or so to keep it in good condition. Concrete, on the other hand, is expensive but needs very little maintenance. Both types can be covered with trellis and smothered with evergreen climbers to conceal them if their position makes that desirable; grape vine, ivy, honeysuckle and climbing roses all make good attractive cover, and the hardy Morello cherry is particularly fine for a north-facing wall.

The shed **(above)** has been covered with a grape vine on a sun-facing doorway and Morello cherry on the shady side. A yew trained over the door **(right)** and pyracantha on the roof provide good cover.

Features of a typical greenhouse

Full-length glass provides maximum light

Metal or wooden structure

Rainwater tank

Trays of seedlings

Automatic window ventilator

Side ventilator

Electric fan

Mist propagator

Greenhouse staging

Pots of rooted cuttings

Automatic blinds

Paved interior

Cistern for an automatic watering system

Electric control panel

The standard model (**above**) is screened from the house by a row of evergreens; a lean-to greenhouse is built onto the house; a small hexagonal construction can be joined to other similar glasshouses to create a complex; the modern geodesic style of greenhouse (**left**) is more difficult to organize.

Most sheds come with optional extras to suit further needs — such as fitted floors, windows or a locking door — and are delivered flat-packed to be erected on site over a stable concrete base.

You may, however, prefer to build your own shed from bricks or timber. The simplest home-made construction is the tiny sentry-box shed commonly seen on allotments. They have a single locking door, and are usually big enough only to store basic tools in, so they can be completely disguised by smothering in an attractive evergreen such as laurel, bay, rhododendron or *Magnolia grandiflora* (leaving only the door free for access).

This pent-roofed shed (**left**) has been covered with a trellis, latticed on the diagonal and grown with rambling red rose and ivy. The tiny shed (**above**) has been smothered with an evergreen.

This area **(above)** has been paved to match the surrounding patio area, and includes plenty of room for playing with wheeled toys, balls and bicycles. If there is an existing patio which you do not want to dig up, you may prefer to build a raised sandpit **(left)**, using recycled timber planks sanded smooth and treated with wood preservative. A wide-planked top helps contain the sand and is more comfortable for playing on.
Play furniture, such as slides **(right)** can be decorative as well as functional.

Pets

When deciding on a location for a pets' corner in your garden, make sure the spot is protected from drafts, cold winds and the worst of the weather, and easily accessible from the house for feeding and cleaning. Hutches for rabbits, guinea-pigs, hamsters and gerbils are quickly and easily made from stout timber and wire netting, and can be raised on legs or set on a bench or table top. Wooden dog-kennels should be situated on a hard surface, such as gravel or paving, and can be brightened with a coat of gloss paint and surrounding tubs of hardy evergreens. Encourage wild birds into the garden by building nesting boxes and bird-tables to the approved designs, and positioning them out of reach of cats and dogs.

Keeping pets in the garden **(right)** provides fun for children of all ages. Make sure that rabbit hutches are strongly made to give adequate shelter.

A smart wooden kennel is easy to make with shaped sections of particle board, and can be 'softened' by adding a few plants in tubs for interest. Shown here is hebe, which is particularly hardy.

Children's areas

Most children love playing outdoors and are quite happy to spend all day in the garden, where they can let off steam and invent a wide variety of games. Such enjoyment of the fresh air and exercise is excellent for them, especially if they can be allocated a properly designed area of their own, ideally near the house where it can be occasionally supervised. This not only keeps them away from your flowerbeds, but can probably contain all the play equipment.

The area should be big enough to dig, play and wallow in without disturbing the rest of the garden. If space is limited, however, consider building up the flowerbeds, retaining them behind low brick walls where they are near paths or paving; enclosure like this should protect plants from bicycles and wheeled toys at least, if not from balls.

There is no reason for children not to be allowed to play in the garden all year round, provided that they are wrapped up warmly in winter. The play area should be paved and well drained to keep it dry in most weathers, and well screened from cold winds and drafts by tough evergreens such as variegated holly or barberry *(Berberis)*, timber fencing or concrete screening blocks — anything sturdy enough to withstand a battering from balls and bikes, or being used as a stockade and battlements. A high wooden palisade of logs makes good strong screening — and, if gaps are incorporated along the side at child's eye-level, it can double as a fort, log-cabin or castle.

Some form of shelter means play can continue even when the weather is wet. A wooden frame with tarpaulin stretched across is simple to make and offers adequate protection from showers. If there is room, a playhouse is always popular, and is also useful for storing large items such as bikes and scooters when not in use. The traditional-style house can be easily made by building a strong wooden frame with walls and roof of waterproof plywood; alternatively, if the age of the children is appropriate, construct a strong log cabin with flat log roof and wooden ladder.

Either a playhouse or a log cabin can be built in a suitable tree on a strong platform for older children to use as a tree-house. Access is again by wooden or rope ladder. If there is no tree big or strong enough, the house can instead be just as easily raised on stilts.

Paving the play area provides a better surface for playing which remains relatively dry at all times if sloping gently. Large paving slabs are more appreciated by children than crazy paving — which is hopeless for hopscotch and making roads; you may prefer, though, to install a timber-decked area which looks softer to the eye and provides an altogether warmer surface. A sunken wading pool or sand-pit within a paved area provides hours of absorbed play but should be equipped with a tight-fitting cover when not in use, not only so that kids cannot hurt themselves by falling in, but also to protect it from animals.

In fact, it is worthwhile sinking the paved play area half a meter (a couple of feet) or so. This provides extra shelter, helps to define the area clearly, and toys are less likely to escape from it into the rest of the garden; any stray sand can easily be swept back in. Such advantages are of course not possible where there is already an existing paved area, but in that case the sand-pit can instead be built up into a raised structure with timber sides and a wide rim all around to help contain the sand.

If there is no tree in the garden, build a 'tree' house

Aviaries can be contructed using strong netting fixed to a wooden framework, leaving a hinged section to provide access for feeding and watering. Grow a bushy plant in a container for the birds to perch on. Ideal is *Viburnum opulus* — Guelder rose — **(right)**, which produces masses of bright red berries irresistible to birds. Two styles of aviary are shown **(left)**: a single-roofed construction for two or three birds, and a more complex design featuring two sheltered perching areas with matching conical roofs.

A paved play area with an integrated wading pool or sand-pit can be protected from cold winds and drafts by building a palisade of timber logs. The log cabin construction (**left**), is securely made with cross battens and an open doorway to provide unlimited play possibilities. A simple but strong wooden ladder offers access to the roof and turns a cabin, fort or house into a ship or castle.

In addition to a sand-pit or wading pool, there should ideally be some form of large play equipment, such as a climbing frame, swing or slide. A climbing frame offers best value: it can grow with the child and is flexible enough to stimulate the imagination for a wide range of play situations as well as providing good exercise. Even a simple structure can become a boat, a castle or a jungle, and has the advantage of being vertically-oriented where space is limited. A wide range of ready-made play frames are available — but it is more fun, and cheaper, to make your own out of good-quality planed softwood. Once a simple frame has been built, accessories such as rope or wooden ladders and swinging ropes can be added, and can be repositioned higher as the children grow.

A bird house (**above**) is simply made by using waterproof plywood and can be fixed to a suitable tree-trunk or the side of a timber-built shed.

An attractive dovecote (**right**) can be constructed in the same way, with a suitably enlarged entrance, mounted on a stout post.

A free-standing bird-table (**left**) encourages many different species of birds to visit the garden.

Playing with a rabbit (**above**) is every child's ambition. A garden hutch can make a dream become a safe reality.

A simple tire swing like the one shown **(left)**, can be constructed using a strong timber frame, stout rope and an old automobile tire.

Swings and slides can also be incorporated into a climbing frame, where they will take up less space than they do free-standing and also extend the play possibilities. But for a simple swing structure, the easiest method is to build a plain wooden frame and hang an old tire from a stout rope.

In the children's area, try to set apart a small piece of ground as a 'gardening' zone in which they can potter and be encouraged to grow things. Even a few tubs and pots of easy-to-grow annuals can teach them the pleasures of gardening — but remember, children like to see results quickly, so choose varieties with fast or spectacular results.

Sunflowers *(Helianthus annuus)* are a well-known favorite, growing up to 3m (10ft), but also popular are the mouse-tail plant

Children love to go barefoot in gardens **(above)**. Make sure there are no sharp stones or other hazards in their play areas.

A wooden play counter **(right)** offers hours of play and useful storage for garden toys and equipment. Its strong wooden frame is covered with particleboard to make a simple top with cupboards below; a pitched roof protects it from showers. A window box attached to one side allows a fast-climbing evergreen to cover the side and roof of the structure, and is also perfect for children to experiment with

Rabbits, hamsters, rats and other rodents need a sheltered corner of the garden for hutches or cages **(left)**. Hutches should be constructed using stout timber frames with wooden plank or particleboard walls and roofs, and heavy-gauge wire netting. All timber should be treated with a non-poisonous wood preservative every one or two years. This hutch has been raised on legs for easier access and to keep it off the damp ground; the cages for hamsters and guinea pigs **(right)**, are designed to stand on a low counter.

(Arisarum proboscideum) which produces a tapering 'mouse-tail', and jumping Jacks *(Impatiens roylei)* of which the wriggly ripe seedpods explode with a loud pop. Quick-growing bright annuals include candytuft *(Iberis amaria)*, cornflowers *(Centaurea cyanus)* and nasturtiums *(Tropaeolum majus)*. Selected edible plants, such as miniature tomatoes and strawberries, can be grown in containers.

Other projects likely to be appreciated by young gardeners include carving words and designs in small squash and watching them grow, and growing small trees from horse chestnuts, sycamore seeds and acorns.

A large sink **(above)** planted with chalk-loving plants which would not survive in a garden with highly acid soil. A well-shaped *Juniperus communis* 'Compressa' and a couple of rough chunks of limestone provide height and background to a good variety of foliage and flowering plants. Creeping thyme *(Thymus serpyllum)*, thrift *(Armeria)*, and house-leeks *(Sempervivum)* with their strange rosettes provide excellent blanket cover.

Effectively filling the gaps with leaves and flowers are *Dianthus*, *Gypsophila* and saxifrage. Limestone chippings sprinkled on the soil help to retain moisture and maintain a good alkali balance in the compost.

A sink filled with acid soil and planted randomly with boulders **(above)** is ideal for growing some of the smaller lime-hating varieties. Miniature rhododendrons are the perfect shrub for this type of garden, available in a wide range of colors with tiny, perfectly-formed flowers.

Sink gardens

Old sinks make excellent miniature gardens, and because they can be raised to any level, are ideal for children or disabled gardeners. They can be delightfully filled with alpines, miniature roses or perhaps even a miniature Oriental landscape with tiny trees, shrubs and temples. If your main garden is particularly acid or chalky, it is also possible to use a sink garden to experiment with dwarf varieties of plants not otherwise open to your selection.

To make a garden properly, the sinks should first be covered with PVA adhesive, followed by a mixture of two parts peat, one part sand, one part cement for a more natural finish. Drainage is essential: stand the sink on wood blocks, bricks or tiles and ensure that the drainage hole remains free (perhaps cover the hole with a broken piece of flower pot to prevent soil causing a blockage). On top of the mixture, put in a good layer of crocks or stones, then a layer of peat to help hold the moisture. Water thoroughly and allow to settle before topping up with a suitable soil mixture, making it fairly stony to aid drainage. Add a few surface rocks for interest, positioning them so that they are half buried by the compost, and start planting your chosen trees and plants, remembering to include some cushion and trailing plants to 'soften' the sides of the container. Finish with a dressing of limestone chippings if the plants are ericaceous, or granite for lime-haters and neutral species.

As with any container in which the roots cannot go very deep to find moisture, watering is vital. Water as and when needed, but do not allow the soil to dry out completely, or it will shrink away from the sides. If this does happen, pricking the surface helps the water to penetrate more easily. Constant feeding encourages plants to grow too bushy in such a miniature setting, so only add a little fertilizer if they begin to look weak and sickly with no obvious signs of pest or disease.

Choose your plants from the vast selection of dwarf and miniature varieties, many of them alpines which adapt well to difficult conditions. Make sure you have some cushion plants such as *Dianthus*, *Draba* and saxifrage, for growing over rocks and between other plants, and trailers for hanging over the edge of the container: gray-green *Linaria alpina*, phlox, St John's wort *(Hypericum)* or *Gypsophila*, all of which have pretty flowers.

Dwarf trees and shrubs are important for adding height and interest to an arrangement: miniature conifers in shades of grey, blue or green, dwarf cypress *(Chamaecyparis)*, juniper *(Juniperus)* and spruce *(Picea)*. Look out for miniature conifers in shades of gray, blue or heather *(Calluna vulgaris* 'Foxii Nana'), or the beautiful miniature roses: pink *Rosa rouletii*, red 'Maid Marion', yellow 'Yellow Bantam' and the white with pink 'Cinderella'.

Dwarf bulbs make a lovely display of delicate blooms against a bristly *Pinus mugo*, dwarf mountain pine.

The raised level of a sink garden adds to the pleasure of growing miniature scented plants such as *Dianthus*, dwarf lavender *(Lavandula stoechas)*, creeping thyme and the lovely miniature roses: red 'Maid Marion' and the pink *Rosa roulettii*. The fine, leafy *Daphne cneorum* produces a mass of scented red blooms.

Small sinks are perfect for creating miniature Japanese landscapes **(above)** in which a Bonsai pine and tiny temple set the scale for a selection of tiny shrubs and plants.

Drainage is vital in sink gardens **(right)**. A crock over the hole should keep it free from compost; above it, a good layer of crocks and pebbles, suitable (usually stony) soil.

Herb gardens

Herb gardens were invariably included in the grounds of European manor houses, not only to provide seasonings and fragrances for the kitchen and parlor, but also as decorative features in their own right. These two examples (**left**) show the variety of color and form that traditional herb gardens display.

The large formal herb garden (**below**) contains a selection of mainly culinary herbs, arranged in well-clipped blocks linked by low hedges of box (*Buxus*).

Herbs offer such a variety of shape, texture, scent and color that their culinary uses seem almost a mere bonus. Even the smallest garden should be able to dedicate a few square meters of soil, or a couple of pots on the patio, to growing a selection of herbs. But if there is a larger space to spare, there is tremendous scope for creating wild sweeps or formal patterns of color and shape.

Most herbs like good drainage and a sunny situation, and are vigorous growers — too vigorous, even, in the case of mints and lemon balm which it is advisable to plant in containers that stand on the patio or are sunk into the soil, to limit their growth. Many herbs attract bees and butterflies to the garden too, especially meadow saffron *(Colchicum autumnale)*, catmint *(Nepeta mussinii)*, santolina, hyssop, bergamot *(Monarda didyma)* and borage *(Borago officinalis)*.

With their subtle shading and variety of foliage and flowers, herbs create many different effects. The informal garden, with plants spilling over each other in a profusion of shapes and colors, aims to look partly overgrown. In fact, each plant has to be chosen carefully to maintain a good contrast of color, height and texture without being swamped by its neighbor.

Formal gardens use the wide variety of herbs to create a very different effect. They are then arranged in very definite geometric shapes, such as curves, rectangles, triangles and circles, defined with neatly clipped hedges of box *(Buxus)*. Herbs are usually kept well spaced and cropped to maintain their shape, so it is best to choose upright, compact varieties or to prune the roots as well as the branches of fast-growing herbs. Among formal designs using herbs are the traditional knots, which take quite a lot of care and maintenance; wheel effects, using brick or concrete to divide the plants; and checkerboard designs in which the herbs are planted in a series of squares. Raised beds are particularly suited to formal herb gardens as they help contain the plants and offer excellent drainage.

Another way to use herbs is in order to provide scented, creeping cover for paths, seats and lawns. Creeping thyme *(Thymus serpyllum)* and Roman chamomile *(Chamaemelum nobile)* soften the edges of stone paths in sunny situations if introduced into the cracks between the slabs; pennyroyal *(Mentha pulegium)* and the tiny *Mentha requienii* do well in shady sites. These herbs can

also be used to make herb seats: simply build up a low bank of earth, lay slabs of paving or timber planks along the top, and plant creeping herbs in the gaps between. The seat should be covered with a sweet-scented living cushion by the following year.

Herbs also grow well on a patio or outside the kitchen door — where culinary varieties are easily accessible for adding to soups, grills and stuffings. Remember to provide good drainage with a generous level of crocks or pebbles, and position them where they receive plenty of sunlight.

However you want to display your herbs, aim for a good contrast of leaf shape and color. For pale and silver foliage, choose rue *(Ruta graveolens)*, woolly thyme *(Thymus pseudolanuginosus)* or wormwood *(Artemisia absinthium)*. For dark leaves, black horehound *(Ballula niger)*, purple basil *(Ocimum basilicum* 'Dark Opal')* and bronze fennel *(Foeniculum vulgare)* are all suitable. Herbs with variegated leaves include pineapple mint *(Mentha suaveolens* 'Variegata')*, golden sage *(Salvia officinalis* 'Icterina')* and variegated lemon balm *(Melissa officinalis* 'Aurea')*. And for bright flowers, choose between: red bergamot *(Monarda didyma)*, blue borage *(Borago officinalis)* and yellow elecampane *(Inula helenium)*.

If there is no room for herbs in the garden, they can be grown successfully in well-drained tubs and containers (**above**) on a patio or near the kitchen door. Place them where they receive plenty of light and sunshine — few herbs thrive in the shade — and spread a good layer of crocks or pebbles in the bottom of the pots to prevent the roots from being waterlogged.

The herb wheel (**above**) has divisions of rosemary, sage, marjoran, chives, thyme and parsley; old bricks make a pleasant edging. In the centre is lemon balm *(Melissa officinalis)*. Invasive plants (**top right**), such as mint, can be contained in a tub or pot which can be set on a patio or sunk in the ground. The concrete-edged checkerboard effect (**right**) is achieved with regular square beds of culinary herbs.

Island beds

Island beds are a valuable feature in garden design, both for small gardens, in which narrow borders only add emphasis to the overall lack of space, and in larger plots where they can be used to break up large areas of lawn. They can be any shape or size to suit their location — formal geometric shapes or natural irregular sweeps, provided that they do not look out of place or create narrow strips of grass that are then difficult to mow. On the whole, they are easier to maintain than the traditional border because they are accessible from all sides and do not have as many tall plants, thus reducing the need for staking.

It is essential to mark the chosen shape accurately before beginning — there is nothing worse than a meandering line that should be straight or an off-square corner. Informal shapes are of course easiest, but should fit the natural contours of the garden if they are not to look out of place. Experiment, using a length of hosepipe as a marker, so that you can stand back and view the shape easily from all angles. Once decided on a design, mark out using a pointed stick or a thin trickle of lime.

To mark out a square or rectangular bed, first make a large set-square out of lengths of wood and use it to make the right-angled corners. This done, mark the shape with pegs and lines, checking the accuracy of the resulting shape by measuring the diagonals to see if they are of the same length.

Circular beds are easily drawn by driving a peg into the ground at the approximate center of the proposed bed. Tie to this a length of twine that is the radius of the required bed, and using it as a pivot, scribe a circle with a sharp stick on the other end of the twine.

Oval beds are marked in a similar fashion but using two pegs with a length of twine approximately three times as long as the distance between them. Knot the twine into a loop, place over the pegs, and using a sharp stick to take up the slack, draw the shape; the closer together the two pegs are, the more circular the oval.

A regular hexagonal shape is easily achieved by drawing a circle using the peg and twine method mentioned above, then using the same radius to mark off six equally-spaced points around the circumference. Joining up the points with pegs and twine gives the hexagonal shape.

When planning the planting of island beds, remember that they can be seen from all sides, and that plants have to be more or less self-supporting, so do not choose anything that grows too tall. Small shrubs and trees are useful for adding height and perennial interest in informal beds, and can also provide the focal point in a more formal arrangement: a bay tree in the center of a circular herbal bed, for example, or the holly in the ericaceous bed of heathers and rhododendrons shown here.

An irregularly shaped bed can be planted

Aim at a good variety of shape and colour when planning island beds. This informally-shaped bed (**below right**) has been planted with perennials: delphiniums, lupins, pampus grass and the giant pom-poms of *Allium gigantum* rise out of a sea of contrasting leaves and flowers.

with perennials rather like the traditional herbaceous borders; taller flowering plants, such as lupins, foxgloves, delphiniums or red-hot pokers *(Kniphofia)* should be placed toward the center. The rest of the bed may contain all your personal favorites, positioned according to color, shape and texture for a good balance of different leaves and flowers: primula, *Gypsophila*, *Anchusa angustifolia*, thrift *(Armeria)*, elephant's ears *(Bergenia)*, astilbe, *Dianthus*, *Salvia*, phlox, *Sedum*, aster, campanula, *Rudbeckia*, *Geum* and pansies are but a few.

The more formal beds are perfect for creating geometric shapes of living color using seasonal plants like those seen and admired in public parks. Mark out your design on the bed first, using pegs and twine or a trail of lime, then plant with areas of single colored bulbs or bright wallflowers for spring, annuals for summer. Low-growing compact annuals with masses of flowers are the most successful and are easier to conform to a shape: *Alyssum*, lobelia, marigolds *(Tagetes)*, verbena, begonias, *Matricara*, petunias and asters all blend together well.

Formal beds of bright-colored annuals grown in neat, geometric shapes are fun to make and provide a glorious show of summer color.

The circular bed (**above**) combines four different heathers and four types of rhododendron around a central holly tree. Heathers can be chosen to provide color all year round, with a wide variety of flowers and foliage from dark green, golden and red tinged needle-like leaves to bronze, red, pink, white and dark purple flowers.

The circular bed (**above**) has been planted with *Salvia*, petunias, marigolds, lobelias, asters, *Matricaria* and *Pyrethrum* to create a mass of reds, golds, blues, yellows and mauves. The large bed (**left**) is more informal, with a variety of different shrubs ranged around a flowering cherry. Here, it is the shape and color of the flowers and foliage that have been balanced to provide a series of contrasting and complementary patterns.

Raised beds

Raised beds can be formal or informal as appropriate to the style of the garden. Dry stone walling, bricks, peat blocks or even old railway sleepers are the usual means of constructing the retaining walls. Providing not only an excellent opportunity to control soil-type and drainage — particularly important in a problem garden — raised beds also offer easier access to plants for the handicapped gardener, and protection for the plants from toys and bicycles when children stray from the paths.

Brick retaining walls look the most formal. They should be at least two to three bricks thick, upon proper concrete foundations. It is a good idea to stake out the site beforehand, using pegs and string to check that corners are square, and to ensure that the size suits your garden, then to leave the foundations 24 hours to make sure it is level. Lay one of the corner bricks first and start working towards the center, making sure that the mortar used is not as solid as the bricks themselves. This ensures that in heavy frost it is the mortar that gives and not the bricks.

Raised beds need careful drainage, depending on their size, the soil character and the local climate. Intermittent gaps left in the brick joints are sufficient in some cases; alternatively, insert small pipes of clay, asbestos, concrete or plastic at 1m (39in) intervals from the bottom to a height about a third of the way up the wall. The pipes should be between 5cm (2in) and 7.5cm (3in) in diameter, and extend the full depth of the wall — and about 30cm (12in) into the soil beneath. If they drain onto a patio or other paved area, remember to provide a gulley to allow the water to run away.

Small trees and shrubs add height and weight to raised beds; but otherwise fill with your favorite annuals for a blaze of color and scent in summer, bulbs for spring and a few evergreens to maintain interest over winter. Always include a selection of good creeping and trailing plants to 'soften' the edges.

For a more natural effect, use dry stone walling to construct your retaining walls, and leave out the occasional stone for interplanting with appropriate plants. This type of bed is ideal for growing alpines, which thrive in a free-draining, rocky setting and can provide color and interest all year round.

Dry stone walls can be laid on sand, hardcore or concrete foundations, and to stand firm should be built with the width of their base equal to half their height, and tapered slightly from bottom to top, yet leaning slightly backward. The actual stones of the wall can be interplanted with alpines for an even softer, more natural effect.

If your garden is on very chalky soil but you wish to grow some of the beautiful lime-hating plants such as rhododendron and magnolia, it is possible to create a lime-free setting for them using raised beds. In this case, use pre-formed peat blocks 30 x 10 x 10cm (12 x 4 x 4in), soaked for 24 hours and laid as you would bricks, for your retaining walls. Line the bottom of the bed with a sheet of strong plastic; top with a good layer of crocks and pebbles for drainage; then fill with a mixture of loam, sand and peat.

There are many dwarf rhododendrons available which are ideal for raised beds — varieties such as *R. yakushimanum* which provide good dense foliage as well as a mass of compact blooms. Camellias, too, offer a fine display of glossy green leaves especially when in flower, which tends to be late winter to mid-spring — a welcome mass of pink, white or deep red flowers. For winter color, witch hazel enjoys an acid soil, and the popular *Hamamelis mollis* brightens the garden with yellow flowers and a distinctive sweet scent.

Informal beds enclosed by dry stone walling (**left**) are ideal for making rock gardens where standard alpines can be grown.

Cross-section of the acid bed retained by peat blocks (**above and right**) shows how a sheet of plastic topped with a good layer of crocks for drainage and suitable compost enables lime-hating plants to be grown in a garden with chalky soil. This bed includes a selection of suitable ericaceous plants.

Beds retained by brick walls tend to look more formal but are perfect if you have children, who all too often ride their bicycles over the flower beds. Some proper system of drainage is important, either by means of drainage pipes built into the brickwork (**above**), or by leaving occasional gaps in the brick joints (**right**) to allow water to drain away.

The small compact bed (**above**) has a small birch as centerpiece, surrounded by colorful summer planting; and the larger arrangement (**right**) a blaze of annuals with a sweet-scented mock orange (*Choisya ternata*): orange *Calendula*, mauve petunias, pink *Dianthus* and the dwarf poppy *Eschscholzia*.

Sunken beds

One of the best ways to treat a deep hollow or a very uneven site is to create a sunken garden out of it, saving a lot of levelling and possibly creating a fascinating feature into the bargain. The soil tends to be poorly drained in such sunken areas, so it is advisable to base any plan around moisture-loving plants, such as roses, or even bog plants, depending on how bad the problem is.

Roses are perfect for making a formal garden, which can be paved with brick or stone and designed to include raised or inset beds of different varieties. Some form of screening adds to the attraction and helps to ward off drafts: a hedge of lavender makes a sweet-smelling and effective wind-break; or you can erect a trellis all around on which to grow climbing or rambling roses such as the scarlet 'Danse du Feu', white 'Climbing Iceberg', or yellow 'Albéric Barbier'.

The main beds can be planted with a selection of standard and bush roses designed to bloom at different times with a complementary range of colors and scents. The large flowered roses (formerly hybrid tea) are particularly useful in that they produce fat blooms from early summer until the first frosts. 'Whisky Mac' has the advantage of a coppery-orange color and a good scent; the popular 'Peace' produces huge pink-edged pale yellow blooms.

Miniature roses grow to about 45cm (18in) high and are perfect for raised beds where they can be seen and smelt more easily. Scented varieties include the pink 'Baby Faurax', white 'Snow Carpet' and orange-yellow 'Darling Flame'.

A more informal-style sunken garden can be constructed using crazy paving and a palisade of old railway sleepers. A circular design looks most attractive planted with evergreen shrubs around the top for extra protection and to 'soften' the timber edging; steps down can be made from timber to match. If the soil tends to be soggy and poorly drained, create a special bog garden with moisture-lovers such as ferns, hostas and lilies.

For spring flowering, choose the lovely yellow globe flower *(Trollius europaeus)*, or bell-flowered plantain lily *(Hosta)*, and for summer you can enjoy blue monkshood *(Aconitum napellus)*, spiraea *(Astilbe)* which has pink, white and red blooms, scarlet monkey flower *(Mimulus)*, yellow ligularia *(Ligularia przewalskii)*, or the striking giant rhubarb *(Rheum palmata)* which produces huge leaves up to 1.5m (5ft) tall and large red flowers.

For late summer and autumn, plant loosestrife *(Lythrum salicaria)*, which produces red, purple and pink flowers, and waxbells *(Kirengeshoma palmata)*.

Roses flourish in a moist soil, making them ideal for sunken gardens. In the rose garden (**below**) a central bed of standards is surrounded by large-flowered bush roses, while ramblers smother the trellis and provide screening all around. Miniatures in raised beds of brick or stone are easier to see and smell than at ground level.

Bog plants grow well in a sunken area with poor drainage. The circular garden (**above**) is made using vertical railway sleepers and crazy paving and features moisture-lovers such as ferns, hostas, iris, lilies and astilbe.

Low growing rockery plants flourish on the scant soil between millstone steps (**left**). Informal steps, framed by dwarf conifers, lead naturally into a sunken garden (**below**).

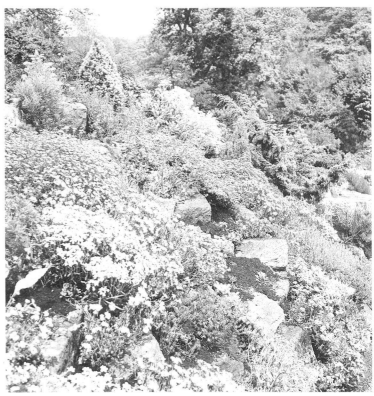

Rockeries look good and fit well into the garden only if the rocks are laid correctly, following any apparent natural strata of the rock, and imitating the natural effects of weathering (**above**). Exposed strata weather and crumble, leaving a shelf of scree and creating a natural outcrop which tilts slightly backwards (**below**).

Rock gardens

The clue to a successful rock garden lies in the positioning of the stones, which should imitate as closely as possible a natural outcrop. Alpines, for example, prefer a sunny, open site with well-drained soil; if you mean to plant them, therefore, prepare by working in some stones and rubble before starting to build. Place large pieces first according to their natural strata, embedding them in the soil and tilting them slightly backwards to allow the moisture to drain to the roots of surrounding plants. Then add smaller stones and areas of scree, leaving pockets of firm soil for the plants above and below the rocks.

There are many ways in which a rock garden can be blended into the overall garden design. If the garden has a natural slope or incline, a rocky outcrop with a grassy bank behind always looks very natural, and can slope down to a planted scree area at the bottom. Alternatively, if there is some feature you wish to hide, the rockery can be built up on top by planting dwarf conifers to add height and depth. Most suitable varieties for this are the cypress *Chamaecyparis lawsoniana* 'Minima Aurea', the juniper *Juniperus communis* 'Compressa' and the spruce *Picea glauca*.

Most nurseries offer a wide selection of alpine plants, many now grown in pots so that they can be planted at any time between early spring and autumn. Aim for a good balance of plants to 'soften' the rocks — creepers, cushion and crevice varieties — and designed to flower at different times so that there is a good display for most of the year.

Creeping and trailing plants are useful for winding between the rocks; many have scented flowers. Creeping thyme grows well in a sunny situation, as does *Alyssum*, rock cress *(Arabis)* and *Aubretia deltoidea* (purple rock cress). St John's wort *(Hypericum)*, with its bright yellow flowers, and purple alpine toadflax *(Linaria alpina)* are also good trailing plants.

Compact cushion-forming plants add interest and color to a flat surface through their round hummocks of foliage and bright flowers. The alpine Drabas produce white or yellow flowers; thrift *(Armeria maritima)* has round heads of pink. Rosette-forming plants are more valued for their unusual fleshy foliage which clings to the rock-face, such as that of the house-leek *(Sempervivum)*, which is quite hardy and available in a wide range of foliage colors from green through to red. There is also a wide selection of plants that flourish on scree too: stonecrop *(Sedum)*, *Verbascum*, which flowers until late summer, and the alpine daisy *(Erigeron)* are all worth considering.

Other alpines virtually guaranteed to produce a fine show of foliage and flowers are the mossy saxifrage, phlox, *Dianthus*, *Lewisia*, astilbe, and the lovely *(Pulsatilla)*.

A rocky outcrop can look particularly effective if it backs onto a raised lawn area (**above**) and features suitable alpines planted in pockets of good soil mixture among the rocks on the vertical face. A natural scree bed forms the base of the structure, made up of stone chippings and grit laid to a depth of about 45cm (18in) on a slight incline to aid drainage.

Planting tall shrubs and trees on top of a rock garden construction adds height and helps to hide any garden eyesore (**below**). Here, conifers provide the background for a variety of alpine plants growing on the rock face, on ledges and in cracks between the boulders.

The above-ground pond (**above**) is pre-cast and has a raised section in the center with a ball jet fountain and matching raised beds of shrubs all round. The very formal pond (**right**) with two-tier fountain can be made using concrete or a flexible liner and has been planted with iris and reedmace (*Typha*).

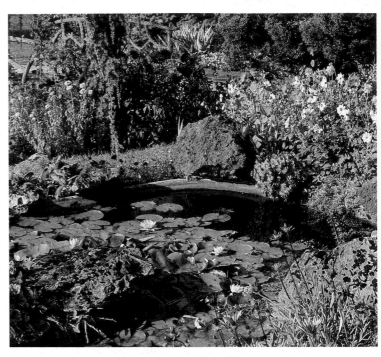

Flowering plants surround this small concrete pond (**above**). Water lilies provide shade for fish.

The bubble fountain (**below**) spills over an old millstone and trickles through the pebbles to a sump below.

Garden ponds

However small, a pond is an asset to any garden; it provides constant interest as its surface changes with variation in light, and beneath there is the chance to observe delicate aquatic plants, fish and other wildlife at close quarters. Any feature involving moving water, such as a fountain or waterfall, is stimulating to the eye, and not only aerates the water for fish and plants, but also creates an air of tranquillity through the soothing sound of trickling or bubbling water.

But an unfenced pond can be dangerous. If there are young children in the family, it is advisable to restrict a pond to a simple bubble fountain — in which the water is pumped over a bed of pebbles into the safety of a concealed sump below — until they are older.

The size and style of a garden pond should be appropriate to your requirements and the overall dimensions of the garden — but it must be at least 38cm (15in) deep to prevent it from freezing solid in winter; to keep goldfish or other fancy fish in, a depth of 75cm (30in) is ideal. The shape can be informal, with gentle sweeping curves framed by boulders, or paved and formal in a circular, square or rectangular design. A formal pond should be marked out using pegs and twine; for an informal effect, use a length of hosepipe making sure the pattern is not too intricate or the water will tend to stagnate. A raised pool can look effective in some settings, especially in a formal garden with a circular pool and a central fountain, maybe surrounded by raised flowerbeds or a paved area with planted containers.

If the garden has room for a large pool area, a series of small pools on different levels offers the option of an informal stream effect, with water tumbling down over boulders to the lowest level before being pumped to the top again. This system works well in formal pools too, creating a series of small waterfalls linking two or three square-paved ponds.

Once the pool is established there is a wide range of features that can be added: fountains in single, double or triple tiers, statues, underwater lights (which are particularly effective if the family enjoys sitting in the garden after dark or the pond is visible from the house) and so on.

There are basically three methods of constructing a pond: using concrete, a preformed shell, or a pond liner — all involve digging a hole to the correct shape and lining with a level layer of sand.

Concrete is less used these days; it is difficult to apply and tends to crack and lose its waterproofing qualities.

Preformed shells are very popular, constructed in fiberglass or reinforced plastic and available in a range of shapes and sizes.

Probably the best and longest-lasting method is to use a sheet of flexible lining material; it should be laid in a pre-dug hole, inclined outward at an angle of about 20°, and with a shelf about 23cm (9in) below the surface for marginal plants. Several 'grades' of lining material are available; the most expensive but toughest one is of butyl rubber. The liner should be anchored with smooth boulders or paving slabs around the sides, adjusted as the pool is filled. The edge of the liner should be covered with turf or cemented with boulders or paving for a good finish. This also prevents sunlight from causing the exposed edges of the

cheaper grades of liner — especially polyethylene — to break down.

A new pond looks rather murky to begin with as its ecological balance adjusts itself. After about ten days, however, it should clear, and plants and fish can be added. A selection of oxygenators such as Canadian pondweed (*Elodea canadensis*) is required to keep the water healthy; these grow from the bottom and can be anchored with strips of lead until they are established. Floating plants, such as frogbit (*Hydrocharis morsus-ranae*) and water soldiers (*Stratiotes aloides*), simply need placing on the surface, but marginal plants like marsh marigolds (*Caltha palustris* and *C. polypetala*), iris and bog bean (*Menyanthes trifoliata*) should be planted in meshed tubs on shelves beneath the surface. Water-lilies and deep water plants should be grown from the bottom in pots of fiber-free soil. When stocking with fish, allow each about 900cm^2 (1sq ft) of pond surface.

If the garden has room for a larger pool complex, a change of levels can create a pleasant waterfall effect. The informal three-level pond (**below**) was made using a flexible rubber liner edged with boulders over which the water spills into the lower pool before being pumped back to the top. The formal pool (**below right**) includes several interesting features: stepping stones to a small island where water is pumped into a trough, a pebble beach, and a paved area with plants to soften the edges.

Swimming pools

Improved methods of construction and installation have meant that swimming pools are far more generally accessible than they used to be, no longer the impossible dream. They come in all shapes and sizes to suit personal requirements and finances, depending especially on whether you are prepared to install it yourself or can afford to pay the retail company to do it for you. No swimming pool is cheap, however, so it is worth sitting back and considering what those requirements really are before you start.

A keen swimmer needs a rectangular pool no smaller than 7.3 x 3.7m (24 x 12ft), with a minimum depth of 2.1m (7ft) at the deep end. If there are children in the family, a shallow end is essential, usually around 1.0m (3.3ft) deep. In fact, if the whole purpose of the pool is really only for them to splash around in, a small above-ground pool would be perfectly adequate.

Before arriving at a final decision on the type of pool you intend to buy it is essential to check that you have sufficient space in terms of the overall dimensions of the garden. As far as possible, moreover, the pool should

not be too conspicuous, yet lie ideally in a sunny site out of the wind. There must be enough space surrounding it for a paved area to prevent dirt and leaves being brushed into the water, a sitting and sunbathing area, some form of screening, and room to store the filtration unit, heater, and possibly changing rooms. Avoid siting the pool near trees or your family will forever be fishing leaves out of the water.

The best — and most expensive — type of swimming pool is the in-ground model, which can be rectangular, L-shaped, kidney-shaped, or any shape you like. Not only costly, it may be difficult to install too: planning permission may be necessary, excavations must be dug, and usually the rest of the garden needs relandscaping afterward. You ought to be very sure that your family really is going to put it to good use before you commit yourself.

Cheaper and easier to install are the above-ground models — which are of course far more difficult to blend into the rest of the garden. If the garden has a slope or change of levels, setting the pool into the side of the slope may help to disguise it; otherwise, you might be able to conceal it with carefully placed evergreens or screening that can double as a windbreak.

All swimming pools need filtering every eight hours, so provision must also be made for

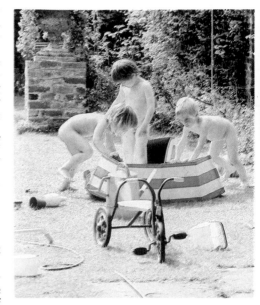

At the first sign of sunny weather children insist on getting the pool out. These small pools (**above**) are ideal for very young children, but do keep a careful eye on them.

For the more ambitious there are larger portable pools (**below**). Used occasionally, these should not cause too much permanent damage to the garden lawn.

Timber decking (**above**) greatly improves the appearance of an above-ground pool and can be used to conceal the filter, pump and cover. The stylish kidney-shaped built-in pool (**left**) has been edged with crazy paving and screened with a well-clipped evergreen hedge. The small changing-room covered in trellis and a fast-growing evergreen blends well into the pool areas. A raised timber-decked area is the perfect setting for a matching timber-clad hot-tub and built-in plunge pool (**below left**). Attractive evergreens planted as screening all around provide adequate privacy as well as a pleasant outlook.

the pump unit and heater. A small building incorporated into the paved area around an in-ground pool can be designed to include changing-rooms and somewhere to store chairs and tables. The appearance of an above-ground model can alternatively be greatly improved by building a raised timber deck around one side of it and using the space below to store pump, heater and cover, and possibly for room to change in too.

Some kind of screening may be desirable, not only for privacy but also if the climate is windy — to help limit the amount of dirt and leaves blowing into the water from the rest of the garden. Cedars, cypresses, firs and pines make good natural screening; alternatively, grow a more formal, curved, clipped hedge using evergreens such as privet *(Ligustrum)*, barberry *(Berberis)*, box *(Buxus)* or yew *(Taxus)*. Bamboo screening, timber fencing or palisades also create a pleasant-looking windbreak that should help the area blend with the rest of the garden.

If the garden is really too small for a full-size swimming pool, you could install a well-screened hot-tub area on the patio complete with plunge pool set into timber decking and outdoor lighting for midnight dips. Screen with bamboo screens, evergreens and tubs of green plants and seasonal flowers.

Sports and games

Playing games in your own back garden is extraordinarily satisfying; even the smallest site has room for a simple pole with a ball on the end for batting practice, or a clock golf putting-green in which a single hole is placed off-center within a small circle of evenly-spaced teeing points. Even on a patio area, if it is paved with slabs alternating in color, giant chess becomes possible using scaled up pieces made from cardboard tubes.

But it is the lawn that is generally the center of sporting activities, especially if it is large enough to double as a croquet, tennis or badminton court. For ball games, however, the grass has to be kept in excellent condition to withstand the wear and tear: be prepared to lavish extra care on it in fertilizing, watering and mowing throughout the season.

If space is limited, remember that courts smaller than the standard size can be just as much fun to play on. A tennis court for slow or junior play can be as small as 30 x 15m (100 x 50ft) and a singles badminton court measures only 12 x 5.2m (39 x 17ft).

It is unlikely for an ordinary garden to have the space for a full-scale bowling green—which also has to be perfectly level or 'crowned' and as smooth as velvet. But you can have a lot of fun playing with a small wooden-framed pitch filled with turf or planted with top-quality grass seed, or levelled with sand for the Italian version, *boccie*. (A smooth, timbered surface in the same type of frame makes a miniature outdoor ten-pin bowling alley.)

A permanent giant chess board can be installed in the garden using contrasting paving slabs for the board, with the pieces made from shaped cardboard drums, large tins or blocks of polystyrene (**above**). To play bowls or *boccie*, make a small pitch by building a wooden framework (**right**): in it lay turf, or plant grass seed for English bowls, or a levelled layer of sand for the Italian version.

Croquet (**right**) is one of the most traditional of lawn games. The hoops can be set out easily to provide a summer's gentle sport.

The space needed

A large lawn area can double as a court for ball games, provided that the turf is kept in good condition with regular dressings of fertilizer and soil compost to compensate for the close mowing needed. The most popular lawn game is tennis, but it does require a large area of grass. Where space is more limited, or the site is uneven, you may have to consider other games such as croquet or badminton. A croquet lawn (**left**) should be as level as possible. The boundary line is divided into 2.1 and 1.1m (7 and 3½ ft) sections with the pegs and hoops set out at 6.4m (21ft) intervals. A tennis court (**center**) needs 23.8 × 11m (78 × 36ft), allowing 4.1m (13½ ft) for each court and 1.4m (4½ ft) for the lines, the length divided into 5.5 and 6.4m (18 and 21ft) sections. Ideally, there should be a farther run-back of 6.4m (21ft) at each end but this can be reduced for home use. A badminton court (**right**) measures 6.1 × 13.4m (20 × 44ft) with 75cm (30in) lines a 4m (13ft) service court, and a 2m (6½ ft) short service area.

PLANTS
FOR
SPECIAL
PURPOSES

Popular ground cover plants

One of the most widely planted ground cover plants is *Hypericum calcinum* (rose of Sharon, also called St. John's wort). It is effective as ground cover but it is not a very interesting plant; it has large golden yellow flowers in summer but does not flower continuously. There are other ground cover plants which grow just as well and can be used to give shades of green, red, gray and variegated foliage.

Hedera canariensis **(below)** provides effective ground cover and is particularly useful for shady areas. It grows quickly in any type of soil. The creamy flowers of *Symphytum grandiflorum* **(bottom)** are a short-lived spring bonus on an excellent ground cover plant that spreads rapidly in sun or shade.

GROUND COVER PLANTS

Botanical name	Common name	Height
Ajuga reptans (Perennial)	Bugle	10–30cm (4–12in)
Alchemilla mollis (Perennial)	Lady's mantle	30–45cm (12–18in)
Berberis candidula (Shrub)	Barberry	60cm (2ft)
Bergenia, various (Perennial)	Saxifrage	30cm (12in)
Calluna vulgaris (Shrub)	Ling, Heather	30–45cm (12–18in)
Cotoneaster dammeri (Shrub)		Prostrate
Epimedium, various (Perennial)	Barrenwort; Bishop's hat	30cm (12in)
Erica carnea (herbacea) (Shrub)	Heather	Up to 30cm (12in)
Euonymus fortunei radicans variegatus (Shrub)		40cm (16in)
Euphorbia, various (Perennial)	Spurge	45cm (18in)
Gaultheria (Shrub)	Partridge berry	*G.procumbens* Prostrate *G.shallon* 1.8m (6ft)
Geranium, various (Perennial)	Cranesbill	20–60cm (8–24in)
Hebe pinquifolia 'Pagei' (Shrub)	Veronica	15–23cm (6–9in)
Hedera, various (Shrub)	Ivy	Spreading
Hosta, various (Perennial)	Plantain lily	38–90cm (15–36in)
Hyperium calycinum (Shrub)	Rose of Sharon	30–45cm 12–18in)
Lavandula (Shrub)	Lavender	30–80cm (12–32in)
Lysimachia nummularia (Perennial)	Creeping Jenny	Prostrate
Mahonia aquifolium (Shrub)	Oregon grape	90–120cm (3–4ft)
Nepeta mussinii (Perennial)	Catmint	30–45cm (12–18in)
Pachysandra terminalis (Perennial)		20–30cm (8–12in)
Polygonum affine (Perennial)	Knotweed	15–23cm (6–9in)
Potentilla 'Mandschurica' (Shrub)	Cinquefoil	30cm (12in)
Prunus laurocerasus 'Zabeliana' (Shrub)		1.2m (4ft)
Pulmonaria angustifolia (Perennial)	Lungwort	30cm (12in)
Santolina chamaecyparissus (incana) (Shrub)	Lavender cotton	45–60cm (18–24in)
Sarcococca humilis (Shrub)	Christmas box; Sweet box	60cm (2ft)
Sedum, various (Perennial)	Stonecrop	30cm (12in)
Symphytum grandiflorum (Perennial)	Russian comfrey	20cm (8in)
Tiarella cordifolia (Perennial)	Foam flower	15–30cm (6–12in)
Thymus serpyllum (Perennial)	Thyme	2.5–10cm (1–4in)
Vinca major (Shrub)	Periwinkle	15–30cm (6–12in)
Vinca minor (Shrub)	Periwinkle	5–10cm (2–4in)

Color	Foliage	Season	Suitable sites
Blue	Multicolored and variegated forms	Mid summer	Heavy clay; shady; chalky
Yellow-green calyces	Light green, hairy palmate leaves	Early to late summer	Heavy clay; chalky; industrial; shady; coastal
Yellow	Evergreen, spiny	Late spring	Heavy clay; chalky; shade; industrial; coastal
Shades of pink, purple and white	Autumn color	Spring and autumn	Heavy clay; coastal. Tolerates dryness and deep shade
White, pink, purple and white	Colored foliage	Mid summer to late autumn	Lime-free; coastal
White, red berries	Evergreen	Summer autumn	Shady; industrial; heavy clay; chalky; coastal
Wide range	Autumn tints	All year	Chalky; heavy clay; industrial
White, pink, purple	Light or dark green bronze, yellow	Late autumn to late spring	Coastal; lime-free
Green-white	Gray-green and variegated white and pink	All year	Chalky; heavy clay; coastal; industrial
Yellow, red bracts	Evergreen	Mid to late spring	Dry sunny
Pinkish white flowers, red or black berries	Evergreen	All year	Lime-free soil
Shades of blue, pink or white	Dense leaves some with autumn tints	Early summer to early autumn	Coastal; heavy clay; industrial
White	Gray-green evergreen	Early summer	Coastal; dry sunny; industrial
	Variegated forms	All year	Heavy clay; industrial
White, purple	Wide color range including variegated forms	Summer	Heavy clay; shady
Yellow	Bright green; variegated forms	Summer	Heavy clay; dry sunny; industrial
Shades of blue and purple, fragrant	Evergreen, aromatic	Summer	Dry sunny
Yellow	Medium green and golden	Summer	Shady
Yellow fragrant flowers, blue-black berries	Evergreen	Spring	Industrial
Lavender blue, fragrant	Gray-green aromatic	Late spring to early autumn	Industrial; heavy clay
White, fragrant	Medium green; variegated form available	All year	Lime-free
Deep pink, rose red	Bright green becoming darker	Summer	Industrial; shady
White	Silver-gray foliage on purple stems	Late spring to early autumn	Industrial; shady
White; dark red fruits, finally black	Willow-like leaves	Evergreen	Industrial; clay
Pink or purple changing to blue	White spotted form available	Spring	Shady; clay
Yellow flowers	Silver-gray aromatic	Summer	Dry sunny
White flowers fragrant	Evergreen	Late winter	Chalk; heavy clay
Pink, yellow, white	Fleshy	Late summer	Dry sunny
White/pink shades	Rough, medium green	Spring	Heavy clay
Cream white	Turning bronze – red in winter	All year	Shady; heavy clay
White, shades of pink and lilac	Aromatic	Summer	Dry sunny
Blue	Evergreen; variegated forms available	Spring to autumn	Industrial; heavy clay
Blue	Evergreen; variegated forms available	Spring to autumn	Industrial; heavy clay

The periwinkle *(Vinca)* provides many reliable and easy ground cover plants which do well in shade and can be planted under hedges. They send out creeping stems that root very easily and, when established, rapidly cover a fair area. The best known are *V. major* with blue flowers (there is a creamy white and green variegated form *V. major* 'Variegata') and *V. minor* 'Bowles' Variety', which has larger, deeper blue flowers. The following are also recommended: *V. minor* 'Alba', white; *V. minor* 'Azurea Flore Pleno', double, sky blue; *V. minor* 'Gertrude Jekyll', glistening white; *V. minor* 'Variegata', leaves variegated creamy white. The greater periwinkles, *Vinca major*, are approximately 35cm (14in) in height, whereas the lesser periwinkles, *Vinca minor*, are about 15cm (6in) high.

Symphytum grandiflorum (Russian comfrey) is a very good ground cover plant. It is like the wild comfrey but grows only to a height of 30cm (1ft). It has evergreen hairy foliage, and small tubular flowers which rise above the foliage in the spring; they are cream with red tips. It can be an invasive plant and should not be planted in confined areas.

Pachysandra terminalis is a glossy-leaved plant growing up to 30cm (1ft) in height. It is difficult to establish but, once started, forms a thick and pleasant low mass. The fragrant early spring flowers are white but inconspicuous. The silver variegated form, 'Variegata', is more attractive but takes even longer to establish than the type plant. *Pachysandra* spreads by underground stolons and should not be planted in small areas adjacent to lawns.

Cotoneaster horizontalis (**above**) is one of several cotoneasters that can be grown as ground cover plants.

Once established, *Pachysandra terminalis* (**right**) spreads vigorously by underground stems to form a dense mass of weed-proof growth. The glossy foliage is evergreen and adorned in spring with small white fragrant flowers. A variegated form is also available.

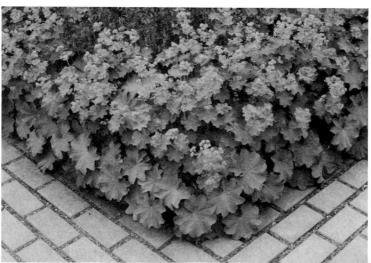

Attractive foliage and fresh yellow-green flowers make *Alchemilla mollis* (**right**) a highly desirable ground cover plant. It will flourish in any moist well-drained soil and seeds itself so readily that it very quickly fills its allotted space.

Ajuga reptans 'Burgundy Glow' (**right**) forms a carpet of bronze foliage dotted with small blue flowers throughout the summer months. An ideal gound cover plant for moist shady locations. It spreads rapidly by vigorous stems that radiate across the surface of the soil.

Planting ground cover

If the area to be covered is overgrown with difficult weeds such as crabgrass, nettles, ground elder, docks or bindweed, treat it all with a suitable weedkiller — avoiding all the plants that are to stay — at least four weeks before planting; check the manufacturer's recommendations. This should kill off the weeds and leave no harmful residue in the soil. Ground cover plants usually spread roughly in a proportion equal to their height and, if required to interlock, the initial planting distance should be 15-25cm (6-10in) or less. The mat type of plants require a planting distance of 30-45cm (12-18in). The very dwarf mat-forming plants such as *Ajuga*, *Sedum* and thyme require spacing at 15-30cm (6-12in).

All weeds must be removed by hoe or by

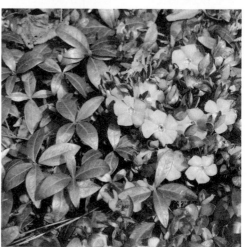

hand until the plants have grown together and become established. This should not be too difficult; the site should have been well cleared before planting.

Replace any plants that die, and remove all dead wood and any rubbish that accumulates in and around the plants. All large tree leaves should be removed to the compost heap; the smaller leaves can be left to help as a natural mulch. In addition, apply a good mulch of well-rotted compost either in the spring or autumn. When planting on a steep bank make sure that the plants are secure and then protect the root area with stones above them. These can be removed when the plants have become established. Replace any soil that has been washed down a bank planting.

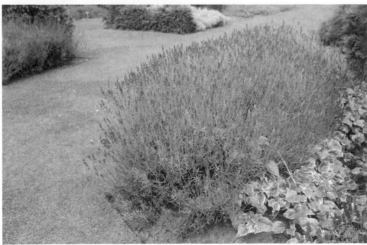

The late winter or early spring fragrant flowers of *Sarcococca humilis* (**above**) are borne amid glossy evergreen foliage. This densely branched shrub grows up to 60cm (2ft) tall and provides good ground cover in moist shady places. One of the most popular ground cover plants is *Vinca minor* 'Bowles' Variety' (**left**). It bears lovely blue flowers all summer long. Several euphorbias can be grown as ground cover. *E. myrsinites* (**top right**) produces plantlets on long spreading stems, and *E. epithymoides* (**center right**) forms dense evergreen bushes that suppress weeds effectively. Both these euphorbias produce bright yellow 'flowers' (really bracts) in spring. For superb fragrance and ground cover too, choose *Lavandula* 'Hidcote' (**right**).

Dwarf hedges

Practically every garden has at least one hedge — usually it marks the boundary and is fairly high, for most people like to have privacy in their gardens. Dwarf hedges are quite a different garden feature. The reason for planting a dwarf hedge is generally to segregate an area from the main part of the garden. A dwarf hedge — up to 60cm (2ft) high — usually has one or more of three primary functions: to act as an internal boundary fence, for example to screen off the vegetable plot, herb garden or cut-flower area; to act as a foil to rose beds or borders, in much the same way as the box hedging used in the Elizabethan knot gardens; or to give an element of cohesion to the overall garden design.

Relatively few plants are suitable for very low hedges of up to our limit of 60cm (2ft), but remember that the final height is dependent partly on how the plants are trimmed or pruned, and partly on how well the situation fits the plant; if it likes the situation, it grows faster and needs more frequent pruning.

Dwarf hedges up to 30cm (1ft)

For very low hedges the choice is limited. Box hedging *(Buxus sempervirens)* must be the first choice: it is evergreen and forms a very neat, formal boundary. But it must be trimmed at least twice a year to prevent it becoming 'leggy'. It has been a popular dwarf hedging plant for centuries. In the latter half of the 16th century, for example, the Elizabethans used box hedging widely in their knot gardens. These were formal gardens of intricate design in which shrubs, flowerbeds or herbs were divided by traditional patterns of hedging. Many fine examples can be seen today.

If box has any disadvantages, one must be that it provides an excellent home for snails, which of course can play havoc with nearby plants, particularly marigolds. The snails also attract birds, which scratch away the soil at the base of the hedge, making frequent mulching a necessity.

An unusual plant for dwarf hedging is *Hebe propinqua*, a dwarf shrub that eventually attains a height of about 30cm (1ft), depending on situation, and requires very little trimming. It is evergreen, and looks for all the world like a dwarf conifer.

The ericas (heathers) make lovely flowering evergreen hedges if they are clipped after flowering; regular trimming is required to keep them within bounds. For gardens on chalk, *Erica carnea* and *Erica darleyensis* should be used. On acid soils all the heaths, including *Calluna vulgaris*, can be grown. Many cultivars of *Erica cinerea* and *Calluna vulgaris* are available, including quite a number of golden-foliaged forms. None of them should be allowed to become leggy.

DWARF HEDGES

Botanical name	Common name	Height	Flower color
Berberis X stenophylla 'Corallina Compacta'	Barberry	30–45cm (12–18in)	Yellow/orange flowers in spring
Berberis X stenophylla 'Gracilis Nana'		30–45cm (12–18in)	Golden yellow
Berberis thunbergii 'Atropurpurea Nana'		30–45cm (12–18in)	Red berries in autumn
Berberis thunbergii 'Erecta'		60cm (2ft)	Pale yellow
Berberis thunbergii 'Rose Glow'		60–75cm (24–30in)	Pale yellow
Buxus sempervirens	Box	30–45cm (12–18in)	
Calluna vulgaris	Ling, Heather	23–60cm (9–24in)	Pink or purple
Erica cinerea	Bell heather	23–30cm (9–12in)	White, deep pink, red and maroon
Erica X darleyensis		Up to 60cm (2ft)	Deep pink
Erica carnea (herbacea)	Heather	Up to 30cm (12in)	White, pink and purple flowers
Forsythia ovata		Up to 60cm (2ft)	Amber yellow
Hebe propinqua	Veronica	30cm (12in)	White
Lavandula 'Hidcote' Lavandula 'Munstead'	Lavender	Up to 90cm (3ft)	Lilac
Rosa	Rose	Many sizes available	Many colors available
Santolina chamaecyparissus (incana)	Cotton lavender	45cm (18in)	Lemon-yellow button flowers

Dwarf hedges up to 60cm (2ft)

Above 30cm (1ft) the choice is much greater. The dwarf forms of *Berberis* make splendid low hedges. Both deciduous and evergreen species are available, and their dense spiny growth makes them completely animal-proof. Flowers, colorful foliage, bright berries and autumn tints can all be provided by varieties of *Berberis*. See the table for the recommended forms.

For early spring flowers of a lovely amber yellow, try *Forsythia ovata*. This adaptable shrub can be kept to 60cm (2ft) by pruning after flowering. Alternatively, a delightful combination of color and fragrance is provided by lavender, which can be grown into a charming dwarf hedge. The gray-green foliage is aromatic, and in mid-summer is topped by compact, highly scented flower clusters. Lavender makes a fairly wide hedge, in comparison with box, and grows well in all types of soils and situations, being particularly

Foliage	Season of interest	Notes
Arching branches, evergreen	Spring	All berberis tolerate most soils that are not waterlogged. They form dense animal-proof hedges. Little pruning is required; merely trim to shape
Dense, evergreen	Spring	
Red-purple turning scarlet in autumn, deciduous	Spring/autumn	
Autumn colors	Spring/autumn	
Shades of pink and rose becoming purple later	Spring/autumn	
Small dark green evergreen leaves	All year	Trim twice a year, mulch frequently
Golden, silvery, bronze and red	Mid summer/late autumn	Lime-free soil
Evergreen	Early summer/ early autumn	Lime-free soil
Evergreen	Early winter/ late spring	Tolerates some lime, but do not plant on thin chalk soils
Evergreen	Early winter/ late spring	Tolerates some lime, but do not plant on thin chalk soils
Deciduous	Spring	Prune after flowering. Tolerates all soils and situations
Resembles a dwarf conifer	Evergreen	Requires little trimming
Aromatic	Mid summer	Prefers sunny situation
Foliage is lost in winter	Early summer, early autumn	Keep to one cultivar to attain even height. *Floribunda* roses are the most suitable. A sunny situation
Gray-green	Evergreen	Prune hard in spring to keep in shape

Box hedging brings a formal touch to a Dutch garden (**above**). Its dense growth and small evergreen leaves make box a supreme dwarf hedging plant. Trim it twice a year to keep it looking neat and guard against the snails that are attracted to its foliage.

The strongly aromatic silver foliage of *Santolina chamaecyparissus* (**left**) provides a perfect foil for brightly colored plants. It grows only 45cm (18in) high and can be trimmed in spring to produce a neat dwarf hedge. For precision gardening an Elizabethan knot garden (**right**) is hard to beat. Box hedging traditionally formed the dividing 'walls' between patches of flowers, shrubs and herbs.

suitable for seashore gardens. It looks natural with stone-work and blends well with other blue-flowered and gray plants. 'Hidcote' and 'Munstead' are particularly suitable varieties for low hedges.

Many roses are candidates for growing into dwarf hedges. The cluster-flowered (or *floribunda*) roses are the most suitable; keep to one cultivar so that an even height can be attained, for no two cultivars have the same habit. Advantageously, roses abound with bloom and many are fragrant. As a disadvantage, however, many roses need regular spraying against aphids, black spot, mildew and rust. And regular pruning and sucker removal are equally essential.

The cotton lavender *(Santolina chamaecyparissus)* can be grown into a striking low hedge on sunny, well-drained soils. The foliage is silver-gray, finely divided and aromatic. In midsummer the mounds are festooned with lemon-yellow flowerheads.

General cultivation

All hedges should be planted in a well prepared soil because they will be there for a long time. Dig the selected area well, at least 90cm (3ft) wide and 45cm (18in) deep. In fact, it is preferable to 'double dig', keeping the topsoil separate from the subsoil. Incorporate plenty of farmyard manure or well-rotted compost at the bottom of the trench. Once the digging is complete allow the soil to settle and sprinkle some general purpose fertilizer on the surface of the planting area and lightly fork it in. Be sure to remove all perennial weed roots when digging.

Use a line when planting to ensure that the hedge is straight; lay out the plants at the required distance and dig the planting holes large and deep enough to take the roots easily. Check the soil mark on the main stem as a guide to planting depth. Place the plant into the hole and work the soil into the roots, lightly firming and filling alternately, and occasionally shaking the plant to get rid of air pockets. When the soil is slightly above soil level, firm in well. On completion, water well and mulch the surface with compost or peat. The aftercare is simple: never let the plants become dry, and spray overhead in hot periods. If the hedge is planted in the autumn, trim all plants (except evergreens) back to 23cm (9in). If they are planted in the spring, trim back lightly and cut them back hard the following spring.

Fragrant plants

It is difficult to define fragrance because it is so subjective; what is fragrant to one person may be uninteresting — or even objectionable — to others. Books on botany tend to ignore fragrance, referring to it insted as 'odor'. Botanically, odor is really all it is: it attracts insects that collect the nectar and pollen and at the same time pollinate the flowers. The fragrance thus helps flowers to carry out their primary function — to produce seeds. Unfortunately, because the modern hybridist works toward bigger and more colorful flowers, fragrance has to some extent diminished in many kinds of cultivated flowers. A special case is the musk *Mimulus moschatus*, which is now almost scentless although its presentday hybrids have many large bright flowers.

Many flower shows have a class for fragrant roses, which are sometimes judged by a blind person who is able to distinguish the scent quality or intensity much better than a sighted judge. The pleasure that fragrant plants bring to blind and partially sighted people is evident from the many public gardens planted especially for their enjoyment.

Fragrant roses

Of all the fragrant cultivated plants, roses stand supreme. The scent from roses can vary from a heavy musk perfume to a light lemony fragrance. At one time it was thought that all deep red roses were fragrant, but today many of them are scentless, and indeed some of the bicolors and pale soft colors are heavily scented.

In general, it is the old-fashioned shrub roses which have the most intense perfume. Many of the modern cultivars actually have little or none at all, although there are exceptions. Yet the old roses, although they may have the advantage of perfume, do have some disadvantages: with some exceptions, they only flower once a year, usually in early to midsummer; they tend to be susceptible to black spot and mildew; the flowers are large, with cabbage-like open centers that are easily damaged by rain; many are too large for the small modern garden; and although most are strong-growing, some tend to have a straggly habit.

Old-fashioned roses look their best planted in a shrub border, where they require little attention except that given to other shrubs plus, if necessary, routine spraying against black spot and mildew.

During the last 40 years a new group of shrub roses has been developed, the modern shrub roses, several of which carry a delightful fragrance. The very popular cluster-flowered (or *floribunda*) roses and the large-flowered (or hybrid tea) roses also contain a number of superbly fragrant varieties. There are also several climbing roses with an agreeable scent. Selected fragrant examples of all these types of roses are described in the table.

Fragrant shrubs

Shrubs can provide fragrance in all seasons, even — in mild climates — winter. This list includes the most widely available shrubs prized for their scented flowers and, in some cases, for their aromatic foliage too.

Buddleia: Butterfly bush
The cultivars of *Buddleia davidii*, justifiably popular for their graceful flower clusters in shades of red, purple, pink and white, also bring superb fragrance to the summer garden. Bushes grow to about 2.4m (8ft) in height and spread.

Chimonanthes: Winter sweet
This is one of several shrubs that provide sweetly-scented flowers during the winter. *Chimonanthes praecox*, which takes several years to establish has pale yellow flowers with a purplish center; *C. p.* 'Luteus' has all-yellow blooms. Both reach a height of about 3m (10ft).

Daphne cneorum (**top left**) and *Daphne odora* 'Aureomarginata' (**center left**) are both prized for their sweet-smelling flowers. *Nicotiana alata* 'Lime Green' (**left**) is also heavily scented.

Choisya ternata: Mexican orange blossom
The common name aptly describes the heady fragrance this shrub offers in spring. Both the white flowers and the glossy, evergreen leaves (when crushed) are fragrant. A superb shrub for a sunny sheltered spot, *Choisya ternata* grows to a height of 2-3m (6½-10ft).

Clethra alnifolia: Sweet pepper bush
Late summer sees the emergence of slender clusters of creamy white scented 'flowers' on this deciduous shrub, which requires a lime-free soil. Grow *C. a.* 'Paniculata' for the most abundant bloom; up to 2.1m (7ft) tall.

Corylopsis
This easily-grown deciduous shrub provides cowslip-scented, pale yellow flowers in early spring. Best grown on acid or neutral soils, *Corylopsis* generally reach a height of 1.5-2.1m (5-7ft). Recommended species are *C. pauciflora*, *C. spicata*, *C. veitchiana* and *C. willmottiae* (up to 3m/10ft tall).

Cytisus battandieri: Moroccan broom
For a tang of pineapple, grow this fast-growing tall shrub, preferably against a warm wall. The cone-shaped yellow flowers appear in midsummer.

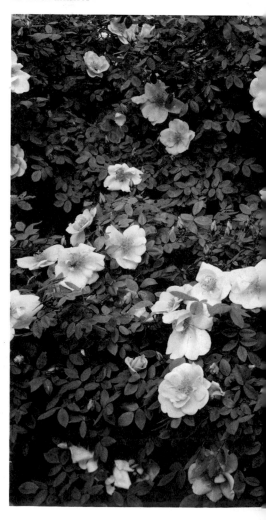

Daphne

The daphnes are among the most fragrant of shrubs. From late winter until early spring the bare stems of the most popular daphne, *Daphne mezereum*, are clothed in sweetly scented blooms of white, pink or purplish red depending on variety. Also in bloom during winter and early spring is *Daphne odora*

Of the floribunda roses 'Arthur Bell' **(above)** is a favorite for its heavy fragrance. Frühlingsgold **(below)** blooms briefly but with a delicious scent.

'Aureomarginata', and as spring turns to summer *D. cneorum, D. X burkwoodii* 'Somerset' and *D. retusa* add their scent to the garden air.

Daphnes range in size from 30cm to 1.5m (1-5ft), and thrive in a moist but well-drained acid soil.

Genista cinerea

This lovely member of the pea family has profuse clusters of fragrant yellow pea flowers in early to mid summer. It forms a bush up to 3m (10ft) tall and 2.4m (8ft) across.

Hamamelis: Witch hazel

For fascinating flowers during cold months it is hard to beat this shrub. Its spidery yellow or reddish-yellow blooms are delicately scented, their strap-like petals able to withstand the severest weather. Choose from *H. X intermedia* 'Jelena' ('Copper Beauty'), yellow-suffused coppery red; *H. mollis*, golden yellow; *H. m.* 'Goldcrest', golden yellow and claret; and *H. m.* 'Pallida', sulphur yellow. All grow slowly to about 3m (10ft) tall.

Jasminum officinale

In a warm, sheltered site the climber jasmine and its variety 'Affine' ('Grandiflorum') can be relied upon for a crop of sweet-smelling white flowers throughout the summer.

OLD ROSES

Botanical name	Height	Flower Color	Flowering season	Notes
Rosa alba 'Königin von Dänemarck'	180cm (6ft)	Soft pink	Mid summer	Specimen bushes reach 180cm (6ft)
Rosa bourboniana 'Boule de Neige'	150cm (5ft)	Rich cream	All summer	Suitable for hedging
Rosa bourboniana 'Madame Isaac de Pereire'	180cm (6ft)	Purple crimson	All summer	Suitable for hedging
Rosa centifolia 'De Meaux'	90cm (3ft)	Pink	Mid summer	Slender growth, light green foliage
Rosa centifolia 'Tour de Malakoff'	210cm (7ft)	Lilac pink	Mid summer	Very vigorous
Rosa chinensis 'Cramoisie Superieure'	90cm (3ft)	Crimson	All summer	Moderately vigorous
Rosa damascena 'Madam Hardy'	150cm (5ft)	Pure white	All summer	Vigorous
Rosa gallica 'Belle de Crecy'	120cm (4ft)	Deep pink	Mid summer	Untidy habit, very few thorns, low growth
Rosa gallica 'Rosa Mundi'	90cm (3ft)	Striped pink, crimson, white	Mid summer	Vigorous
Rosa rugosa 'Blanc Double de Coubert'	150cm (5ft)	Pure white	All summer	Suitable for hedging
Rosa rugosa 'Mrs Anthony Waterer'	120cm (4ft)	Deep crimson	All summer	Suitable for hedging, vigorous

MODERN SHRUB ROSES

Botanical name	Height	Flower Color	Flowering season	Notes
R. 'Chinatown'	180cm (6ft)	Bright yellow	Repeat flowering	Suitable for hedging
R. 'Frühlingsgold'	180cm (6ft)	Primrose	Early summer	
R. 'Penelope'	180cm (6ft)	Light pink	Repeat flowering	Suitable for hedging

FLORIBUNDA

Botanical name	Height	Flower Color	Flowering season	Notes
R. 'Arthur Bell'	1m (3.3ft)	Yellow to cream	All summer	Vigorous upright growth
R. 'Elizabeth of Glamis'	75cm (30in)	Light salmon shaded orange	Early to mid summer	
R. 'Escapade'	90cm (3ft)	Rosy violet with a white eye	All summer	Disease resistant
R. 'Fragrant Delight'	75cm (30in)	Orange salmon	All summer	Very vigorous
R. 'Korresia'	90cm (3ft)	Bright yellow	All summer	
R. 'Margaret Merril'	90cm (3ft)	Pearl white	Repeat flowering	
R. 'Southampton'	105cm (3.5ft)	Apricot orange	Repeat flowering	Suitable for hedging

HYBRID TEA

Botanical name	Height	Flower Color	Flowering season	Notes
R. 'Admiral Rodney'	105cm (3.5ft)	Light rose pink	Early summer to mid autumn	
R. 'Fragrant Cloud'	90cm (3ft)	Coral red	Early summer to mid autumn	Vigorous and upright
R. 'Prima Ballerina'	105cm (3.5ft)	Deep rose pink	Early summer to mid autumn	Very vigorous
R. 'Red Devil'	105cm (3.5ft)	Light red	Early summer to mid autumn	Vigorous and upright
R. 'Wendy Cussons'	1m (3.3ft)	Rose red to deep pink	Early summer to mid autumn	Vigorous and bushy
R. 'Whisky Mac'	75cm (2.5ft)	Amber yellow	Early summer to mid autumn	

CLIMBING ROSES

Botanical name	Height	Flower Color	Flowering season	Notes
R. 'Compassion'	3m (10ft)	Pink to apricot-pink	Repeat flowering	
R. 'Maigold'	3.4m (11ft)	Apricot yellow	Early summer	Vigorous pillar or wall rose
R. 'New Dawn'	2.7m (9ft)	Light pearl pink	Repeat flowering	Bushy pillar rose
R. 'Rosy Mantle'	2.5-3.5m (8-10ft)	Rose pink	Repeat flowering	
R. 'Zephirine Drouhin'	2.7m (9ft)	Deep pink	Repeat flowering	Thornless, vigorous.

The highly fragrant flowers of *Osmanthus* (below) and *Syringa* (bottom).

Lavandula

In any discussion of fragrance, the lavender cannot be overlooked. Its familiar silver-gray aromatic foliage and highly scented flowers in blue, violet, white and pink enrich the garden from mid summer until early autumn.

Lonicera: Honeysuckle

Of the popular climbing honeysuckles, *L. periclymenum* 'Belgica' and 'Serotina' can be recommended for their yellow and purple scented flowers in early and mid summer to autumn respectively. Of the bush varieties, *L. fragrantissima* bears creamy white fragrant blooms from mid winter until early spring.

Magnolia sieboldii

This magnolia produces a succession of lemon-scented white cup-shaped flowers from late spring until late summer. It forms a shrub up to 3m (10ft) tall.

Mahonia

The mahonias are at their best from mid winter until early spring, sporting bright yellow fragrant flowers in clusters or slender spikes against a foil of glossy evergreen foliage. Choose from these recommended mahonias: *M. aquifolium*, golden yellow; *M. X media*, mimosa yellow; *M. X media* 'Buckland', deep yellow; *M. japonica*, lemon-yellow.

Myrtus communis: Common myrtle

In a sunny sheltered location, the common myrtle scents the summer air with its creamy white solitary flowers. The evergreen foliage is a dark glossy green, and aromatic when crushed. Bushes grow to a height and spread of 3m (10ft).

Osmanthus

It is impossible to pass close to an osmanthus bush in spring without stopping to savor its rich perfume; the white flower clusters nestling amid the dense evergreen foliage are powerfully fragrant. *O. delavayi* is the most popular species; *O. X burkwoodii* (also known as *Osmarea burkwoodii*) is similar and just as fragrant. Both shrubs grow slowly to over 2m (6½ft) in height.

Philadelphus: Mock orange

This is a genus rich in fragrant plants. The traditional mock orange is *P. coronarius*, celebrated for its flat, single, white, scented blooms in summer. This shrub reaches 3m (10ft) tall and more, but there are plenty of more compact hybrids suitable for small gardens. Among these, *P.* 'Belle Étoile' is worthy of mention, its pink tinged white flowers borne on a bush reaching 2m (6½ft) tall. *P.* 'Manteau d'Hermine' is even smaller, no more than 1m (39in) in height, and bears double creamy white blooms. The largest of these so-called 'modern hybrids' is *P.* 'Virginal', well-loved for its generous clusters of large double or semi-double strongly fragrant flowers, growing to 3m (10ft) tall.

Rhododendron (Azalea)

The *Occidentale* hybrids of deciduous azaleas sport some superbly fragrant shrubs. The pink-flowered 'Graciosa', and 'Irene Koster', the yellow-opening white 'Bridesmaid', and the pink-flushed white 'Superba'. All bring pastel shades and delicious perfume to the garden in late spring.

Rubus tridel 'Benenden'

This adaptable member of the bramble family brings scent into the late spring garden with its large single white flowers, each with a central boss of bold stamens. It grows quickly to a height of 3m (10ft).

Sarcococca: Christmas box, sweet box

For late winter fragrance and a useful ground cover plant choose *S. humilis*, a dwarf evergreen shrub up to 60cm (2ft) in height. The flowers are white, and followed by blue-black berries.

Skimmia japonica

Justly prized for its bright crops of autumn and winter berries, this compact evergreen shrub has several forms that bear fragrant spring flowers. Notable among these is *S. j.* 'Fragrans', a male clone that bears dense clusters of white flowers giving off a lily-of-the-valley perfume.

Spartium junceum: Spanish broom

A long season of honey-scented flowers grows on this hardy deciduous shrub. From early summer until early autumn its erect green stems are smothered with bright yellow fragrant pea-like flowers. Excellent for seashore locations, it can reach up to 3m (10ft).

Sweet peas (below) bring perfume to the garden from summer into autumn.

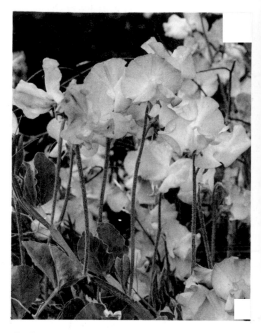

Syringa vulgaris hybrids: Lilac

What a rich resource of fragrant shrubs these hybrids represent! All thrive in full sun on a wide range of soils, being particularly suited to chalky soils. Colors range from pure white through creamy-yellow, shades of blue, lilac and red to a rich claret-mauve. Choose from single-flowered cultivars such as 'Souvenir de Louis Spaeth', wine red, and 'Vestale', white, or the double-flowered cultivars such as 'Charles Joly', dark purple-red, or 'Madame Lemoine', creamy yellow opening white. The flowering period lasts for about three weeks between late spring and early summer, depending on the cultivar.

Viburnum

For winter and early spring fragrance, *V. X bodnantense* and *V. farreri (fragrans)* have much to offer. Both grow to 2.4m (8ft) in height and bear clusters of rose-tinted white flowers that can survive fairly cold weather. As spring merges into summer, the pink buds of *V. X burkwoodii* and *V. carlesii* open to reveal light flowerheads of richly scented white flowers.

Annuals and perennials

The annual, biennial and herbaceous perennial plants provide plenty of fragrance during the summer. Predominant among them are: the sweet rocket *Hesperis matronalis*, sweet peas (*Lathyrus* species), many species of primula, violas, sweet Williams, *Dianthus* (pinks) in variety, wallflowers, nasturtiums (particular the 'Gleam' hybrids), sweet-scented candytuft, lily-of-the-valley, peonies, bergamot (*Monarda*), catmint (*Nepeta*), sweet alyssum, stocks, mignonette and polyanthus.

Long-flowering shrubs

Many shrubs have only one short flowering season that may not last for more than one or two weeks. Some flower — or can be induced to flower — a second or even a third time, but for each such shrub the flowering period is comparatively shorter still and on each successive occasion there are fewer flowers. Others, conversely, have a succession of flowers which may go on for a very long time: these provide the main focus of this section.

The most outstanding of shrubs for flowering is the common gorse, *Ulex europaeus*, which flowers continuously and which long ago gave rise to the old saying 'Love is in season when the gorse is in flower'. But gorse is certainly not a shrub for the average garden: it tends to be straggly and is very prickly.

Among garden shrubs the first prize for long flowering must go to the cinquefoil, *Potentilla*. The flowers are not particularly spectacular but they are very numerous and appear constantly from early summer until late autumn. The plant always looks colorful and charming. It is perfectly hardy, not reliant on any special position (although it does best in a fairly sunny location: in shade the flowers are greatly reduced); given proper drainage, cinquefoil grows on any, even limy, soils. In fact, it is surprising that it is not more widely grown. It forms an attractive plant, provided that it receives an occasional trimming to remove old seedpods and dead leaves — an essential measure if it is not to look unkempt in winter. There are many cultivars, ranging in color variation from white through cream to red; the predominant color is golden yellow. A selection is featured in the Table. All the potentillas are worth growing; the average height is about 90cm (3ft). They require little attention from the gardener, once established, and are ordinarily pest- and disease-free.

Almost equally highly to be recommended — perhaps it would be equally if it were completely hardy in temperate regions — is *Abutilon megapotamicum*, a wall shrub that flowers continuously in a warm, sunny position in mild areas, but that in colder areas has a flowering season from mid-spring to the first frosts. Its conspicuous pendulous flowers have a red calyx, yellow petals, and purple-brown anthers; the overall effect resembles nothing so much as a ballet dancer in purple-brown shoes and a yellow dress topped by a green cap. It likes the sun and does best in well drained soil, although it is tolerant of slightly limy soils. On chalk subsoils, however, it becomes chlorotic (i.e. the leaves turn yellow).

Again only just less commendable is the fuchsia family. Although they too cannot be classed as completely hardy, even after being cut down by the frost many of them grow rapidly in the spring and flower from mid-summer to the next frosts. In mild or coastal

Among the longest flowering plants are the lovely *Abutilon megapotamicum* (**above**) and *Potentilla fruticosa* 'Elizabeth' (**left**).

gardens the stems are not killed; nevertheless, to ensure good flowering they should be cut back to the ground in the spring. Fuchsias which are planted out in permanent positions benefit from a mulch of peat or compost over their crowns in the winter. None of them is fussy about soil or position, but all thrive on well drained good soil in a semi-shaded site. The flowers of the fuchsia are bell-shaped, pendulous, and surmounted by four colored segments of the calyx: a very delightful flower. There is quite a variation of color in the family, but to date no yellow or wholly blue ones. The most hardy of them is *F.* 'Riccartonii', but its flowers are small and not so spectacular as the larger-flowered types; it can be used as a hedging plant. Some recommended cultivars for border planting are featured in the Table; the final two recommended species *F. magellanica* 'Variegata' and *F. m.* 'Versicolor' have small flowers but lovely variegated foliage.

The St John's wort or *Hypericum* is also justly popular: its lemon or buttercup yellow flowers are both bright and superbly shaped, borne with remarkable freedom from mid summer to mid autumn. The best is *Hypericum* 'Hidcote', a superb hardy semi-evergreen of compact habit, approximately 1.8m (6ft) high with a similar spread. Its golden yellow flowers, the largest of any of the hardy hypericums, are produced in bursts over the flowering season; the shrub also grows well in most soils and is in the main trouble-free, thriving particularly in light shade and in a well drained position, with a moist subsoil.

Further commendation must go also to the family of camellias, especially to *C. japonica* and its cultivars. The garden value of these is high because not only are the flowers large,

beautiful and of delightful coloration, they are in addition produced over a long period — throughout spring. The foliage is as hardy as that of a laurel but unfortunately the flowers are not, and damage can occur from a hard frost. Although the flowers are tender, though, the camellia makes up for this by producing a good crop of buds — so many, in fact, that it is necessary to thin them out on smaller plants. They are much more lime-tolerant than rhododendrons and thrive in a good acid or neutral peaty soil. It is important to feed them regularly (this is often forgotten) because they soon exhaust the soil in the enormous effort to produce the crops of heavy, solid flowers that they bear. An annual mulch of compost and a light dressing of general fertilizer should be given, plus two or three liquid feeds in the autumn when the buds are being formed. The Table lists several recommended cultivars. The *C. reticulata* and *C. saluenensis* hybrids are not quite as hardy as *C. japonica*.

The heather family must similarly be highly commended because although no single one flowers for more than four months, through a judicious selection by the gardener of the kinds and cultivars they can flower all the year round. But for this an acid soil is essential. The ling *(Calluna vulgaris)*, the Dorset heath *(Erica ciliaris)*, *Erica cinerea*, and their many cultivars, are all lime-haters; *E. carnea (herbacea)* and *E. X darleyensis* are lime-tolerant, however. All are in general tolerant of semi-shade but flower best in full sun. When planted in heather borders they associate well with dwarf rhododendrons and dwarf conifers, and because many cultivars have colored foliage, the beds look colorful even when out of flower. They have few enemies, and the only attention is the removal of dead flowers.

Camellia reticulata (**top**), a vivid pink.   The popular *Fuchsia* 'Mrs Popple' (**above**).

LONG-FLOWERING SHRUBS

Botanical name	Common name	Height	Flower color
Abutilon megapotamicum		1.8-2.4m (6-8ft)	Yellow petals, red calyx, purple-brown anthers
Calluna vulgaris and cultivars	Heather, Ling	23-60cm (9-24in)	Pink, purple, crimson and white
Camellia japonica		1.8-2.4m (6-8ft)	Red
C.j. 'Adolphe Audusson'			Blood red
C.j. 'Alba Simplex'			White
C.j. 'Apollo'			Rose red
C.j. 'Chandleri'			Red, white blotches
C.j. 'Donckelarii'			Red, marbled white
Camellia reticulata			Rose pink
Camellia saluensis			Soft pink
Clematis		1.8-9m (6-30ft)	
C. 'Comtesse de Bouchard'			Soft rose pink
C. 'Ernest Markham'			Petunia red
C. 'Hagley Hybrid'			Shell pink
C. 'Jackmanii Superba'			Violet-purple
C. 'Marie Boisselot'			White
C. 'Nelly Moser'			Pale mauve, carmine bar
C. 'The President'			Deep purple-blue
C. 'Ville de Lyon'			Carmine red
C. 'W.E. Gladstone'			Lavender
Erica ciliaris	Dorset heath	30-45cm (12-18in)	White, pink, red
Erica cinerea	Bell heather	23-30cm (9-12in)	White, deep pink red, purple
Erica X darleyensis		Up to 60cm (2ft)	Deep pink
Erica carnea (herbacea)	Heather	Up to 30cm (12in)	White, pink, purple
Fuchsia		Up to 1.2m (4ft)	
F. 'Chillerton Beauty'			Pink/violet
F. 'Empress of Prussia'			Scarlet
F. 'Ethel Wilson'			Pale/dark pink
F. 'Flash'			Red
F. 'Genii'			Cerise/violet
F. 'Madame Cornelissen'			Red/white
F. 'Margaret'			Scarlet/cerise
F. 'Mrs Popple'			Scarlet/violet-purple
F. 'Reading Show'			Scarlet/deep blue
F. 'Tom Thumb'		Dwarf var.	Light carmine
F. 'Wilson's Pearls'			Red/white
F. magellanica 'Variegata and *F.m.* 'Versicolor'			
Hamamelis mollis	Witch hazel	3m (10ft)	Golden yellow
H.m. 'Goldcrest'			Golden yellow, claret red at base
H.m. 'Pallida'			Sulphur yellow
H.X. intermedia 'Jelena'	Copper beauty		Yellow suffused with coppery red
Hypericum 'Hidcote'	St John's wort	Up to 1.8m (6ft)	Golden yellow
Mahonia X media 'Buckland'		2.4m (8ft)	Deep yellow
Mahonia X media 'Charity'			Deep yellow
Mahonia X media			Mimosa yellow
Potentilla fruticosa arbuscula	Cinquefoil	90cm (3ft)	Clear yellow
P.f. 'Farreri'			Buttercup yellow
P.f. 'Katherine Dykes'			Soft canary yellow
P.f. 'Nana Argentea'		60cm (2ft)	Yellow
P.f. 'Red Ace'		90cm (3ft)	Red
P.f. 'Vilmoriniana'			Cream white
Prunis subhirtella 'Autumnalis'	Autumn cherry	Up to 7.6m (25ft)	White
Rosa	Roses	Many sizes available	Many colors available
Viburnum X bodnantense		2.4m (8ft)	Pink and white
V. farreri (fragrans)		2.4m (8ft)	White, pink in bud
V. tinus	Laurustinus	Up to 3m (10ft)	White, pink in bud

Roses have a long flowering period, although to be strictly accurate it is really a succession of bursts of flowering. They also have some fairly marked disadvantages, the main one being that they have many enemies — including aphids, black spot, mildew and rust — and therefore require spraying at two-week intervals; suckering is also a problem. The most floriferous type is the cluster-flowered, or *floribunda*, which gives almost continuous flowers from early summer until mid autumn. The large-flowered hybrid tea roses and the modern shrub roses tend to be recurrent flowering in early to mid summer and again in late summer and early autumn. There are many cultivars and many colors, so the choice is huge. Particularly recommended are the 'Iceberg', white; 'Evelyn Fison', bright deep red; and 'Southampton', apricot orange; the large-flowered (hybrid tea) roses 'Silver Jubilee', peach pink and cream; 'Grandpa Dickson', lemon yellow; and 'Red Devil', light red; and the shrub roses 'Fred Loads', light orange vermilion; 'Chinatown', bright yellow; and 'Ballerina', light pink with a white eye. .

The large-flowered clematis are among the most colorful of flowering climbing plants, and have a long flowering season from early summer to early autumn. They are often spectacular, are fairly adaptable, but not too easy to establish. Their site should be chosen with care: they like their 'heads' in the sun and their roots in the shade, growing best in a good loamy soil in which well-rotted manure and a little lime in some form have been mixed. In general, the clematis flowers prolifically in full sun, but some of the paler cultivars — such as

Foliage	Flowering period	Notes
Bright green ovate leaves	Late spring to autumn	Thrives best in a sunny position against a wall in well drained soil. On chalky soil leaves may turn yellow
Golden, silvery bronze or red	All year	Lime-free soil
Evergreen, glossy	Late winter/late spring	Neutral soil. Regular feeding is important
Evergreen, glossy		
Evergreen, glossy		
Evergreen, glossy		
Evergreen, glossy		
Evergreen, glossy		
Veined		Not as hardy as *C. japonica* or *C. reticulata*
Glossy green hairless leaves	Early summer to late autumn	Head in the sun, roots in the shade. Mulch annually. Water well in dry periods. Prune in early spring to keep in shape
Pale and dark green evergreen	Mid summer to early winter	Lime-free soil
Evergreen dark and light green and copper colored	Mid summer to early winter	Lime-free soil
Evergreen	Early winter to late spring	Lime-tolerant. Trim back in late spring
Light green, bronze, dull yellow	Late autumn to late spring	Trim back in late spring
	Mid summer to mid autumn	Cut back to soil level in early spring. Mulch root area in late autumn
Green		
Green		
Green, red veins		
Green		
Yellow-green		
Green, red veins		
Green		
Green		
Green, red veins		
Pale green		
Green, red veins		
Variegated foliage		
Green hazel-like leaf	Early winter to early spring	Good autumn leaf colors
Green hazel-like leaf		
Green hazel-like leaf		
Green hazel-like leaf		
Semi-evergreen	Mid summer to mid autumn	
Evergreen	Early winter to early spring	Tolerates all soils including chalk
Evergreen		
Evergreen		
	Early summer to late autumn	Tolerates most situations. Remove old seedpods and dead leaves. Trim to shape when established
Silvery leaves		
Silver leaves		
Small green leaves	Late autumn to early spring	When established flowers well
Green, deciduous	Repeat flowering throughout summer	*Floribunda* types give the most continuous flowering
Gray-green	Late autumn to early spring	Young foliage is bronze
Green netted red	Late autumn to early spring	Good autumn color
Evergreen	Late autumn to late spring	

'Nelly Moser' — tend to bleach when exposed in a hot, sunny position. A selection of recommended cultivars is featured in the Table.

Several winter-flowering shrubs provide a long season of bloom in mild climates. Witch hazel *Hamamelis* has many fine cultivars that are clothed in spidery, frost-resistant yellow flowers throughout the winter until very early spring. They are first-rate shrubs which require little attention and thrive in all types of soils. As a bonus, the deciduous foliage turns through beautiful shades of yellow in the autumn.

Mahonias also offer yellow flowers during the same period. Long spreading and ascending racemes of flowers, mostly fragrant, are borne above attractive evergreen foliage. They grow in all soils, including chalky. Birds can be a problem, however, for they find the flower buds a great delicacy.

A tree to be recommended for a long flowering season is *Prunus subhirtella* 'Autumnalis', which produces semi-double white flowers intermittently from late autumn until early spring. It flourishes on all types of soils and can be cut for winter decoration.

Viburnum offers a wide variety of long-flowering shrubs. *Viburnum farreri (fragrans)* and *V. X bodnantense* bear superb white fragrant flowers from late autumn until early spring. They are almost maintenance-free, needing just a light trimming to keep them in shape. *Viburnum tinus* (the laurustinus) is an evergreen shrub that provides white flowers during the same period against its own backdrop of glossy leaves.

The superb pink and peach flowers of the hybrid tea rose 'Silver Jubilee' (**above**) appear in flushes throughout the summer months. An excellent disease-resistant rose with glossy green foliage.

133

Plants for butterflies and bees

A hundred years ago, beehives were an essential feature of most gardens. Nowadays much of the honey for sale is labelled 'Produce of Several Countries' and beehives are rarely seen in gardens. The bee is a great ally of the gardener; its fertilizing efficiency among fruit blossom has no equal and probably exceeds its value as a producer of honey. Bees range far and wide collecting pollen and nectar. Not so the butterfly, which does not collect nectar but feeds on it. There are therefore different requirements for bees and for butterflies.

The worker bee collects nectar and pollen and requires masses of good nectar-producing flowers. It is able, through its foot hooklets, sticky foot pads and strong legs, to cling to a wildly swaying flower and remove the nectar with its tube-like tongue. The nectar is pre-digested in the bee's crop where, by the addition of enzymes from the bee's glands, it is turned into honey. The pollen is collected into a special sac for feeding the growing bees in the hive.

The butterfly, on the other hand, has very weak legs, is not able to cling and to feed itself, requires a stable, roughly horizontal platform where it can rest and suck up the nectar through its very long proboscis. Such platforms are available on plants which have long spikes or panicles of flowers. A butterfly can, for example, sit on a *Buddleia* spike and sip the nectar but would find it impossible to do the same thing on a broom *(Cytisus)* flower.

Plants to attract bees

A beekeeper's garden should therefore contain many plants which produce masses of heavy nectar-bearing flowers during the summer — but the period can be longer or shorter depending on the weather. In any case, the bees' working season is longer than this, and extends from early spring until early autumn, mid-summer being the peak time. The bee is very selective — it has a keen sense of smell — but in general all flowers are inspected and, if found acceptable, are worked. Plants which have a mass of flowers on each stem and open sequentially are the favorites. Nectar is produced constantly while a flower is open, and it can consequently be visited by several bees during the day. The ideal garden for bees is one which has masses of flowers all the summer and is close to the hive.

The flowers can be borne on annuals, perennials, shrubs or trees, so the choice is wide, but some seem all the same to attract bees more than others — and they are not necessarily the ones with large colorful flowers.

Many garden plants attract bees and butterflies to their blooms. The early spring red flowers of *Ribes sanguineum* (**top left**) emanates a heavy musk-like fragrance that draws bees to them. Throughout the summer bees visit the pink blooms of *Sidalcea malviflora* (**top right**). *Buddleia davidii* (**center left**) acts as a 'magnet' to butterflies from mid-summer until autumn, so much so that it has gained the popular name of butterfly bush. Bees and butterflies also visit the dense flower clusters of *Solidago* 'Golden Showers' (**center right**). These are borne on stems up to 90cm (3ft) tall. Bees are attracted in mid-summer to the tiny flowers of the low-growing *Thymus serpyllum* 'Bressingham Pink') (**bottom left**) and the elegant cup-shaped blue flowers of *Campanula carpatica* (**bottom right**).

Shrubs

Among shrubs, the cotoneaster is particularly popular. This group of shrubs contains many useful forms; all have masses of small pink-tinged white flowers set in groups among the foliage, followed by a crop of red or orange berries. Some good ones are:

C. conspicuus 'Highlight', an evergreen, mound-forming shrub of medium size, flowers white followed by orange berries.

C. X 'Cornubia', a vigorous semi-evergreen up to 6m (20ft) that has a profusion of flowers which are followed by red berries. A very attractive shrub if space is available.

C. franchetii, useful for hedging, a semi-evergreen, white flowers, orange-scarlet berries.

C. horizontalis, the well known 'herring-bone' shrub, deciduous with good autumn color and red berries, and invaluable for north or east walls, or for covering banks and so on.

Others worth growing are *C. salicifolius rugosus* and *C. simonsii*.

Berberis has many species that are well loved by bees; they include:

B. darwinii, one of the finest evergreen flowering shrubs, with masses of orange flowers.

B. X stenophylla, evergreen, with a profusion of yellow flowers.

B. thunbergii, deciduous, with brilliant autumn color and red berries.

B. wilsoniae, deciduous, good autumn color and coral berries.

Heather honey is one of the most delicious, and the heathers can be grown in many gardens. For gardens that are not limy, *Calluna vulgaris* (ling) and its many cultivars make a lovely dwarf shrub border in the summer. Gardens that are slightly limy can be planted with *Erica carnea (herbacea)* and *E. X darleyensis* and their cultivars; they flower through the winter.

A number of other shrubs are also attractive to bees. The brooms *(Cytisus)*, which are commonly yellow but have a wide selection of colors from white through to dark red, flower profusely in early summer. They are admirable subjects for dry, poor conditions and if pruned back to the old wood after flowering, can be kept to a uniform height. They tend to be short-lived but can readily be raised from seed. The lavender *(Lavandula)*, particularly the cultivars 'Hidcote' and 'Munstead', are good for dwarf hedges. The firethorn *(Pyracantha)* is useful for walls or as a specimen shrub. The flowering currant *(Ribes sanguineum)* has curious musk-like scent. Rosemary *(Rosmarinus officinalis)* makes a lovely shrub with gray-green foliage and slate blue flowers that attract bees. *R. officinalis* 'Benenden Blue' has bright blue flowers.

Trees

All fruit trees attract bees. Particularly effective is the crab apple; the best ones to grow are *Malus* 'Golden Hornet', which has bright yellow fruits, and *M.* 'John Downie', which has large conical, bright orange and red fruits ideal for crab-apple jelly. In many commercial orchards the owners often ask their local beekeepers to move their hives into the orchards during blossom time. This is done not for altruistic motives but to ensure a good apple crop, because many of the popular cultivars require pollen from at least two other cultivars to ensure good pollination — and thus more apples. Two such apple cultivars are 'Bramley Seedling' and 'Cox's Orange Pippin'. Also useful in a beekeeper's garden are currants (both red and black), gooseberries, pears, plums and strawberries.

Although the willow *(Salix)* is not considered to be a flowering tree, the bees are very fond of the catkins which appear in the spring; *S. caprea* 'Pendula', known as the Kilmarnock willow, is recommended for small gardens in that its maximum height is 3m (10ft), but try alternatively *S. repens* (creeping willow) which has stems crowded with small catkins in the spring.

Vegetables

Vegetables too help the beekeeper. The legumes (beans and peas), especially lima

The heavily scented flowers of *Matthiola* (**top**) attract bees to their rich supplies of nectar. There are many garden varieties.

The long flowering period of *Helenium autumnale* (**above**) allows bees ample opportunity to visit these bright daisy-like flowers.

beans and to a lesser extent French and string beans, have masses of nectar-producing flowers from late spring until the first frosts. Squash, peppers and tomatoes also flower in roughly the same period but do not produce the same quantity of flowers. Of all these vegetables, the lima and string or kidney beans are the bees' favorites.

Herbaceous plants

A well stocked herbaceous border is a good source of nectar, and herbaceous perennials are usually in full flower when bees are at their busiest in early and mid summer. A perennial flowering plant produces masses of flowers which enable the bees to work continually on them. The globe thistle *(Echinops ritro)* is well loved by bees, who frequently crowd onto the spiky globe-like heads.

The perennial flowers that particularly attract bees are: *Aquilegia; Campanula; Dianthus* (pinks); *Echinops ritro* (globe thistle); *Helenium; Lilium; Lythrum; Monarda* (bergamot); *Phlox*, border cultivars; *Sidalcea; Solidago* (golden rod) and *Veronica*.

Annuals and biennials which are well liked by bees include: *Alyssum; Antirrhinum; Cheiranthus* (wallflowers); *Digitalis* (foxgloves); *Matthiola* (stocks, all types); *Reseda* (mignonette) and *Tropaeolum* (nasturtiums, particularly the 'Golden Gleam' varieties).

Many alpine and rock plants are well worked by the bees. Their particular favorites are: *Alyssum* in variety; *Arabis; Aubretia; Mimulus; Phlox*, alpine types; *Sedum* in variety; *Thymus* in variety; and the dwarf *Veronicas*. The early foraging bees also work the many bulbous flowers both in the rock garden and in the spring flowering borders.

Plants to attract butterflies

Of the plants most liked by butterflies, first and foremost is the *Buddleia*. This shrub is aptly also named the butterfly bush, and seems to be such an attraction to butterflies that during its flowering period, it is frequently covered with them.

Hebe 'Midsummer Beauty' is a close second choice; moreover, if the first spent flowers are cut off, it has the advantage of producing a second crop of flowers. *Sedum spectabile* and its cultivars make lovely alighting platforms for butterflies in the late summer. *Solidago* (golden rod) in its many cultivars are also very attractive to butterflies.

All these kinds of plants provide a reasonably stable platform for the butterfly, enabling it to rest — which is very important — and at the same time, providing close-at-hand nectar.

If it becomes necessary to spray plants because of aphid or fungus attacks, always spray either in the morning or late afternoon (preferably between 8 and 10 a.m. and 5 and 7 p.m. in the summer). At these times few insects are on the wing and bees are not active.

PLANTS FOR CUTTING

The range of plants which can be used as cut flowers is much wider than is generally supposed, for the market growers commonly restrict their variety to the minumum that is commercial so as to maximize the use of space, packaging and transport. This inevitably results in a reduced selection for the purchaser. But the amateur gardener need not be concerned by such problems, and can grow whichever plants may be thought suitable for house decoration.

The average garden today is small, and becoming smaller. If flowers are to be cut from display borders, the resulting gaps left may be unsightly. So it is a good idea, if cut flowers are to be a continuing requirement, to allocate a space somewhere in the garden specifically to the growing of flowers to be cut — a cut flower area. Allotments are often used for this purpose, and generally provide good growing conditions; cut flower allotments also brighten up what otherwise are predominantly vegetable-growing zones.

Cut flowers are, on the whole, annuals or biennials and perennials; some cut flowers are provided by shrubs and trees (like lilac) but they are distinctly in the minority. The cutting of some flowers from several shrubs is actually beneficial to the health of the plants; the flowers can be lovely too. But keen floral arrangers use all kinds of plants for flowers, foliage and seed-heads.

This selection of flowers to cut is intended as a starter list.

Camellias (*Camellia* species), when established, have lovely sprays of large, colorful flowers with deep green glossy foliage; they last well in water. Spring is their time for flowering. Daphne flowers (*Daphne* species) are very fragrant: one stem can scent a room. They do not really like being cut, but one or two stems' loss do no harm to the plant, which flowers in spring and summer. The forsythias (species of the shrub *Forsythia*) genuinely benefit from cutting. A harbinger of spring, the plant's golden-yellow flowers can be cut in bud to open indoors. The 'Hortensia' hybrids of the hydrangeas add body to a flower arrangement in mid-summer; *Hydrangea paniculata* produces large spikes of flowers in the late summer. The winter-flowering jasmine *(Jasminum nudiflorum)* is invaluable during late winter and early spring; *J. revolutum* produces lovely golden-yellow flowers in summer.

The rose genus *(Rosa)* provides cut flowers from mid-summer until mid-autumn in so many colors that the choice is almost endless. The end of each cut stem should be split to allow it to take up water. From late spring to autumn the various forms of the shrub *Spiraea* give color and elegance; the bridal wreath *(S. arguta)* has white flowers, and *S. X bumalda* 'Anthony Waterer' has crimson flowers throughout the summer. The lovely heads of the flowers of the lilac *(Syringa* species) vary in color from white through to deep purple in spring and early summer. The leaves should be removed from cut stems or the flowers tend to droop. Viburnums (*Viburnum* species) can be used as cut flowers but should not be cut back too much. *V. X burkwoodii* has fragrant pink budded white flowers in early spring; *V. carlesii* produces rounded clusters of pure white flowers with a daphne-like fragrance.

The cutting of flowers from shrubs should be carried out with great care, leaving no snags, and maintaining the overall shape of the bush. All shrub flower stems should be split to enable the stem to take up water.

Annuals and perennials

Annuals, and some perennials grown as biennials, are a fruitful source of cut flowers. Grown from seed in one year they are very rewarding, although the sowing, the pricking out (with half-hardy annuals also the hardening off) and the planting out are all time-consuming. Hardy annuals can be sown where they are to flower, of course, either in the autumn or in the early spring.

The following selection includes many of the best.

The annual asters (*Callistephus* species) make lovely flowers all summer, with colors' from white through to deep purple. Half-hardy annuals, they tend to suffer from wilt, but the many types available are all well worth growing. The pot marigold (*Calendula* species), a hardy annual, repeats bloom all summer, bearing masses of orange and yellow-orange flowers. All spent flower heads should be removed to prolong the display. The hardy annual cornflower *(Centaurea cyanus)* has flowers in many colors from white to purple in countless shades. Wallflowers (*Cheiranthus* species) are perennials but are usually grown as biennials; they provide many lovely colors, with pastel shades from lemon yellow to deep, rich reds. The Siberian wallflower *C. X allionii* has attractive flowers in yellow and orange.

The hardy annual chrysanthemums are better known for the autumn-flowering types than the annual ones; *C. carinatum* has fern-like foliage and bright daisy-like flowers, yellow through to deep red, most with a zonal eye of yellow. *Clarkia elegans*, another hardy annual, bears masses of double flowers on slender stems and in colors of white, pink and cerise. The same colors may be found on the half-hardy annual *Cosmea*, sometimes called cosmos; it has pretty fern-like foliage. A hardy annual often available from a florist is the rocket larkspur, *Delphinium ajacis* — and rightly so. It has slender stems of stock-like flowers in white, pink, red and deep blue, and many intermediate colors. The flowers of the blanket flower *Gaillardia* — a plant that may be hardy or half-hardy annual or perennial — are single or double, mostly yellow, flame and red, often edged in contrasting shades. They make splendid summer border displays. Of the hardy annual *Godetia*, the single and double flowers, some frilled, are in many shades of white, pink and red. *Gypsophila*, also known as baby's breath, is a hardy annual which has a delicate froth of tiny white flowers on a widely branching stem, ideal for use in combination with sweet peas (see below). The mallow (*Lavatera* species) is a superb flower for cutting: the rose-pink, silver-pink and white flowers are borne on strong stems; the best are *L. trimestris* 'Mont Blanc', *L.* 'Loveliness' and *L.* 'Silver Cup'.

Another first-class flower for cutting is the sweet pea *(Lathyrus odoratus)*; available in many shades from white to deep purple, this hardy annual is fragrant and can be grown to many heights between 30cm (12in) and 1.8m (6ft). Also a hardy annual, Love-in-a-mist *(Nigella damascena)* has pretty blue flowers much like those of the cornflower, followed by decorative seed-heads. *Rudbeckia* makes an excellent cut flower, in colors from yellow to mahogany, some possibly bicolored. Among the best of these hardy and half-hardy annuals are *R.* 'Marmalade', golden orange; *R.* 'Rustic Dwarfs', mahogany-tipped and variegated orange; *R.* 'Irish Eyes', golden yellow with a bright yellow center — all of these varieties of *R. hirta*, the black-eyed Susan. The sweet

These plants provide excellent cut flowers: from left to right, *Gladiolus* 'Extremist', dusty mauve; *Lavatera trimestris* 'Silver Cup', pink; *Crocosmia masonorum*, vivid orange; *Aconitum napellus* 'Bicolor', blue-and-white hooded flowers.

scabious (*Scabiosa* species) also gives a fine selection of colors, from white to purple. A new cultivar of this hardy annual called 'Paper Moon' has soft lavender flowers which eventually shed their petals to leave papery spheres with a blue eye. And finally, the half-hardy annual zinnias (*Zinnia* species) provide gaily-colored flowers of substance in white, gold, bronze, cerise, red, and many intermediate shades.

Perennials

A herbaceous border can give a good supply of cut flowers during the summer months. Perennials are generally taller than annuals, have stiffer stems, and produce their best flowers when they are well established, after three years, despite commonly being left very much to their own devices after the first year in many gardens. They appreciate a yearly mulching and a dressing of a good general fertilizer in the spring to give of their best. The flower stems need some support against wind damage, for which twiggy branches are ideal. To maintain the quality of the flowers and to prevent overcrowding, they should be dug out and split up at least once every five years — although to this rule there are one or two exceptions such as *Aster amellus* cultivars, *Eryngium* and peonies.

Once a border has been emptied, dig it over thoroughly and incorporate plenty of well-rotted manure or compost before sprinkling in some general fertilizer at a rate of 60gm per m² (2oz per sq yd) and forking it in lightly. Prior to replanting, divide the plants into three or four pieces and use only one outside piece for replanting; discard the rest.

There are many perennials to choose from; the following selection includes many of the best.

Achillea
A long-lasting cut flower on tall 1.2m (4ft) stems, its flowers are golden yellow from mid-summer until early autumn, borne in large, flat heads; the foliage is deeply cut and aromatic. The best cultivars are 'Gold Plate' and 'Parker's Variety'.

Aconitum: Monkshood
The blue and white or violet-blue flowers are carried on stems 120 to 135cm (4 to 4½ft) tall from mid-summer until early autumn. Supports are required if grown in open positions.

All parts of this plant are poisonous — flowers, stems and roots: wash hands thoroughly after handling. The two best cultivars are 'Spark's Variety' and 'Bressingham Spire'.

Aster amellus
This is a superb border plant, of which the best varieties are *A*. 'King George', deep blue, 60cm (2ft) tall; *A*. 'Jacqueline Genebrier', pink, 90cm (3ft); and *A*. 'Violet Queen', 45cm (1½ft). *Aster X frikartii*, a hybrid between *A. amellus* and *A. thomsonii*, bears lovely orange-centered blue flowers on stout stems up to 75cm (30in) tall. All flower in late summer and early autumn.

Astrantia: Masterwort
Astrantias make good cut flowers, with gray and white or pink and white intricate flowers decorated with a mass of stamens. Height: 40-75cm (15-30in). Flowering periods vary throughout the summer.

Campanula: Bellflower
The *Campanula* genus is a large and diverse one. Most of them are blue in many shades, light pink and white. *C. lactiflora* offers many good cultivars, 1.2m (4ft) in height. *C. latifolia*, 100cm (3½ft), and *C. persicifolia*, 90cm (3ft), also have many cultivars. They flower from early summer to early autumn.

Chrysanthemum maximum: Shasta daisy
This flower and its cultivars are also advantageous to the flower arranger; their white or pale cream single, semi-double, double or fimbriated flowers are held on stiff stems 75-90cm (2½-3ft) in height. The flowering period is mid- to late summer.

Crocosmia and Curtonus: Montbretia
These bulbous plants commonly grow to be so crowded in an average garden that their true worth goes unrecognized. *Crocosmia masonorum* is the best of the genus: it has graceful, arching stems carrying vivid orange flowers at a height of 75cm (2½ft). There are several cultivars in all, with slight variations in color, flowering from mid-summer to early autumn.

Dahlia
A large and diverse genus, dahlias are available in many colors, some mixed, from white through red to the deepest purple. The single varieties are the best for floral ar-

rangements. Height: 45-120cm (1½-4ft). The flowering period is mid-summer until early autumn.

Dianthus: Pink, Border carnation
These are lovely — and common — cut flowers in white, pink, red and intermediate shades, and have pleasant fragrance. Height: 15-30cm (6-12in). They flower in mid-summer.

Eryngium: Sea holly
Very eye-catching, very prickly plants with blue flowering heads, these grow to a height of 45-90cm (1½-3ft) and flower in mid-summer.

Gypsophila
G. paniculata is the perennial form; *G*. 'Bristol Fairy' and *G*. 'Flamingo' are white and double pink respectively. Height: 120cm (4ft). The flowering period is mid-summer until early autumn.

Helenium: Sneezewort
A sun-loving and very free-flowering plant, the sneezewort has yellow, orange or mahogany flowers. Recommended cultivars are *H*. 'Moerheim Beauty', *H*. 'Gold Fox' and *H*. 'Bressingham Gold'. Height: 60-110cm (2½-3ft). It is in flower from early summer until mid-autumn.

Scabiosa: Scabious, Pincushion flower
One of the well-known flowers at florists', the colors of the scabious vary from white to light and dark blue. The best ones are *S*. 'Clive Greaves', deep blue, *S*. 'Moonstone', light blue; and *S*. 'Miss Willmott', white. Height: 75cm (2½ft). The flowering period lasts from early autumn, but the plant does not do well in clayey soils.

All of these plants are good garden plants and amply repay care and attention.

Bulbous plants suitable for cutting comprise another elite group. Daffodils, including narcissi, are perhaps the most commonly available at the florists'. Gladioli should be planted in sequence from early spring onward to prolong the flowering times; doing this, the season can be extended for flowers from mid-summer to early autumn. Tulips come into flower in spring and are available in many colors.

Rudbeckia hirta 'Marmalade' (**far right**) produces 10cm (4in) golden blooms that are excellent for indoor decoration. Daffodil 'Fortune' (**center right**) one of many daffodils well-loved for their spring blooms. *Syringa* flowers (**right**) last well in water.

Plants for drying

There are many plants that can be dried or otherwise preserved for ornamental purposes and used in virtually permanent flower arrangements. Many plants — particularly the herbs, for example — are also dried for use in the kitchen. Preserved ornamental plants were great favorites of the Victorians, who dried, pressed and oiled all manner of plant material. Today this method of prolonging the beauty of plants is experiencing a comeback.

Dried flowers and leaves provide long-lasting decorative arrangements; moreover — and much more than is generally the case at present — they can be used to complement the cut flowers which in winter are so expensive to buy. Requiring little attention, they have only to be dusted from time to time. Dried flowers and leaves can be used in containers, for pictures and plaques, and in swags (three-dimensional arrangements which can be hung up on a wall without a frame).

Suitable plants
The Table features a wide range of plants suitable for drying or preserving. Many of the flowering plants can be sown and gathered in one season: the hardy and half-hardy annuals.

The half-hardy annuals should be sown in gentle heat during the early spring in seed pans, and after germination should be pricked out in seed trays when the first true leaves have appeared. Grow them on until late spring, and harden them off in a cold frame before planting them in a border in early summer.

The hardy annuals can be sown where they are to flower in mid-spring, when weather conditions are suitable and the soil is warm; sow thinly. After their germination, thin out to 23cm (9in) apart. All these annuals thrive in well prepared soil in a sunny position and require little attention.

The two hardy biennials in the Table, *Dipsacus* (teasel) and *Lunaria* (honesty), should be planted as seed in early summer for flowering the same time the following year.

The parts of the plants that are suitable for preserving include the flowers, the seed-heads, the foliage and the fruit. Some of the most fascinating plants for preservation are the ornamental gourds, which can be grown in the same way as squash. Sow the seeds in pots or boxes in a frame or greenhouse in spring. Plant out early in summer, depending on the weather, and water freely, giving liquid fertilizer as necessary. Train the stems onto a trellis or similar support in order to avoid slug damage and soil splashes. Cut the inedible fruits when they are large enough to handle, wash them and lay them out in a well ventilated room out of the sun for about eight weeks. Many colors and patterns of gourds can be grown from one packet of mixed seed.

The stately flower spires of *Verbascum* (**above**) grace the perennial border during mid-summer. The seed-heads that follow are excellent subjects for drying.

Drying technique
The method used for drying plant material uses the fact that when a plant dies, a change takes place which leaves it a facsimile of itself when alive, but brown where once it was green. When the life of a plant comes to an end, it stops taking up water, which is not replaced as it evaporates; the plant then shrivels and dies. The ones to dry, therefore, are those that die back gracefully, retaining their shape. They tend to have a finely branching, strong, rigid structure, able by itself to support the dead tissue and so retain the shape even when completely dehydrated. This retention is particularly good if the final water evaporation is gradual.

It is far better to dry plants indoors. Some plants do dry naturally out of doors, but they can be damaged by weather conditions. Other plants tend to shrivel when drying and instead, for good results, require pressing.

Drying is most successfully effected by bunching and hanging. Cut the flowers and seed-heads for hanging up to dry. Flowers must be in good condition — avoid misshapen heads or any that have been damaged — and should be neither moist nor yet fully open. Seed-heads should be cut when they are beginning to dry on the plant. Care must be taken when gathering thistles, pampas grass and bulrushes for these all break readily and should be cut when half developed. Tie the stems of the plant material in small bunches, with a hanging loop, and ensure that the flowers or seed-heads do not rub each other. Remove any leaves — without special measures (see below) they do not dry successfully and commonly become patchy and increase the humidity as the water evaporates.

Hang the plant material up to dry in the dark. The bunches should be hung upside down, which gives a better shape to the flowers and seed-heads, and prevents a drooping appearance. If the drying is too slow the colors may fade. A warm place with a free circulation of air — *not* the inside of a cupboard — gives the best results.

Store the dried plants for future use where they were dried or in boxes without lids, layering with tissue-paper to avoid crushing. Dried material is fragile, so great care is needed.

Preserving foliage
All foliage to be preserved should be cut when the leaves are fully grown and at their best. The time required to treat the leaves is dependent on the type of leaf.

Foliage is normally better preserved with glycerine than dried. The glycerine is mixed with water in a solution made up of one part of glycerine to two parts of boiling water, but it must be cold when used. Stir the solution well when mixing. It can be used over and over again. The newly-picked stems take up the mixture, and the water evaporates but the glycerine remains in the leaf cells. Because of the water loss, the natural color is not retained, so the leaves turn brown, dark green or blue-gray, or variations of these colors depending on the plant composition. The results, though, are tough and long-lasting. The plant material must of course be treated while it is still absorbing water, for the solution must be carried to every part of the foliage.

Arranging dried plants
Dried plant material which loses its shape can be 'revived' by holding it over the spout of a steaming kettle for a few seconds and then reshaping quickly. If the material is flat it can be lightly ironed — use a warm iron: this is certainly the best method for large leaves.

When arranging dried plant material, you can support it with modeling clay, dry plastic foam or a frog. If natural flowers or foliage are also used, the stem ends of the dried material should be dipped in candle wax to prevent them from taking up water.

The purple flowers of *Lunaria annua* (**below**) are replaced by flat seed-pods.

The prickly flower-heads of *Dipsacus fullonum* (**below**) dry well.

PLANTS FOR DRYING

Botanical name	Common name	Height	Flower color	Foliage	Decorative feature
Allium, various (Bulb)	Onion (and related plants)	23-120cm (9-48in)	Lilac, blue, gold white, red	Gray-green	Seed-head/fruit
Althaea (Biennial)	Hollyhock	90-180cm (3-6ft)	Many colors but not blue	Gray-green	Seed-head/fruit
Amaranthus caudatus (Half-hardy annual)	Love-lies-bleeding	90cm (3ft)	Red/dark red	Pale green, netted red	Flowers
Ammobium alatum (Half-hardy annual)	Winged everlasting	45-60cm (18-24in)	White and yellow	Gray	Flowers
Angelica archangelica (Perennial)	Holy ghost	1.8-3m (6-10ft)	Yellow-green	Aromatic	Seed-head/fruit
Briza media (Grass)	Quaking grass	30-45cm (12-18in)	Golden nodding flowers	Small heart-shaped purple-brown spikes on thin stalks	Seed-head/fruit
Bromus brizaeformis (Grass)	Ornamental oats	40-120cm (16-48in)	Purplish red panicles	Pale green	Seed-head/fruit
Castanea sativa (Tree)	Sweet chestnut	Up to 21.3m (70ft)	Cream	Shiny, lance-shaped	Foliage
Celosia argentea 'Plumosa' *C.a.* 'Cristata' (Half-hardy annuals)	Prince of Wales' feathers Cockscomb	23-60cm (9-24in)	Red, yellow orange	Light green	Flowers
Clematis vitalba (Climbing shrub)	Travellers joy, Old man's beard	Climber	Greenish white	Glossy green hairless leaves	Seed-head/fruit
Cortaderia, various (Grass)	Pampas grass	1.2-2.1m (4-7ft)	Gold, rose, silver	Bluish green evergreen	Seed-head
Cucurbita pepo (Half-hardy annual)	Ornamental gourd	Climber	Yellow	Large, green	Fruit (gourd)
Dipsacus fullonum (Hardy biennial)	Teasel	45cm-2m (18in-6½ft)	Pink or white	Lance-shaped, green	Seed-head
Fagus, various (Tree)	Beech	Grow as a hedge		Elliptical leaves green, copper and purple	Foliage
Gomphrena, various (Half-hardy annual)	Everlasting globe amaranth	30cm (12in)	Orange, yellow, purple, pink and white	Bright green	Flowers
Helichrysum (Half-hardy annual)	Straw flower	90-120cm (3-4ft)	Many colors available	Pale green	Flowers
Helipterum, various (Hardy annual)	Everlasting	45cm (18in)	Yellow	Woolly, almost white	Flowers turn green after drying
Helleborus corsica (Perennial)	Hellebore	60cm (2ft)	Yellow-green	Thick and spiny	Foliage
Koelaria glauca (Grass)	Blue meadow grass	60cm (2ft)	Intense blue	Blue	Seed-head
Lagarus ovatus (Grass)	Hare's tail grass	45cm (18in)	Fluffy white heads	Pale green	Seed-head
Limonium, various (Half-hardy annual)	Statice, everlasting	30cm (12in)	Many colors	Green	Flowers
Liriodendron tulipifera (Tree)	Tulip tree	over 18m (60ft)	Yellow-green with orange markings	Squarish leaves turn yellow in autumn	Foliage
Lunaria annua (Hardy biennial)	Honesty	75cm (30in)	Silvery seed pods	Dark green	Seed-head
Moluccella laevis (Half-hardy annual)	Bells of Ireland	60cm (2ft)	Spikes of white flowers with pale green calyx	Pale green	Flowers
Nicandra physaloides (Hardy annual)	Shoo-fly plant	Up to 90cm (3ft)	Pale blue	Globular fruits enclosed by green and purple calyces	Fruiting branches Seed-head
Nigella damascena (Hardy annual)	Love-in-a-mist	45cm (18in)	Blue. Multi-colored form available	Feathery shape, green	Seed-head
Panicum violaceum (Grass)	Millet	90cm (3ft)	Green and violet	Pale green	Seed-head
Papaver orientale (Perennial)	Oriental poppy	60-90cm (2-3ft)	Shades of pink and red, white	Silver-green	Seed-head/fruit
Physalis franchetii (Perennial)	Chinese lantern	60cm (2ft)	Globular orange fruits in a papery calyx	Pale green	Seed-head/fruit
Setaria italica (Grass)	Foxtail millet	45cm (18in)	Panicles of reddish gold	Pale green	Seed-head
Triticum spelta (Grass)	Ornamental wheat	60cm (2ft)	Biscuit color	Biscuit color when ripe	Seed-head
Verbascum, various (Perennial)	Mullein	90-180cm (3-6ft)	Wide range of colors		Seed-head/fruit
Xeranthemum annuum (Hardy-annual)	Immortelle	60cm (2ft)	Shades of pink, purple-lilac and white	Gray-green	Flowers. They keep their color after drying
Zinnia, various (Half-hardy annual)		15-75cm (6-30in)	Many colors, flowers round with thick petals	Gray-green	Flowers

Ornamental vegetables

Ornamental vegetable borders are now seen in many public parks and gardens; professional flower-arrangers, well aware of the possibilities, have also caught on, with the result that ornamental cabbage leaves for example are often on display in exhibition halls, especially used cleverly as backgrounds in large and small floral arrangements. What a pity it is, then, that the average gardener seems to ignore vegetables altogether as a source of color and beauty, that when planting summer flowering borders vegetables are generally the last plants to be considered — a pity indeed, for many of them have lovely flowers, fruit and foliage.

The string bean, for instance, flowers from mid-summer to the first frosts; its various cultivars have flowers of red, red and white, soft pink, white, and creamy white. And the beans themselves can be green, red-streaked green, or purple — after all. vegetables planted in a border provide not only color and texture but something to eat too.

The thistle-like flowerheads of the globe artichoke (**above**) are carried atop a stately plant that may reach 90cm or more (35in), depending on variety. In a border it makes a fine architectural subject; its gray-green foliage acting as a foil for more colorful plants. 'Rhubarb' chard (**right**) is a variety of Swiss chard or leaf beet that has highly decorative deep red stems and dark bronze foliage in late summer to early autumn. Ornamental cabbages (**center**) make a fine show in a mixed border. The shades of cream, pink and red mixed with the natural greens of these familiar vegetables produce quite outstanding results.

Planning a vegetable border

As with flowers, a vegetable border can be planned to give a colorful display during the whole of the summer. One suggestion is to plan the background with one or two globe artichokes interspersed with groups of string beans on tripods, poles or a trellis, using different-colored cultivars in each group. In the middle of each border plant several tomatoes with red and golden fruits, and a pepper if the border is sited in warmth and sunshine. Interplant with groups of beetroot, carrots and ruby or rainbow chard (artichoke), and edge with parsley or red-leaved lettuce. What could be more colorful?

With the exception of the globe artichoke — a perennial, so one-year-old plants should be planted — all the vegetables grown for use in a vegetable border should be sown in pots or boxes in early spring, either in a greenhouse or a frame. When the seedlings are large enough to handle, at the first true leaf, they should be pricked out into boxes or planted singly in 5cm

Cabbage

The most popular vegetable for foliage is the ornamental cabbage. Packets of mixed seeds can be purchased containing many variations in color: cream, green in several shades, pink, red and rose. Cabbage grows well in most good garden soils, although precautions should be taken against club root. Sow the seeds in early spring under glass, and when they are large enough to handle pot the seedlings in 7.5cm (3in) pots. Once they are established a selection can be made of the colors required for planting out in early summer. The plants retain their color for the whole of the season.

Carrot

The best cultivars for foliage are 'Chantenay Red Cored' and 'Sutton's Favourite'.

Globe artichoke

'Green Globe' is an ideal variety: it requires a space of at least 60cm (2ft) and has globular thistle-like blue heads of flowers and grey-green foliage. A very statuesque plant. Height: 90cm (3ft).

Kale (or borecole)

Several types of kale produce ornamental foliage. The topknot of the plant resembles the ornamental cabbage but is much taller. Height: 30-90cm (1-3ft). Good varieties to choose are 'Red and White Peacock Mixed' and 'Westland Autumn'.

Kohlrabi

Try the variety 'Purple Vienna'. This interesting vegetable has purple marking on the bulb and on the leaves.

Leaf beet

Sometimes called silver beet or Swiss chard. The cultivar 'Rhubarb' has crimson stems and dark foliage; 'Rainbow' has red, orange, purple, yellow or white stems, the foliage varying with the color of the stem.

Lettuce

There are many decorative lettuce varieties, including 'Continuity', red-tinged outer leaves; 'Red Salad Bowl', deeply cut and curled leaves, bronze-green shading to deep crimson; and 'Salad Bowl', fresh green curled leaves.

Orach

Atriplex hortensis 'Rubra', also known as mountain spinach. A quick-growing plant with crimson leaves. Height: 1.2-1.5m (4-5ft).

Parsley

An excellent decorative plant with deep green curled foliage, ideal for borders or beside paths. Two good cultivars to try are 'Curlina' and 'Paramount Imperial Curled'. Parsley is slow to germinate in open ground; for preference therefore use one of the indoor seed-raiser packs now available.

Vegetables for flower effect

Asparagus pea

This edible podded pea bears masses of chocolate-purple flowers followed by winged seedpods: these must be used when of a length no greater than 2.5cm (1in). It flowers and crops for about ten weeks. (The peas have an asparagus-like flavor.)

String beans

This strong-growing climbing plant has cultivars with pink, red, red and white, and white flowers. It can be used for clothing a trellis, growing on a tripod or spreading over canes set up wigwam-fashion, and if plenty of moisture is available flowers continuously from mid-summer until the first frosts. Good cultivars include 'Achievement', red flowers; 'Butler', red flowers, stringless; 'Enorma', red flowers; 'Mergoles', white flowers, stringless; 'Painted Lady', red and white flowers; 'Sunset', pink flowers; 'White Achievement', white flowers. Height: 1.8m (6ft). The string bean is the most rewarding of all vegetables.

Vegetables for fruit effect

Ornamental corn

Zea mays, also known as maize. In a warm, sheltered corner that receives full sun and has a fertile soil, try growing some ornamental corn plants. The cobs are not edible but can be dried for decorative use. The most spectacular variety is 'Rainbow', which produces striking multicolored cobs.

Sweet pepper

This plant, *Capsicum*, can be grown only in a warm, sunny border. Try the variety 'Triton', which grows to a height of 30cm (1ft) with golden yellow fruits. 'Canape' has deep green fruits which turn red when ripe; height: 45cm (18in). All the peppers are very ornamental, showy plants.

Tomato

For an outdoor border the indeterminate (single-stem) cultivars are best; bush cultivars take up too much space. They should be trained to a stout cane and allowed to grow to a height of 1.2m (4ft); all side shoots should be removed, and feeding should commence when the first truss of fruit has set. The best cultivars include 'Alicante', a very popular tomato with bright red fruits, it ripens early and has delicious flavor; 'Gardener's Delight', which produces large crops of small red fruits, sweet-flavored, on long trusses; 'Golden Sunrise', medium-sized pale orange fruits with distinctive sweet flavor; 'Marmande', large, irregular red fruits with firm flesh and very few seeds — this is the standard Continental tomato; 'Sweet 100', very similar to 'Gardener's Delight', masses of small red tomatoes with good flavor, produced on long trusses; 'Tigerella', medium-sized fruits of excellent sweet-sharp flavor, ripening to red with golden stripes.

(2in) pots; once they are established, they should then be repotted in 10-12cm (4-5in) pots for a time before transplanting into the border. Make sure that the plants do not become pot-bound — that the pots do not become solid with roots — or they will not take kindly to being planted out at all.

The border should be well prepared in the same way as the vegetable garden. Dig thoroughly and incorporate plenty of well-rotted compost. After digging, let the soil settle before sprinkling 70gm per m² (2oz per sq yd) of a general fertilizer, plus a handful of bonemeal, onto the surface and lightly forking it in. At this stage, mark out the intended vegetable positions to ensure that the plants will be in the best place to achieve the desired effect. After planting, water well.

Vegetables for foliage effect

Beet

Globe varieties such as 'Burpee's Golden' produce decorative foliage.

COLOR
IN THE
GARDEN

Color Introduction

Color has a strong effect on the emotions. A garden that contains only the various greens of leaves seems restful but may in time become boring. Yet a garden completely filled with bright-colored flowers is certainly exciting — but may equally quickly become tiring. The story is told of a man who, having been taken to admire a bed of particularly bright geraniums, begged to be led away to cool his eyes on the parsley. There seems to be a good scientific reason for that reaction. If one stares for a while at an area of bright red and then closes one's eyes, an image of green appears briefly against the darkness. It is as if the surfeit of red has produced a need for green to complement it; in fact, green is known as the complementary color for red.

Sunlight is composed of all the colors that appear in a rainbow or when it is split up by a prism: this is direct light. What we actually see when looking at objects around us is the light they reflect. The colors that the eye registers from them can all be made by mixing yellow, red and blue pigments (with the addition of black or white to darken or lighten them and so make the different shades and tints). If the three primary colors are placed around a circle numbered like a clock face, with yellow at the top (12), red at 4 and blue at 8 and the intermediate colors made by mixing any two of these are filled in in between, so that orange-yellow is at 1, orange at 2, orange-red at 3, red-violet at 5, violet at 6, blue-violet at 7, blue-green at 9, green at 10 and yellow-green at 11, it will be found that all the complementary colours face one another across the clock. Red is seen to be complementary to green, orange to blue and so on all around the color circle.

But the color clock tells us something more. The nearer the colors are on the clock face, the more they harmonize. Broadly speaking all color associations can be split up into harmonies and contrasts, the former less violent to the senses than the latter. This violence can be reduced by introducing linking colors, shown on the clock face between those that are contrasting too much for satisfaction. The softest harmonies of all are produced by the paled or darkened tints and shades of the full colors.

Armed with such information it is possible to approach color planning in the garden in a very logical and systematic way. Appreciation of this has grown rapidly among gardeners in recent years thanks to the activities of flower arrangers, particularly at flower shows. The fine floral exhibits that are such an admired feature of many shows demonstrate the effective use of color and form, and because flower arrangers have been trained, or have trained themselves, in both they usually also make good garden designers.

In borders of flowers there are several ways in which color can be used. The simplest is to restrict each border to a limited range of colors — for example, to use only white flowers and gray or silver-leaved plants with perhaps a just a touch of light yellow, blue, pink and mauve; to go entirely for strong colors in a limited range, such as blue and purple or red, orange and yellow; or to make quiet harmonies with soft blues, pinks and cream. The effects so produced may be lively or sad, stimulating or restful, but they can never jar the senses by dissonance.

Another safe method is to arrange the colors in a border in a progressive sequence, starting with white and pale yellow at one end and gradually working up to the strongest oranges, reds and crimsons at the other end. Alternatively, if there is sufficient length, these strong colors could be set in the center and the color sequence appear in reverse, not necessarily with the same flowers, to either end. Such arrangements are sometimes referred to as rainbow borders because they roughly follow the sequence of colors in a rainbow, but usually with marked differences in shade and intensity.

This is another feature of color that must be considered. Of course, not all colors are fully saturated or intense: in practice they occur in an infinite variety of intensities and gradations which an artist simulates by adding white, black or brown or by diluting the color with more solvent. Flowers exhibit innumerable gradations of this kind and can thus be chosen to give the precise effect that is sought.

Most flower borders are planned neither for a limited color range nor for a rainbow effect, but are filled with colors randomly distributed. Unless all the plants are carefully placed in relation to their neighbors, the effect can be insipid or tiresome to the eye. It takes some ingenuity to arrange a border without having any clashes, but one method of sorting out such problems before actually committing oneself to plant is to write the names, colors, heights and flowering times of all the plants to be used on little circles or ovals of cardboard and then move these about on an outline plan of the border until a satisfactory mix is achieved. Flowering time is important for it is no use planning some fine color association only to find that the colors do not appear at the same time. Height is also a useful piece of information: comparison shows at a glance whether any plant is likely to be concealed by a taller one growing next to it.

Green, gray, silver and white, whether in flowers or foliage, can be used to break up all the other colors and prevent clashes between them. The advantage of leaves over flowers is that they are usually present for much longer. There are a great many variations of green and gray and even, oddly enough, of white, partly because the latter is often not quite pure, but also because of the differences in the surface texture of petals or in the way they are arranged, both of which affect the way in which they reflect light.

Color can also be used to play tricks with perspective. Some colors (especially the strong ones), are seen more clearly than others (mainly the weak ones), and so they seem to be closer to the eye. If a long border is planted so that the colors range progressively toward the weaker, for example starting with the full-blooded crimsons, purples, reds and oranges at one end and gradually toning down to the pale mauves, pinks, creams and white at the other end (much in the manner already described for a rainbow border), it appears even longer than it really is when viewed from the strong-colored end and shorter than it is when seen from the weak-colored end.

There are no unbreakable rules in the use of color. Some would say that the bluish reds should never be mixed with the yellowish reds because they clash. But that clash may be precisely the effect desired. I remember once asking a very sensitive and clever garden-maker why she had planted orange alstroemeria in the middle of a lot of flowers in the magenta range — and receiving the reply that it was to make fools ask questions. Theatrical designers often get away with the most outrageous color combinations, using them to stir the senses and create a peak of excitement. Nevertheless, what may be fully justified on the stage for a performance that continues only for an hour or so may be intolerable in a garden that has to be lived with. If in doubt, try the colors you like on a sheet of paper, using paints or crayons; place a splodge of each desired color against another and gradually built up from this.

One difficulty in communicating ideas about color is the very meager vocabulary on the subject that most of us have. Color charts are useful — if the person with whom we are trying to communicate has access to the same color chart. If not, terms such as Tyrian rose and Turkey red have little meaning. Color descriptions in nursery and seed catalogues can accordingly be very misleading; often, one catalogue appears completely to contradict another. The ideal is to see the plants flowering before deciding to use them — but that is a counsel of perfection that is rarely practical. In the following lists of some suggested plants arranged according to the color of their flowers I have tried to use only familiar terms, such as lavender-blue, violet-purple and rose-pink, although I know that again each of these covers a fairly wide range of color.

The bright pinks of *Phlox paniculata* varieties and roses provide bold splashes of color in the garden. The large heart-shaped leaves of the tree *Catalpa bignonioides* 'Aurea' provide a refreshing shade of yellow-green to the darker foliage greens. But the balance of color is never constant; as the seasons change so new plants come into flower as others fade. Timing is therefore an important part of planning color in the garden. It is also vital to know the mature size and shape of garden plants; subjects chosen carefully for their color may be overshadowed by taller plants as the garden develops.

Arranging the colors of the rainbow in a circle (**left**) helps to show which ones clash and which ones are complementary. Colors facing each other directly across the circle are complementary and likely to clash. Those that lie close together around the circle harmonize with each other and can be used as links between the contrasting colors.

Borders composed of just one or two colors, such as this pink and silver one (**left**), often produce more effective color schemes than those mixing many hues. The cascading mounds of azaleas in full flower (**right**) are effective through the sheer 'weight' of their color.

The double pink flowers of *Prunus* 'Kanzan' (**left**) form a restful backdrop to the bright early spring blooms of polyanthus and *Myosotis*.
Yellow and pink form a simple yet strikingly effective combination in this mixed planting of *Helianthemum* and *Dianthus* (**above**).

Yellow flowers

Yellow is a color that raises strong feelings. In its most concentrated form it is a penetrating and dominant color that some people find unbearable. A colleague of mine complains of the yellow rash that breaks out when the daffodils flower in spring. Letters deploring the acid yellow of rape fields in flower in summer appear in some British newspapers. Yet yellow is essential to most garden designers — a cheerful and compelling color freely available at most seasons, and unsurpassed for making exhilarating displays when combined with red and orange. It can also be used to brighten up blues and purples, especially in its lighter forms, such as primrose, sulphur, lemon and mimosa yellow.

Some gardeners like yellow so much that they plant yellow borders or even yellow

Tagetes 'Lemon Queen' (**left**) forms a bright foreground to this garden border. The yellow pea-like flowers of *Genista aetnensis* (**right**) appear during mid- and late-summer. They are borne in loose clusters on a shrub reaching up to 6m (20ft) in height.

Crocus chrysanthus

Fritillaria imperialis

Laburnum 'Vossii'

Limnanthes douglasii

Kerria japonica 'Pleniflora'

Koelreuteria paniculata

SPRING / SUMMER

ANNUALS/BEDDING

Cheiranthus cheiri
(Wallflower)
Height: 25-45cm (10-18in)
Spread: 20-25cm (8-10in)
Soil: Ordinary
Site: Sunny
'Cloth of Gold'
'Golden Monarch'
'Primrose Monarch'

Limnanthes douglasii
(Poached egg flower)
Height: 15cm (6in)
Spread: 23cm (9in)
Soil: Ordinary
Site: Open
Pale yellow and white

Pansy
Height: 15-23cm (6-9in)
Spread: 15cm (6in)
Soil: Ordinary
Site: Sun or shade
'Clear Crystals', golden yellow
'Coronation Gold', deep golden yellow
'Sunny Boy', yellow and black
'Yellow Bedder', bright yellow

Polyanthus
Height: 20cm (8in)
Spread: 15cm (6in)
Soil: Ordinary
Site: Sun or moderate shade
'Triumph Yellow', deep yellow

Antirrhinum (SUMMER)
(Snapdragon)
Height: 38-45cm (15-18in)
Spread: 23cm (9in)
Soil: Ordinary
Site: Open
'Regal Yellow'
'Yellow Monarch'

BULBS

Crocus
Height: 10cm (4in)
Spread: 7.5cm (3in)
Soil: Ordinary
Site: Open or light shade
'Large Yellow', daffodil yellow
C.chrysanthus 'Cream Beauty', cream
C.chrysanthus 'E.A. Bowles', deep butter yellow

Fritillaria imperialis
(Crown Imperial)
Height: 75cm (30in)
Spread: 25cm (10in)
Soil: Rich
Site: Open
'Lutea Maxima', golden yellow

Hyacinth
Height: 25cm (10in)
Spread: 15cm (6in)
Soil: Ordinary
Site: Open
'City of Haarlem', pale yellow

Narcissus (Daffodil)
Height: 30-50cm (12-20in)
Spread: 15cm (6in)
Soil: Ordinary
Site: Sun or light shade
'Carlton', light yellow
'February Gold', deep yellow
'Golden harvest', deep yellow
'Spellbinder', sulphur yellow
'Trevithian', lemon yellow
'Yellow Cheerfulness', light yellow

Tulip
Height: 30-60cm (12-24in)
Spread: 10cm (4in)
Soil: Ordinary
Site: Open
'Beauty of Apeldoorn', creamy yellow flushed orange
'Bellona', daffodil yellow
'Golden Harvest', lemon yellow
'Golden Springtime', deep yellow
'West Point', daffodil yellow

Allium moly (SUMMER)
Height: 25cm (10in)
Spread: 7.5cm (3in)
Soil: Ordinary
Site: Sun or partial shade
Buttercup yellow

PERENNIALS

Alyssum saxatile
(Gold dust)
Height: 23cm (9in)
Spread: 23cm (9in)
Soil: Ordinary
Site: Open
'Golden Queen', bright yellow
'Citrinum', lemon yellow

Doronicum
(Leopard's bane)
Height: 20-90cm (8-36in)
Spread: 20-30cm (8-12in)
Soil: Ordinary
Site: Sun or light shade
D.cordatum, marigold yellow
D.plantagineum, 'Harpur Crewe', marigold yellow

Euphorbia
(Spurge)
Height: 15-45cm (6-18in)
Spread: 30cm (12in)
Soil: Ordinary
Site: Sunny
E.myrsinites, sulphur yellow
E.polychroma (epithymoides), lime yellow

Trollius
(Globe flower)
Height: 45-60cm (18-24in)
Spread: 25cm (10in)
Soil: Ordinary, moist
Site: Sun or semi-shade
'Canary Bird', lemon yellow
'Golden Queen', orange yellow

Achillea filipendulina (SUMMER)
Height: 90cm (36in)
Spread: 30cm (12in)
Soil: Ordinary
Site: Open
'Coronation Gold', marigold yellow
'Moonshine', canary yellow

SHRUBS/TREES

Azalea, deciduous
Height: 1.5m (5ft)
Spread: 1.2m (4ft)
Soil: Acid, no lime
Site: Open or light shade
Rhododendron luteum, deep yellow
'Klondyke', orange-yellow

Cytisus praecox
(Broom)
Height: 1.2m (4ft)
Spread: 90cm (3ft)
Soil: Ordinary
Site: Open
Sulphur yellow

Forsythia
(Golden bells)
Height: 2-2.4m (6-8ft)
Spread: 1-1.2m (3-4ft)
Soil: Ordinary
Site: Sun or light shade
'Lynwood', daffodil yellow

Kerria japonica
(Jew's mallow)
Height: 1.2-1.8m (4-6ft)
Spread: 90cm (3ft)
Soil: Ordinary
Site: Sun or shade
Buttercup yellow

Laburnum
(Golden chain)
Height: 4.8-7m (16-23ft)
Spread: 3-4.5m (10-15ft)
Soil: Ordinary
Site: Open
'Vossii', golden yellow

Cytisus (SUMMER)
(Broom)
Height: 1.8-4m (6-13ft)
Spread: 1.2-2m (4-6ft)
Soil: Ordinary
Site: Open
C.battandieri, light yellow
'Cornish Cream', cream
'Golden Sunlight', deep yellow

gardens. There is a notable example of the latter at Crathes Castle in Scotland, a garden divided into a number of sections, several of which are devoted to single colors, one of which is yellow. Here, much of the foliage as well as the flowers is yellow or lime green, and white is the only other color admitted. It is always a center of interest and also of controversy between the yellow-lovers and the yellow-haters.

Because it is so clearly seen, yellow can be used to define shapes even at a considerable distance. At Dawyck, another Scottish garden (but one that differs greatly from Crathes Castle in being mainly woodland), a great 'river' of golden daffodils flows down a wide grassed ride between the forest trees on a hillside to finish up in a huge 'lake' of daffodils in the meadow below. Only white would make a similarly clearcut contrast to the green of turf and tree foliage.

Although yellow is such a basic flower color it almost disappears from trees and shrubs after summer, its place taken by the yellowing foliage of deciduous species and the yellow color of some ripening fruits. Yellow-flowered bulbs are also lacking in autumn with one notable exception, the sternbergias, which look superficially like golden crocuses though they are totally unrelated. Only the shortage of supply prevents this lovely and easily grown flower from being much more widely used and appreciated.

Potentilla fruticosa

Solidago 'Goldenmosa'

Sternbergia lutea

Hypericum calycinum

Zinnia 'Pacific Gold'

Rudbeckia fulgida 'Goldsturm'

AUTUMN

Calendula (Pot marigold) *Height:* 30-45cm (12-18in) *Spread:* 25cm (10in) *Soil:* Ordinary *Site:* Open 'Lemon Queen', lemon yellow 'Yellow Gitana', golden yellow	**Nasturtium** *Height:* 30cm (12in) *Spread:* 25cm (10in) *Soil:* Ordinary *Site:* Sunny 'Golden Gleam', golden yellow	**Nicotiana** (Sweet tobacco) *Height:* 75cm (30in) *Spread:* 25cm (10in) *Soil:* Ordinary *Site:* Sun or shade 'Lime Green', pale yellow-green	**Tagetes** (Marigold) *Height:* 15-90cm (6-36in) *Spread:* 15-25cm (6-10in) *Soil:* Ordinary *Site:* Sunny 'Diamond Jubilee', bright yellow 'First Lady', light yellow 'Gold Lady' golden yellow 'Showboat', deep yellow *T.signata* 'Golden Gem' *T.signata* 'Lemon Gem' 'Yellow Boy'	**Rudbeckia** (Coneflower) *Height:* 45cm (18in) *Spread:* 30cm (12in) *Soil:* Ordinary *Site:* Open 'Marmalade', marigold yellow and black	**Zinnia** *Height:* 25-60cm (10-24in) *Spread:* 20cm (8in) *Soil:* Ordinary *Site:* Sunny 'Pacific Yellow', bright yellow 'Peter Pan', golden yellow 'Yellow Ruffles', saffron yellow
Gladiolus *Height:* 60-90cm (24-36in) *Spread:* 20cm (8in) *Soil:* Ordinary *Site:* Open 'Flowersong', daffodil yellow 'Green Woodpecker', lime yellow 'Landmark', cream	**Iris xiphium** (Dutch iris) *Height:* 75cm (30in) *Spread:* 10cm (4in) *Soil:* Ordinary *Site:* Open 'Yellow Queen', deep yellow	**Lilium** (Lily) *Height:* 1-1.5m (3½-5ft) *Spread:* 25cm (10in) *Soil:* Acid, no lime *Site:* Sun or dappled shade 'Connecticut King', daffodil yellow 'Destiny', lemon yellow 'Limelight', chartreuse yellow *L.monadelphum*, light yellow *L.pyrenaicum*, greenish yellow *L.testaceum*, apricot yellow		**Dahlia** *Height:* 30-90cm (24-36in) *Spread:* 45-90cm (18-36in) *Soil:* Ordinary *Site:* Open 'Claire de Lune', light sulphur yellow 'Glory of Heemstede', primrose 'Klankstade Kerkrade', sulphur yellow 'Yellow Frank Hornsey', clear yellow	**Sternbergia lutea** *Height:* 10cm (4in) *Spread:* 7.5cm (3in) *Soil:* Ordinary *Site:* Sunny Buttercup yellow
Anthemis tinctoria *Height:* 75cm (30in) *Spread:* 45cm (18in) *Soil:* Ordinary, well drained *Site:* Sunny 'E.C.Buxton', sulphur yellow 'Grallagh Gold', deep yellow	**Geum** *Height:* 60cm (24in) *Spread:* 23cm (9in) *Soil:* Ordinary *Site:* Open 'Lady Stratheden', marigold yellow	**Ligularia clivorum** *Height:* 90cm (36in) *Spread:* 60cm (24in) *Soil:* Ordinary *Site:* Open or light shade 'Gregynog Gold', deep yellow	**Lysimachia punctata** (Yellow loosestrife) *Height:* 90cm (36in) *Spread:* 45cm (18in) *Soil:* Ordinary *Site:* Open or light shade Bright yellow	**Rudbeckia** (Coneflower) *Height:* 60-180cm (2-6ft) *Spread:* 45cm (18in) *Soil:* Ordinary *Site:* Sunny 'Goldquelle', chrome yellow 'Goldsturm', deep yellow and black 'Herbstonne', butter yellow	**Solidago** (Golden Rod) *Height:* 60-120cm (2-4ft) *Spread:* 60cm (2ft) *Soil:* Ordinary *Site:* Sun or light shade 'Goldenmosa', mimosa yellow 'Golden Wings', sunflower yellow
Genista (Broom) *Height:* 45cm-6m (18in-20ft) *Spread:* 60cm-3m (2-10ft) *Soil:* Ordinary *Site:* Open *G.aetnensis*, light yellow *G.hispanica*, gorse yellow *G.tenera (virgata)*, bright yellow	**Koelreuteria paniculata** (Golden grain tree) *Height:* 4.8-7m (16-23ft) *Spread:* 4-5.2m (13-17ft) *Soil:* Ordinary *Site:* Sunny Light yellow	**Potentilla** (Shrubby cinquefoil) *Height:* 45-120cm (18in-4ft) *Spread:* 90cm (3ft) *Soil:* Ordinary *Site:* Open 'Elizabeth', soft yellow 'Goldfinger', marigold yellow 'Primrose Beauty', primrose yellow	**Senecio** (Shrubby ragwort) *Height:* 90cm (3ft) *Spread:* 90cm (3ft) *Soil:* Ordinary, well drained *Site:* Sunny, sheltered 'Sunshine' (*S.greyi*), marigold yellow	**Hypericum** (St John's wort) *Height:* 1.2m (4ft) *Spread:* 90cm (3ft) *Soil:* Ordinary *Site:* Open or light shade 'Hidcote', buttercup yellow	**Spartium junceum** (Spanish broom) *Height:* 2.4m (8ft) *Spread:* 1.2m (4ft) *Soil:* Ordinary *Site:* Open Daffodil yellow

Orange flowers

Because it is a mixture of red and yellow, orange combines the penetrating qualities of both these colors. It is the color usually chosen for the clothing of those who, while at work, are at risk from fast-moving traffic because it catches the eye at a distance so exceptionally well. In the garden it can be used in a similar way to attract attention, and it is also useful in association with reds and yellows to create explosions of color. The opposite approach is to contrast orange with blue as, for example, by planting *Lilium bulbiferum* against a background of *Campanula lactiflora* or mixing *Kniphofia galpinii* with the lavender and yellow daisy flowers of *Aster frikartii*.

It is not a color that covers a very wide range of variations, like pink or purple, nor is it found naturally in a great many species, least of all among temperate-zone trees. But it is a color that has been brought into many hybrids by deliberate breeding and selection, and so it is among cultivated varieties, rather than those existing in the wild, that it must mainly be sought.

In some species, orange is available only in mixture. For example many beautiful shades of orange exist in Iceland poppies *(Papaver nudicaule)*, but the seed that is commonly offered also gives salmon pink, yellow and pink flowers: a delightful mixture, but not one that could be recommended to those seeking plain orange for a particular color scheme. The same is true of the delightful little Welsh poppy, *Meconopsis cambrica*, the seed of which usually gives both yellow and orange forms, but because this species is perennial it is possi-

Cheiranthus

Rhododendron (Azalea)

Euphorbia griffithii 'Fireglow'

Berberis darwinii

Tagetes erecta 'Orange Jubilee'

Dahlia

	SPRING					SUMMER
ANNUALS/BEDDING	**Cheiranthus allionii** (Siberian wallflower) *Height:* 30cm (12in) *Spread:* 23cm (9in) *Soil:* Ordinary *Site:* Sunny Bright orange	**Pansy** *Height:* 15-23cm (6-9in) *Spread:* 15cm (6in) *Soil:* Ordinary *Site:* Sun or shade 'Clear Crystals Orange', apricot 'Imperial Orange Prince', deep orange 'Orange Bedder', clear orange	**Polyanthus** *Height:* 20cm (8in) *Spread:* 15cm (6in) *Soil:* Ordinary *Site:* Sun or moderate shade 'Monarch Giant Orange', shades of orange			**Antirrhinum** (Snapdragon) *Height:* 20-40cm (8-16in) *Spread:* 15-25cm (6-10in) *Soil:* Ordinary *Site:* Open 'Regal Apricot', apricot and orange 'Orange Monarch', deep orange and cerise
BULBS	**Crocus** *Height:* 10cm (4in) *Spread:* 7.5cm (3in) *Soil:* Ordinary *Site:* Open or light shade *C.ancyrensis*, bright orange *C.chrysanthus* 'Zwanenburg', yellow and red-bronze	**Fritillaria imperialis** (Crown imperial) *Height:* 75cm (30in) *Spread:* 25cm (10in) *Soil:* Rich *Site:* Open 'Aurora', bronzy orange 'Rubra Maxima', tangerine	**Hyacinth** *Height:* 25cm (10in) *Spread:* 15cm (6in) *Soil:* Ordinary *Site:* Open 'Gypsy Queen', yellow and light tangerine	**Narcissus** (Daffodil) *Height:* 30-50cm (12-20in) *Spread:* 15cm (6in) *Soil:* Ordinary *Site:* Sun or shade 'Fortune', yellow and orange 'Sempre Avanti', cream and orange 'Texas', yellow and tangerine	**Tulip** *Height:* 30-60cm (12-24in) *Spread:* 10cm (4in) *Soil:* Ordinary *Site:* Open 'De Wet', golden orange 'Marechal Niel', yellow and light orange 'Orange Nassau', bronzy orange 'Orange Sun', orange and carmine	**Gladiolus** *Height:* 60-90cm (2-3ft) *Spread:* 20cm (8in) *Soil:* Ordinary *Site:* Open 'Albert Schweitzer', tangerine 'Atlantic', tangerine 'Orange Chiffon', orange and salmon 'Prince Bernhardt', vermilion-orange
PERENNIALS	**Euphorbia griffithii** (Spurge) *Height:* 60-75cm (24-30in) *Spread:* 30cm (12in) *Soil:* Ordinary *Site:* Sun or partial shade 'Fireglow', red-orange	**Trollius** (Globe flower) *Height:* 45-60cm (18-24in) *Spread:* 25cm (10in) *Soil:* Ordinary, moist *Site:* Sun or partial shade 'Orange Princess', orange 'Fireglobe', light orange				**Geum** (Avens) *Height:* 30-45cm (12-18in) *Spread:* 23cm (9in) *Soil:* Ordinary *Site:* Open *G.borisii*, deep orange *G.* 'Fire Opal', coppery-orange
SHRUBS/TREES	**Azalea, deciduous** *Height:* 1.5m (5ft) *Spread:* 1.2m (4ft) *Soil:* Acid, no lime *Site:* Open or dappled shade 'Gibraltar', red-orange 'Christopher Wren', orange-yellow 'Klondyke', orange-gold	**Berberis** (Barberry) *Height:* 1-3m (3½-10ft) *Spread:* 60-180cm (2-6ft) *Soil:* Ordinary *Site:* Open *B.darwinnii*, orange *B.linearifolia*, red-orange *B.stenophylla* 'Coccinea', red buds, orange flowers	**Rhododendron** *Height:* 1.2-3m (4-10ft) *Spread:* 1.2-2.4m (4-8ft) *Soil:* Acid, no lime *Site:* Open or dappled shade 'Goldsworth Orange', light orange and apricot *R.dicroanthum*, deep orange			**Buddleia globosa** (Orange ball tree) *Height:* 3-4m (10-13ft) *Spread:* 2-2.4m (6-8ft) *Soil:* Ordinary *Site:* Sunny Light orange

ble to select the orange-flowered plants and discard the yellow, a stratagem of little use with the short-lived, if not definitely biennial, Iceland poppies.

Similarly, although there are few orange-flowered selections of polyanthus, it is now usual for this color to be included in mixtures with yellow, pink and red. With these it is not difficult to select the orange-flowered plants and increase them by division after flowering, for they live for several years.

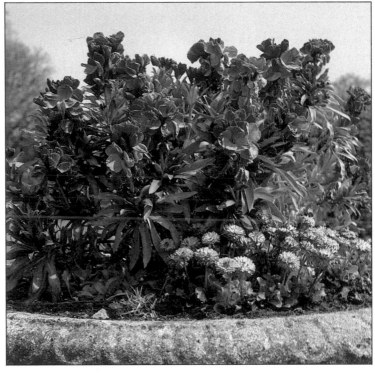

For beautiful shades of orange in late spring *Cheiranthus X allionii* (**left**) has much to offer. The Siberian wallflower thrives in any well-drained soil in a sunny location and should be planted in autumn for color the following spring.

The vivid orange of marigolds such as *Tagetes erecta* 'Orange Jubilee' (**left**) is a bold and useful color for summer bedding schemes and borders.

Crocosmia

Zinnia 'Peter Pan Orange'

Kniphofia galpinii

AUTUMN

Calendula (Pot marigold) *Height:* 30-45cm (12-18in) *Spread:* 25cm (10in) *Soil.* Ordinary *Site:* Open 'Geisha Girl', reddish orange 'Orange King', deep orange 'Radio', deep orange	**Dimorphotheca** (Star of the veldt) *Height:* 30cm (12in) *Spread:* 15cm (6in) *Soil:* Ordinary *Site:* Sunny 'Giant Orange' ('Goliath'), orange	**Tagetes** (Marigold) *Height:* 15-90cm (6-36in) *Spread:* 15-25cm (6-10in) *Soil:* Ordinary *Site:* Sunny 'Apollo', orange 'Orange Lady', deep orange 'Orange Jubilee', light orange *T.signata* 'Tangerine Gem', tangerine	**Rudbeckia hirta** (Coneflower) *Height:* 60cm (24in) *Spread:* 30cm (12in) *Soil:* Ordinary *Site:* Open 'Rustic Dwarf', yellow with bronzy orange	**Tithonia speciosa** (Mexican sunflower) *Height:* 75cm (30in) *Spread:* 25cm (10in) *Soil:* Ordinary *Site:* Sunny Tangerine	**Zinnia** *Height:* 25-60cm (10-24in) *Spread:* 20cm (8in) *Soil:* Ordinary *Site:* Sunny 'Orange Ruffles' 'Peter Pan Orange'
Ixia (African corn lily) *Height:* 40cm (16in) *Spread:* 10cm (4in) *Soil:* Ordinary, well drained *Site:* Sunny, warm 'Afterglow', orange-buff 'Conqueror', orange-red	**Lilium** (Lily) *Height:* 1-1.5m (3½-5ft) *Spread:* 25cm (10in) *Soil:* Acid, no lime *Site:* Sun or dappled shade *L.bulbiferum*, orange *L.davidii willimotiae*, deep red- orange *L.hansonii*, yellow-orange *L.pardalinum*, deep red-orange		**Dahlia** *Height:* 30-100cm (12-39in) *Spread:* 45-90cm (18-36in) *Soil:* Ordinary *Site:* Open 'Jescot Julie', burnt orange and purple 'Shirley Alliance', soft orange 'Sweitzer's Kirkarde', shades of orange	**Lilium** (Lily) *Height:* 1-1.5m (3½-5ft) *Spread:* 25cm (10in) *Soil:* Acid, no lime *Site:* Sun or dappled shade *L.henryi*, pale orange	
Helenium (Sneezewort) *Height:* 90cm (3ft) *Spread:* 30cm (1ft) *Soil:* Ordinary *Site:* Open 'Coppelia', coppery-orange	**Hemerocallis** (Day lily) *Height:* 90cm (3ft) *Spread:* 60cm (2ft) *Soil:* Ordinary *Site:* Open or light shade 'Cartwheels', light orange 'Doubloons', orange 'Kwanso Plena', buff-orange, double flowers	**Ligularia clivorum** *Height:* 90cm (3ft) *Spread:* 60cm (2ft) *Soil:* Ordinary *Site:* Open or light shade 'Desdemona', orange	**Crocosmia** (Montbretia) *Height:* 60-75cm (24-30in) *Spread:* 25cm (10in) *Soil:* Ordinary *Site:* Sunny, warm 'Jackanapes', yellow and orange *C.masonorum*, tangerine	**Kniphofia** (Red hot poker) *Height:* 75-120cm (30-48in) *Spread:* 30-45cm (12-18in) *Soil:* Ordinary *Site:* Open *K.galpinii*, orange 'Loddon Variety', red-orange	
Helianthemum (Sun rose, rock rose) *Height:* 20-40cm (8-16in) *Spread:* 25-45cm (10-18in) *Soil:* Ordinary, alkaline *Site:* Sunny 'Ben Fhada', orange and yellow 'Ben Nevis', coppery orange 'Firedragon' (Mrs Clay), red- orange	**Potentilla** (Shrubby cinquefoil) *Height:* 90cm (3ft) *Spread:* 90cm (3ft) *Soil:* Ordinary *Site:* Open 'Tangerine', light coppery- orange				

Red flowers

There are many different shades of red, from scarlet and vermilion to crimson and magenta, and their effect on the senses is very different. Someone once said that red burned holes in the landscape, but the reference must surely have been to the reds at the yellow end of the range where the colors that are very difficult to assimilate chiefly occur. The bluer reds, including the much maligned magentas, are often much easier to place and far less strident, especially if they are accompanied by a good deal of green.

Of course, stridency may quite legitimately be an end. It can be used to draw the eye to any spot in the garden. If brilliant reds are associated with yellow or white the effect is even more compelling. At Sissinghurst Castle in England the vivid vermilion *Lychnis*

chalcedonica has been used most effectively against a background of *Achillea* 'Coronation Gold', but this was in an area of the garden where nearly all the colors are in the yellow-orange-red range with the intention of producing a gay and stimulating environment. It is no accident that this compartment of the garden is in front of the cottage in which Sir Harold Nicolson had his study, for he liked bright colors, whereas his wife, Vita Sackville-West, who planted it for him, preferred softer, more muted color schemes.

In gardens a scattering of red here and there can create so many different focal points that the result is restless and confusing. It may be preferable to keep such strong colors together and allow them to drift away quite gently into quieter pinks, blues, mauves,

creams and white. But it is always safe to mix greens of any kind with red, except perhaps the sharper lime greens, and this is one very satisfactory way of bringing them into tune with the garden as a whole. It is fortunate that rhododendrons grow best in woodland for there are many intense shades of red among them and these colors are toned down and made acceptable by the dappled shade and also by the predominant greenness of the setting. In Britain it is even more fortunate that the only rhododendron species that has found the climate so congenial that it has leapt the garden fence and naturalized itself extensively in the countryside, is *rhododendron ponticum* with its relatively quiet color range in the blue-mauves and light purples.

Many plants used in bedding schemes are

Malus

Tulip

Escallonia

Gladiolus

Embothrium coccineum

Pelargonium zonale

	SPRING			SUMMER		
ANNUALS/BEDDING	**Dianthus barbatus** (Sweet William) *Height:* 45cm (18in) *Spread:* 25cm (10in) *Soil:* Ordinary *Site:* Open 'Messenger Scarlet' 'Scarlet Beauty'	**Matthiola incana** (East Lothian stocks) *Height:* 45cm (18in) *Spread:* 25cm (10in) *Soil:* Ordinary, well drained *Site:* Sunny, sheltered 'Kelvedon Crimson' 'Kelvedon Scarlet'	**Polyanthus** *Height:* 20cm (8in) *Spread:* 15cm (6in) *Soil:* Ordinary *Site:* Sun, or moderate shade 'Monarch Scarlet'	**Antirrhinum** (Snapdragon) *Height:* 20-40cm (8-16in) *Spread:* 15-25cm (6-10in) *Soil:* Ordinary *Site:* Open 'Regal Bright Scarlet' 'Regal Crimson'	**Begonia semperflorens** *Height:* 25cm (10in) *Spread:* 15cm (6in) *Soil:* Ordinary *Site:* Open 'Danica Rose' 'Danica Scarlet'	**Dianthus caryophyllus** (Carnation) *Height:* 45cm (18in) *Spread:* 25cm (10in) *Soil:* Ordinary with lime *Site:* Open 'Crimson Knight' 'Scarlet Knight'
BULBS	**Anemone blanda** *Height:* 10cm (4in) *Spread:* 10cm (4in) *Soil:* Ordinary *Site:* Sun, or light shade 'Radar', carmine and white	**Hyacinth** *Height:* 25cm (10in) *Spread:* 15cm (6in) *Soil:* Ordinary *Site:* Open 'Jan Bos', carmine 'Tubergen's Scarlet'	**Tulip** *Height:* 30-60cm (1-2ft) *Spread:* 10cm (4in) *Soil:* Ordinary *Site:* Open 'Apeldoorn', scarlet 'Electra', carmine 'Holland's Glory', orange red 'Red Riding Hood', signal red	**Allium sphaerocephalum** *Height:* 60cm (2ft) *Spread:* 10cm (4in) *Soil:* Ordinary *Site:* Open Red, maroon	**Gladiolus** *Height:* 60-90cm (2-3ft) *Spread:* 20cm (8in) *Soil:* Ordinary *Site:* Open 'Firestone', vermilion 'Oscar', crimson	**Lilium** (Lily) *Height:* 75cm (30in) *Spread:* 25cm (10in) *Soil:* Ordinary, with added peat *Site:* Sun or dappled shade 'Cinnabar', deep red 'Enchantment', nasturtium red 'Lilium Tigrinum', orange-red
PERENNIALS	**Bergenia** *Height:* 30cm (12in) *Spread:* 45cm (18in) *Soil:* Ordinary *Site:* Sun or shade 'Abendglut', rosy red 'Ballawley', crimson	**Paeonia officinalis** (Peony) *Height:* 75cm (2½ft) *Spread:* 45cm (18in) *Soil:* Ordinary, rich *Site:* Open 'Rubra Plena', deep crimson	**Viola** *Height:* 10cm (4in) *Spread:* 15cm (6in) *Soil:* Ordinary *Site:* Sun or partial shade 'Arkwright's Ruby', mahogany red and maroon	**Astilbe** *Height:* 45-60cm (18-24in) *Spread:* 30cm (12in) *Soil:* Ordinary, moist *Site:* Sun or light shade 'Fanal', crimson 'Jo Ophorst', ruby-red	**Geum** *Height:* 60cm (2ft) *Spread:* 20cm (10in) *Soil:* Ordinary *Site:* Open 'Mrs Bradshaw', signal red	**Hemerocallis** (Day lily) *Height:* 90cm (3ft) *Spread:* 45cm (18in) *Soil:* Ordinary *Site:* Open or light shade 'Stafford', bright mahogany red
SHRUBS/TREES	**Azalea, deciduous** *Height:* 1.5m (5ft) *Spread:* 1.5m (5ft) *Soil:* Acid, no lime *Site:* Sun, or dappled shade 'Coccinea Speciosa', orange-red 'Dr M. Oosthoek', deep orange-red 'Royal Command', vermilion	**Malus** (Crab apple) *Height:* 4.5-6m (15-20ft) *Spread:* 3.5-4.5m (12-15ft) *Soil:* Ordinary *Site:* Open 'Lemoinei', deep carmine 'Profusion', wine-red	**Ribes sanguineum** (Flowering currant) *Height:* 2-2.5m (6½-8ft) *Soil:* Ordinary *Site:* Sun or shade 'Pulborough Scarlet', light crimson	**Cistus** (Rock rose) *Height:* 60-100cm (2-3½ft) *Spread:* 45-60cm (1½-2ft) *Soil:* Ordinary or alkaline *Site:* Warm, sunny 'Purpureus', carmine and maroon 'Sunset', deep magenta	**Escallonia** *Height:* 2.5-3m (8-10ft) *Spread:* 2.5-2.5m (6½-8ft) *Soil:* Ordinary *Site:* Sunny, sheltered 'Crimson Spire', crimson 'Donard Brilliance', rose red	**Embothrium coccineum** (Fire bush) *Height:* 4-6m (13-20ft) *Spread:* 2.5-3m (8-10ft) *Soil:* Acid, no lime *Site:* Sunny, sheltered 'Lanceolatum', deep scarlet

red; tulips in the spring, geraniums, begonias, scarlet salvias and numerous others in the summer. Many of these plants come from much warmer countries than the cool temperate regions in which they are planted, and they do bring an exotic warmth that can be welcome in the formal, obviously man-made settings in which bedding plants are commonly used.

Salvia 'Blaze of Fire' (**right**) is an apt name for this extremely popular bedding plant. It bears bright scarlet blooms from mid-summer until autumn on stems 30cm (12in) high. The exquisite flowers of *Tulipa* 'Red Riding Hood' (**left**) are borne in mid-spring above beautifully variegated foliage. This 20cm (8in) tulip is an excellent choice for rockeries. Plant the bulbs in late autumn in well-drained soil. A sunny sheltered spot will suit them.

 Fuchsia

 Lychnis

 Weigela

 Dahlia

 Aster novi-belgii

 Schizostylis

AUTUMN

Pelargonium zonale (Zonal-leaved geranium) *Height:* 45cm (18in) *Spread:* 30cm (12in) *Soil:* Ordinary *Site:* Sunny 'Sprinter', scarlet 'Vulcan', dark red	**Impatiens sultanii** (Busy Lizzie) *Height:* 15-20cm (6-8in) *Spread:* 20-25cm (8-10in) *Soil:* Ordinary *Site:* Sun or shade 'Blitz', orange-scarlet 'Carmine Baby', carmine	**Petunia** *Height:* 23cm (9in) *Spread:* 23cm (9in) *Soil:* Ordinary *Site:* Sunny 'Dwarf Resisto Scarlet' 'Red Cloud', deep scarlet	**Callistephus** (Annual aster) *Height:* 25-60cm (10-24in) *Spread:* 25cm (10in) *Soil:* Ordinary *Site:* Open or semi-shade 'Milady Rose Red'	**Salvia splendens** *Height:* 30cm (12in) *Spread:* 25cm (10in) *Soil:* Ordinary *Site:* Sunny 'Blaze of Fire', scarlet	**Verbena** *Height:* 15cm (6in) *Spread:* 30cm (12in) *Soil:* Ordinary *Site:* Sunny 'Blaze', scarlet 'Sparkle', scarlet and white
			Dahlia *Height:* 30-90cm (1-3ft) *Spread:* 45-90cm (1½-3ft) *Soil:* Ordinary *Site:* Open 'Bacchus', blood red 'Majuba', cardinal red	**Schizostylis** (Kaffir lily) *Height:* 45cm (18in) *Spread:* 23cm (9in) *Soil:* Ordinary *Site:* Sunny, warm *S. coccinea* 'Major', deep scarlet	
Lychnis *Height:* 60-90cm (2-3ft) *Spread:* 30cm (12in) *Soil:* Ordinary *Site:* Sunny *L. chalcedonica*, scarlet *L. coronaria*, deep magenta	**Paeonia lactiflora** (Chinese peony) *Height:* 70-90cm (2½-3ft) *Spread:* 45cm (18in) *Soil:* Ordinary *Site:* Sunny 'Felix Crousse', carmine 'Mons. Martin Cahuzac', crimson	**Papaver orientale** (Oriental poppy) *Height:* 75cm (2½ft) *Spread:* 45cm (18in) *Soil:* Ordinary *Site:* Sunny 'Goliath', light crimson 'Marcus Perry', scarlet and black	**Aster novi-belgii** (Michaelmas daisy) *Height:* 30-90cm (1-3ft) *Spread:* 45-60cm (18-24in) *Soil:* Ordinary *Site:* Sun or light shade 'Carnival', deep carmine 'Freda Ballard', deep red 'Winston S. Churchill', carmine	**Lobelia cardinalis** *Height:* 60cm (2ft) *Spread:* 30cm (12in) *Soil:* Ordinary, rather moist *Site:* Open or light shade *L. cardinalis*, grenadier red 'Queen Victoria', light crimson	**Phlox** *Height:* 90cm (3ft) *Spread:* 30-40cm (12-16in) *Soil:* Ordinary *Site:* Sun or light shade 'Brigadier', orange-red 'Starfire', deep red
Fuchsia *Height:* 30-100cm (1-3½ft) *Spread:* 25-60cm (10-24in) *Soil:* Ordinary *Site:* Sunny, sheltered 'Margaret', scarlet and violet 'Mrs Popple', signal red and violet 'Rufus', bright red	**Spiraea japonica** *Height:* 1.2m (4ft) *Spread:* 1.5m (5ft) *Soil:* Ordinary *Site:* Open 'Anthony Waterer', carmine	**Weigela** *Height:* 1.5-2.5m (5-8ft) *Spread:* 1.2-2m (4-6½ft) *Soil:* Ordinary *Site:* Open 'Bristol Ruby', deep carmine	**Hebe** (Shrubby veronica) *Height:* 1-1.5m (3½-5ft) *Spread:* 1-1.2m (3½-4ft) *Soil:* Ordinary *Site:* Sunny, sheltered 'Simon Delaux', crimson	**Hydrangea macrophylla** *Height:* 1.5-2m (5-6½ft) *Spread:* 1-1.2m (3½-4ft) *Soil:* Alkaline for red flowers *Site:* Sun, or semi-shade 'Hamburg', rose-red deepening to crimson 'Westfalen', carmine	

flowers

There are a great many plants with pink flowers — yet no one ever seems to make a pink garden or even a pink border. Perhaps it is too miscellaneous a color for that, scarcely a true color in its own right but paler versions of red, red-purple and orange-red. The first gives the true pinks, such as that of apple blossom and dog roses; the second the mallow pinks, carmine pinks, lilac pinks and mauve pinks; the third the salmon pinks, peach pinks and shell pinks. All these are essentially link colors, admirable for blending the stronger hues into the overall color scheme whatever that may be. In general it seems wise to use them either in harmonies with other colours closely related to them — the mauve pinks with the blues and the salmon pinks with the oranges rather than the other way around—or,

alternatively, as strong contrast: soft pink London Pride with blue primroses and polyanthuses or purple tulips, salmon pink roses with the deepest blue delphiniums.

Yet, even after all this, it remains true that most pinks are easy to handle, unaggressive, and so unlikely to produce strong reactions from those who view them. The addition of white makes them even more harmless yet agreeable particularly, for example, when *Lavatera* 'Silver Cup' and *L.* 'Mont Blanc' are planted together. Carpets of pink *Claytonia sibirica* can be made in thin woodland or beneath groups of deciduous trees with white and mauve wood anemones and the fuller blue of bluebells, either British or Spanish, without raising an eyebrow. The worst that could be said of such schemes is that they are pretty

Anemone 'Albert Schweitzer'

Rhododendron 'Pink Pearl'

Camellia x williamsii 'Donation'

Astilbe x arendsii

Escallonia 'Apple Blossom'

Geranium endressii 'Wargrave Pink'

	SPRING				SUMMER	
ANNUALS/BEDDING	**Matthiola incana** (East Lothian stocks) *Height:* 45cm (18in) *Spread:* 25cm (10in) *Soil:* Ordinary, well drained *Site:* Sunny, sheltered 'Kelvedon Exquisite', pink	**Myosotis** (Forget-me-not) *Height:* 25-30cm (10-12in) *Spread:* 20cm (8in) *Soil:* Ordinary *Site:* Sun or shade 'Carmine King', rose-pink	**Polyanthus** *Height:* 25cm (10in) *Spread:* 15cm (6in) *Soil:* Ordinary *Site:* Sun or moderate shade 'Pacific Giants Pink', shades of pink 'Triumph Pink', shades of pink		**Antirrhinum** (Snapdragon) *Height:* 38-45cm (15-18in) *Spread:* 23cm (9in) *Soil:* Ordinary *Site:* Open 'Coral Monarch' coral-pink 'Regal Rose', rose-pink	**Cleome spinosa** (Spider flower) *Height:* 90cm (36in) *Spread:* 25cm (10in) *Soil:* Ordinary *Site:* Open 'Rose Queen', rose-pink
BULBS	**Anemone blanda** (Windflower) *Height:* 10-15cm (4-6in) *Spread:* 10cm (4in) *Soil:* Ordinary *Site:* Sun or partial shade 'Charmer', clear pink	**Hyacinth** *Height:* 25cm (10in) *Spread:* 15cm (6in) *Soil:* Ordinary *Site:* Sunny 'Anna Marie', bright pink 'Lady Derby', rose-pink 'Pink Pearl', carmine-pink	**Scilla campanulata** (Spanish bluebell) *Height:* 38cm (15in) *Spread:* 15cm (6in) *Soil:* Ordinary *Site:* Sun or shade 'Rosea', soft pink	**Tulip** *Height:* 20-60cm (8-24in) *Spread:* 10cm (4in) *Soil:* Ordinary *Site:* Open 'Clara Butt', salmon-rose 'Elizabeth Arden', salmon-pink 'Mariette', bright rose-pink 'Peach Blossom', deep pink	**Allium** *Height:* 20-38cm (8-15in) *Spread:* 10cm (4in) *Soil:* Ordinary *Site:* Open *A.cernuum*, soft rose-pink *A.ostrowskianum*, purplish pink	**Gladiolus** *Height:* 60-90cm (24-36in) *Spread:* 20cm (8in) *Soil:* Ordinary *Site:* Open 'Columbine', soft pink and white 'Delacroix', pink and red 'Miss America', deep pink 'Peter Pears', shrimp-pink
PERENNIALS	**Arabis caucasica** (Rock cress) *Height:* 15cm (6in) *Spread:* 30cm (12in) *Soil:* Ordinary, alkaline *Site:* Open 'Rosabella', soft pink	**Bergenia** *Height:* 30cm (12in) *Spread:* 45cm (18in) *Soil:* Ordinary *Site:* Sun or shade *B.cordifolia*, mauve-pink *B.purpurascens*, deep-pink *B.schmidtii*, light pink	**Paeonia officinalis** (Peony) *Height:* 75cm (30in) *Spread:* 45cm (18in) *Soil:* Ordinary *Site:* Open 'Rosea Superba', rose-pink	**Saxifraga urbium** (London pride) *Height:* 30cm (12in) *Spread:* 25cm (10in) *Soil:* Ordinary *Site:* Open or shady Soft pink	**Astilbe** *Height:* 45-60cm (18-24in) *Spread:* 30cm (12in) *Soil:* Ordinary, moist *Site:* Sun or light shade 'Betsy Cuperus, pale pink 'Bressingham Beauty', warm pink 'Ostrich Plume', coral-pink	**Dianthus plumarius allwoodii** (Pinks) *Height:* 15-30cm (6-12in) *Spread:* 25cm (10in) *Soil:* Ordinary, alkaline *Site:* Open 'Doris', soft salmon-pink and rose 'Excelsior', rose-pink 'Inchmery', pale pink
SHRUBS/TREES	**Azalea, evergreen** *Height:* 1-1.2m (3½-4ft) *Spread:* 1-1.2m (3½-4ft) *Soil:* Acid, no lime *Site:* Dappled shade 'Blaauw's Pink', light cerise pink 'Fedora', deep pink 'Hinomayo', soft pink 'Kirin', deep rose 'Rosebud', rose-pink	**Camellia** *Height:* 2-2.4m (6½-8ft) *Spread:* 1.2-1.5m (4-5ft) *Soil:* Moderately acid *Site:* Dappled or half shade 'Anticipation', deep rose 'Debbie', rose-pink 'Donation', orchid-pink 'Elegans', peach-pink	**Prunus** (Cherry) *Height:* 3-6m (10-20ft) *Spread:* 1-6m (3½-20ft) *Soil:* Ordinary *Site:* Open 'Accolade', pale rose-pink 'Amanogawa', shell pink 'Kanzan', purplish pink 'Pink Perfection', bright rose-pink	**Rhododendron** *Height:* 1.2-3m (4-10ft) *Spread:* 1.2-2.5m (4-8ft) *Soil:* Acid, no lime *Site:* Open or dappled shade 'Betty Wormald', deep rose-pink 'Bow Bells', silvery pink 'Cynthia', deep rose 'Mrs G. W. Leak', rose-crimson 'Pink Pearl', lilac-pink	**Cistus** (Rock rose) *Height:* 60-100cm (2-3½ft) *Spread:* 60-100cm (2-3½ft) *Soil:* Ordinary or alkaline *Site:* Sunny *C.albidus*, rose *C.* 'Silver Pink', soft pink *C.skanbergii*, clear pink	**Clematis** (Virgin's bower) *Height:* 2.5-3m (8-10ft) *Spread:* 150cm (5ft) *Soil:* Ordinary, alkaline *Site:* Open 'Comtesse de Bouchard', light rose-pink 'Hagley Hybrid', shell pink

The funnel flowers of *Sidalcea* 'Rose Queen' (**left**) appear from early summer until early autumn on stems 75cm (30in) tall. Color is used to good effect in this classic garden setting (**right**). Against a bold background of foliage plants of various shapes and hues phlox and roses provide the key color interest in shades of pink.

rather than exciting, and that the gardener who makes them may be described as playing safe rather than playing to the gallery.

The public reaction to pink flowers is ambiguous. Rose growers report that there is greater demand for red and yellow roses than for pink, although no tulip has ever been more popular than 'Clara Butt' (usually planted with a groundwork of forget-me-nots), which the lovely glowing pink lily-flowered tulip 'Mariette' looks set to rival. Probably the most popular of all Chinese peonies is 'Sarah Bernhardt' which is apple-blossom pink. And everyone rejoices when the pink-flowered Japanese cherries bloom in spring, particularly Kanzan, which has been so freely planted that there is now an élite opposition to it on the grounds that it is too common.

Hemerocallis 'Pink Damask'

Kolkwitzia amabilis 'Pink Cloud'

Petunia 'Resisto Rose'

Calluna vulgaris

Colchicum speciosum

Sedum spectabile 'Autumn Joy'

AUTUMN

Godetia
Height: 30cm (12in)
Spread: 15cm (6in)
Soil: Ordinary
Site: Sun or light shade
'Sybil Sherwood', salmon pink

Lavatera rosea
Height: 75cm (30in)
Spread: 45cm (18in)
Soil: Ordinary
Site: Open
'Silver Cup', rose-pink

Petunia
Height: 23-30cm (9-12in)
Spread: 23cm (9in)
Soil: Ordinary
Site: Sunny
'Pink Satin', soft pink
'Resisto Rose', rose-pink

Aster
Height: 25cm (10in)
Spread: 20cm (8in)
Soil: Ordinary
Site: Sun or shade
'Meteor', rose-pink
'Mllady Rose'
'Pink Magic', light pink

Lilium
(Lily)
Height: 1.5m (5ft)
Spread: 30cm (12in)
Soil: Acid
Site: Open or dappled shade
'Pink Perfection', mauve-pink

Colchicum speciosum
Height: 15cm (6in)
Spread: 15cm (6in)
Soil: Ordinary
Site: Open or light shade
Lilac-pink

Dahlia
Height: 30-100cm (12-39in)
Spread: 45-90cm (18-36in)
Soil: Ordinary
Site: Open
'Cherrio', deep cerise
'Gerrie Hock', silvery pink
'Piper's Pink', deep pink
'Richard Marc', bright pink and lemon

Nerine bowdenii
Height: 60cm (24in)
Spread: 25cm (10in)
Soil: Ordinary, well drained
Site: Sunny, warm
Deep rose-pink

Geranium endressii
Height: 40cm (16in)
Spread: 45cm (18in)
Soil: Ordinary
Site: Open or light shade
'Wargrave Pink', baby-pink

Hemerocallis
(Day lily)
Height: 90cm (3ft)
Spread: 45cm (18in)
Soil: Ordinary
Site: Open
'Pink Damask', buff-pink

Sidalcea
Height: 75-120cm (30-48in)
Spread: 30cm (12in)
Soil: Ordinary
Site: Open
'Loveliness', shell-pink
'Rose Queen', mallow-pink

Anemone hybrida
(Japanese windflower)
Height: 60cm (24in)
Spread: 25cm (10in)
Soil: Ordinary
Site: Sun or shade
'Bressingham Glow', deep rose-pink
'Lady Gilmour', light pink

Aster novae angliae and A.novii belgii
(Michaelmas daisy)
Height: 30-90cm (12-36in)
Spread: 25-30cm (10-12in)
Soil: Ordinary
Site: Sun or shade
'Alma Potschke', salmon-pink or rose
'Fellowship', mid pink
'Harrington's Pink', baby-pink
'Patricia Ballard', purplish pink

Sedum spectabile
Height: 45cm (18in)
Spread: 30cm (12in)
Soil: Ordinary
Site: Sunny
'Autumn Joy', salmon-rose deepening to coppery rose
'Brilliant', rose-pink

Escallonia
Height: 2.5-3m (8-10ft)
Spread: 1.2-2m (4-6½ft)
Soil: Ordinary
Site: Sunny, sheltered
'Apple Blossom', pink and white
'Edinensis', pale pink
'Langleyensis', muted rose-pink

Kolkwitzia amabilis
(Beauty bush)
Height: 2.4-3m (8-10ft)
Spread: 120-150cm (4-5ft)
Soil: Ordinary
Site: Open
Clear pink and cream

Lavatera olbia
(Tree mallow)
Height: 1.5-2m (5-6½ft)
Spread: 1-1.2m (3-4ft)
Soil: Ordinary, well drained
Site: Sunny
'Rosea', bright rose-pink

Calluna vulgaris
(Heather, ling)
Height: 23-60cm (9-24in)
Spread: 23-30cm (9-12in)
Soil: Acid, no lime
Site: Open
'H. E. Beale', light pink
'Peter Sparkes', deep pink

Ceanothus delineanus
(Californian lilac, mountain sweet)
Height: 2m (6½ft)
Spread: 1m (3½ft)
Soil: Ordinary
Site: Sunny, sheltered
'Perle Rose', rose-pink

Hebe
(Shrubby veronica)
Height: 90-120cm (3-4ft)
Spread: 60-90cm (2-3ft)
Soil: Ordinary
Site: Sunny, sheltered
'Carnea', light rose-pink
'Great Orme', rose-pink

Violet and purple flowers

The hinterland between blue and red is occupied by the wide range of purples and violets. There is, of course, no hard and fast line drawn at either end of this great band of colors beyond which one can say that one is a blue, not a blue-purple, or that another is a red not a red-purple. Each of us registers colors in our own individual way, and classifies them accordingly. But it is equally true that all violets and purples contain some elements of both blue and red. They can be made by combining white light of varying intensity passed through red and blue filters, or they can be mixed on an artist's palette with varying proportions of blue and red paint.

But having said that, one has still told only a small part of the story, for violet and purple colors — like all the others — are subject to an

infinite number of variations produced by other agencies which dull or brighten the color or modify it in other ways. There are some flowers that are such a dark purple as to appear almost black; such flowers can be found among both hellebores and tulips, such as the one well named 'Queen of Night'. The iris family is also good at producing these very dark colors; they turn up frequently in the fritillaries. Right at the other end of the scale are the very light violets and purples to which we give such names as mauve, lilac and lavender.

Deep purple is a rich color to handle in the garden — one can easily have too much of it — but in moderation it is highly valuable. It is not perceived as sharply as red or yellow, and so can be used to give dark shades to color com-

positions and to tone down colors that might otherwise claim too much attention. These dark purples and the lighter shades of purple and violet are blending colors useful in linking more clamorous colors with the greens and browns that almost invariably form the background and carpet of the garden. Light blue irises look even more delightful when planted with mahogany red *Viola* 'Arkwright's Ruby' and lilac purple *Allium christophii*, a combination in which all the colors are muted and the effect is totally restful. Equally harmonious is an association of purple irises with violet-blue hardy geraniums and sulphur yellow *Alchemilla mollis*. There is really no end to the satisfying combinations that can be devised using purple and violet as the unifying colors.

 Aubrieta

 Magnolia liliiflora 'Nigra'

 Erica

 Cheiranthus cheiri

 Primula denticulata

 Syringa

	SPRING				SUMMER	
ANNUALS/BEDDING	**Cheiranthus cheiri** (Wallflower) *Height:* 25-45cm (10-18in) *Spread:* 20-25m (8-10in) *Soil:* Ordinary *Site:* Sunny 'Ruby Gem', ruby-violet	**Matthiola incana** (East Lothian stocks) *Height:* 45cm (18in) *Spread:* 25cm (10in) *Soil:* Ordinary *Site:* Sunny, sheltered 'Kelvedon Purple'	**Lunaria biennis** (Honesty) *Height:* 90cm (3ft) *Soil:* Ordinary *Site:* Open or light shade Red-purple		**Alyssum maritimum** *Height:* 10cm (4in) *Spread:* 15cm (6in) *Soil:* Ordinary *Site:* Open 'Royal Carpet', deep violet-purple 'Wonderland', red-purple	**Amaranthus caudatus** (Love-lies-bleeding) *Height:* 75cm (30in) *Spread:* 30cm (1ft) *Soil:* Ordinary *Site:* Open Crimson-purple
BULBS	**Allium** *Height:* 60-90cm (2-3ft) *Spread:* 10cm (4in) *Soil:* Ordinary *Site:* Sunny A. aflatuenense, deep blue-purple A. christophii, lilac purple	**Crocus** *Height:* 10m (4in) *Spread:* 8cm (3¼in) *Soil:* Ordinary *Site:* Open or light shade 'Pickwick', heliotrope and white 'Remembrance', deep blue-purple	**Tulip** *Height:* 38-71cm (15-28in) *Spread:* 20cm (8in) *Soil:* Ordinary *Site:* Open 'Bleu Aimable', lilac-mauve and violet-purple 'Maytime', lilac-purple 'Purple Star', red-purple 'Queen of the Night', deep maroon-purple		**Brodiaea laxa** *Height:* 45cm (18in) *Spread:* 10cm (4in) *Soil:* Ordinary, well drained *Site:* Sunny, warm Violet-purple	**Gladiolus** *Height:* 60-90cm (2-3ft) *Spread:* 20m (8in) *Soil:* Ordinary *Site:* Open 'Blue Conqueror', blue-purple 'Blue Isle', petunia purple G. byzantinus, magenta
PERENNIALS	**Aubrieta** *Height:* 15cm (6in) *Spread:* 25m (10in) *Soil:* Ordinary, alkaline *Site:* Open 'Dr Mules', deep violet-purple 'Greencourt Purple', violet-purple	**Phlox** *Height:* 10-15cm (4-6in) *Spread:* 15cm (6in) *Soil:* Ordinary *Site:* Open P. douglasii 'Waterloo', red-purple P. subulata 'Temiscaming', red-purple	**Pansy** *Height:* 10cm (4in) *Spread:* 15m (6in) *Soil:* Ordinary *Site:* Sun or shade 'Clear Crystals', violet-blue, deep blue-purple with black blotch 'Prince Henry', violet-purple	**Primula** (Primrose) *Height:* 15cm (6in) *Spread:* 15cm (6in) *Soil:* Ordinary *Site:* Open or light shade P. denticulata, blue-mauve 'Wanda', red-purple	**Aconitum** (Monkshood) *Height:* 90cm (3ft) *Spread:* 30cm (1ft) *Soil:* Ordinary *Site:* Sun or shade 'Bressingham Spire', blue-violet 'Spark's Variety', deep blue-purple	**Agapanthus** (African lily) *Height:* 45-90cm (18-36in) *Spread:* 45cm (18in) *Soil:* Ordinary *Site:* Sunny, sheltered 'Headbourne Hybrid', light to deep violet
SHRUBS/TREES	**Daphne** *Height:* 60-90cm (2-3ft) *Spread:* 45-60cm (18-24in) *Soil:* Ordinary with peat *Site:* Open D. collina, blue-purple D. mezereum, red-purple	**Erica** (Heath, heather) *Height:* 15-25cm (6-10in) *Spread:* 25cm (10in) *Soil:* Ordinary *Site:* Open E. carnea 'King George', red-purple E. carnea 'Vivellii', red-purple E. darleyensis, rosy purple E. mediterranea, red-purple	**Magnolia** *Height:* 2.5-4.5m (8-15ft) *Spread:* 2-4m (6½-13ft) *Soil:* Moderately acid *Site:* Open or dappled shade M. liliiflora 'Nigra', deep reddish purple M. soulangeana 'Lennei', rose-purple	**Syringa** (Lilac) *Height:* 1-4m (3¼-13ft) *Spread:* 1-2.5m (4-8ft) *Soil:* Ordinary *Site:* Open 'Charles Joly', deep reddish purple 'Katherine Havemeyer', lavender-purple S. microphylla, blue-lilac	**Abutilon** *Height:* 3-5m (10-16½ft) *Spread:* 1.5m (5ft) *Soil:* Ordinary *Site:* Sunny, sheltered A. suntense, blue-violet A. vitifolium, light mauve	**Buddleia** (Butterfly bush) *Height:* 2.4-3m (8-10ft) *Spread:* 2m (6½ft) *Soil:* Ordinary, alkaline *Site:* Open 'Black Knight', dark violet-purple 'Royal Purple', plum purple

The rich purple blooms of *Clematis* 'Jackmanii Superba' (**left**) appear from mid-summer until early autumn on twining stems that reach over 3m (10ft) high on suitable supports. This is one of the popular large-flowered hybrids. Lavender (**right**) provides a summer harvest of delicate violet flowers with the added bonus of a superb fragrance. Even the gray-green foliage of this charming plant is aromatic.

Abutilon suntense

Amaranthus caudatus

Clematis 'The President'

Clematis 'Barbara Jackman' *Geranium*

Salvia splendens

AUTUMN

Echium plantagineum *Height:* 30cm (12in) *Spread:* 23cm (9in) *Soil:* Ordinary *Site:* Open Blue-purple	**Heliotropium peruvianum** (Heliotrope) *Height:* 38-45cm (15-18in) *Spread:* 25cm (10in) *Soil:* Ordinary *Site:* Open 'Marine', violet-purple	**Petunia** *Height:* 23-30cm (9-12in) *Spread:* 23cm (9in) *Soil:* Ordinary *Site:* Sunny, warm 'Marina', deep blue-violet 'Resisto Blue', deep blue-violet	**Salvia splendens** *Height:* 30cm (1ft) *Spread:* 25cm (10in) *Soil:* Ordinary *Site:* Sunny 'Royal Purple', deep blue-purple		
			Colchicum speciosum *Height:* 15cm (6in) *Spread:* 8cm (3¼in) *Soil:* Ordinary *Site:* Open or light shade 'Lilac Wonder', amethyst	**Dahlia** *Height:* 30-100cm (1-3¼ft) *Spread:* 45-90cm (18-36in) *Soil:* Ordinary *Site:* Open 'Carousel', deep purple 'Hallmark', pink-lavender 'Hamari Girl', pink-lavender 'Lavengro', deep lavender and bronze 'Reveille', red-maroon and white	
Delphinium (Larkspur) *Height:* 90-180cm (3-6ft) *Spread:* 45cm (18in) *Soil:* Ordinary *Site:* Open 'Black Knight', deep blue-purple 'Nimrod', royal purple 'Strawberry Fair', mulberry purple	**Erigeron** (Fleabane) *Height:* 45-60m (18-24in) *Spread:* 30-45cm (12-18in) *Soil:* Ordinary *Site:* Open 'Darkest of All', deep violet 'Foerster's Liebling', red-purple	**Geranium** *Height:* 25-30cm (10-12in) *Spread:* 30cm (12in) *Soil:* Ordinary, alkaline *Site:* Sun or partial shade *G. himalayense* (grandiflorum), deep violet-blue *G. pratense* 'Plenum Coeruleum', lavender, double flowers	**Aster novi-belgii** (Michaelmas daisy) *Height:* 30-90cm (1-3ft) *Spread:* 25-30cm (10-12in) *Soil:* Ordinary *Site:* Sun or light shade 'Coombe Rosemary', violet-purple 'Gayborder Royal', crimson-purple 'Jenny', violet-purple	**Liriope muscari** *Height:* 30cm (1ft) *Spread:* 25cm (10in) *Soil:* Ordinary *Site:* Sunny Violet-mauve	**Phlox** *Height:* 60-90cm (2-3ft) *Spread:* 30cm (1ft) *Soil:* Ordinary *Site:* Sun or shade 'Aida', crimson-purple 'Hampton Court', heliotrope 'Vintage Wine', red-purple
Clematis (Virgin's bower) *Height:* 2.5-3m (8-10ft) *Spread:* 1.5m (5ft) *Soil:* Ordinary, alkaline *Site:* Open 'Barbara Jackman', blue and petunia purple 'Jackmanii Superba', deep blue-purple 'The President', deep blue-purple			**Calluna vulgaris** (Heather, ling) *Height:* 20-60m (8-24in) *Spread:* 23-30cm (9-12in) *Soil:* Acid, no lime *Site:* Open 'Mullion', light purple 'Robert Chapman', light purple	**Clematis** (Virgin's bower) *Height:* 2.5-3m (8-10ft) *Spread:* 1.5m (5ft) *Soil:* Ordinary, alkaline *Site:* Open 'Kermesina', red-purple 'Royal Velours', deep purple	**Hebe** (Shrubby veronica) *Height:* 60-180cm (2-6ft) *Spread:* 60-90cm (2-3ft) *Soil:* Ordinary *Site:* Sunny, sheltered 'Autumn Glory', violet-purple 'Carl Teschner', deep violet-purple 'Midsummer Beauty', lavender purple

Blue flowers

Blue is sometimes described as a 'depressing' color, but 'relaxing' would be both kinder and nearer to the truth. Borders devoted almost entirely to blue are an attractive and restful feature of many gardens. But almost invariably the description is interpreted broadly to include related colors in the violet-purple range, and possibly some grey, silver and white as well.

Both yellow and white liven up blue in a striking but quite different way, as may be seen by comparing flowers which actually combine them, for example blue polyanthus and *Chionodoxa luciliae*. The polyanthuses almost always have a yellow eye, which both warms and brightens the flowers, whereas the chionodoxa has a white center which makes it even cooler than it would be without it. It is

In late winter and early spring the charming blue, white-centered flowers of *Chionodoxa luciliae* (**left**) brighten the garden with their color. Growing only 15cm (6in) high, this bulbous plant is excellent for growing at the front of the border. *Meconopsis betonicifolia* (**right**) bears these striking blue flowers up to 7.5cm (3in) across in mid-summer. Grow in a semi-shaded sheltered spot. Water freely in summer.

Anemone blanda 'Blue Pearl'

Rhododendron 'Susan'

Hyacinthus orientalis 'Ostara'

Veronica gentianoides

Wisteria floribunda 'Macrobotrys'

Muscari armeniacum 'Heavenly Blue'

	SPRING			SUMMER	
ANNUALS/BEDDING	**Myosotis** (Forget-me-not) *Height:* 25-30cm (10-12in) *Spread:* 20cm (8in) *Soil:* Ordinary *Site:* Sun or shade 'Royal Blue', deep blue	**Pansy** *Height:* 15-23cm (6-9in) *Spread:* 15cm (6in) *Soil:* Ordinary *Site:* Sun or moderate shade 'Azure Blue', sky blue 'Blue Bedder', dark blue 'Clear Crystals'	**Polyanthus** *Height:* 15-25cm (6-10in) *Spread:* 15cm (6in) *Soil:* Ordinary *Site:* Sun or moderate shade 'Pacific Giant', blue shades	**Ageratum** *Height:* 10-45cm (4-18in) *Spread:* 15cm (6in) *Soil:* Ordinary *Site:* Open *A.houstianum*, soft blue 'Blue Danube', violet-blue 'Blue Mink', soft blue	**Anchusa capensis** *Height:* 23cm (9in) *Spread:* 23cm (9in) *Soil:* Ordinary *Site:* Open 'Blue Angel', ultramarine
BULBS	**Anemone blanda** *Height:* 10-15cm (4-6in) *Spread:* 10cm (4in) *Soil:* Ordinary *Site:* Sun or light shade *Atrocoerulea*, deep blue	**Chionodoxa** (Glory of the snow) *Height:* 10-15cm (4-6in) *Spread:* 10-15cm (4-6in) *Soil:* Ordinary *Site:* Open *C.gigantea*, pale blue *C.luciliae*, sky blue and white	**Hyacinth** *Height:* 25cm (10in) *Spread:* 15cm (6in) *Soil:* Ordinary *Site:* Open 'Delft Blue', light blue 'King of the Blues', medium blue 'Ostara', deep blue	**Muscari** (Grape hyacinth) *Height:* 15cm (6in) *Spread:* 8cm (3¼in) *Soil:* Ordinary *Site:* Open or light shade 'Blue Spike', light blue 'Heavenly Blue', gentian blue *M. tubergeniana*, dark and light blue	**Allium coeruleum** *Height:* 60cm (2ft) *Spread:* 10cm (4in) *Soil:* Ordinary *Site:* Sun Deep cornflower blue	**Iris xiphium** (Dutch iris) *Height:* 75cm (30in) *Spread:* 10cm (4in) *Soil:* Ordinary *Site:* Open 'Purple Sensation', violet blue 'Wedgwood', wedgwood blue
PERENNIALS	**Aquilegia glandulosa** (Altai mountain columbine) *Height:* 38cm (15in) *Spread:* 23cm (9in) *Soil:* Ordinary, well drained *Site:* Open Sky blue and white	**Omphalodes verna** *Height:* 15cm (6in) *Spread:* 15cm (6in) *Soil:* Ordinary *Site:* Open Forget-me-not blue	**Pulmonaria angustifolia** (Lungwort) *Height:* 20cm (8in) *Spread:* 20cm (8in) */Soil:* Ordinary *Site:* Sun or shade 'Azurea', gentian blue	**Veronica gentianoides** *Height:* 45cm (18in) *Spread:* 25cm (10in) *Soil:* Ordinary *Site:* Open Pale blue	**Anchusa** (Alkanet) *Height:* 90cm (3ft) *Spread:* 30cm (1ft) *Soil:* Ordinary, well drained *Site:* Open 'Loddon Royalist', Oxford blue	**Campanula** (Bellflower) *Height:* 25-150cm (10in-5ft) *Spread:* 20-30cm (8-12in) *Soil:* Ordinary *Site:* Sunny *C.carpatica* 'Isobel', deep blue *C.glomerata* 'Superba', deep violet blue *C.latiloba* 'Percy Piper', deep lavender blue *C.persicifolia* 'Telham Beauty', light lavender blue
SHRUBS/TREES	**Ceanothus, evergreen** (Californian lilac, mountain sweet) *Height:* 30cm-6m (1-20ft) *Spread:* 2-3m (6½-10ft) *Soil:* Ordinary *Site:* Sunny, warm C. 'Cascade', light blue *C.impressus*, deep blue	**Rhododendron** *Height:* 1.2-3m (4-10ft) *Spread:* 1.2-2.5m (4-8ft) *Soil:* Acid, no lime *Site:* Open or dappled shade 'Blue Bird', lavender blue 'Blue Peter', lavender blue *R.augustinii*, violet blue 'Susan', light heliotrope	**Rosmarinus** (Rosemary) *Height:* 60-90cm (2-3ft) *Spread:* 45-60cm (18-24in) *Soil:* Ordinary, well drained *Site:* Sunny, warm 'Miss Jessup's Upright' (Pyramidalis), violet blue 'Severn Seas', deep violet blue	**Wisteria** ((Wistaria) *Height:* 3-15m (10-50ft) *Spread:* 2-4m (6½-13ft) *Soil:* Ordinary *Site:* Sunny *W.floribunda*, violet blue *W.sinensis*, mauve blue	**Abutilon** *Height:* 3-5m (10-16½ft) *Spread:* 1.5m (5ft) *Soil:* Ordinary *Site:* Sunny, sheltered *A.suntense*, blue-violet *A.vitifolium*, pale blue	**Ceanothus delineanus** (Californian lilac, mountain sweet) *Height:* 2m (6½ft) *Spread:* 90cm (3ft) *Soil:* Ordinary *Site:* Sunny, sheltered 'Gloire de Plantières', deep blue 'Gloire de Versailles', light blue 'Topaz', medium blue

strange that some people actually object to the yellow eye of the polyanthus and have succeeded in removing it by prolonged breeding and selection. The result is a much drabber flower: most people prefer the normal combination of blue and yellow.

These flowers give a practical lesson in the way in which blue can be best used in the garden in association with yellow or white. Many species actually occur in two or even all three colors. There are all yellow and all white primroses and polyanthuses as well as blue ones, white and cream delphiniums to go with the blue varieties, both blue and white campanulas, and many more such examples.

Blue also blends well with the related purples, but too much of this, unrelieved by any brighter colors, can produce too somber

an effect. Blue and red can be a dangerously clashing combination, yet it is traditional to mix scarlet geraniums with blue lobelia and, although the result may make color-sensitive viewers shudder, there is no doubt that most people find it stimulating.

There is a close chemical relationship between the dyes that produce blue, purple, red and pink flowers, which is strikingly exemplified by the behavior of the manifold varieties of the common mop-head and lacecap hydrangeas. In acid soils all the colors are in the blue and blue-purple range; remove these same plants to alkaline soil and the flowers change to pink, red or red-purple. White-flowered hydrangeas, having no pigment to be worked on, are immune to this color change caused by soil chemistry.

Muscari tubergeniana

Anchusa azurea

Hydrangea macrophylla 'Blue Wave'

Campanula carpatica

Convolvulus 'Blue Flash'

Lobelia erinus 'Crystal Palace'

				AUTUMN	
Convolvulus minor *Height:* 30cm (12in) *Spread:* 30cm (12in) *Soil:* Ordinary *Site:* Open 'Blue Flash', deep blue, white and yellow 'Royal Ensign', ultramarine and yellow	**Centaurea cyanus** (Cornflower) *Height:* 30-90cm (1-3ft) *Spread:* 20cm (8in) *Soil:* Ordinary *Site:* Open 'Blue Diadem', Oxford blue 'Jubilee Gem' (dwarf), Oxford blue	**Lobelia** *Height:* 10-15cm (4-6in) *Spread:* 15-20cm (6-8in) *Soil:* Ordinary *Site:* Open 'Crystal Palace', dark blue 'Mrs Clibran', medium blue and white	**Nigella damascena** (Love-in-a-mist) *Height:* 45cm (18in) *Spread:* 23cm (9in) *Soil:* Ordinary *Site:* Open 'Miss Jekyll', cornflower blue	**Aster** *Height:* 25cm (10in) *Spread:* 20cm (8in) *Soil:* Sun or shade 'Blue Magic' 'Milady Blue'	**Salvia patens** *Height:* 60cm (2ft) *Spread:* 45cm (18in) *Soil:* Ordinary, well drained *Site:* Sunny, warm Gentian blue
Ixiolirion pallasii *Height:* 45cm (18in) *Spread:* 10cm (4in) *Soil:* Ordinary *Site:* Sunny, warm Deep blue				**Crocus speciosus** *Height:* 10cm (4in) *Spread:* 8cm (3¼in) *Soil:* Ordinary *Site:* Open or light shade Violet	
Delphinium elatum (Larkspur) *Height:* 90-180cm (3-6ft) *Spread:* 45cm (18in) *Soil:* Ordinary *Site:* Open 'Blue Bees', light blue 'Blue Heaven', various shades of blue 'Blue Jay', medium blue	**Echinops** (Globe thistle) *Height:* 90-120cm (3-4ft) *Spread:* 45cm (18in) *Soil:* Ordinary *Site:* Open 'Taplow Blue', deep lavender blue	**Eryngium** (Sea holly) *Height:* 90cm (3ft) *Spread:* 30cm (1ft) *Soil:* Ordinary, well drained *Site:* Open *E.alpinum*, steel blue *E.tripartitum*, deep blue	**Iris** *Height:* 90-120cm (3-4ft) *Spread:* 30cm (1ft) *Soil:* Ordinary, alkaline *Site:* Open *I.germanica* varieties, various shades of blue with other colors *I.sibirica*, light to deep violet blue	**Aconitum** (Monkshood) *Height:* 120cm (4ft) *Spread:* 30cm (1ft) *Soil:* Ordinary *Site:* Sun or light shade 'Audrey', lavender blue 'Marie Ballard', light blue 'Mistress Quickly', violet blue	**Ceratostigma plumbaginoides** (Leadwort) *Height:* 30cm (1ft) *Spread:* 25cm (10in) *Soil:* Ordinary, well drained *Site:* Sunny, sheltered Gentian blue
Hydrangea macrophylla *Height:* 1-2m (3½-6½ft) *Spread:* 1.2-2m (4-6½ft) *Soil:* Acid for blue flowers *Site:* Sun or semi-shade 'Blue Wave', light heliotrope 'Generale Viscomtesse de Vibraye', forget-me-not blue	**Lavandula** (Lavender) *Height:* 45-60cm (18-24in) *Spread:* 30cm (12in) *Soil:* Ordinary, alkaline *Site:* Open 'Grappenhall', lavender blue 'Hidcote', deep lavender blue			**Caryopteris clandonensis** (Blue spiraea) *Height:* 90cm (3ft) *Spread:* 60cm (2ft) *Soil:* Ordinary, well drained *Site:* Open 'Kew Blue', deep blue	**Perovskia atriplicifolia** *Height:* 1-1.5m (3½-5ft) *Spread:* 90cm (3ft) *Soil:* Ordinary, well drained *Site:* Sunny Lavender blue

White flowers

White is the great harmonizer. It is all the rainbow colors combined, reflected to the eye unaltered and in balance and, since it contains all the colors, it does not clash with any of them. It is also the great enlivener, the one that can be used to bring light into dark places and to brighten up color combinations that are becoming too somber.

Some people say that they do not like white flowers because they remind them of funerals. It would be just as apposite and far more cheerful to think of white as the wedding color.

White gardens or white borders have been fashionable in Britain, but the most satisfactory of them are rarely devoted exclusively to white flowers. Silver and gray foliage is brought into them and also cream, light lemon and pale shades of pink, blue and mauve. In this way white is made to seem even whiter and the whole composition is given greater molding and variety.

The opposite approach to this is to use white for the boldest of contrasts with scarlet

or crimson or the deepest blues and purples. Many plants produce varieties with both white and strongly colored flowers. In border phloxes, for example, there are bright red and deep purple varieties as well as white, and roses offer almost every imaginable shade of red and crimson as well as the purest of whites in varieties such as 'Iceberg' and 'Ice White'. Dahlias are equally versatile in this respect and petunias offer a wide selection of strong colors to go with snowy whites.

Color schemes of all kinds are influenced by the size and texture of the flowers that produce them. There is a fundamental difference in the effect produced by the filmy clouds of white *Gypsophila* 'Bristol Fairy' or *Clematis flammula* and the more substantial blocks of white produced by white hydrangeas or

Arabis caucasica

Amelanchier lamarckii

Crocus

Choisya ternata

Saxifrage

Narcissus 'Actaea'

	SPRING					**SUMMER**
ANNUALS/BEDDING	**Bellis perennis 'Monstrosa'** (Double daisy) *Height:* 15cm (6in) *Spread:* 15cm (6in) *Soil:* Ordinary *Site:* Open 'Fairy Carpet', white and rose	**Matthiola incana** (East Lothian stocks) *Height:* 45cm (18in) *Spread:* 25cm (10in) *Soil:* Ordinary, well drained *Site:* Sunny, sheltered 'Kelvedon White'	**Polyanthus** *Height:* 25cm (10in) *Spread:* 15cm (6in) *Soil:* Ordinary *Site:* Sun or moderate shade 'Triumph White'			**Alyssum maritimum** *Height:* 10cm (4in) *Spread:* 15cm (6in) *Soil:* Ordinary *Site:* Open 'Little Dorrit' 'Snow Carpet'
BULBS	**Anemone blanda** (Windflower) *Height:* 10-15cm (4-6in) *Spread:* 10cm (4in) *Soil:* Ordinary *Site:* Sun or partial shade 'Alba' 'White Splendour'	**Crocus** *Height:* 10m (4in) *Spread:* 8cm (3¼in) *Soil:* Ordinary *Site:* Open or light shade *C. chrysanthus* 'Snow Bunting' 'Jeanne d'Arc'	**Erythronium** (Dogs tooth violet) *Height:* 15-20cm (6-8in) *Spread:* 20cm (8in) *Soil:* Plenty of humus *Site:* Dappled shade 'White Beauty'	**Narcissus** (Daffodil) *Height:* 30-50cm (12-20in) *Spread:* 15cm (6in) *Soil:* Ordinary *Site:* Sun or light shade 'Actaea', small yellow and red cup 'Ice Follies', crown is cream at first 'Mount Hood' 'Silver Chimes', cup is cream 'Tresamble', touch of cream	**Tulip** *Height:* 30-60cm (12-24in) *Spread:* 10m (4in) *Soil:* Ordinary *Site:* Open 'Diana' 'Purissima' 'Schoonoord' 'White Triumphator'	**Galtonia candicans** (Summer hyacinth) *Height:* 90cm (3ft) *Spread:* 23cm (9in) *Soil:* Ordinary *Site:* Open
PERENNIALS	**Arabis caucasica** (Rock cress) *Height:* 15cm (6in) *Spread:* 30cm (12in) *Soil:* Ordinary, alkaline *Site:* Open 'Alba', single flowers 'Alba Plena', double flowers	**Iberis** (Candytuft) *Height:* 10-45cm (4-18in) *Spread:* 20cm (8in) *Soil:* Ordinary *Site:* Open *I. semperflorens* *I. sempervirens*	**Primula** (Primrose) *Height:* 10-30cm (4-12in) *Spread:* 15cm (6in) *Soil:* Ordinary *Site:* Shade *P. denticulata* 'Alba' *P. vulgaris* 'Snow Queen'	**Saxifraga** (Mossy saxifrage) *Height:* 8-20cm (3¼-8in) *Spread:* 20cm (8in) *Soil:* Ordinary *Site:* Partial shade 'Harstwood White' 'Pearly King' 'Wallacei'	**Viola cornuta 'Alba'** (Horned violet) *Height:* 15-20cm (6-8in) *Spread:* 15cm (6in) *Soil:* Ordinary *Site:* Partial shade	**Astilbe** *Height:* 45-60cm (18-24in) *Spread:* 30cm (12in) *Soil:* Ordinary, moist *Site:* Sun or light shade 'Irrlicht' 'White Gloria'
SHRUBS/TREES	**Amelanchier** (Snowy mespilus) *Height:* 4-5m (13-16½ft) *Spread:* 3-4m (10-13ft) *Soil:* Ordinary *Site:* Open *A. laevis* *A. lamarckii*	**Choisya ternata** (Mexican orange blossom) *Height:* 120-150cm (4-5ft) *Spread:* 120m (4ft) *Soil:* Ordinary *Site:* Sunny, sheltered	**Clematis montana** *Height:* 6m (20ft) *Spread:* 2m (6½ft) *Soil:* Ordinary *Site:* Open There are also pink varieties	**Magnolia** *Height:* 2-5m (6½-16½ft) *Spread:* 2-4m (6½-13ft) *Soil:* Moderately acid *Site:* Open *M. stellata* *M. soulangeana* 'Alba Superba' *M. soulangeana* 'Lennei Alba'	**Prunus** (Cherry, almond) *Height:* 1-6m (3½-20ft) *Spread:* 60cm-4m (2-13ft) *Soil:* Ordinary *Site:* Open 'Avium Plena', double flower *P. glandulosa* 'Alba Plena', double flowers *P. yedoensis*, bluish white 'Shirotae', semi-double flowers 'Tai-Haku', single flowers	**Deutzia** *Height:* 2-2.5m (6½-8ft) *Spread:* 1-1.5m (3½-5ft) *Soil:* Ordinary *Site:* Open *D. magnifica* *D. scabre candidissima*

White varieties of *Matthiola incana* (**left**) provide freshness to the border in mid-summer. In full sun and on poor soils the papery blooms of *Cistus X cyprius* (**right**) are borne in profusion during the summer months. These Mediterranean shrubs are ideal for planting on dry sunny banks. The almond-scented flowers of *Prunus yedoensis* (**far right**) grace this elegant tree in early spring. Several named forms are available.

Chrysanthemum maximum. There is even a difference between the effect of single and double flowers of the same species — a more solid white from the double white arabis than from the single white wild form, for instance — which is why such differences are noted when describing these flowers below.

There are also many white-flowered climbers, most of all among the roses which range all the way in vigor from the 3m (10ft) 'Swan Lake' to the 10m (33ft) 'Kiftsgate', all of which can be used as backgrounds or allowed to mingle with other plants or spill out of trees. Clematis varieties of moderate vigor and sweet peas are particularly eligible minglers that are unlikely to smother the host plants used as support, and can make charming color associations with them.

Galtonia candicans

Magnolia stellata

Chrysanthemum maximum

Ornithogalum umbellatum

Spiraea prunifolia 'Plena'

Viburnum tomentosum 'Mariesii'

				AUTUMN	
Iberis amara (Candytuft) *Height:* 30cm (12in) *Spread:* 15cm (6in) *Soil:* Ordinary *Site:* Open 'White Spiral'	**Gypsophila** (Baby's breath) *Height:* 45cm (18in) *Spread:* 23cm (9in) *Soil:* Ordinary *Site:* Open 'Covent Garden White'	**Lavatera rosea** *Height:* 60cm (2ft) *Spread:* 45cm (18in) *Soil:* Ordinary *Site:* Open 'Mont Blanc'	**Petunia** *Height:* 23-30cm (9-12in) *Spread:* 23cm (9in) *Soil:* Ordinary *Site:* Sunny 'Resisto White' 'Snow Cloud' 'White Joy'	**Aster** *Height:* 25cm (10in) *Spread:* 20cm (8in) *Soil:* Ordinary *Site:* Sun or shade 'Milady White'	
Gladiolus *Height:* 60-90cm (2-3ft) *Spread:* 20cm (8in) *Soil:* Ordinary *Site:* Open 'Alba Nova' 'Purity' 'Sancerre' 'Summer Snow'	**Lilium** (Lily) *Height:* 90-120cm (3-4ft) *Spread:* 25cm (10in) *Soil:* Ordinary *Site:* Sun or dappled shade *L. candidum* *L. martagon* 'Album' *L. regale*, flushed light yellow and purple	**Ornithogalum umbellatum** (Star of Bethlehem) *Height:* 15cm (6in) *Spread:* 15cm (6in) *Soil:* Ordinary *Site:* Sun or partial shade		**Acidanthera murielae** *Height:* 75cm (30in) *Spread:* 15cm (6in) *Soil:* Ordinary, well drained *Site:* Sunny, warm Purple blotch	**Dahlia** *Height:* 30-90cm (1-3ft) *Spread:* 45-90cm (18-36) *Soil:* Ordinary *Site:* Open 'Easter Sunday', creamy white 'Mistill Delight' 'White Klankstad' 'Wooton Wedding'

Chrysanthemum maximum
(Shasta daisy)
Height: 60-90cm (2-3ft)
Spread: 30cm (12in)
Soil: Ordinary
Site: Open
'Beauté Nivelloise', single
   flowers
'Wirral Supreme', double
   flowers
	Dianthus plumarius
	(Pinks)
	Height: 15-30cm (6-12in)
	Spread: 25cm (10in)
	Soil: Ordinary, alkaline
	Site: Open
	'Mrs Sinkins'
	'White Ladies'
		Gypsophila paniculata
		Height: 90cm (3ft)
		Spread: 60cm (2ft)
		Soil: Ordinary, alkaline
		Site: Open
		'Bristol Fairy', double flowers
			Paeonia lactiflora
			(Chinese peony)
			Height: 90cm (3ft)
			Spread: 45cm (18in)
			Soil: Ordinary
			Site: Sun or partial shade
			'Duchesse de Nemours'
				Aster novi-belgii
				(Michaelmas daisy)
				Height: 30-90cm (1-3ft)
				Spread: 25-30cm (10-12in)
				Soil: Ordinary
				Site: Sun or shade
				'Snowsprite'
				'White Ladies'
					Cimicifuga
					Height: 120-150cm (4-5ft)
					Spread: 45cm (18in)
					Soil: Ordinary
					Site: Half or dappled shade
					C. racemosa, ivory
					C. simplex 'White Pearl'

Escallonia iveyi
Height: 3m (10ft)
Spread: 1.5m (5ft)
Soil: Ordinary
Site: Sunny, sheltered
	Philadelphus
	(Mock orange)
	Height: 1.2-3m (4-10ft)
	Spread: 1.2-1.5m (4-5ft)
	Soil: Ordinary
	Site: Open
	'Beauclerk'
	'Belle Etoile', flushed purple
	'Sybille', flushed purple
	'Virginal', double flower
		Spiraea
		Height: 1.2-2.5m (4-8ft)
		Spread: 1.2-2m (4-6½ft)
		Soil: Ordinary
		Site: Open
		S. prunifolia, double flowers
		S. vanhouttei
		S. veitchii
			Viburnum
			Height: 2.5-3m (8-10ft)
			Spread: 1.2-2.4m (4-8ft)
			Soil: Ordinary
			Site: Open
			V. opulus sterile, ball shaped
			   flower clusters
			V. plicatum, ball shaped flower
			   clusters
			V. plicatum tomentosum, flat
			   flower clusters
				Erica
				(Heath, heather)
				Height: 15-60cm (6-24in)
				Spread: 25cm (10in)
				Soil: Acid, no lime
				Site: Open
				E. ciliaris 'Stoborough'
				E. cinerea 'Alba Major'
				E. cinerea 'Alba Minor'
					Potentilla fruticosa
					(Shrubby cinquefoil)
					Height: 1-1.2m (3½-4ft)
					Spread: 60cm (2ft)
					Soil: Ordinary
					Site: Sunny
					'Abbotswood', starts in
					   summer

Silver and gray foliage

Plants with silver or gray leaves have become so important to garden designers that whole books have been written about their selection and use, and some nurseries specialize in them. They can be used in gardens in two quite different ways: either as a relieving contrast to flower colors or, alternatively, in areas devoted almost exclusively to the silver or gray foliage, with flowers playing a definitely subordinate role, if admitted at all. Silver and gray gardens of the latter kind have become fashionable and, because many of the plants that have such leaves come from naturally dry climates, they can usually be grown with particular success in the gravel gardens which have also gained greatly in popularity in recent years.

Like white, silver and gray do not clash with anything and so can be used with any other foliage or with any flowers. Yet some combinations seem more satisfactory than others. Both silver and gray make delightfully restful combinations with blue and purple. Lavender and nepeta can actually supply both the gray leaves and the blue flowers, but many other combinations can be devised in which foliage and flowers come from different sources; silver *Cineraria maritima*, for example, with purple heliotrope or blue *Salvia patens*.

Pink flowers with gray foliage is another association almost certain to please, and again one may note that it occurs automatically when garden pinks, varieties of *Dianthus plumarius*, are planted. But by far the commonest natural alliance is between silver and gray leaves and yellow flowers, as in some gazanias, many senecios, *Santolina*, euryops and numerous verbascums.

Silver and gray also occur in much larger plants, including some big shrubs and trees. The willow-leaved pear, *Pyrus salicifolia* 'Pendula', is a particularly beautiful small tree that can be used as a centerpiece in a silver-gray scheme, and there are also many silvery or blue-gray conifers, some of which remain small either permanently or for a good many years. These small conifers combine particularly well with heathers, many of which have pink or reddish purple flowers and some have the added attraction of gray, yellow or copper-colored leaves.

Many silver- and gray-leaved plants retain their leavers in winter, although very few look their best at that time. Often the silver or gray

Anaphalis triplinervis 'Summer Snow'

Helichrysum splendidum

Pyrus salicifolia 'Pendula'

Senecio 'Sunshine'

Artemisia ludoviciana 'Silver Queen'

Stachys lanata

Leaves retained all the year

Artemisia tridentata
Shrub
Height: 1.2m (4ft)
Spread: 60cm (2ft)
Soil: Ordinary
Site: Sunny
Grey leaves

Centaurea cineraria
Sub-shrub
Height: 45cm (18in)
Spread: 30cm (12in)
Soil: Ordinary
Site: Sunny
Long, indented, white woolly leaves

Convolvulus cneorum
Sub-shrub
Height: 45cm (18in)
Spread: 30cm (12in)
Soil: Ordinary
Site: Sunny, sheltered
Narrow silvery leaves

Eucalpytus gunnii
Tree
Height if pollarded: 2-3m (6½-10ft)
Spread if pollarded: 1.2m (4ft)
Soil: Ordinary
Site: Sunny, sheltered
Rounded silvery blue leaves

Helichrysum splendidum
Shrub
Height: 60cm (2ft)
Spread: 45cm (18in)
Soil: Ordinary, well-drained
Site: Sunny
Small silvery leaves

Senecio cineraria
Sub-shrub
Height: 60m (2ft)
Spread: 30cm (1ft)
Soil: Ordinary
Site: Sunny
Deeply lobed white woolly leaves
'White Diamond' and 'Ramparts' are good varieties

Leaves from spring to autumn only

Achillea argentea
Herbaceous perennial
Height: 15cm (6in)
Spread: 25cm (10in)
Soil: Ordinary, well-drained
Site: Sunny
Small silvery leaves, small white flowers in late spring

Achillea taygetea
Herbaceous perennial
Height: 30cm (12in)
Spread: 38cm (15in)
Soil: Ordinary, well-drained
Site: Sunny
Finely divided grey leaves, pale yellow flowers in summer

Anaphalis nubigena
Herbaceous perennial
Height: 30cm (12in)
Spread: 30cm (12in)
Soil: Ordinary, well-drained
Site: Sunny
Small silvery leaves, pearly white flowers in autumn

Anaphalis triplinervis
Herbaceous perennial
Height: 38cm (15in)
Spread: 38cm (15in)
Soil: Ordinary, well-drained
Site: Sunny
Silvery grey leaves, pearly white flowers in autumn

Anthemis cupaniana
Herbaceous perennial
Height: 30cm (12in)
Spread: 30cm (12in)
Soil: Ordinary
Site: Sunny
Finely divided grey leaves, large white daisies in summer

Antennaria dioica
Herbaceous perennial
Height: 10cm (4in)
Spread: 15cm (6in)
Soil: Light, well-drained
Site: Sunny
Small silvery leaves becoming green in winter, pink flowers in late spring

Euryops acreus
Shrub
Height: 30cm (1ft)
Spread: 30cm (1ft)
Soil: Ordinary
Site: Sunny
Small grey-blue leaves, small yellow daisies in late spring

Festuca ovina glauca
(Fescue grass)
Perennial
Height: 25cm (10in)
Spread: 20cm (8in)
Soil: Light, well-drained
Site: Sunny
Narrow blue-grey leaves

Helichrysum petiolatum
Herbaceous perennial
Height: 20cm (8in)
Spread: 60cm (2ft)
Soil: Ordinary, well-drained
Site: Sunny
Heart-shaped grey leaves

Leucanthemum hosmarense
Sub-shrub
Height: 23cm (9in)
Spread: 30cm (1ft)
Soil: Gritty, well-drained
Site: Sunny
Finely divided silver-grey leaves, large daisies in spring and summer

Onopordon arabicum
Biennial
Height: 2.5m (8ft)
Spread: 45cm (18in)
Soil: Ordinary
Site: Sun or partial shade
Broad, almost white leaves, purple thistle flowers in summer

Pyrus salicifolia 'Pendula'
(Willow-leaved pear)
Tree
Height: 4-5m (13-16½ft)
Spread: 3m (10ft)
Soil: Ordinary
Site: Sunny
Narrow silvery leaves

appearance is produced by a dense covering of silky hairs or down developed by the plant to cut down water loss by evaporation from the leaf surface and so enable it to survive periods of drought. In damp climates, this covering collects moisture and may become sodden, possibly even causing the leaves to decay. Even without this final disaster, rain-soaked plants can look very bedraggled.

All silver- and gray-leaved plants succeed best in well-drained soil and open, sunny places. Many like soil that contains lime, either as chalk or limestone.

Stachys lanata (**left**) is a favorite plant, prized for its silver gray foliage.

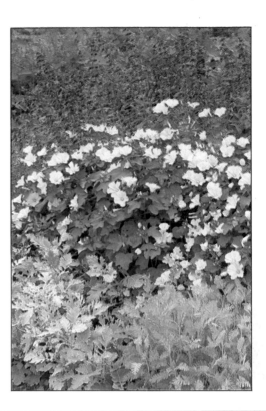

Gardens featuring silver and white plants (**right**) have a clean crisp appearance that generates a restful atmosphere. Many types of plants have silvery foliage, from low-growing perennials to stately trees. All can be used to good effect in the garden, especially with bold contrasting colors of seasonal bedding plants.

Verbascum bombyciferum

Artemisia schmidtiana

Ballota pseudodictamnus

Senecio 'Sunshine' (S. greyii)
Shrub
Height: 90cm (3ft)
Spread: 90cm (3ft)
Soil: Ordinary
Site: Sunny
Rounded grey leaves

Lavandula angustifolia
(Lavender)
Shrub
Height: 45-60cm (18-24in)
Spread: 30cm (12in)
Soil: Ordinary, well-drained
Site: Sunny
Narrow grey leaves

Stachys lanata
(Lambs ears)
Herbaceous perennial
Height: 25cm (10in)
Spread: 25cm (10in)
Soil: Ordinary, well-drained
Site: Sun or partial shade
Lance-shaped white woolly leaves and purplish-rose flowers. 'Silver Carpet' is a low-growing variety without flowers

Teucrium fruticans
(Shrubby germander)
Height: 90cm (3ft)
Spread: 60cm (2ft)
Soil: Light, well-drained
Site: Sunny
Narrow silvery leaves, lavender flowers in summer

Artemisia absinthium
Sub-shrub
Height: 75cm (30in)
Spread: 45cm (18in)
Soil: Ordinary
Site: Sunny
Finely divided silvery leaves. 'Lambrook Silver' is a specially good variety

Artemisia arborescens
Sub-shrub
Height: 90cm (3ft)
Spread: 60cm (2ft)
Soil: Ordinary
Site: Sunny
Finely divided silvery leaves

Artemisia ludoviciana
Herbaceous perennial
Height: 60cm (2ft)
Spread: 23cm (9in)
Soil: Light, well-drained
Site: Sunny
Silvery grey leaves

Artemisia schmidtiana
Herbaceous perennial
Height: 23cm (9in)
Spread: 20cm (8in)
Soil: Light, well-drained
Site: Sunny
Finely divided silvery leaves

Ballota pseudodictamnus
Herbaceous perennial
Height: 60cm (2ft)
Spread: 45cm (18in)
Soil: Poor or ordinary
Site: Sunny
Pale green leaves becoming white woolly

Cynara cardunculua
(Cardoon)
Herbaceous perennial
Height: 1.5m (5ft)
Spread: 60cm (2ft)
Soil: Light, deep
Site: Sunny
Large, deeply divided silver-grey leaves

Romneya coulteri
(Californian tree poppy)
Sub-shrub
Height: 1.5m (5ft)
Spread: 60cm (2ft)
Soil: Light, well-drained
Site: Sunny, sheltered
Silver-grey leaves, large white poppies in late summer

Santolina chamaecyparissus
(Lavender cotton)
Sub-shrub
Height: 60cm (2ft)
Spread: 45cm (18in)
Soil: Ordinary
Site: Sunny
Small silver-grey leaves

Verbascum bombyciferum
(Mullein)
Biennial
Height: 1.5m (5ft)
Spread: 30cm (1ft)
Soil: Ordinary
Site: Sunny
Large white woolly leaves, pale yellow flowers in summer

Veronica incana
Herbaceous perennial
Height: 10cm (4in)
Spread: 30cm (12in)
Soil: Ordinary, fertile
Site: Sun or partial shade
Narrow silver-grey leaves, dark blue flowers in late summer

Red/yellow foliage

Flowers come and go but leaves are there for months on end, even throughout the year if the plant is an evergreen. So it is very important to consider foliage when color-planning the garden. Although most leaves are green, there is an enormous variation even in this color alone. There are the blue-greens of rue, some hostas and aquilegias, the narrow-leaved grass *Festuca ovina* 'Glauca', and many other plants; deep laurel greens; much livelier lime greens; muted sage greens; real gray-greens; and many more.

In addition to all this there is a diversity of other foliage colors, some of which would not have survived in the wild but were seized on by gardeners appreciative of their decorative merit and propagated by vegetative means because most would not reproduce the

unusual leaf color from seed. There are yellow leaves, purple leaves, and some that are various shades of red, bronze or copper. All these colors can be just as effective as those of flowers, and can be used in precisely the same way to create harmonies and contrasts, to be eye-catchers (and for this, some of the all-yellow leaves such as those of *Catalpa bignonioides* 'Aurea', *Robinia* 'Frisia' and *Gleditsia* 'Sunburst' are particularly effective), or to tone down other colors which, on their own, may prove too strident.

Red, purple, bronze and copper make little or no difference to the vigor of plants. But when leaves are yellow, overall growth is usually slower, and the plant — be it tree, shrub or herbaceous perennial — may not grow as large as its normal green counterpart.

Yellow is also in general most fully produced when the light intensity is good; the color may tend to become dull and greenish in the shade. Most yellow-leaved trees and shrubs can be planted in full sun. A few, however — notably the golden elders *(Sambucus)* — may suffer leaf scorch if the sunshine is too intense, and for these a position in good light but shaded from the sun around midday is best.

To all these leaf colours may be added the various colors of bark: the coral red of *Acer palmatum* 'Senkaki', the much deeper reds of the dogwoods *Cornus alba* and *C. sanguinea*; the yellow or orange of various willows such as the golden weeping willow *(Salix chrysocoma)* and two forms of the white willow *(S. alba)* named 'Chermesina' ('Britzensis' in some catalogues) and 'Vitellina'; the cinnamon of

Acer japonicum
'Aureum'

Humulus lupulus
'Aureus'

Juniperus media
'Old Gold'

Robinia pseudoacacia
'Frisia'

Taxus baccata
'Semperaurea'

Acer palmatum
'Atropurpureum'

YELLOW LEAVES

PERENNIALS

Hosta fortunei 'Aurea'
(Plantain lily)
Height: 45-75cm (18-30in)
Spread: 45cm (18in)
Soil: Ordinary
Site: Sun or partial shade
Young leaves soft yellow

Humulus lupulus 'Aureus'
(Hop)
Height: 6m (20ft)
Spread: 2m (6½ft)
Soil: Ordinary
Site: Open
Young leaves bright yellow

Milium effusum 'Aureum'
(Millet grass)
Height: 60cm (2ft)
Spread: 30cm (1ft)
Soil: Ordinary
Site: Open
Yellow

Valeriana phu 'Aurea'
(Valerian)
Height: 90cm (3ft)
Spread: 30cm (1ft)
Soil: Ordinary
Site: Open or light shade
Young leaves bright yellow

SHRUBS

Acer japonicum 'Aureum'
(Japanese maple)
Height: 3-4m (10-13ft)
Spread: 2m (6½ft)
Soil: Ordinary
Site: Open
Soft yellow

Calluna vulgaris
(Heather, ling)
Height: 20cm (8in)
Spread: 25cm (10in)
Soil: Acid, no lime
Site: Open
'Gold Haze', light yellow
'Robert Chapman', bronze and yellow

Cornus alba 'Aurea'
(Red-barked dogwood)
Height: 2-3m (6½-10ft)
Spread: 1.2m (4ft)
Soil: Ordinary, moist
Site: Open
Soft yellow

Ligustrum ovalifolium 'Aureum'
(Golden privet)
Height: 2-3m (6½-10ft)
Spread: 90-120cm (3-4ft)
Soil: Ordinary
Site: Open
Yellow

Lonicera nitida 'Baggesen's Gold'
Height: 90cm (3ft)
Spread: 90cm (3ft)
Soil: Ordinary
Site: Open
Yellow, becoming greenish yellow

Ribes sanguineum 'Brocklebankii'
(Flowering currant)
Height: 2-2.5m (6½-8ft)
Spread: 1.2m (4ft)
Soil: Ordinary
Site: Sun or light shade
Yellow

TREES/CONIFERS

Acer negundo 'Auratum'
(Box elder)
Height: 4.5-6m (15-20ft)
Spread: 3-4m (10-13ft)
Soil: Ordinary
Site: Open
Pale yellow

Catalpa bignonioides 'Aurea'
(Indian bean tree)
Height: 4.5-6m (15-20ft)
Spread: 5m (16½ft)
Soil: Ordinary
Site: Sunny
Soft yellow

Cupressus, Chamaecyaris and Cupressocyparis
(Cypress)
Height: 6-12m (20-39ft)
Spread: 3-5m (10-16½ft)
Soil: Ordinary
Site: Sunny
'Castlewellan Gold', greenish yellow
'Ellwood's Gold', yellow tipped
'Filifera Aurea', yellow
'Goldcrest', soft yellow
'Lanei', golden yellow

Gleditsia triacanthos 'Sunburst'
(Honey locust)
Height: 4.5-6m (15-20ft)
Spread: 3-4m (10-13ft)
Soil: Ordinary
Site: Sunny
Changing from deep to light yellow

Juniperus media
(Juniper)
Height: 60-120cm (2-4ft)
Spread: 2-4m (6½-13ft)
Soil: Ordinary
Site: Open
'Aurea', young leaves sulphur yellow
'Old Gold', bronzy-yellow

Robinia pseuodoacacia 'Frisia'
(False acacia)
Height: 5-9m (16½-30ft)
Spread: 3-4m (10-13ft)
Soil: Ordinary
Site: Sunny
Light yellow

Acer griseum; the shining mahogany of *Prunus serrula*; and the white of good forms of the common birch as well as exotic birches such as *Betula ermanii* and *B. papyrifera*.

In a few plants it is only the young growth that has colorful leaves. This is true of the herbaceous valerian named *Valeriana phu* 'Aurea', which has yellow leaves at first, and also two fine shrubs, *Pieris formosa* and *Photinia fraseri*, both of which have red leaves when young. They are very handsome for a few weeks in spring but relapse into greenness in summer.

Several varieties of *Cotinus coggygria* have striking purple foliage. These and the green-leaved forms are often suffused with superb shades of reds, yellows and oranges during autumn (right).

Cotinus coggygria

Pieris formosa

RED AND PURPLE LEAVES

Ligularia dentata 'Desdemona'
Height: 90cm (3ft)
Spread: 60cm (2ft)
Soil: Ordinary
Site: Open or light shade

Phormium tenax 'Purpureum'
(New Zealand flax)
Height: 2m (6½ft)
Spread: 60cm (2ft)
Soil: Ordinary
Site: Sunny, sheltered

Rheum palmatum 'Atrosanguineum'
(Ornamental rhubarb)
Height: 2m (6½ft)
Spread: 90cm (3ft)
Soil: Ordinary or moist
Site: Open
Leaves red-purple beneath

Sambucus
(Elder)
Height: 2.5-3m (8-10ft)
Spread: 1.2-1.5m (4-5ft)
Soil: Ordinary
Site: Open or light shade
S.nigra 'Aurea', yellow
S.racemosa 'Plumosa Aurea', yellow, leaves much divided

Spiraea japonica 'Goldflame'
Height: 1.2m (4ft)
Spread: 1.5m (5ft)
Soil: Ordinary
Site: Open
Leaves copper-yellow when young

Corylus maximus 'Atro Purpurea'
(Filbert)
Height: 2.5m (8ft)
Spread: 2m (6½ft)
Soil: Ordinary
Site: Open or partial shade
Bark purple

Cotinus coggygria
(Smoke tree, Venetian sumach)
Height: 2-3m (6½-10ft)
Spread: 2-2.5m (6½-8ft)
Soil: Ordinary
Site: Sunny
'Foliis Purpureus', plum purple
'Royal Purple', deep red-purple

Photinia fraseri
Height: 3-6m (10-20ft)
Spread: 1.8m (6ft)
Soil: Ordinary
Site: Sunny, sheltered
'Red Robin', young leaves bronze-red

Pieris
(Lily-of-the-valley-bush)
Height: 2.4-8m (8-26ft)
Spread: 2-2.4m (6-8ft)
Soil: Acid, no lime
Site: Open or dappled shade
P. 'Forest Flame', young leaves red becoming cream
P.formosa 'Wakehurst', young leaves bright red

Taxus baccata
(Yew)
Height: 2.5-5m (8-16½ft)
Spread: 0.6-3m (2-10ft)
Soil: Ordinary
Site: Sun or shade
'Davastonii Aurea', wide spreading, leaves edged yellow
'Fastigiata Aurea', narrowly erect, leaves edged yellow
'Semperaurea', bright yellow
'Standishii', columnar, yellow

Acer palmatum 'Atropurpureum'
(Japanese maple)
Height: 2-3m (6½-10ft)
Spread: 2m (6½ft)
Soil: Ordinary
Site: Open or dappled shade
Red-purple

Acer platanoides 'Crimson King'
(Norway maple)
Height: 9-18m (30-60ft)
Spread: 8m (26ft)
Soil: Ordinary
Site: Open
Beetroot purple

Fagus sylvatica 'Fastigiata'
(Dawyck beech)
Height: 9-18m (30-60ft)
Spread: 3m (10ft)
Soil: Ordinary, alkaline
Site: Open
'Dawyck Purple', leaves purple

Prunus cerasifera 'Nigra'
(Cherry plum)
Height: 6-7m (20-23ft)
Spread: 4-5m (13-16½ft)
Soil: Ordinary
Site: Open
Very dark purple

Variegated foliage

Some leaves combine several colors — usually white, cream or yellow with green — but there are also pink, red and purple variegations in some plants. Such colors are not natural to the plant — although variegations do appear among wild plants — but correspond to reactions to various events: sometimes to virus infection, sometimes to mutations affecting only certain layers of tissue which may in turn determine whether the variegation appears in stripes, or as an edging to the leaf, or as a central blotch in it. All may be regarded as freaks, useful if the variegation is attractive, merely curious if it is ugly. In the wild,. such freaks soon disappear because they are almost invariably less vigorous than the normal green-leaved type. Gardeners may, however, find them useful for various decorative pur-

poses, and keep them going mainly by vegetative means. Very occasionally, a variegation can be inherited by seed, a notable example being a white blotched variety of honesty *(Lunaria biennis)* which, because it is a biennial, can be kept going only by seed. This variation is unusual not only in being seed-borne but also in that it does not appear until the second year.

Variegations can be very decorative, especially when several colors combine, as shades of pink and cream do in the young leaves of the sycamore *Acer pseudoplatanus* 'Brilliantissimum' or in the leaves of some varieties of New Zealand flax *(Phormium)*.

Because of the way in which variegations originate there is often a risk that some growths may revert to the original green-

leaved form. Because these green-leaved stems are almost certain to be more vigorous and faster-growing than the variegated ones, any that appear must be removed as soon as possible or they may take over completely. Some variegated trees are grafted high up on main stems of the green-leaved type; with these there is an ever-present danger that stems may appear lower down on this main stem and quickly starve out the variegated head. Pruning to get rid of such green-leaved stems can be carried out at any time, even in summer. The offending stem must be removed cleanly right down to the trunk or to the variegated branch from which it has grown, with no stump left to give rise to a new crop of green stems.

The degree of variegation sometimes dif-

Hosta fortunei 'Albopicta'

Hedera helix 'Glacier'

Ilex aquifolium

Pachysandra terminalis 'Variegata'

Cornus alba 'Spaethii'

Elaeagnus pungens 'Maculata'

PERENNIALS

Brunnera macrophylla 'Variegata'
Height: 45cm (18in)
Spread: 45cm (18in)
Soil: Ordinary
Site: Sun or shade
White blotched

Hosta
(Plantain lily)
Height: 45-75cm (18-30in)
Spread: 45cm (18in)
Soil: Ordinary
Site: Sun or partial shade
H. albomarginata, leaves edged cream
H. fortunei 'Albo Marginata', leaves edged white
H. 'Frances Williams'
H. 'Thomas Hogg'
H. undulata, leaves white variegated

Iris
Height: 60cm (2ft)
Spread: 30cm (1ft)
Soil: Ordinary, alkaline
Site: Open
I. foetidissima 'Variegata', white striped
I. pallida 'Aureo Variegata', yellow striped
I. pallida 'Variegata', cream striped

SHRUBS/TREES

Acer negundo 'Variegatum'
(Box elder)
Height: 4.5-6cm (15-20ft)
Spread: 3.4m (10-13ft)
Soil: Ordinary
Site: Open

Acer pseudoplatanus 'Brilliantissimum'
(Sycamore)
Height: 3-6m (10-20ft)
Spread: 3-5m (10-16½ft)
Soil: Ordinary
Site: Open
Young leaves pink and cream

Aralia elata 'Variegata'
(Angelica tree)
Height: 2-4m (6½-13ft)
Spread: 1.5cm (5ft)
Soil: Ordinary
Site: Sunny, sheltered
Large, compound, creamy-white and green

Phormium tenax 'Variegatum'
(New Zealand flax)
Height: 2cm (6½ft)
Spread: 60cm (2ft)
Soil: Ordinary
Site: Sunny, sheltered
Cream striped leaves

Scrophularia aquatica 'Variegata'
(Water betony)
Height: 90cm (3ft)
Spread: 45cm (18in)
Soil: Ordinary, moist
Site: Open
Cream variegated

Sisyrinchium striatum 'Variegatum'
Height: 60cm (2ft)
Spread: 30cm (1ft)
Soil: Ordinary
Site: Open
Leaves gray-green striped white

Fuchsia magellanica
Height: 1.2-2m (4-6½ft)
Spread: 90cm (3ft)
Soil: Ordinary
Site: Sun or light shade
'Variegata', cream border to leaf
'Versicolor', leaves gray-green, pink and cream

Hebe andersonii 'Variegata'
(Shrubby veronica)
Height: 90cm (3ft)
Spread: 60cm (2ft)
Soil: Ordinary
Site: Sunny, sheltered
Cream variegated

Hedera (Ivy)
Height: to 6m (20ft)
Spread: 1.2-2m (4-6½ft)
Soil: Ordinary
Site: Sunny for variegation
H. colchica dentata 'Variegata', pale yellow
H. helix 'Glacier', grey-green and white
'Goldheart', dark green and yellow
'Goldheart' 'Marginata Elegantissima, gray-green white and pink.

Borders featuring mixed foliage plants (**right**) can be just as effective and attractive a part of the garden as those overflowing with bright flowering plants. Many people prefer the sculptural and subtle qualities such borders offer. Plants with variegated leaves are high on the list of favored foliage subjects. These are available in all types, from ground-cover perennials to shrubs and climbers.

Euonymus fortunei 'Emerald and Gold'

fers considerably from branch to branch. This is particularly noticeable with golden-variegated hollies which may produce some stems with wholly yellow leaves. It might seem clever to make cuttings of these stems and so produce a wholly golden holly, but plants that have no chlorophyll with which to manufacture food quickly die. The apparently all yellow-leaved trees and shrubs actually do have some chlorophyll, but it is masked by the yellow color (whereas the yellow-variegated parts of the holly leaf have no chlorophyll at all). The same applies to white variegation — the more there is of it, the weaker is the plant. Another peculiarity of some variegations is that it is not carried in the root: take root cuttings from a white- or yellow-variegated Japanese angelica *(Aralia elata)*, for example, and all the resulting plants are green-leaved.

Weigela florida 'Variegata'

Weigela (young shoots)

Cornus alba 'Elegantissima'
Height: 2-3m (6½-10ft)
Spread: 1.2m (4ft)
Soil: Ordinary, moist
Site: Open

Cornus alternifolia 'Variegata'
(Dogwood)
Height: 2-2.5m (6½-8ft)
Spread: 1.8m (6ft)
Soil: Ordinary
Site: Open
Leaves edged with white

Cornus controversa 'Variegata'
(Dogwood)
Height: 4-5m (13-16½ft)
Spread: 3-4cm (10-13ft)
Soil: Ordinary
Site: Sunny, sheltered
Cream variegated

Cotoneaster horizontalis 'Variegatus'
Height: 15cm-6m (6in-20ft)
Spread: 1-3cm (3-10ft)
Soil: Ordinary
Site: Open or light shade

Elaeagnus pungens
(Oleaster)
Height: 2-3cm (6½-10ft)
Spread: 1.5m (5ft)
Soil: Ordinary
Site: Sun or shade
'Aurea', yellow edge
'Maculata', yellow center

Euonymus fortunei
Height: 15-60cm (6-24in)
Spread: 60cm (2ft)
Soil: Ordinary
Site: Sun or shade
'Emerald and Gold', yellow variegated
'Emerald Gaiety', white variegated
'Variegatus', gray-green edged white

Ilex (Holly)
Height: 3-15m (10-50ft)
Spread: 3m (10ft)
Soil: Ordinary
Site: Sun or shade
'Argentea Marginata', edged white
'Golden King', broadly edged yellow
'Golden Queen', edged yellow
'Madame Briot', yellow variegated
'Silver Queen', broadly edged white

Kerria japonica 'Variegata'
(Jew's mallow)
Height: 1.2-1.8m (4-6ft)
Spread: 90cm (3ft)
Soil: Ordinary
Site: Sun or shade
White variegated

Pachysandra terminalis 'Variegata'
Height: 15-20cm (6-8in)
Spread: Indeterminate, plant 15cm (6in) apart
Soil: Ordinary, moist
Site: Shady
White variegated

Rhamnus alaterna 'Argenteo-variegata'
(Buckthorn)
Height: 1.5-3m (5-10ft)
Spread: 1.5cm (5ft)
Soil: Ordinary
Site: Open
White variegated

Vinca
(Periwinkle)
Height: trailing
Spread: Indefinite, plant 30-45cm (12-18in) apart
Soil: Ordinary
Site: Sun or shade
V. major 'Variegata', yellow variegated
V. minor 'Aureovariegata', yellow variegated
V. minor Variegata', ivory white variegated

Weigela florida 'Variegata'
Height: 2-2.4m (6½-8ft)
Spread: 1.5m (5ft)
Soil: Ordinary
Site: Open
Creamy white border to leaf

Autumn fruits/winter blooms

As autumn advances, nature takes over and brings everything into harmony with color schemes based on yellow, brown, copper, bronze, crimson and scarlet. Much of the color is provided by the ripening leaves of deciduous trees and shrubs, but ripening fruits also play their part and in gardens may actually play a major role in the display. Because these also mainly follow the red and yellow pattern, with only occasional diversions into more esoteric colors such as lilac, blue and white, there is little opportunity for violent contrasts in devising color schemes. Indeed, it would be true to say that most of the famous autumn color gardens show few obvious signs of having been consciously arranged but occur rather as creative collections of autumn foliage and fruit-bearing plants.

What does become important when planning for autumn fruits is to ensure that the selection and conditions are right for fruit production. Many plants have devised mechanisms to ensure that their seeds are produced by cross-pollination from other plants of the same kind, rather than by self-fertilization with their own pollen. The reason for this is that inbreeding tends to magnify constitutional weaknesses, whereas cross-breeding helps to maintain vigor.

So important is this to the survival of species that some plants have developed mechanisms which make self-pollination impossible. Plants may produce flowers of one sex only — male flowers on one, female on another — so that unless plants of both sexes are grown reasonably close together, no fruits can be produced. Rarely, gardeners have been able to break down this (dioecious) mechanism by searching for and preserving the odd mutant that produces flowers of both sexes. *Pernettya* 'Bell's Seedling', for example, is an hermaphrodite variant of a dioecious plant. Such freaks can be increased vegetatively and can be very useful.

With other plants, the mechanisms are more subtle and less absolute. Apples, for example, bear fruit when fertilized with their own pollen, but do it more freely when fertilized with pollen from another apple tree. No comprehensive studies of this kind of partial self-sterility have been carried out for ornamental plants, however, so it is wise to assume that it exists and to plant more than one tree or bush of each species chosen.

Cotoneaster horizontalis

Skimmia japonica

Aucuba japonica

Gaultheria procumbens

Ilex aquifolium

Pernettya mucronata

RED AND ORANGE	SHRUBS/TREES			OTHER COLORS	
Arbutus unedo (Strawberry tree) *Height:* 3-5m (10-16½ft) *Spread:* 1.5m (5ft) *Soil:* Ordinary, alkaline *Site:* Open Strawberry-like fruits for a long period	**Aronia arbutifolia** (Red chokeberry) *Height:* 2-3m (6½-10ft) *Spread:* 1.2m (4ft) *Soil:* Ordinary, not too much lime *Site:* Open Berries small and red	**Aucuba japonica** (Spotted laurel) *Height:* 2-3m (6½-10ft) *Spread:* 1.2m (4ft) *Soil:* Ordinary *Site:* Open or shade Red berries only produced on female bushes, such as 'Salicifolia' and 'Variegata', in the presence of a male plant such as 'Crassifolia' or 'Crotonifolia'	**Berberis aggregata, rubrostilla** and **wilsoniae** (Barberry) *Height:* 1-1.2m (3¼-4ft) *Spread:* 90cm (3ft) *Soil:* Ordinary *Site:* Open Small coral-red berries freely produced	**Berberis darwinii** (Barberry) *Height:* 3m (10ft) *Spread:* 1.5m (5ft) *Soil:* Ordinary *Site:* Open Small black berries with white bloom	**Callicarpa bodinieri** *Height:* 2-2.5m (6½-8ft) *Spread:* 1.2m (4ft) *Soil:* Ordinary, well drained *Site:* Sunny Lilac-blue berries
Cotoneaster *Height:* 15cm-6m (6in-20ft) *Spread:* 1-3m (1¼-10ft) *Soil:* Ordinary *Site:* Open or light shade *C. conspicuus decorus*, bright red *C. franchetii*, scarlet *C. horizontalis*, deep red *C. microphyllus*, deep red *C. salicifolius*, bright red *C. simonsii*, bright red	**Euonymus** *Height:* 2.5-4m (8-13ft) *Spread:* 1.2m (4ft) *Soil:* Ordinary *Site:* Open or light shade *E. europaeus*, red fruits, orange seeds *E. latifolius*, red fruits, orange seeds *E. yedoensis*, rose pink fruits, orange seeds	**Gaultheria procumbens** *Height:* 5cm (2in) *Spread:* Indefinite, plant 20cm (8in) apart *Soil:* Acid, no lime *Site:* Shade Bright red berries	**Hippophae rhamnoides** (Sea buckthorn) *Height:* 3-5m (10-16½ft) *Spread:* 1.2m (4ft) *Soil:* Ordinary *Site:* Open Small orange berries on female plants in presence of a male	**Gaultheria miqueliana** *Height:* 30cm (1ft) *Spread:* 30cm (1ft) *Soil:* Acid, no lime *Site:* Shade White or pink berries	**Ilex aquifolium** (Holly) *Height:* 3-15m (10-50ft) *Spread:* 3m (10ft) *Soil:* Ordinary *Site:* Sun or shade 'Bacciflora', bright yellow berries
Ilex aquifolium (Holly) *Height:* 3-15m (10-50ft) *Spread:* 3m (10ft) *Soil:* Ordinary *Site:* Sun or shade Red berries on most female plants e.g. 'J.C. van Thol', 'Madame Briot', 'Scotica', in presence of a male plant	**Malus** (Apple) *Height:* 4.5-6m (15-20ft) *Spread:* 4-5m (13-16½ft) *Soil:* Ordinary *Site:* Open 'Dartmouth', red and yellow 'John Downie', orange and red 'Red Sentinel', deep red 'Veitch's Scarlet', bright red	**Pyracantha** (Firethorn) *Height:* 3-4m (10-13ft) *Spread:* 1.5m (5ft) *Soil:* Ordinary *Site:* Sunny 'Lelandei', orange red 'Orange Glow', orange red 'Mojave', orange red 'Watereri', red	**Rosa moyesii 'Geranium'** *Height:* 2.5m (8ft) *Spread:* 1.2m (4ft) *Soil:* Ordinary *Site:* Open Large flask-shaped red hips	**Mahonia aquifolium** (Oregon grape) *Height:* 1.2m (4ft) *Spread:* 1.2m (4ft) *Soil:* Ordinary *Site:* Sun or shade Small black berries with white bloom	**Pernettya mucronata** *Height:* 60-150cm (2-5ft) *Spread:* 90cm (3ft) *Soil:* Acid, no lime *Site:* Open Globular berries, white, red, crimson, lilac or purple produced by female plants in presence of a male
Ruscus aculeatus (Butcher's broom) *Height:* 90cm (3ft) *Spread:* 45cm (18in) *Soil:* Ordinary *Site:* Shade Globular red berries	**Skimmia** *Height:* 60-120cm (2-4ft) *Spread:* 60cm (2ft) *Soil:* Ordinary *Site:* Sun or shade *S. japonica*, scarlet berries on female plants in presence of male *S. reevesiana*, scarlet berries	**Stranvaesia davidiana** *Height:* 3-6cm (10-20ft) *Spread:* 2m (6½ft) *Soil:* Ordinary *Site:* Sun or light shade Holly-red berries	**Sorbus** (Rowan, mountain ash) *Height:* 6-9m (20-30ft) *Spread:* 3-5m (10-16½ft) *Soil:* Ordinary *Site:* Open *S. aucuparia*, orange to scarlet *S. sargentiana*, bright red	**Symphoricarpos** (Snowberry) *Height:* 1.2-2m (4-6½ft) *Spread:* 90cm (3ft) *Soil:* Ordinary *Site:* Sun or shade *S. albus*, globular white berries *S.* 'Doorenbos Hybrids', pink or white berries *S. orbiculatus*, magenta berries	

Sometimes there are unexplained differences between the behavior of two plants of the same kind. The first *Cotoneaster conspicuus decorus* I planted failed to produce any of its brilliant red berries. A friend gave me a seedling from his own well-fruited bush — and that has continued to fruit prodigiously for the past twenty years or so. I have no idea how those two bushes differed, but it does point the lesson that if failures of this kind do occur, it is wise to look for another plant from a parent of proved fertility.

The winter garden

In temperate climates in which many plants drop their leaves in the autumn, color in winter is inevitably greatly reduced. Evergreens remain to create new patterns and new contrasts with the delicate tracery of branches of deciduous trees and shrubs. At this time evergreens with yellow leaves can become quite startling in their apparent brilliance due, in part, to the lack of competition. I have on several occasions stopped my car because I thought I had seen an unexpected winter flower, only to find that it was a golden privet or a gold variegated *Elaeagnus*.

However, there are flowers even in mid-winter, in milder climates, and some are capable of making a considerable display. Most notable are the witch hazels — at their

peak in mid-winter — and they are closely followed by snowdrops, which can make great carpets of white. Golden winter aconites can look like an early flowering of celandines, and there are other small bulbs which brave the winter in order to be free of the competition of plants flowering later.

Some of the most useful and readily available of these winter flowers are listed here, but there are others. In fact, more than one whole book has been devoted to the fascinating possibilities of the temperate garden in winter.

Clerodendrum trichotomum fargesii

Sorbus aucuparia

Helleborus orientalis

Eranthis hyemalis

Chaenomeles speciosa (lagenaria)

Hamamelis mollis

WINTER FLOWERS Perennials/Bulbs —		WINTER FLOWERS Shrubs —	
Clerodendrum trichotomum *Height:* 3m (10ft) *Spread:* 2.5m (8ft) *Soil:* Ordinary *Site:* Sunny Small turquoise blue berries	**Cotoneaster** *Height:* 15cm-6m (6in-20ft) *Spread:* 1-3m (3¼-10ft) *Soil:* Ordinary *Site:* Open or light shade *C. frigidus,* light yellow 'Exburiensis', yellow	**Crocus tomasinianus** *Height:* 5cm (2in) *Spread:* 7.5cm (3in) *Soil:* Ordinary *Site:* Open 'Barr's Purple', purple-lilac 'Taplow Ruby', red-purple 'Whitewell Purple', mauve-purple	**Eranthis hyemalis** (Winter aconite) *Height:* 5cm (2in) *Spread:* 10cm (4in) *Soil:* Ordinary *Site:* Dappled or half shade Bright yellow	**Azara microphylla** *Height:* 3-4m (10-13ft) *Spread:* 1.5m (5ft) *Soil:* Ordinary *Site:* Sun or shade, sheltered Tiny yellow flowers with a vanilla fragrance	**Camellia sasanqua** *Height:* 2-3m (6-10ft) *Spread:* 1.5m (5ft) *Soil:* Moderately acid *Site:* Dappled shade, sheltered White, pink or rose-red
Leycesteria formosa (Himalayan honeysuckle) *Height:* 2.4m (8ft) *Spread:* 1.2m (4ft) *Soil:* Ordinary *Site:* Sun or shade Aubergine-purple fruits	**Malus** (Apple) *Height:* 4.5-6m (15-20ft) *Spread:* 4-5m (13-16½ft) *Soil:* Ordinary *Site:* Open 'Golden Hornet', yellow 'Golden Siberian', yellow	**Galanthus nivalis** (Snowdrop) *Height:* 15-25cm (6-10in) *Spread:* 15cm (6in) *Soil:* Ordinary *Site:* Shade 'Atkinsii', white and green, single 'Flore Pleno', white and green, double flowers	**Helleborus niger** (Christmas rose) *Height:* 25cm (10in) *Spread:* 30cm (12in) *Soil:* Ordinary *Site:* Shade White	**Chaenomeles** (Japanese quince, japonica) *Height:* 1-3m (3-10ft) *Spread:* 1.5m (5ft) *Soil:* Ordinary *Site:* Sun or shade 'Cardinalis', light crimson 'Knap Hill Scarlet', orange scarlet 'Moerloosii', pink and white 'Nivalis', white 'Simonii', blood red	**Chimonanthus praecox** (Winter sweet) *Height:* 1.5-3m (8-10ft) *Spread:* 2m (6½ft) *Soil:* Ordinary *Site:* Sunny, warm Pale greenish yellow and purple
Pyracantha (Firethorn) *Height:* 3-4m (10-13ft) *Spread:* 1.5m (5ft) *Soil:* Ordinary *Site:* Sunny 'Buttercup', yellow *P. rogersiana flava,* yellow 'Shawnee', deep yellow	**Sorbus** (Rowan, mountain ash) *Height:* 6-9m (20-30ft) *Spread:* 3-5m (10-16½ft) *Soil:* Ordinary *Site:* Open *S. aucuparia xanthocarpa,* amber *S. hupehensis,* white and pink *S.* 'Joseph Rock', light yellow becoming amber *S. vilmorinii,* pink becoming paler or white	**Helleborus orientalis** (Lenten rose) *Height:* 38cm (15in) *Spread:* 30cm (12in) *Soil:* Ordinary *Site:* Shade White, pink and purple	**Iris, bulbous** *Height:* 10-15cm (4-6in) *Spread:* 10cm (4in) *Soil:* Ordinary *Site:* Sunny *I. histrioides,* light blue *I. reticulata,* light blue to deep violet-purple	**Hamamelis mollis** (Chinese witch hazel) *Height:* 3-4m (10-13ft) *Spread:* 2.4m (8ft) *Soil:* Modertely acid, no lime *Site:* Open or partial shade Yellow, paler in variety 'Pallida'	**Jasminum nudiflorum** (Winter jasmine) *Height:* 1-2m (3-6ft) *Spread:* 90cm (3ft) *Soil:* Ordinary *Site:* Sun or shade Daffodil yellow
		Iris unguicularis (Algerian iris) *Height:* 30cm (1ft) *Spread:* 30cm (1ft) *Soil:* Ordinary, well drained *Site:* Sunny, warm Pale to mid blue	**Leucojum vernum** (Spring snowflake) *Height:* 20cm (8in) *Spread:* 10cm (4in) *Soil:* Ordinary *Site:* Sun or light shade White and green	**Rhododendron mucronulatum** *Height:* 2.4m (8ft) *Spread:* 1.2m (4ft) *Soil:* Acid, no lime *Site:* Dappled shade Deep magenta	**Viburnum fragrans (farreri)** *Height:* 2-3m (6½-10ft) *Spread:* 2-3m (6½-10ft) *Soil:* Ordinary *Site:* Open Pink-tinged white

TREES
&
SHRUBS

The elegant *Sorbus* 'Lutescens' (**top**) is prized for the flush of silvery young leaves it bears in spring. It is not fussy over soil and position. Quite different in shape and leaf form is the wide-spreading *Juniperus x media* 'Pfitzerana Aurea' (**above**). Such conifers are ideal as ground cover and specimen plants. The full splendor of *Nyssa sylvatica* (**right**) is realised during the autumn, when its foliage turns to glorious shades of red, yellow and orange.

Perhaps we should start by defining our terms. A tree is a woody plant with a central stem, usually referred to as a trunk, from which branches may radiate. In contrast to a tree with its central trunk, a shrub produces a number of woody outgrowths from its roots. If we think of the oak as a typical tree, then the rose is a typical shrub.

When considering trees we tend to think of large plants, and of shrubs as smaller, but dimensions do not always fit such definitions. Some of the Himalayan climbing roses grow into and over very large trees, whereas many trees may be happier amid an alpine garden than elsewhere. It is convenient, although unscientific, to refer to the smaller trees — say, those under 1.5m (5 ft) — as bushes, as long as we also bear in mind that what may eventually become a large tree may perfectly well begin in the garden as a bush.

Most trees grow upward, but there are a few trees (notably some junipers) which hug the ground and eventually cover a large area. When thinking of planting a tree, it is rare for anybody to consider such a plant as *Juniperus pfitzerana* — but a tree it is. Sometimes the distinction between a shrub and a tree is tenuous.

Most rhododendrons are technically trees, but in their youth so many of their branches seem to come from soil level that they have a shrub-like appearance. It is only when they become very old that their genuinely arboreal nature is apparent. Consequently, most of us think of rhododendrons as shrubs, and it does no harm to go on doing so. Both shrubs and trees are woody, after all, and it is this feature that tends to set them apart from other denizens of the garden.

One of the great gardening writers of the last century wrote in 1871: '. . . a few trees and shrubs, a plot of grass and comfortable walks (are) the three first essentials of a garden'. To this he added a herbaceous border, and claimed that anything else was mere embellishment. Nowadays, gardens are ordinarily smaller than was usual in the 1870s, but the essential truth of his statement remains valid. With large gardens there can be no question that he was absolutely right.

Siting trees in the garden

Trees are one of the most permanent features of the garden, so their siting is a matter of the utmost importance. Herbaceous plants, bulbs, or even small shrubs, can be transplanted if placed where they subsequently do not appeal. Trees once established, on the other hand, must be regarded as fixtures. It is in fact not impossible to move large trees, at considerable expense in both money and time, but it is certainly not practical for an amateur. Far better before planting your tree to give thought to all the possible advantages and disadvantages.

There are a number of uses for trees, apart from that of pure ornament. In a small garden, for example, a tree can be the focal point for the whole design. There can be more than one focal point. Alternatively, trees can be planted round the perimeter, to mark the limits of the garden and provide a pleasing background for other plants; they can be used to provide shade, to provide spectacle in blossom, flower or attractive foliage; to provide color in spring, autumn, or even in winter; and it would seem that there are few requirements of a gardener that a tree cannot be found to supply.

The main disadvantage of trees is that they grow slowly, so that it may be many years before they achieve the desired effect. Another drawback is that the larger trees have an equally large root system under the ground which must take nourishment from the soil, to the impoverishment of other plants. This need not, of course, be catastrophic, for the nutrients can be replaced either by chemicals or by garden composts and animal waste.

Some trees are poisonous. If there are young children in the vicinity, do not plant laburnum, for instance: the seeds are toxic, and small children may mistake them for peas and eat them with dire, possibly fatal, consequences. Even worse, the only part of the yew that is *not* poisonous is the red, fleshy cup that encloses the seed: it is this that children might well be tempted to taste, and by itself it would do them no harm — but if they bit into the internal seed that the cup surrounds, they would quickly become very ill.

Of course there are plenty of suitable trees besides laburnum or yew, but with young children you can never be too careful. Thorny trees could also cause distress. Hawthorns, if they have a decent trunk, are probably out of the reach of the young, but gleditsias may have thorns on their trunks. There is, however, a thornless form of the most common gleditsia —*G. triacanthos,* known as 'Inermis' — so if you wish to see at close quarters the delicate, fern-like leaves of the honey locust, it can be done without the risk of laceration.

Another disadvantage of trees is that the ground around them becomes extremely dry, because the canopy of leaves above may be so thick that nothing can grow underneath. This is not such a disadvantage with deciduous trees (which shed their leaves in autumn) for spring bulbs and such early-flowering subjects as primroses grow happily underneath them, just as they do in the wild, and in the dry area just beyond the effects of the canopy Mediterranean plants such as cistus and the shrubby euphorbias may find conditions to their liking.

Many of the disadvantages of trees can thus be overcome with a little forethought — the ever-present watchword of the tree planter. Before planting, you should have some idea of the final dimensions of your chosen tree. If you decide to plant a cedar, let's say, what you will probably start with is a rather small stick, maybe 90cm (3ft) high and 30cm (12in) across ... which gets taller and wider every single year, as year follows year — and 200 years is not an excessive age for a cedar — so you

The autumn tints are just beginning to show on this *Acer palmatum* 'Osakazuki' (**far left top**). Gradually the whole tree will turn a brilliant fiery red. The range of colors and leaf shapes among conifers is very wide. This blue spruce, *Picea pungens glauca* (**far left bottom**), forms a medium-sized tree with young foliage a striking shade of blue. Aptly named the Golden Rain tree *Koelreuteria paniculata* (**left**) bears abundant yellow flowers in mid-summer. Grow this medium-sized tree in good loam in a sunny position.

should bear the enormous eventual tree in mind when planting the tiny sapling. Patience may be required to wait to see it at all from indoors at first — but later, if you have planted it too close to the house it will eventually take all the light away and your electricity bill will soar.

It is a sound rule of thumb that no potentially large tree should be planted nearer the house than 10m (33ft); 15m (50ft) is preferable. Tree roots can also damage a house's foundations, so the farther away from the house that forest trees are planted the better. Smaller trees may have additional dangers. Poplars, willows and alders in the wild tend to grow in wet places; their roots are particularly suited for seeking out water. Should there be the smallest fissure in nearby underground drainpipes, the roots of these subjects seek them out, enter, and crack them or block them with their roots. With these plants it is necessary to find out beforehand where your drainage system runs, and to be careful not to plant any of these subjects in its vicinity. Elsewhere in the garden they do no harm, and indeed, placing a weeping willow near a small pond is a favorite ploy of garden designers.

Types of trees

Trees may be divided into angiosperms and gymnosperms or, more colloquially, into broadleaved trees and conifers. The broadleaved trees include some plants with needle-like foliage, such as the tree heather, and

at the same time the seed heads of alders are shaped much like pine cones, but in spite of these unusual forms the distinction is generally quite clear. All trees are either deciduous — losing their leaves in the autumn, overwintering with bare branches, and producing fresh leaves in the spring — or evergreen, which keep their leaves throughout the winter. In fact, with some evergreens the leaves remain on the tree for several seasons; with others, the old leaves tend to fall away as the new leaves emerge.

The reason that some plants are evergreen whereas others are deciduous is not always clear-cut. Most oaks are deciduous, for example — but some, such as the cork and holm oaks, are evergreen. Usually it would seem that where winters are ordinarily extremely cold, dark, and with frequent strong winds, the tendency is for trees to be deciduous. They are less likely to be damaged by storms and, in that their leaves need daylight in which to function, the disadvantage of the loss of daylight in winter is minimized. Although this sounds

logical, there are plants such as holly which remain evergreen even in regions where short days occur annually, and in the same contrary fashion, the inhabitants of the coldest and stormiest regions in extreme latitudes are commonly evergreen pines and firs.

The ornamental value of trees

Fortunately the gardener need not be concerned about why a plant should be evergreen or deciduous, just with the results. Evergreen trees certainly enliven the garden during the winter months, but many of them tend to look a little heavy during the summer. Moreover, the delicate tracery of boughs and branchlets of deciduous trees during the winter often has its own fascination — so, if space allows, a judicious mixture of deciduous and evergreen trees probably gives the happiest result.

Deciduous trees can have other attractions during the winter. Many of them have attractive wood. The glistening white, cream, or pale pink trunks of various birches, for instance, contrast happily with the almost thread-like twigs of the past year's growth. The green and white striations of the snake-bark maples, of which there are a number, are particularly striking at this season, as is the flaking cinnamon bark of *Acer griseum* and the polished mahogany-like appearance of the trunks of the Tibetan cherry, *Prunus serrula.*

In other deciduous plants it is the young wood that is colored. The coral-bark maple *Acer palmatum* 'Senkaki', is coral-pink; the young growths of some varieties of *Salix alba* are especially vivid — 'Vitellina' is orange-yellow and 'Chermesina' has red bark. Another willow, *Salix irrorata,* has young wood that is purple overlaid with a silvery bloom. It is certainly possible to have color in the garden in winter without evergreens.

Nevertheless, evergreens are naturally also colorful at this period. *Elaeagnus pungens* 'Maculata', which has gold splashes in the center of its dark green leaves, gives an impression of sunshine even during the dullest days. There are a number of silver and yellow variegated hollies which look attractive throughout the year but are at their best during the winter. Some columnar conifers, mainly the thujas and false cypresses, have either golden or steel-blue foliage, as do some of the larger conifers such as the blue cedar, *Cedrus atlantica* 'Glauca', and the blue spruce *Picea pungens glauca,* of which a number of named forms exist. These large blue conifers are not altogether suitable for small gardens, where a single blue tree can be simply overwhelming; when surrounded by trees of more ordinary coloration, the effect is less intense.

Colorful foliage is not confined to winter. There are a number of deciduous trees which have golden or variegated foliage, producing a longer display than either flowers or colored fruits do. The effect is enhanced if the variegated trees are used with restraint among green-leaved trees. Such restrained use should also apply to trees with purple leaves, such as the popular *Prunus cerasifera* 'Pissardii' and the purple beech. These look splendid in the spring as the leaves are unfurling, when the sun makes them glow like rubies, but they begin to look a bit heavy as the summer advances . . . and the purple beech does nothing at all in the autumn, when the green-leaved ones are turning golden.

Some leaves, indeed, achieve color only at one season. *Pieris formosa forrestii* has flowers like the lily-of-the-valley in spring, followed by young growth that is a vivid red, contrasting with the green leaves of the previous season. In fact, the young growths are more showy than the flowers. Another evergreen, *Photinia X fraseri,* also has young growths in various shades of red, from the coppery red of 'Robusta' to the bright red of 'Red Robin'. Many trees have silvery young leaves, including several rhododendrons and the whitebeam, *Sorbus aria.* In others, such as the Indian horse chestnut, *Aesculus indica,* and the Golden Rain tree, *Koelreutera paniculata,* the young leaves are bronzy. The young leaves of *Maackia chinensis* are a curious mixture of slate-blue and silver; the tree looks spectacular for a fortnight, but is rather dull thereafter.

Even more trees turn brilliant colors in the autumn. One of the most useful, although small, has the unwieldy name of *Malus tchonoskii;* it has an upright habit. Its leaves are silver, and turn a succession of flame-like tints before they fall in the autumn. Some of the maples previously mentioned for their handsome bark also color red and gold before the leaves fall; those of the coral-bark maple, *Acer palmatum* 'Senkaki', on the other hand, turn butter yellow. *Acer palmatum* 'Osakasuki' turns a really fiery scarlet. The tupelo, *Nyssa sylvatica,* which is inconspicuous for most of the year — you may have to search to find the small greenish flowers at all — suddenly transforms itself into a pillar of fire. The Golden Rain tree, which has almost all the advantages — handsome young leaves, attractive mature foliage, late yellow flowers, followed by bronzy bladder-like capsules — closes its repertoire with golden, or occasionally scarlet, tints.

Tree shapes

The shapes of trees are significant. Basically, trees grow as pyramids: the older, lower branches extend for some distance, while the younger, upper ones progressively do so less and less. In a garden without competition from others, trees maintain this shape for a long time. In forests, as the trees enlarge, the light is cut off from the lower branches, which die and fall off to expose the trunk. In a situation without competition, if a bare trunk is required, you may have actually to saw away the lower branches. Many nurserymen provide what are termed 'standards', in which the trunk (not infrequently of another species) is already formed. Standard amelanchiers, for example, are frequently amelanchiers budded onto the trunk of a whitebeam; and standard cherries are almost always budded onto a trunk of the wild cherry. In such cases it is essential to keep the trunk clear, or the stock may overtake the plant you require.

Shapes can alter, however. Many trees that are normally pyramidal have both fastigiate and weeping forms. Fastigiate trees are like spires in outline; the side branches rise perpendicularly rather than horizontally. The Lombardy poplar is a good example. Such forms are usually called 'fastigiata' in catalogues. Weeping trees have branches that tend to droop, with the branchlets hanging down. These are usually called 'pendula' in the catalogues, and the weeping willow is among the best known. A third type comprises the 'tabular' trees — those in which both branches and branchlets are horizontal, so that the trees look like a series of layers. The Cedar of Lebanon is a good example. In general, trees seem to be tabular by nature: no unusual tabular shapes have been recorded. As they age, some trees become round-topped and others flat, but not before the trees have acquired their full dimensions.

Weeping
Hybridization and selective breeding have produced a number of beautiful weeping trees, notably weeping willows and birches.

Conical
Many trees, especially conifers, assume a conical shape when mature. In a forest the lower branches may not develop fully.

Fastigiate
These trees have a narrow columnar shape. Prime examples are the Lombardy poplar and many garden forms of conifers.

Spreading
Most broadleaved trees assume an open spreading shape with a rounded top. The oak tree is a classic example of this type of growth.

Planting trees in the garden

The actual operation of planting trees requires care and forethought. It makes comparatively little difference whether the trees arrive from the nursery lifted from the ground or whether they have been kept in containers. It is claimed that container-grown trees can be planted at any time of the year, even when they are in flower, but this is only true to a limited extent. It is generally not the state of the tree when purchased that is important, as much as the ease with which it can become established. And to become established means making abundant root growth during its first season. A plant removed from a container in midsummer normally survives, it is true, but makes little growth for the rest of the year — and so is more vulnerable to a bad winter, and is certainly slower again to get away in the following season.

In theory, the container-grown plant should get away more rapidly if planted at the correct season. This does not always happen, however, often because the roots have become so convoluted in their containers that unless they are teased out when planted, they take a long time to penetrate the soil in the garden. This has been found actually to be the case in some nurseries where plants that have unexpectedly made no significant growth have been lifted, and it has been seen that the roots have found it impossible to escape from the original soil ball, and have thus remained potbound. Unlikely though it sounds, therefore, it is best, if the container seems excessively full of roots, to shake the soil off the roots and try to rearrange them in a normal spread.

In nature most trees send down one long root to anchor the plant, and then send out roots in all directions to gather nourishment from the soil. In a container all the roots are forced into the shape of the container. In fact, they become distorted. So although one of the advantages of the potted plant is that it can be planted without disturbing the roots, there is also the fact that, to a limited extent, the roots become damaged just by being grown in a restricted space.

Sometimes the grower has no choice. Brooms have a long taproot, breaking which kills the plant. Brooms must on that account be grown in pots before planting out; it is very doubtful whether brooms lifted from the open ground would transplant successfully. It has also been found that clematis are very difficult to move unless grown in pots. Apart from these few exceptions, the majority of trees move quite happily from the open ground.

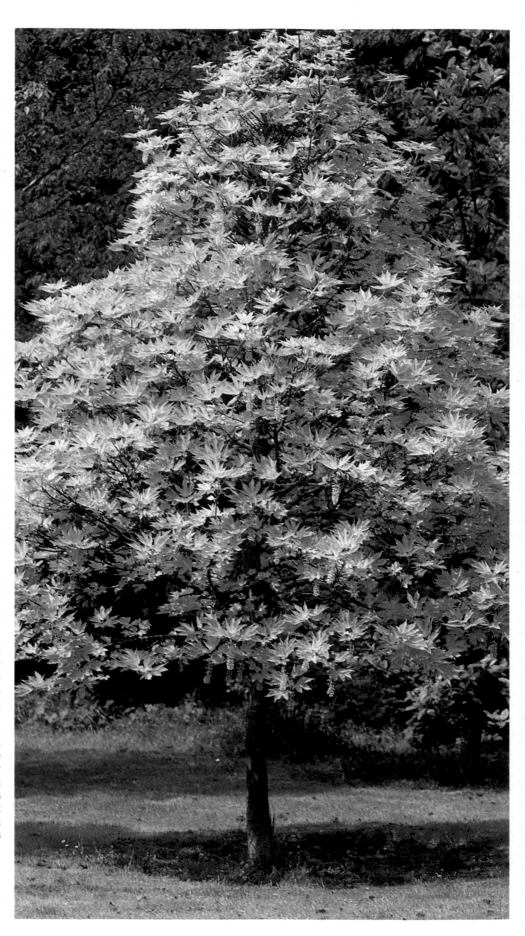

Acer pseudoplatanus 'Prinz Handjery' (**right**), a small tree for garden planting.

How to plant trees

First dig a hole large enough to take the roots of the tree and loosen the soil at the bottom to a depth of at least 30cm (12in).

Insert a tree stake securely into the ground on the side facing the direction of the prevailing wind (i.e. into the wind).

Set the tree in the hole, carefully spreading out the roots. To prevent infection trim off any damaged or broken roots.

Add well-rotted manure or peat before returning the soil. Firm down and attach the tree to the stake with adjustable ties.

Prune the branches of newly planted bare-rooted trees by about one third to compensate for any damage sustained by the roots.

Having watered the tree thoroughly, apply a mulch around the base of the tree to a depth of 5cm (2in) to conserve moisture in the soil.

When to plant trees

The period for planting trees varies somewhat according to the habit. Deciduous trees have an obvious dormant period when leaves are off them, and so are best moved at any suitable time between late autumn and early spring. Evergreens seem to be best moved either in mid-autumn or in mid-spring, although they are never fully dormant. If they are moved in mid-autumn, the soil is still warm enough to encourage some root growth before the cold weather discourages the roots from elongating. Similarly, by mid-spring the soil is warming up again and the roots should start to grow at once.

Whether you prefer the autumn to the spring may depend to a certain extent on where you live. Where spring is usually rather dry, autumn would seem to be a better time to plant evergreens, whereas where spring is wetter, spring may be preferred. It is not critical which of these seasons you choose, however, rather a matter of convenience. Deciduous trees have a longer period during which they can be planted, but since mid- to late winter may be very frosty or even bitterly cold, late autumn and early winter are usually preferable.

Obviously, the main purpose behind all the methodology in planting trees is to get them established and growing as soon as possible. One way of actively encouraging this is to keep the tree out of the soil for as short a time as possible — which may entail preparing the site before the plant arrives. Of course some adjustment may be necessary, depending on the size of plant you then obtain, but some general spade-work can be carried out in advance. Excavate a circular hole about 1.2m (4ft) in diameter and 45cm (18in) deep. With a fork, loosen the soil for a further 30cm (12in) at the bottom of the hole.

When planting a tree in the lawn, remove the turf around the hole so as to make a bed at least 2m (6½ft) — or preferably 3m (10ft) — in diameter (with the planting hole in the center). Grass might otherwise take a lot of nutrients from the soil at the expense of the tree; indeed, one way of restricting the growth of trees is to allow a lawn to come up close to the trunk. (You may wish to do this much later, but not with a new tree.)

When the tree arrives, examine the roots and take off with secateurs any parts that may be cracked or split. Set the tree in the hole and ensure that the soil level is the same as that in which the tree was originally growing. Because there will inevitably be some subsidence as the soil firms down, heap up the soil a few centimetres above the old soil level, but not more. For many trees it is bad to be planted too deeply and, in the case of rhododendrons, it may prove fatal. It is at this time that you may have to make adjustments either upwards or downwards to your original excavation. Sprinkle some peat or well-rotted manure around the roots and cover them with soil. Then add a scattering of bonemeal or hoof and horn, or some slow-release chemical fertilizer.

The next thing is to stake the tree. Unless it is given time to establish itself in your garden, it will be very susceptible to the effects of wind. Rocking can harm the tree in two ways: it can break the roots, and it can cause an abraded hole through the outer layers to appear round the bottom of the trunk, into which rain can seep and rot the wood. So a good stake, although expensive, is essential, and is most easily inserted before you fill in the hole. It should be about 15cm (6in) from the trunk and carefully situated on the side of the prevailing wind, i.e. into the wind. Now fill in

the hole simultaneously treading the earth firmly around the roots. Once this is done, attach the tree to the stake. It is possible to buy adjustable ties which have a buckle, enabling you to loosen the tie as the trunk expands over the years. Wire or rope might chafe the trunk and cause damage, so a tie must be fairly wide and flexible.

However much care has been taken at the nursery, the roots of your new tree will have sustained some damage, so it is sound policy to lighten their burden and shorten the aerial parts of the tree by about one-third. In this way the roots are able to supply what is left. Conditions during the first year are critical for the tree, so make sure the soil does not dry out. Moisture is best retained with a mulch; put this on in spring when the soil has become moist. Peat, farmyard manure or shredded bark are all suitable mulches, and should be put on to a depth of 5cm (2in). Garden compost, leaf mold or bracken are also suitable. A mulch is essential for the first year; repeated in succeeding years, growth is that much more rapid.

On no account should trees be planted when the ground is waterlogged or frozen. If such conditions do obtain when the plants arrive, they will be quite happy for some time in a cool shed; the roots should be covered in sacking, especially if frost is likely, but they do not need to be warm. If water lies for any length of time in the hole you have dug, you have probably chosen an unsuitable site and must think again. Many trees are unsuitable for soils with a high water table — but a local nurseryman should be able to advise you on this. It makes little difference with shallow-rooted plants such as rhododendrons, but some of the larger trees die if their roots descend to permanent water.

Small deciduous trees

The choice of trees, although for many reasons far less than it was some ten years ago, is still large, and we should perhaps start by considering small deciduous trees. By 'small', a final height of around 10m (33ft) is implied. Alphabetically, we should no doubt begin with *Abutilon vitifolium* and its hybrid *A. X suntense*. Rapid in growth, these are bushes rather than trees, with grayish leaves and lavender or deep mauve flowers in early summer; the flowers look like small hollyhocks. Usually the plant is not very long-lived, but it comes very rapidly from seed.

Many of the maples are rather too large for this category, but most of the snake-barks grow at moderate latitudes, as do the Japanese maples, which are forms of *Acer palmatum* cultivated for many centuries in Japan. Although they eventually make small trees, they are very slow-growing and take many years even to exceed bush dimensions. They resent excessive wind, but otherwise present few problems, although chalky soil might prove unsuitable. There are forms with green, variegated and purple leaves; many of them color brilliantly in the autumn; and the young wood of 'Senkaki' has been mentioned already. The snake-barks include *A. capillipes, A. davidii, A. grosseri, A. pennsylvanicum* and *A. rufinerve:* all make small trees with striated trunks, and most also have good autumn color. Giving the trunks a good scrub with a brush in the autumn shows them to the best advantage. *Acer griseum* has peeling bark, revealing cinnamon-colored wood below and the most gorgeous autumn tints. It has apparently been known to make quite a large tree — but it grows almost infinitely slowly. Another species of *Acer*, the sycamore, is far too large for this section but has two dwarf forms with showily colored young leaves: *A. pseudoplatanus* 'Brilliantissimum' and 'Prinz Handjery'. The young leaves, often described as shrimp pink, fade to greenish yellow.

The amelanchier is a marvellous small tree, with purplish young leaves, white flowers in late spring, and good autumn colors. Its botanical name is *Amelanchier X lamarckii*, but it is just as likely to turn up in catalogues as *A. canadensis, A. laevis* or *A. grandiflora*. Whatever alias it goes under, it is a first-rate small tree. Its Chinese relative, *A. asiatica*, has a more graceful habit and flowers even more freely. It does not turn color in autumn but may then produce a second crop of flowers.

Berberis are usually regarded as smallish shrubs, but in suitable conditions some can attain quite a size; most of them are evergreen, however. But plants of the Carminea group, such as 'Barbarossa', can quickly reach 2m (6½ft). The yellow flowers open in early summer, but it is autumn when fruits and leaves turn crimson that the plant is at its best. *Berberis temolaica* can reach 3m (10ft), and has glaucous blue leaves on arching stems which make an impressive foliage feature. The plant is sometimes rather slow to re-establish itself after being moved.

Most of the buddleias tend to be shrubby in appearance, although they do have a short trunk. In the case of *Buddleia alternifolia*, though, it is worth shaping the tree to have a visible trunk at least 1m (3¼ft) tall so that its weeping character becomes evident. It has narrow, silvery leaves, and in mid-summer the branches are covered with small, fragrant lavender flowers. It is one of the most delightful small trees of any description. The common butterfly bush, *B. davidii*, seems to produce its best effects if annually pruned hard in early spring, making a rather awkward-looking plant for part of the year. This treatment does, however, result in longer panicles of flowers in late summer. There are a number of color forms varying from white through various shades of mauve and violet to red and crimson-purple; 'Harlequin' has the

leaves variegated with ivory. In sheltered districts it is worth growing the large *B. colvilei*, which bears large crimson flowers in early summer. Young plants are frost tender, but older plants seem hardy. The showiest of all buddleias, it may reach 8m (26ft).

The Judas tree, *Cercis siliquastrum*, rarely exceeds 6m (20ft) in height, although it may spread sideways to a greater extent. Before the kidney-shaped leaves emerge, rosy purple pea-shaped flowers wreathe the branches and

Acer palmatum   Amelanchier
                 X lamarckii

Cercis siliquastrum

Cornus alba   Buddleia davidii

Cornus kousa chinensis (**left**) develops into an elegant small tree with large white flower bracts in mid summer. *Cornus florida rubra* (**below left**) produces its floral display in late spring and early summer. Rose-pink bracts surround the tiny flowers. *Amelanchier X lamarkii* (**right**) bears a mass of white spring blooms. For a deep pink spring show choose *Cratagus oxyacantha* 'Rosea Flore Pleno' (**below**).

may even sprout from the trunk. A few years' waiting achieves the full effect. Spring frosts may affect the flowers, which open in late spring; the tree is actually native to the Mediterranean and so unsuitable for very cold districts.

Clerodendrum trichotomum is more a large shrub than a tree, but it can reach 4.5m (15ft) or more. There are few late-flowering shrubs, but this one is at its best in early autumn, when it produces panicles of white, fragrant flowers

about 2.5cm (1in) across and backed by dark crimson sepals. If the autumn is warm enough these may be followed by bright blue fruits which make an extraordinary addition to the repertoire of colored fruits. Another large, late-flowering shrub is the Chilean *Colletia armata*, which covers itself in mid-autumn with small, fragrant white flowers. It is ferociously spiny, making gorse seem quite innocuous — but it does give a fine display at a time when there is little else, growing up to 2.4m (8ft) in height.

The dogwoods form an important group of garden plants, although their flowers are not outstanding. Three species — *Cornus florida, C. nuttallii* and *C. kousa chinensis* — have small flowers surrounded by large white bracts (pink in *C. florida rubra*) so that they give the effect of being covered with flowers. *C. florida* seems only to flower well in milder regions — coloring vividly in autumn — but the other two are more hardy, *C. kousa chinensis* being the best. The latter can in time make a tree up to 7m (23ft) tall, but such large plants are rare; the others are smaller. In addition, *C. kousa* can

produce large red fruits like strawberries in autumn, although these are rarely seen if there is only one plant present. Cross-fertilization seems to improve the chances of this fruiting. *C. kousa* flowers in mid-summer; the others about three weeks earlier. In the same genus, *Cornus alba* is a suckering shrub that grows up to 3m (10ft) high with brilliant red bark, at its best in 'Sibirica'. 'Spaethii' has less brilliant wood, but the leaves are variegated with gold so that it is ornamental in summer as well as in winter. *Cornus controversa* makes a sizeable tree with tabular branches on which heads of cream flowers open in late spring. It is rather too large for this section, but its variegated form ('Variegata') remains a small tree rarely exceeding 6m (20ft). It has the same tabular habit, and the leaves have attractive silver variegation, making this one of the most appealing of small trees.

The *Corylopsis* group of shrubs bear racemes of flowers that look like large catkins. The earliest to flower is *C. pauciflora*, which needs an acid soil. It has primrose flowers in early spring. The others also have yellow flowers; one of the best is *C. willmottiae* 'Spring Purple', which can reach 2m (6½ft) or more, and in which the young leaves are plumcolored. Mid-spring is the season for *Corylopsis*, for the flowers can be ruined by spring frosts.

The 'smoke' or 'wig' tree, *Cotinus coggygria*, is noteworthy for its circular leaves and the curious threads that surround the small flowers and give a smoky impression. The plants can reach 4m (13ft) high, but are usually smaller. Most forms color well in the autumn and have threads that are fawn in hue; in 'Purpureus', however, the threads are pinkish. There are a number of purple-leaved forms with different names: 'Royal Purple', for example, has dark purple leaves. They all tend to turn crimson before falling.

The hawthorns, species of *Crataegus*, are splendid small trees with white flowers,

Corylopsis pauciflora   Crataegus   Cornus kousa chinensis   Acer capillipes   Acer griseum   Cotinus coggygria

colored fruits, and often good autumn color. Forms of May, *C. oxycantha,* have been found with double white flowers, and single and double red and pink flowers. These are showy when in bloom but have little to offer at other times. One of the best of the remaining species is the Washington thorn, *C. phaenopyrum,* which does not open its flowers until mid-summer, when flowering trees are scarce. Later it bears haws that look as if they had been dipped in scarlet sealing-wax; there are also splendid autumn tints in the foliage. The cockspur thorn, *C. crus-galli,* has very long thorns, up to 7.5cm (3in) long, but makes up for that with large, handsome flowers, large red fruits and a superb autumn display. Closely allied, but with even longer thorns, is *C. macracantha.* There are few species in this genus which are not good small trees.

Deutzias are delightful shrubs closely allied to the syringas but with smaller flowers in racemes. They rarely exceed 2m (6½ft) in height, although *D. scabra* can reach 3.6m (12ft). The flowers are mainly white, but there are some pale purple flowers such as 'Mont Rose' and 'Perle Rose'. They are shrubs rather than trees, and are delightful garden plants. Most flower in early summer, but *D. gracilis* comes out in late spring; *D. scabra* may well wait until mid-summer.

The oleasters contain both evergreen and deciduous species. Of the latter the Silver Berry, *Elaeagnus commutata,* is a suckering shrub with young leaves which really do look as though they were made from silver. *Elaeagnus angustifolius* can eventually make a moderate-sized tree with silvery willow-like leaves, small but extremely fragrant flowers, and eventually a polished trunk. It grows rapidly but seems to take its time to make a sizeable base; it is rather thorny.

In an acid soil, the various species of *Enkianthus* are well worth growing. They all make small shrubs — usually less than 2m (6½ft) high — and have remarkably sym-

In an acid soil *Ucryphia glutinosa* (**right**) will bear large white flowers in late summer and put on a splendid display of red and orange foliage in autumn. The snowdrop trees, *Halesia* (**below** and **below right**), are well named for the rows of droopy white flowers that adorn the branches in late spring. *Laburnum* 'Vossii' (**far right**) is prized for its early summer show of yellow, slightly fragrant flowers in pendulous racemes.

metrical growths, with the leaves in whorls. The bell-shaped flowers emerge at the same time as the leaves, and in the most frequently grown, *E. campanulatus,* they are pale yellow tipped with red. It can make a small tree up to 3.6m (12ft), and the leaves generally color well in the autumn. If obtainable, *E. chinensis* makes a larger plant. The heather family really does require an acid soil, though.

Eucryphia glutinosa is a glorious small tree with pinnate leaves which usually color well before falling, and in late summer white flowers up to 6cm (2¼in) across, looking like single roses. It prefers an acid soil and is the only deciduous species in cultivation.

Good autumn color is not always easy to obtain on chalky soils, but the spindle tree, *Euonymus europaeus,* is a small tree that in autumn is bright with pink, orange-seeded fruits and flaming leaves. 'Red Cascade' is a particularly good fruiting clone. *E. latifolius* is rather more of a shrub, but has larger leaves and fruits which mature in early autumn.

Exochordas are spreading bushes with long

Elaeagnus angustifolius   *Genista aetnensis*   *Laburnum 'Vossii'*   *Exochorda X macracantha*   *Ekianthus campanulatus*   *Hamamelis japonica*

racemes of white flowers in late spring. *E. racemosa* is the most usually seen, and needs an acid or neutral soil. The larger, flowered hybrid *E. X macracantha*, however, tolerates some alkalinity as do most of the other species.

Most of the ash trees are too large for this section — but if it can be obtained, *Fraxinus mariesii* is one of the most elegant of small trees, with purplish young leaves, heads of creamy flowers in early summer, followed by purple keys (seeds). It is difficult to obtain but very rewarding.

The Mount Etna broom, *Genista aetnensis*, makes a tree up to 3m (10ft) with mainly leafless twigs covered in yellow pea-like flowers in mid-summer. The snowdrop trees, *Halesia*, require an acid soil but make very handsome small trees, covered with white, snowdrop-like flowers in late spring.

The witch hazels, *Hamamelis*, are noted mainly for their spidery yellow flowers which open at any suitable time from early winter to early spring. They tend to spread outwards rather than grow upward and are not rapid in growth, although they start to flower when quite small. The Chinese witch hazel, *H. mollis*, is perhaps slightly preferable to *H. japonica*, but both are excellent plants. There are also hybrids between them, some — such as 'Diane' — that have reddish flowers; 'Jelena' is coppery. The leaves of witch hazels color well before falling.

From New Zealand come two valuable late-flowering small trees, *Hoheria glabrata* and *lyalii*, which produce clusters of flowers like large cherry blossom at mid-summer. Their vulnerability to severe winter frosts may account for their relative rarity in temperate gardens. They are rapid in growth, with quite handsome grayish leaves, and are well worth the risk.

The superb Golden Rain tree, *Koelreutera paniculata*, which we have already mentioned, has been known to exceed a height of 10m (33ft), but this is fairly unusual; it is a plant no garden should be without.

The beauty bush, *Kolkwitzia amabilis*, makes a large spreading bush which covers itself with pink, yellow-throated bell-shaped flowers in early summer. The foliage is also quite attractive, although not exciting. Laburnum has very poisonous seeds, but the falling racemes of yellow flowers in early summer are extremely attractive, particularly in the hybrid usually known as 'Vossii', which has extra-long racemes.

Magnolias must be among the most popular of all flowering trees. The most frequently seen is *M. X soulangeana*, which bears white flowers, some with a blotch of purple at the base of the petals. There are also purple flowers in 'Lennei', which also flowers later than most, and reddish flowers in 'Picture' and 'Rustica rubra'. 'Alba Superba' is pure white. Although they eventually make trees to 10m (33ft), they are slow growers, but they flower from an early age. In districts where spring frosts are frequent, *M. sinensis* — which has hanging white flowers with a boss of crimson stamens — may be preferable. It does not flower until early summer. *M. wilsonii* is very similar. In sheltered districts, the huge-flowered *M. campbellii*, and *M. sargentii robusta*, which has pink, red, white or purple flowers, may be grown but they come into flower in early spring, are susceptible to wind damage, and do not flower until well-grown, so they are suitable only for sheltered gardens and patient gardeners. Smaller trees with smaller white flowers are provided by the hybrids *M. X loebneri* and *M. X proctoriana*; these start to flower quite soon. *M. X loebneri* 'Leonard Messel' has pale purple flowers.

The crab apples, species of *Malus*, make delightful small trees with attractive flowers; some species also have attractive fruits. There are also a number of hybrids with purple leaves. So many good ones are available that it is best to see a collection. *M. baccata* is one of the best for fruit; *M. spectabilis* 'Riversii' has delightful semi-double pink flowers; and *M. tchonoskii* has silver young leaves and a very spectacular autumn display.

In acid soil, the sorrel tree, *Oxydendrum arboreum*, makes an attractive tree with flowers like the lily-of-the-valley in late summer and very brilliant autumn colors. It seems slightly temperamental, but where it grows well it is an unusual feature in any garden.

The mock orange, *Philadelphus*, tends to make bushes rather than trees, and the genus contains some desirable plants. *P. purpurascens* has white flowers with purple calices and is one of the first to appear in early summer. *P. coronarius* is the best known and has forms with golden and with variegated leaves. Some of the hybrids, however, are even better plants: 'Etoile Rose' is a smallish bush with a purple blotch at the base of the petals; 'Virginal' has double flowers; and *P. incanus* makes a much larger shrub and does not flower before mid-summer.

Prunus, the almonds, plums and cherries, is a very large genus of small trees, all highly

Magnolia soulangiana   *Malus baccata*   *Malus tchonoskii*   *Euonymus europaeus*   *Oxydendrun arboreum*   *Prunus sargentii*

suitable for the garden. One of the best, if a largish tree is needed, is *P. sargentii,* which covers itself in pink cherry blossom in early spring and turns crimson before the leaves fall in the autumn. Two species, *P. maackii* and *P. serrula,* are grown for their bark rather than their flowers. There are so many gems that again it is best to view a collection.

The willow-leaved pear, *Pyrus salicifolia,* makes a very attractive small tree with pendulous branches, silvery leaves, and the usual pear blossom.

Most rhododendrons are evergreen, but the azaleas contain some attractive deciduous species. Apart from the hybrids, particularly appealing are *R. albrechtii,* which has plum-purple flowers, and *R. schlippenbachii,* with large pink flowers; they do, however, flower in early spring, and so may be damaged by frosts. The North American *R. vaseyi,* which has smaller pink flowers, flowers later and might be more reliable in severe climates.

Robinias make attractive small trees with ferny leaves and racemes of purplish flowers — but they are very brittle, and must be sheltered from strong winds. The best known, *R. pseudoacacia,* is a large tree. The golden-leaved 'Frisia', on the other hand, seems of more moderate dimensions. *R. hispida* and *R. viscosa* are agreeable small trees.

The elders, *Sambucus* species, make small trees, and some of the golden-leaved forms of

S. *nigra* and S. *racemosa* are among the best golden trees for the garden. S. *racemosa* also has attractive red fruits. S. *canadensis* 'Maxima' has cream flower-heads up to 30cm (12in) across, followed by almost black fruits.

The genus *Sorbus* includes both the rowans and the whitebeams. For red fruit none is better than S. *aucuparia,* of which 'Edulis' has the largest fruits. S. *cashmiriana* has pink flowers and large pendulous white fruits; 'Joseph Rock' has yellow fruits and good autumn color. S. *esserteauana* 'Flava' also has yellow fruits. S. *hupehensis* has glaucous blue leaves and pale pink fruits, as has the small graceful S. *vilmorinii.* Silver leaves are the main attraction of the whitebeam S. *aria.*

Stewartias are again attractive small trees for acid soils. They have white flowers in mid- and late summer, and usually good autumn

The large blooms of *Prunus* 'Shirotae' (**far left**) smother the branches of this compact Japanese cherry tree in spring. The blooms are pure white and fragrant, carried in long drooping clusters. An excellent garden tree growing up to 6m (20ft) in height. For delicate sprays of yellow-green foliage choose *Robinia pseudoacacia* 'Frisia' (**left**). This attractive tree, up to 6m (20ft) tall, will grow in any garden soil and tolerate polluted air. For an acid soil plant *Styrax japonica* (**above**). The white flowers are borne profusely in midsummer.

colour. S. *koreana* and S. *sinensis* eventually have handsome trunks with flaking bark. They resent being moved.

Styrax, with hanging white flowers at midsummer, are attractive small trees but slightly tender; they too require an acid soil. S. *japonica* is the easiest to obtain, and one of the best.

Syringas include all the lilacs and a number of pink-flowered hybrids called S. X *josiflexa,* of which 'Belicent' is probably the best. S. *velutina palibiniana* is a dwarf lilac which usually flowers in spring and again in autumn.

The viburnums include winter flowerers such as *V. X bodnantense,* berrying shrubs such as the Guelder rose *V. opulus* and *V. betulifolium,* fragrant flowers as in *V. carlesii* and its hybrids, and showy flowers as in the tabular *V. plicatum.* These tend to be bushy in habit, but can be trained with a trunk.

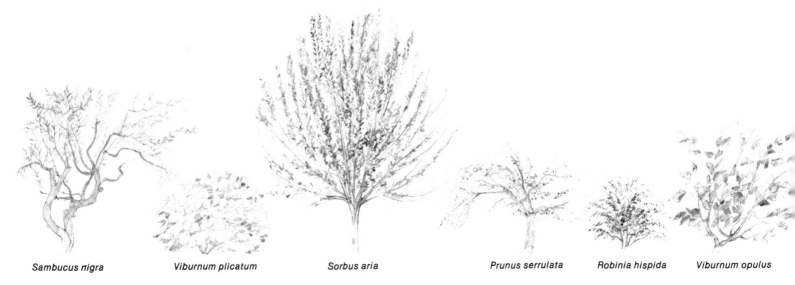

Sambucus nigra   *Viburnum plicatum*   *Sorbus aria*   *Prunus serrulata*   *Robinia hispida*   *Viburnum opulus*

Small evergreen trees and shrubs

Among the smaller evergreen shrubs the genus *Arbutus* is known from its fruits as the strawberry tree. Unlike most ericaceous plants, both the strawberry tree and its hybrid with the eastern Mediterranean *A. andrachne* known as *A. X andrachnoides,* are lime-tolerant. Both also flower and fruit at the same time, in late autumn. The rather more tender *A. arachne* flowers in spring. Apart from attractive fruits and flowers, strawberry trees also have ornamental cinnamon-colored bark. The Californian madrona, *A. menziensii,* can make a larger tree and has panicles of white flowers in late spring followed by small orange fruits, also in panicles. This requires specifically acid soil and is on the tender side.

Azaras are smallish trees from Chile, with leaves of differing sizes opposite each other, and heads of fragrant but small yellow flowers in late winter and early spring. The plants do not tolerate too prolonged frosts.

In suitable districts, *Berberis darwinii* can make a small tree, although in cooler situations it is rarely more than a large bush. Its orange flowers are conspicuous in spring, but less colorful than the orange-red flowers of *B. linearifolia,* which always remains a smaller plant. The dark blue berries are covered with a plum-like bloom in the autumn.

The bottle brushes, species of *Callistemon,* do not like severe frosts. *C. citrinus* 'Splendens', however, which has crimson bottle brushes and rigid, needle-like leaves, is reasonably easy to cultivate; the yellow *C. salignus* seems even hardier. They grow readily and rapidly from the dust-like seeds, at least in the early stages. Acid soil seems preferable. The flowers girdle the twigs, which continue to elongate briefly after the buds have formed. The color comes not from petals but from filaments of the stamens.

Acid soil is also necessary for the camellias, but in spite of their exotic appearance the majority are hardy even in very cold districts. They flower in early spring, so it is as well to locate them where they do not catch the early morning sun — where, in fact, the flowers if frosted overnight can thaw out slowly, so possibly escaping damage. Most popular are the various cultivars of *C. japonica,* occurring in single, semi-double, and fully double forms, in colors ranging from deep red through pinks to white; some even have striped petals; one or two have fringed petals. They also vary in habit: some spread and others are erect — but all flower in early and mid-spring. They start flowering when quite small but can eventually make fairly sizeable trees, although they are rather slow-growing.

In 1924 George Forrest introduced *Camellia saluenensis* from China, which bears pale pink flowers in late winter. A delightful shrub in itself, albeit more tender than *C. japonica,* it has been much used as a parent in hybrids, which are often better garden plants than *C. japonica.* One of these hybrids is *C. X williamsii,* from which a number of cultivars have been developed, flowering from late winter to late spring. 'Donation' is probably the best known of these. Most of the plants are various shades of pink; 'Francis Hanger', however, has white flowers. A good example of hybrid vigor is 'Salutation', which is perfectly hardy but which has *C. saluenensis* and *C. reticulata* — both somewhat tender species — as its parents. *C. reticulata* has the larger flowers, but both need a fairly mild climate to survive. *C. saluenensis* has alternatively been crossed with the small-flowered *C. cuspidata* to produce 'Cornish Snow', which has small white flowers in very early spring and attractive copper-colored young growth. Although the flowers are small, they are produced with great freedom. In very mild districts it may be possible to grow *C. grantha-*

Pyrus salicifolia

Sorbus aucuparia

Sambucus racemosa

Syringa velutina palibiniana

Arbutus unedo

Berberis darwinii

miana, a plant from Hong Kong, with large white flowers in early winter followed again by coppery young growth. *C. sasanqua* has small flowers in winter, but seems to experience difficulty in flowering in too temperate climes, apparently requiring a consistently hot summer to initiate flowers.

Ceanothus tend to succumb to severe winters, but they come up rapidly from cuttings. No other tree has such fine blue flowers. With the exception of the hybrids 'Burkwoodii' and 'Autumnal Blue', they all flower in late spring or early summer. The earliest to flower is also one of the largest, *C. arboreus,* of which 'Trewithen Blue' has the best color. Most of the species come from the western USA, mainly California, which indicates its ideal conditions. The genus can hybridize in the wild, and in fact the reasonably hardy *C. X veitchianus* is one of such natural hybrids; 'Cascade' makes a weeping tree. *C. thyrsiflorus* is one of the hardiest of the species. 'Autumnal Blue' and 'Burkwoodii' flower from mid-summer to early autumn but do not make so massive a display at any one time as do the spring flowerers.

Cistus are mainly rather small bushes, although *C. ladanifer* can attain 3m (10ft) in height. They come up rapidly from seed or from cuttings, but they can succumb to prolonged winter frosts — in any case, they are not very long-lived plants. The flat, rose-like flowers open over a long period in late spring and early summer, but each flower lasts only a day to be replaced by another flower the next day. *C. albidus* has silvery leaves and rather muddy purple flowers. During winter, the leaves of *C. laurifolius* — one of the hardiest species — turn glaucous gray. The bud-scales of the white-flowered *C. populifolius* are bright red. *C. ladanifer* has large white flowers with a crimson blotch in the center; it seems to do best on acid soil, whereas the other species grow in any soil. All need a sunny situation.

The larger cotoneasters are mainly

The bright blue blooms of *Ceanothus x veitchianus* (**above**) are borne in profusion during late spring and early summer. A sunny spot and light soil will suit it best. White flowers smother the arching stems of *Cotoneaster conspicuous* (**right**) in early summer. Bright red berries follow in the autumn.

Erica lusitanica (**above**) may reach 3m (10ft) high. The pink flower buds formed in winter open in early spring into fragrant white flowers. The superb deep pink blooms of *Kalmia latifolia* 'Clementine Churchill' (**right**) grace this 1.5m (5ft) bush in mid-summer. Grow kalmias in a lime-free soil.

evergreen. Most are grown for their numerous colored fruits. The exception is *C. conspicuus,* some forms of which are prostrate and are commonly trained to fall over walls or down banks. They have quite large white flowers in early summer, produced singly along the branches, followed by large crimson berries in the autumn. Most of the others are moderate trees belonging to the 'Watereri' group of hybrids between *C. salicifolius* and the deciduous *C. frigidus.* These have heads of rather dull cream flowers in mid-summer, followed by great heads of red or yellow fruits in autumn. The fruits of 'Salmon Spray' are (not surprisingly) salmon pink; those of 'Rothschildianus' are creamy yellow. *C. lacteus* and *C. glaucophyllus serotinus* flower in late summer and retain their fruits until late winter.

Crinodendron hookeranum, the Japanese

lantern tree, is a gem albeit on the tender side. Its crimson, drooping, lantern-like flowers open in late spring or early summer. Like so many Chilean shrubs, it needs shade around the roots and an acid or neutral soil. Once established, it usually regenerates, although it can be damaged during severe winters: the flower buds are formed in autumn and a bad winter may therefore disrupt the next season's flowers.

There are at least two evergreen species of *Elaeagnus* which deserve mention. *E. macrophyllus* has almost circular leaves, silver on both sides when young but later only on the underside, and small but very fragrant white flowers in mid or late autumn. *E. pungens* 'Maculata', with a bright gold splash in the center of each leaf, is one of the glories of the winter garden; it spreads more widely than it

Cotoneaster frigidus   Embothrium coccineum   Elaeagnus pungens   Erica arborea   Ceanothus arboreus
                                  lanceolatum

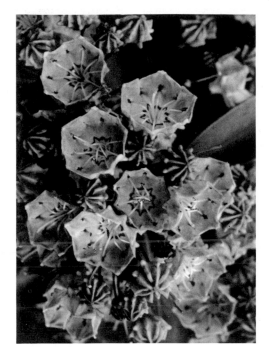

ascends, and grows rapidly. The variegation is not apparent in the leaves before they are fairly well developed — so patience and considerable caution is required before removing shoots that look as though they are reverting.

The Chilean fire bush *Embothrium coccineum lanceolatum* is yet another spectacular Chilean requiring acid soil and shade for its roots. It dislikes root disturbance, so must be brought into the garden as a young plant, preferably container-grown; it also likes a fairly moist root run. The rather spire-like small tree's branches, when mature, are covered with spidery orange-scarlet flowers in late spring and early summer, and justify all the trouble required to grow this shrub successfully.

There are three tree heathers suitable for temperate gardens: the rosy purple *Erica australis,* which is also the tenderest; *E. arborea,* which can form a true tree in sheltered districts, and which has fragrant white flowers in mid- to late spring; and the smaller but earlier-flowering *E. lusitanica,* which has pink buds that open to white flowers in early spring. All need acid soil. In milder districts, some of the South African species, like *E. canaliculata* — which can reach 5m (16ft) — might be tried.

Escallonias are fairly low-growing for the most part, with arching stems and heads of pink or red flowers from early summer to early autumn. *E. X iveyi,* however, is a much larger tree, up to 5m (16ft) tall, with white flowers in late summer and early autumn. Many of the hybrids grow excellently near the sea, seemingly impervious to salt spray.

The evergreen eucryphias are generally somewhat tender, but there are two hybrids with the hardier Chilean deciduous *E. glutinosa* that grow in most places with acid soil. *E. X intermedia* 'Rostrevor' is a hybrid between *E. glutinosa* and *E. lucida* from Tasmania: it makes a fairly upright small tree which does not flower before maturing, but then covers itself in small white flowers in late summer and early autumn. *E. X nymansensis* 'Nymansay' makes a columnar small tree with large white flowers in late summer and early autumn. Both hybrids have white flowers much like single roses in appearance.

Fatsia japonica — more popular in the last century — makes a handsome foliaged evergreen, with large palmate leaves and heads of greenish flowers in late autumn. There is an attractive variegated-leaved form.

Garrya elliptica is grown for its ornamental catkins, which on male plants may be up to 7.5cm (3in) long; those on female plants are much shorter. The trees are at their best in mid- and late winter, and grayish-green in color. Female plants produce quite showy purple fruits in autumn. The plant rarely exceeds 2.5m (8ft) in height, and can be damaged in severe winters (as might be expected of a Californian plant).

Halimium atriplicifolium, a close relative of the cistus, has silvery leaves and bright yellow flowers up to 3.5cm (1½in) across in early summer. It makes a moderate bush and is very desirable, but it is tender and suitable only where moderate winters are to be expected.

Some of the hoherias are evergreen. One of the best is *H. sexstylosa,* which has shiny green poplar-shaped leaves and clusters of white flowers in early autumn. It makes a small tree, up to around 5m (16½ft), and is the hardiest of the evergreen species, but can be damaged in very severe winters.

Most of the kalmias are small shrubs for the alpine garden, but *K. latifolia,* the calico bush, can make a bush up to 1.5m (5ft) tall, with rhododendron-like leaves and panicles of pink flowers at mid-summer. The flowers are saucer-shaped and up to 2.5cm (1in) across: pale pink when open, but deep pink in bud. The bush needs an acid soil and a fairly well-lit situation. 'Clementine Churchill' is so deep a pink as to be described as red in catalogues.

The bay, *Laurus nobilis,* can exceed the 10m (33ft) limit, but for most purposes should be considered here. It is grown mainly for its glossy, aromatic leaves, much used in cuisine. It can be damaged in bad winters, but usually regenerates.

There are a number of *Leptospermum* species in cultivation, all requiring an acid soil and all unable to tolerate too cold a winter. The manukas of New Zealand are most often seen making small trees up to 4.5m (15ft) tall, with small leaves and somewhat starry flowers in early summer, varying in color from white through pink to deep red; some cultivars have double flowers, such as 'Red Damask'. *L. lanigerum (pubescens),* with silvery leaves, and the not dissimilar *L. cunninghamii,* are less tender and have white flowers. *L. cunninghamii* flowers later than other species, in mid-summer.

The privets contain a few ornamental small

Fatsia japonica   *Garrya elliptica*   *Kalmia latifolia*   *Laurus nobilis*   *Eucryphia X nymansensis*   *Cotoneaster conspicuus*

trees with handsome leaves and panicles of creamy flowers in late summer and early autumn. *Ligustrum japonicum* and *L. lucidum* can make sizeable trees, up to 7m (23ft) or more. *L. lucidum* has two attractive variegated forms. It is common to think of privets as evergreens, but in fact most species are deciduous. The golden-leaved common privet, *L. ovalifolium* 'Aureum' can make a noble specimen if planted on its own.

Of the evergreen magnolias, *M. grandiflora* has large, fragrant cream flowers throughout the summer and early autumn. It needs wall protection in cold areas; elsewhere, it can make a large, round-headed tree. Although it also requires a good depth of soil, the acidity or alkilinity seems inconsequential. Of the various named clones, the underside of the leaves of 'Exmouth' is covered with reddish brown 'fur' (tomentum), and 'Goliath' starts to flower much sooner than other cultivars. The other evergreen magnolias — *M. delavayi*, which has very large leaves and short-lived flowers in late summer, and *M. nitida*, with shining leaves and moderate flowers in late spring — are tender plants and do not tolerate very severe winters.

Mahonias are useful bushes that usually flower in late autumn and through the winter. They have large, spiny, pinnate leaves up to 30cm (12in) long which are generally tinged purple when emerging. The best seem to be the hybrids between *M. japonica* and *M. lomariifolia,* known as *M. X media,* with cultivars such as 'Charity', 'Buckland' and 'Winter Sun', all with heads of racemes of yellow flowers which open at any time from late autumn to late winter or early spring. *M. japonica,* which has a bushy habit and pale yellow flowers smelling of lily-of-the-valley is more likely to open in late winter or early spring; *M. lomariifolia,* with its gawky habit and deep yellow flowers, usually obliges in early winter. The plants all grow vigorously but must be left to bush out at their own rhythm:

removing the growing point only causes it to produce a replacement. *M. pinnata,* of garden origin, makes a small bush with deep yellow flowers in mid- and late spring. All the plants have quite handsome bluish fruits.

The myrtles are useful evergreens for their late flowering and, in suitable districts, attractive and edible fruits. One of the best is *M. apiculata (luma),* which can make an attractive small tree with light brown bark peeling to reveal the cream-colored wood beneath. The flowers open in late summer and early autumn. *M. cheken* is a smaller tree with a slightly later flowering season. The European *M. communis* also flowers in mid and late summer; it makes a bush up to 4m (13ft) high. All the myrtles like full sun and a sheltered situation.

There are a large number of evergreen olearias, often known as daisy bushes, which have the advantage of flowering quite late in the season. The most frequently seen is *O. X haastii,* with rather small, rounded leaves and heads of fragrant white daisies in late summer. *O. avicenniifolia,* often offered (incorrectly) as *O. albida,* has pointed leaves and wider corymbs of flowers in early autumn. *O. phlogopappa (gunniana)* flowers in late spring. *O. macrodonta* has holly-like leaves and flowers in early summer; and *O. stellulata* 'Splendens' (also known as *O. gunniana* 'Splendens') has flowers in late spring of lavender blue or pale pink.

Osmanthus armatus has holly-like leaves and fragrant white flowers in mid-autumn; the leaves of *O. heterophyllus,* alternatively, are even more holly-like but the flowers open in early spring.

The evergreen photinias contain some interesting trees, of which the hybrids between *P. glabra* and *P. serrulata* — known as *P. X fraseri* — are remarkable for their brilliantly-colored young growths. 'Red Robin' has almost cerise growths, and usually flushes two or three times in the season. In any case, once the plants are large enough they can be clipped

Rhododendron yunnanense (**above**) produces masses of pale pink flowers in late spring. It is evergreen in mild sites but may lose some leaves during hard winters. It will thrive in lime-free soil and dappled shade.

The abundant white flowers of *Pyracantha rogersiana* (**right**) give way to a generous crop of autumn berries. An excellent hardy shrub for sun or shade. Many viburnums are suitable for garden planting. One of the best is *Vibrunum tinus* (**far right**). The flat heads of white flowers are borne through winter until early spring.

in early summer to encourage a second flush of growth. 'Robusta' has rather more coppery-colored new growth. It is said to be hardier than other clones — but none seems particularly tender.

With equally brilliant new growth is *Pieris formosa forrestii,* which bears flowers like the lily-of-the-valley. This has been crossed with *P. japonica* to derive 'Forest Flame', which has slightly narrower and shorter leaves that soon turn pink and then cream before turning green. *P. japonica* 'Bert Chandler' seems identical, except that it has the narrow leaves and smaller dimensions of *P. japonica*. *P. japonica* itself is a smaller bush with coppery young growth and flowers in early spring, before *P. formosa*. There are forms with pink flowers —

Ligustrum lucidum   *Olearia haastii*   *Photinia X fraseri*   *Pieris formosa forrestii*   *Rhododendron*   *Ligustrum ovalifolium*   *Mahonia japonica*

'Christmas Cheer' and 'Daisen' — and an attractive slow-growing cultivar with variegated leaves.

Pyracanthas tend to make tall bushes, much like hawthorns but evergreen, with heads of white flowers in early summer and brilliant red, orange or yellow fruits in autumn and early winter. *P. coccinea* 'Lalandei', which has scarlet fruits, is most often seen, but *P. atlantioides* 'Aurea' and *P. rogersiana* 'Flava' have good yellow fruits. *P. angustifolia* has orange fruits.

The most popular of flowering evergreen trees and bushes are the rhododendrons, for which an acid soil is essential. They have a long flowering period from winter to late summer and grow in most situations, although

dappled shade suits the majority. The so-called hardy hybrids grow in full sun. All tend to flower profusely, although not always annually, and with smaller plants great benefit is derived by removing the flower heads as soon as they have faded to prevent them from forming seed. They vary in height from prostrate bushes to sizeable trees, and there seems to be some correlation between the size of the leaves and the amount of light they enjoy: apparently, the more light is available, the smaller the leaf. Many, like the hardy hybrids, have the flowers in large trusses; others, such as the attractive *R. yunnanense,* have azalea-like flowers in groups of three. A number, such as *R. bureavii, R. mallotum* and *R. fulvum,* have the young leaves covered in orange tomentum which persists on the underside; yet others, such as *R. thomsonii, R. cinnabarinum roylei* and *R. campanulatum aeruginosum,* have glaucous blue-green leaves so that the foliage is often as ornamental as the flowers. This is particularly so with the large-leaved plants of the *falconeri* and *grande* groups. These big-leaved trees are not effective in very windy districts, for the leaves can be easily damaged. *R. sinogrande* can produce leaves 80cm (32in) long and 30cm (12in) wide. The young leaves of all these big-leaved species are delightfully silvery.

Apart from very many rhododendron species, there are also numerous hybrids. The

season starts in late winter with *R. dauricum* and *R. mucronulatum,* small bushes with magenta flowers, and ends in late summer with the large tree *R. auriculatum,* which has large fragrant white flowers not produced on young specimens.

There are a few useful evergreen viburnums, of which the laurustinus (*Viburnum tinus*), with heads of white flowers which open from early winter to late spring, is deservedly popular. A Mediterranean plant, it can suffer in bad winters but is nevertheless not as tender as its more attractive form from the Canary Islands, *V. rigidum. Viburnum X burkwoodii* has the fragrant *V. carlesii* in its parentage, and correspondingly bears fragrant flowers in late spring and early summer. 'Anne Russell' and 'Park Farm Hybrid' are clones from this cross. *V. davidii* makes a mound-shaped bush and tends to be unisexual so two or more plants should be grown together. The dull white flowers, which open in early summer, are followed by turquoise-blue fruits that persist throughout the winter in some climates and are then very striking.

'Pink Pearl' (**below**) is a popular hybrid for garden planting. The rose-pink flowers, fading in colour as they mature, are borne on vigorous shoots in early summer. In moist sheltered conditions the shrub will grow over 4.5m (15ft) in height and spread. This evergreen hardy hybrid, in common with all other rhododendrons, needs an acid soil to flourish. In chalky soils prepare a peat bed in which to grow these beautiful shrubs and trees.

Viburnum tinus   *Pyracantha*

Large trees

The larger trees — of anything from 10m to 60m (33ft to 200ft) or more tall — not surprisingly take a long time to reach full dimensions, although most are fairly sizeable after ten years. They therefore require considerable patience on the part of the gardener before their full potential is achieved. Because they are such permanent garden features, the bigger trees need positioning and selecting with unusual care.

Among the *acers* are some sizeable examples. The box elder, *A. negundo,* has pinnate leaves and makes a moderate-sized tree. The white variegated 'Variegatum' is deservedly popular for its conspicuous leaves, but 'Auratum', with golden leaves, is also attractive. The Norway maple, *A. platanoides,* is a rapid grower and has heads of green flowers in mid-spring before the leaves unfurl; at that time it looks very attractive, although appearing rather heavy later. 'Crimson King' and 'Schedleri' have purple leaves and purplish flowers. *A. rubrum* has quite brilliant red flowers in mid-spring and may color well in the autumn. 'Schlesingeri' is said to be of particularly good autumnal color. Plants on acid soils, however, always seem to color better than those on alkaline. *A. saccharinum,* the silver maple, has leaves that are silvery below and usually of good autumn color; again it is a rapid grower. The sugar maple, *A. saccharum,* turns vivid red in the autumn in northern USA but is less spectacular in milder areas.

The horse chestnuts are splendid trees, with panicles of flowers in late spring. *Aesculus carnea* is comparatively small, although large enough for this section, and has reddish panicles in late spring and early summer. The horse chestnut itself, *A. hippocastanum,* on the other hand, has white

flowers with reddish stamens. 'Baumannii' has double flowers and so does not produce chestnuts. The Indian horse chestnut, *A. indica,* is the best of the lot: the emerging leaves are bronzy, and the panicles open a month later than other horse chestnuts, in early to mid-summer.

The Tree of Heaven, *Ailanthus altissima,* has very large leaves like an enormous ash, up to 1.2m (4ft) long; it does well in towns.

The alders, species of *Alnus,* have no objection to moist situations but are otherwise not very brilliant. Yet 'Aurea' and 'Ramulis Coccineis' — cultivars of *A. incana* — have yellow young shoots and leaves, and the catkins, which appear in early spring, are at that time red and showy.

The birches contain some of the most handsomely barked trees, but are very territorial, throwing out surface roots well beyond the spread of the canopy. The bark of *Betula albosinensis* tends to be pinkish; that of *B. lutea* is amber-colored; shining white bark is alternatively provided by *B. ermanii, B. jacquemontii* and the European *B. pendula.* The cultivar 'Youngii' makes a very attractive weeping

The splendid *Catalpa bignonioides* (**left**) bears showy flowers (**above**) in mid-summer, followed by slender seedpods.

Fraxinus excelsior 'Pendula' (**below**), a magnificent tree.

form of this last species. The North American *B. papyrifera* also has attractive bark, and may additionally have quite handsome gold leaves in autumn. The birches are difficult to distinguish — but are most attractive.

The sweet chestnut, *Castanea sativa,* has long, rather foetid catkins in mid-summer, and has both white and yellow variegated forms.

Catalpas are useful trees for their late flowering — at mid-summer or just after — but

Acer platanoides *Aesculus hippocastanum* *Alnus* *Betula pendula* *Betula papyrifera* *Corylus colurna* *Davidia involucrata* *Eucalyptus gunnii*

are comparatively short-lived; specimens are said to decline after fifty years. *C. bignonioides* is the commonest, and has panicles of flowers like small foxgloves, white with yellow or purple markings. 'Aurea' has golden yellow leaves. *C. fargesii,* from China, has pinkish flowers.

The Turkish hazel, *Corylus colurna,* unlike most of the hazels, makes a large tree with a fine spring display of catkins and curiously corrugated bark. Specimens over 18.5m (60ft) are not uncommon.

The dove tree, *Davidia involucrata,* has leaves much like those of a lime tree, but after a few years covers itself in late spring with heads of inconspicuous flowers, each surrounded by two large white bracts of papery consistency up to 30cm (12in) in length and about 10cm (4in) across. A flowering specimen is a magnificent sight. Although it looks so exotic it seems unmoved even in very cold winters.

Eucalyptus gunnii, from Tasmania, is the hardiest of these Australasian trees and soon attains a moderate size. The emerging leaves are attractively silvery. *E. niphopilia* has attractive green, gray and cream bark, but is rather slow in growth.

The beeches are handsome trees of large dimensions; the best are forms of the European *Fagus sylvatica.* Of the various forms, 'Purpurea' and 'Riversii' have purplish leaves; 'Heterophylla' is the cut-leaved beech, with lobed, rather narrow leaves; 'Rohanii' is a purple-leaved slow-growing form of this; 'Dawyck' is a fastigiate (steeply conical) form, and 'Pendula' is a weeping form. All seem to thrive in any type of soil, although 'Rohanii' seems to be slower in growth than the others.

The manna ash, *Fraxinus ornus,* has heads of small white flowers in late spring and early summer, and the usual pinnate ash leaves. *F. sieboldii* is similar, but is said to have good autumn color; it may be difficult to obtain. The common ash, *F. excelsior,* has no beauty of flower, but 'Jaspidea' has yellowish wood that is bright in winter, and 'Pendula' makes a tent of green.

Gymnocladus dioicus is rather slow growing but has some of the largest leaves to be found in any garden. They are pinnate and pinkish when unfurling, turning a clear yellow before falling. The young wood is silver-gray and handsome during the winter. Apparently, the beans were used as a substitute for coffee by early settlers in North America.

The hollies include a number of medium-sized, rather slow-growing trees which can make perfect pyramids; alternatively, the lower branches can be removed to display the smooth trunk. To obtain berries, plants of both sexes should be planted. Most of the arboreal (tree-like) forms are either from the European *Ilex aquifolium,* the common holly, or from its hybrid with the Canary holly *I. perado* known as *I. X altaclarensis,* which has larger, less spiny leaves than the common holly. Of all these there are quite a few yellow and white variegated forms — usually with misleading names. Thus 'Golden King' is a female plant, and 'Golden Queen' is male. *I. latifolia,* from Japan, has extremely large leaves and requires a sheltered situation. Patience is needed with hollies; they resent moving, and must be brought into the garden as small plants.

The walnuts, species of *Juglans,* make attractive trees with perfumed leaves and edible fruits. The ordinary walnut comes from *J. regia.* All are slowish growers and usually take a long time before they start to fruit.

Liquidambar styraciflua has maple-like leaves and, once it is well established, good autumn color. The tulip tree, *Liriodendron tulipifera,* has oddly-shaped leaves like a horse's saddle, which turn a good yellow before falling. Its flowers are greenish with an orange base, and not showy.

The southern beeches are rapid growers, although not very long-lived. *Nothofagus antarctica,* which has very small leaves and rather twisted growths, is among the most attractive.

Paulownias make handsome flowering trees, with their panicles of blue-purple in late spring. The best seems to be *P. fargesii,* which flowers sooner than the better known *P. tomentosa,* which may have its flowers damaged in winter whereas those of *P. fargesii* seem less likely to be affected. Trees can reach a height of 20m (65ft).

Poplars are rapid in growth but are not among the most attractive of large trees. The young leaves of the *canadensis* group, however, are attractively copper-colored, and the white poplar, *Populus alba,* has silvery leaves. *P. X generosa* can increase at the rate of 2m (6½ft) per year. The necklace poplar, *P. lasiocarpa,* has very large, red-veined leaves but seems hard to preserve.

The various oaks, species of *Quercus,* make attractive slow-growing trees; a collection should be inspected to find one suitable for the specific conditions. The red oak, *Q. rubra,* seems to be the fastest grower.

Robinia pseudoacacia is the well-known false acacia, which has fragrant white flowers in early summer. *R. X ambigua* makes a smaller tree with pale pink flowers of which 'Bella Rosa' and 'Decaisneana' are the best cultivars.

The lime tree, *Tilia,* has fragrant flowers at mid-summer; the most attractive is the weeping silver lime, *T. petiolaris,* which has pendulous branches and silver undersides to the leaves. It is probably a form of *T. tomentosa,* also with silver undersides to the leaves.

Zelkovas make very attractive slow-growing trees, not unlike elms but with no propensity to disease. *Z. carpinifolia* and *Z. sinica* are both splendid — but *Z. serrata* has the added bonus of good autumn color.

Fagus sylvatica

Fagus sylvatica 'Dawyck'

Fraxinus exelsior

Juglans regia

Populus alba

Hardly recognizable as a conifer, the curious *Ginko biloba* (**above**) is botanically classified as one. *Juniperus communis* 'Compressa' (**right**) is ideal for planting in a rock garden. It grows slowly to form a dwarf column. For even smaller spaces *Picea abies* 'Little Gem' (**below**) forms compact mounds.

Conifers

Conifers differ from the other plants so far discussed in that they have no beauty of flower, although occasionally the fruits are ornamental. Most either have thin, needle-like leaves, or their twigs are covered with overlapping scale-like leaves. Conifers are among the oldest surviving plants and can be found in all climates, from the Arctic to the tropics. Usually they are very intolerant of atmospheric pollution — it seems always to be the conifers which are the first victims of acid rain, for example — and they are thus generally unsuitable for town gardens. Soil reaction (acid or alkaline) seems often of little importance, but it is known that young conifers, in particular, live in symbiosis with a fungus that 'infects' the roots; the roots actually make little growth if the fungus is not present. Spent hops appear to stimulate the growth of the fungus, and should be forked in (if obtainable) when the conifers are being planted. Fortunately the fungus appears to be naturally present in most soils. The great majority of conifers are evergreens, but there are some deciduous ones, including some of the most attractive.

I also include among the conifers — but only because otherwise it has no category of its own — the maidenhair tree, *Ginkgo biloba*, which seems to have survived unchanged for some 160 million years. Deciduous, it has stalked, fan-shaped leaves like a frond of maidenhair fern, which turn a clear yellow before falling. Plants are unisexual, and the fruits are plum-like, yellow in color — and offensive to the nose when the flesh is crushed (although the seeds are eaten in the East). Usually it takes a pyramidal tree, but there are fastigiate forms, and also a pendulous variant that is less consistent.

The dawn redwood, *Metasequoia glyptostroboides*, was known only as a fossil until 1941 when a stand was discovered in China. It makes a tall, conical tree up to 35m (116ft) high in the wild, and develops a buttressed trunk. A rapid grower, in spring it covers itself with bright green needle-like leaves which turn russet in autumn before falling. It seems to do best in a fairly moist situation. Propagation from cuttings is easy; used occasionally as a hedging plant, it is best as a single specimen.

The swamp cypress, *Taxodium distichum*, is not dissimilar but grows, as its English name implies, in very wet situations. Mature trees may throw up 'knees' — woody outgrowths from the roots up to the surface and above, which convey oxygen to the roots in waterlogged soil. Vivid green young leaves turn russet before they fall. The tree requires either acid or neutral soil, but otherwise seems trouble-free.

The best-known deciduous conifers are the larches: almost all are large trees with very vivid young green leaves. Larches make excellent specimens; probably the best is a hybrid of unknown provenance known as *Larix X pendula*, which makes a large tree with long hanging branchlets up to 1m (3¼ft) in length, so that a well-grown tree is extremely handsome. It is thought to be a hybrid between the European *L. decidua* and the North American *L. laricina*; the plant has been known since 1739. The Japanese larch *L. kaempferi*, much like the European larch, has a clone 'Blue Haze' which has glaucous-blue leaves — seemingly an unnecessary refinement in a larch.

Abies, the silver fir, is a genus of large trees in which the cones are large and held pointing upward; the broad needles are silvery on the underside. The young growths are often damaged by late spring frosts. Most species seem to do best in regions of high rainfall, although the Mediterranean *A. cephalonica* and *A. pinsapo* are exceptions. Most of the species make very large trees, with branches emerging in whorls up the trunk. *A. delavayi*

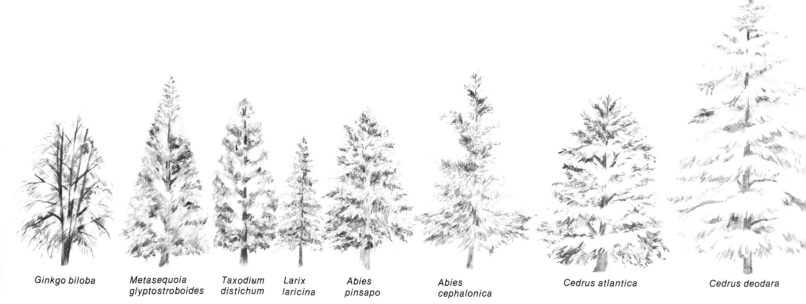

Ginkgo biloba | Metasequoia glyptostroboides | Taxodium distichum | Larix laricina | Abies pinsapo | Abies cephalonica | Cedrus atlantica | Cedrus deodara and *A. speciosa* have bluish cones. *A. koreana* has violet cones, but is a much smaller tree and slow growing; its cones apparently form at quite an early age.

The cedars also all make large, handsome trees, pyramidal at first but later flat-topped with a tabular habit. Although given different specific names, the differences between *Cedrus atlantica*, *C. deodara* and *C. libani* are very slight. The deodar has pendulous branchlets and is slightly more ornamental when young; it also has a reputation for being more tender. There is an attractive glaucous form of *C. atlantica*. None of the cedars is a rapid grower.

The spruces, species of *Picea*, may be confused with the silver firs, but the cones always droop and there are small peg-like projections where old needles have fallen. The classic Christmas tree is the Norway spruce, *P. abies*, of which there are many variants, including a number of dwarf forms. The North American *P. breweriana* and the Himalayan *P. smithiana* are among the most beautiful of mature trees, with very long pendulous branchlets that turn the tree into a green fountain. But they are slow growers and do not produce these hanging growths until well matured. *P. pungens* 'Glauca' has glaucous-blue leaves; 'Koster' seems the best form of this, but 'Globosa' and 'Hoopsii' are naturally shorter and more suitable in restricted spaces.

The pines, species of *Pinus*, have needles in bundles generally longer than those of the other genera discussed. In some of the rather tender Mexican pines, such as *P. montezumae*, the needles may be up to 25cm (10in) long. Pines generally make attractive trees, pyramidal when young, with branches in whorls and more flat-topped when mature, and with very ornamental trunks. The Scots pine, *P. sylvestris*, is among the best, but most species are pleasant to look at, and all make largish trees eventually.

The hemlocks, species of *Tsuga*, have a rather more graceful habit and are distinguished by their small cones. The Douglas fir, *Pseudotsuga menziesii*, is a rapid grower. The Californian redwoods, the giant *Sequoiadendron giganteum* and the almost equally large *Sequoia sempervirens* — the tallest tree in cultivation, at 110m (366ft) — are all excellent subjects… where space allows.

The conifers with overlapping scale-like leaves are rather more tolerant of pollution than those with needles, but naturally do not enjoy it. Between the two groups come the junipers, some of which have needles whereas others have scales. They are mainly small plants, although the pencil cedar *J. virginiana* can make a sizeable tree which has an attractive columnar habit. The savin, *J. sabina*, is a large prostrate tree which can cover very large areas in the wild. The young leaves are needles, whereas the mature leaves are scales. Two of the best forms — 'Hicksii' with glaucous leaves, and 'Tamariscifolia' with green leaves — have needles and no scales. *J. X media* 'Pfitzerana' makes a spreading horizontal tree with scale-like leaves. 'Blue Cloud' has glaucous scales.

The false cypress, chamaecyparis, usually makes a columnar tree with scale-like leaves, but some of the forms of *C. obtusa* and *C. pisifera* retain their juvenile needles. Forms of Lawson's cypress, *C. lawsoniana*, are widely available, ranging from the blue-gray 'Allumii' to the rather dwarf 'Aurea Densa' with golden foliage, and there are innumerable variations in between. The Nootka cypress, *C. nootkatensis*, tolerates the coldest conditions. The true cypresses (of the genus *Cupressus*) are commonly somewhat frost-tender coming as they do from such areas as California and the Mediterranean. Most make very attractive columnar trees.

So do the species of *Thuja*, not easily distinguished from *Chamaecyparis* and again tending to make handsome columnar specimens. *T. occidentalis* 'Rheingold', a slow-

The dark foliage of *Chamaecyparis notkatensis* 'Glauca' (**above left**) is formed in flat sprays tightly clothed in scale-like leaves. *Taxus baccata* 'Fastigiata' (**above**) develops into a dense column of dark green foliage. *Abies koreana* (**left**) is prized for its neat shape and attractive purple cones.

growing conical bush with gold foliage, is among the most popular of smaller conifers. Forms of *T. plicata*, on the other hand, can make extremely large specimens. All the species have proved very variable, and it is only by viewing a collection that a suitable selection can be made.

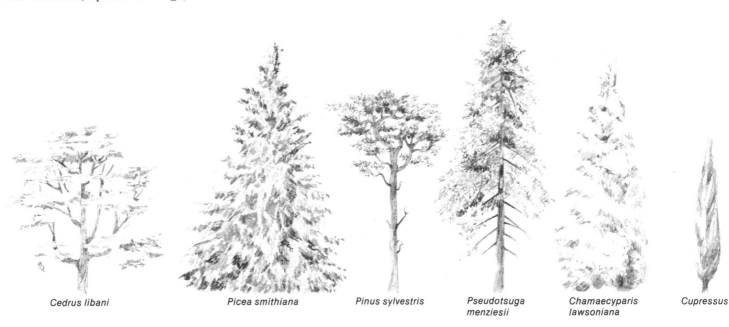

Cedrus libani   *Picea smithiana*   *Pinus sylvestris*   *Pseudotsuga menziesii*   *Chamaecyparis lawsoniana*   *Cupressus*

192

THE
HEALTHY
GARDEN

Planning and maintenance

Good health in the garden inevitably manifests itself as beauty, and is successfully achieved in two stages: correct initial planning, and proper maintenance thereafter. The maintenance not only involves the usual attention to feeding and protection but also includes the control of diseases and pests. All this care is made easier, and more effective, where the initial planning anticipates the eventual development of the mature garden.

Right from the start of the planning stage every need of each plant must be taken into account, including food, water, air, light and warmth. The soil on the site should also be analyzed to determine its chemical nature. Most soils are either slightly acid or slightly the opposite (alkaline): there is no cause for alarm in a finding of either in reasonable degree. Only extremes of acidity or alkalinity create difficulties, particularly as to the choice of plants. The soil analysis also gives guidance on the type of fertilizers that may be required before planting; once that consideration is taken care of, the first on the list of a plant's basic needs — food — can be checked off as reasonably secure.

The second need — water — is made easier by looking after the soil's moisture-holding capacity. Its physical condition should preferably be neither extremely light (sand) nor extremely heavy (clay), but should have enough fiber in it to hold moisture, and enough grit to drain freely. Whatever the soil is deficient in, however, can be added before planting. The natural supply of moisture depends on the weather, though, and it is wise not to rely exclusively on it. Hoses and watering-cans must be available to meet shortages.

Two other basic needs — air and light — require that the site not be overshadowed, and that the plants should not be so close to one another as to blind or choke each other. Nor should they be too close to a wall or fence. Spacing between plants must allow room for each plant to grow to maturity.

As for warmth, all that is needed on a permanent outdoor site is a screen of some kind to protect plants from strong drying winds until they are fully established. Without such protection, growth may be checked.

Even when the garden has been carefully planned, the soil adequately prepared, and the planting carried out, the first stage cannot be considered complete until the plants are settled. Daily checking may help them to settle, perhaps treading the soil around some plants and giving others a drink.

The next stage in a healthy garden — maintenance — means much more than keeping out pests and diseases, although that is certainly important. Plants have to mature and

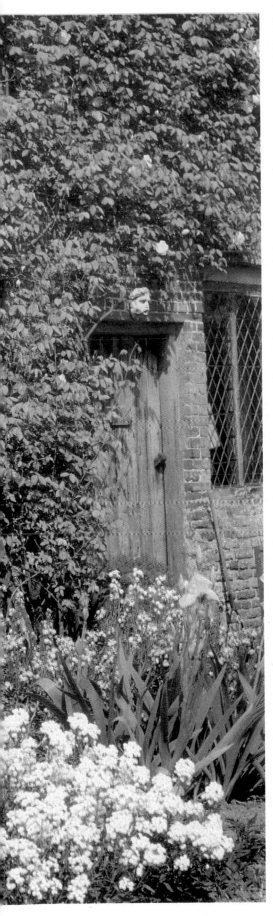

they need help to see that they grow up strong and healthy. They may need staking, tying, and removal of dead flowers; some need feeding, some pruning, and nearly all need weeding.

Weeding is one of the most important jobs in any garden but it is especially in a healthy garden, where tidiness means cleanliness. A weed is a plant in a place it is not wanted. As a plant, it is competing with the rest of the garden for a proportion of everything — all the available food, water, light and air; it is also a potential refuge for pests and diseases. That is why weeds must be removed before they reach maturity, long before they produce seed.

It helps plants to be surrounded by a healthy environment. The rest of the planted garden, and the paths, walls, fences, buildings, machines, equipment, tools and sundry items — all must be kept clean. The list is long, and includes even such garden features as heaps of stones, plant debris, and discarded pots and boxes, each of which can harbor pests.

Greenhouses and garden frames need particular attention because they are full of plant material which becomes a potential source of infection when plants die or are discarded. Such structures also have cozy corners in which pests can nest. Paintwork must be maintained or cracks develop, to be avidly seized upon by harmful bacteria. Pots and boxes that have been used for plants must be cleaned immediately after use, and put away, so that they do not become contaminated.

Other buildings — toolshed, potting shed, or garage — which house any garden machines, tools or equipment need attention on similar lines. Even a handful of grass clippings left in the mower grass-box can go moldy and create trouble.

Fences need an application of wood preservative put on in winter and brushed thoroughly into all the crevices. Soil must never be piled against woodwork or the wood rots. Walls are more easily kept free from plant pests and diseases, but fill in holes from which the mortar has fallen out, and keep them clear of debris and weeds.

When clearing away weeds and plant debris, never just dump it in a corner and call it a compost heap. Such a dump may well become a nuisance and is certainly a likely breeding-place for pests and diseases. Compost heaps must be carefully built up with the right mixture of materials so that they ferment in a controlled fashion. Woody material is slow to break down and it is usually better to burn it. But a bonfire can itself be a hazard, giving off fumes if burning slowly, so an incinerator is much better for disposing of such material. Any plant material known to contain pests or disease should of course be put on the incinerator and not on the compost heap.

Techniques and aids

Having planned and planted the garden, the essential is to start a routine of maintenance to keep it in good health. Today, there is a surprisingly wide range of techniques and equipment available to assist the gardener: certainly the modern garden-owner has things a lot easier than previous generations ever did — look back a little and consider the time when the gardener coped with all the problems without scientific aids. He would search his plants regularly for signs of pest damage — and knew just where to look for the insects. Caterpillars, grubs, slugs, earwigs — anything big enough to get hold of — he would pick off and drop into a jar containing salt. Smaller creatures, such as aphids, he would crush between his thumbnail and the leaf on which he found them. On the soil near a plant salt would be placed to deter crawling pests; fresh soot could also be used in a similar way. So the gardener's only equipment for these techniques was the jar of salt... and that was optional.

One successful early pesticide that is still in use is derris dust, made by crushing the root of the plant of that name. From ancient times it was known that derris is poisonous to fish: pieces of root were thrown into the water to stupefy the fish so that they could be easily netted. Derris (active ingredient, rotatone) is

An annual border **(left)** glows with health at the height of summer, but only constant attention will keep pests and diseases away. Fortunately, many remedies are now available.

A clean well-ordered greenhouse set within a paved area **(above)** is an ideal arrangement for a healthy garden. Insect pests and infections can proliferate in untidy corners.

used in horticulture both as a dust and as a liquid, for the control of aphids, caterpillars, red spider mite and thrips. It has the small drawback that sprayed food-crops must not be picked for at least 24 hours after treatment. And there is the added limitation in an ornamental garden that it must not be allowed to drift onto a garden pool where it could of course kill the fish.

Some of the most fearsome poisons were once popular garden pesticides: arsenic and cyanide, for instance. And even among modern, more sophisticated, garden chemicals there are still some which must not be used on food crops within two weeks of harvesting, although — unlike arsenic and cyanide — they may be considered safe in an ornamental garden.

Techniques have advanced from the primitive method of applying pest-killer dust by sprinkling it through the fingers to the modern dispenser — a disposable, cylindrical, pliable container operated simply by squeezing to puff out a cloud of dust.

One early method of applying insecticides in liquid form was to use a bulbous syringe, operated by simply squeezing the bulb. Today, popular sprays have a pump incorporated so as to pressurize the container and send out a fine spray through a plastic rubber tube and brass lance.

Even as designers were producing ever more efficient sprayers, scientists were searching not only for improved chemicals, but for a way of making them stay longer on the plant instead of running straight off. At one time, soft soap solution became a favorite because it is sticky enough to remain for a while on the leaves. Soft soap and quassia chips made a spray that was highly successful against greenfly on roses.

After soft soap came modern detergents to serve as what were called 'wetters' or 'spreaders' to help the pesticides and fungicides adhere to the plants. Spray chemicals are now sold complete with wetters.

A further scientific development has been the formulation of a type of spray called 'systemic', so called because it is absorbed into the plant's vesicular system (into its sap stream). It means that the pest does not even have to be on the plant at the time of spraying, for the plant remains lethal to pests for as long as the chemical is in its sap stream.

The first systemics stayed active in the sprayed plant for months, which meant that

roses, for example, needed only one spray per season. Such a long period of residual toxicity, however, had its dangers, especially in that the insecticides used were poisonous to humans and had to be kept well away from food crops. New systemics were therefore developed that would stay in a plant long enough to knock out the pests, but not long enough to cause danger were they to drift on to a food crop.

There are still nevertheless a number of domestic garden chemicals, including systemics, which must not be used on food crops too close to the time at which the food is to be eaten. The fact that a spray is for use on a flower border does not mean that no precautions are needed: it is surprisingly all too easy for other plants to become contaminated through spray drift or spillage.

A typical warning on a spray can states that 'food crops must not be harvested for (so many) days after spraying'. Whatever the number of days specified is, try to avoid using any chemicals carrying such a warning altogether if there are food plants in your garden or your neighbor's garden, in case by accident some of the spray should get on to the wrong plant.

Problem Anticipation and Control

The old gardener's close inspection of every plant in his hunt for pests is no longer essential. Nor is his intimate knowledge of the pests, both insects and fungi, and their habits. Furthermore, it is now possible to keep the garden in a clean and healthy state with a minimum of plant inspection, and even to cut out the inspection almost entirely, exercising pest control by routine sprays aimed at keeping the whole garden protected. Caution, however, remains necessary.

Maintaining a look-out for garden pests and diseases is in any case not as difficult as it may seem, because in a clean, healthy garden any plant in trouble is conspicuous enough for most people to notice. It generally lacks the brightness of leaf color and sturdiness of stem that it ought to have; it may even be droopy. There may be holes in leaves where they have been chewed, or the leaves may be distorted where the sap has been sucked out.

One good reason for watching for such signs is that whatever trouble they indicate is likely to spread to neighboring plants. So when a damaged plant is found, all surrounding plants should also be checked. A caterpillar that hatches out on one plant and starts chewing then moves on to other plants. Spray immediately, and cover as much of the garden as is affected.

If the pest is in a rose-bed, spray the whole bed and any other roses. Spray the whole

Stunning displays of ornamental garden plants (**far left**, **left** and **below left**) rely on a host of preventative measures to keep them in full health. Decorative plants are often more susceptible to certain pests and diseases than their wild counterparts and may need special care to help them avoid or survive their ravages. When using garden chemicals be sure to do so in strict accordance with the instructions supplied with the particular product.

garden if there is doubt. You can spot any slugs or snails that are causing damage by the slimy trails they leave on the ground.

Once the specific source of the trouble is identified, choose a spray suitable for dealing with that individual problem. That is not difficult to do, particularly with advice, but if in doubt collect a permanent 'First-Aid Kit' of wide-spectrum items on hand to use.

Against pests, spray with fenitrothion;
Against fungi, use benomyl;
Against slugs and snails, use slug bait based on either metaldehyde or methiocarb.

It is neither sufficient nor wise to rely on just these few substances despite their general effectiveness, however, and your collection should also contain far more specific remedies to individual problems. There are two reasons for this. First, a specific remedy is one designed to cover a very small range of pests or diseases: there should be no need to protect a plant from something it may never suffer from anyway. Second, and more important, a remedy used constantly eventually ceases to be effective. This can happen when a pest escapes the full treatment and gets only a tiny dose which acts rather like an inoculation and renders the pest immune to further doses of the chemical. In the event of not being able to find a specific remedy and having to use the first-aid items frequently, the following advice on alternatives in both substance and technique may be useful.

As an alternative to fenitrothion, try derris;
As an alternative to benomyl, try a copper-based fungicide;
Alternate the two slug baits metaldehyde and methiocarb rather than keeping to one.

A further choice sometimes difficult to make is between dusts and liquid sprays. Given the choice, use whichever is the more convenient: chemically they are equally effective. In showery weather, however, dust may have the disadvantage of being washed off too quickly; it is also sometimes possible for a fine spray at high pressure to get into crevices that dusts cannot reach. But judge for yourself.

All garden chemicals should be handled with great care. Always wear rubber gloves, for even those substances recognized as safe and non-poisonous should not be allowed to get onto the skin or the clothing — or in fact anywhere except on to the plant for which they are intended (and the ground beneath it). If by accident any of these chemicals does get on to the hands, or worse still on to vulnerable places like the eyes or mouth, it must be washed off immediately. Furthermore, before using any chemical labelled as poison, be sure you know its antidote, and have it handy.

Have a safe, locked cupboard, out of children's reach, in which to keep all the chemicals. As you put each chemical into the cupboard, read the label carefully so that you know what you are storing. Read it again when you take the chemical out to use it, in case you have forgotten a warning. Avoid spilling or splashing when mixing a spray.

Do not attempt to spray in windy weather. It is surprising how far a fine spray can be carried by the wind.

Do not spray in strong sunshine either, when plants could be scorched by sun striking the droplets.

Do not spray when bees are active; wait until dusk when they have gone back to their hives.

Never use the watering-can for chemicals other than plant foods. Nor should a sprayer that has been used for pesticides or fungicides be used for any other purpose, not even for weed-killers or for plain water. Conversely, residue after a can has been used for a weed-killer can also kill plants if water or a pesticide is later used from that can.

For that reason it is not enough simply to have separate cans or sprayers: it is essential that *all* equipment be thoroughly washed out immediately after use. The term 'immediately' may seem to suggest unnecessary haste, but it is vital that the washing be done before any chemical residue has time to dry. In fact, when using several cans or sprayers, each should be filled with clean water after use and then set down to await the full washing out. Accident reports prove all the same that mistakes are frequently made.

The following pages attempt to provide a clear guide to help you to identify your garden foes — pests and diseases — and select suitable remedies. When in doubt, however, use one of the 'First-Aid' treatments; these should be kept always in stock. With them keep a good sprayer, of the type which incorporates a pressure pump and hand lance, maintained always to be in good, clean, working order.

Garden pests

Any creature that enters the garden and does something to impair the beauty or development of a plant is called a pest. When pest damage becomes unacceptable, we need to control it by reducing the pest's numbers, but there is no excuse at all, however, for attempting annihilation or an overkill. Certainly there is no need to endanger the whole insect population, friend and foe alike.

Never spray open blooms, where friendly insects may be at work, and never let spray drift out of sight or over a hedge where it might reach a neighbor or an innocent animal.

When your plants appear to need help, see if the following check-list of pests and the means of getting rid of them is of any help to you. Having chosen a chemical remedy, handle it with the maximum possible care.

Ants

Ants are more of a nuisance than a pest, but they encourage aphids and transport them to clean plants — in fact they are less likely to operate where there are no aphids. Aphid control (see below) is thus a help to ant control.

Ants love dry soil like that usually found in rockeries (where their tunnelling can cause havoc by loosening stones), but their additional fondness for sweet things can lead to

their undoing. Mix equal quantities of borax powder and fine granulated sugar, and place half-teaspoonfuls of the mixture where they are working. Workers then carry quantities of the poison back to their nests to be shared out, and all eat fatal doses. There are also several proprietary ant-killers available, most of them based on sodium tetraborate.

Aphids (blackfly and greenfly)

Aphids infest a vast range of plants, causing damage by sucking the sap, mainly from young shoots. They breed rapidly, especially in warm conditions, and repeated sprays may be needed to keep them under control. Derris, fenitrothion, malathion, or systemic insecticides can all be used in sprays.

Aphid, woolly

Colonies of this pest cover themselves with white, waxy 'wool' which it is difficult to penetrate with spray. Protected thus fairly securely they do severe damage to the bark of the tree or shrub they are infesting — such as hawthorn, cotoneaster and pyracantha. The wound they make is then prone to attack by canker spores.

The waxed colonies can be removed with a small brush dipped in denatured alcohol or by a forceful jet of aphicide spray — derris or fenitrothion are useful aphicides. Tree wounds caused by the pest should be treated with a canker paint.

Capsid bug

Chrysanthemums, dahlias and several other flowers commonly have holes in their leaves made by this pest. Spray with fenitrothion or pirimiphos-methyl.

Caterpillar

The countless types of caterpillars attack a large range of plants. Picking off the pests by hand is still one of the most useful controls, but for a chemical control use derris, pyrethrum, pirimiphos-methyl, or HCH.

Chafer grub

This fat, curved grub of the chafer beetle feeds on the roots of many flower plants for a large part of the year. Its attack on the roots of chrysanthemums and dahlias is sometimes fatal. It is a long-term nuisance, taking two years to mature. The adult beetle eats holes in leaves, but such damage is rarely serious. The grub is the real menace — and can be controlled by raking bromophos into the soil.

Cuckoo spit See Froghopper.

Earthworm

Although the earthworm does a lot of good to the soil, and is to be appreciated in most parts of the garden, its presence in a lawn is distinctly unwanted. Its casts do considerable damage: whenever dry enough to be crumbled, however, they should be knocked down.

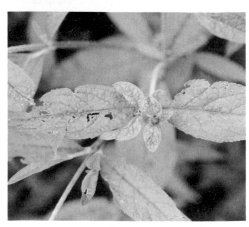

Caterpillars make short work of juicy foliage; these (**left**) are eagerly chewing a willow leaf. Pick off the caterpillars or treat with suitable chemicals. Aphids (**above**) are the bane of most gardeners' lives. They are attracted to roses and can cause extensive damage to young shoots. Systemic insecticides that work from 'inside' the plant are very effective against aphids. The grub of the chafer beetle (**above right**) attacks the roots of many garden plants such as chrysanthemums and dahlias. Chemical control is possible. Holes in leaves may be caused by many agents. This leaf (**right**) has suffered capsid bug damage. A spotted appearance followed by brown-rimmed holes are typical symptoms.

In circumstances in which worms become even more of a nuisance, they can be cleared through the use of chlordane worm-killer applied according to the maker's directions.

Earwig
Blooms of dahlia, chrysanthemum and many other plants are commonly damaged severely by this pest. To trap them, hang small plant pots half filled with hay upside down on canes. The pest feeds at night, and after feeding is attracted to the hay in the pot as a place to rest. On checking the pots each morning, it should be possible to reduce the numbers in quick time. To protect plants without trapping, there are several effective insecticides available, including fenitrothion, HCH and trichlorphon.

Flea beetle
The name follows from the curious fact that this little beetle jumps like a flea, attacking *Alyssum* and wallflower, among others, and making a multitude of holes in their leaves. Spray or dust with derris or HCH.

Froghopper or spittlebug
The effect of this creature is known as cuckoo spit, because of the mass of froth in which each froghopper hides. The froghopper is a tiny pinkish insect about 3mm (1/8in) long. Lavender, rosemary and carnations are particularly likely to be attacked. The damage done is small and can be reduced by just knocking off the froth with a jet of water. For chemical control, spray forcefully with HCH, fenitrothion or malathion.

Gallfly
These tiny mites feed on the stems of trees and shrubs, and the internal irritation causes the tree to produce lumps — galls — which enclose the mite and protect it. Because of this wooden barrier it is difficult to achieve chemical control. The damage done is not severe, but can spoil the tree's appearance.

Leafcutter bee
Neat, semicircular pieces are cut from the leaves of roses, laburnum and other plants by the female bee in order to make her nest. Damage is rarely significant although it occasionally occurs on a large scale. If it becomes unacceptable, watch till the bee reveals her nest, probably in decayed wood or old brickwork, and attack there with HCH.

Leafhopper
Almost any plant is liable to attack by this insect, which jumps (hops) if disturbed when feeding on the undersides of leaves. Attacked leaves take on a pale, mottled look; if the attack is severe, the entire plant becomes unsightly. There are also suspicions that the insect transmits virus diseases.

Control with fenitrothion or malathion.

Leaf miner
Pale, irregular, twisting lines on a leaf give away the fact that this insect grub is tunnelling under the skin. There are several species of leaf miner and various plants are attacked, but chrysanthemums are particularly vulnerable; damage to them can sometimes be fatal. In turn, however, leaf miners are vulnerable to repeated sprays with HCH, especially if started immediately the first signs of attack are seen.

Alternatively, examine the tunnelling carefully; where it ends is where the miner has stopped to rest. Cut open the leaf at that spot and the little pest can be removed forthwith.

Leatherjacket
The tough skin of this crane-fly larva gives it the name — and also indicates why control is difficult. It feeds on plant roots and can cause substantial bare patches when operating under lawns. It can also cause the deaths of young plants. Where the soil surface is kept loose, birds can reduce the infestation. For chemical control when deemed essential, use methiocarb and rake it in thoroughly. On lawns, spread a plastic sheet at night in damp weather; the pests then come to the surface under the sheet ready to be disposed of the next morning.

Mole
The chief food of the mole is the earthworm,

Cuckoo spit (**left**) is an apt description of the froth that appears on some plants. In the froth lie the froghoppers that produce it as a sort of 'smoke screen'. The froth and the froghoppers can be washed off with water. The symmetrical patterns produced by the leaf cutter bee (**above left**) are easily identifiable. It is the female bee taking home leaf pieces for her nest that causes all the trouble. Ideally, destroy the nest. These really quite attractive insects (**above**) are leafhoppers. Besides causing leaves to pale they may also transmit plant viruses. The leafminer plots a telltale trail (**above right**) as the grub journeys through the tissues of a leaf. Leatherjackets (**right**) are the tough-skinned larvae of the cranefly.

and so chlordane worm-killer on lawns can be an effective control. Beneath shrubs and plants its tunnelling may be fatal, but getting rid of the tunneller is difficult because it travels long distances. Putting a smoke dispenser in the tunnel under its latest mole-hill is not likely to be immediately effective, therefore. Trapping, however, calls for skill and experience; and smoke-generating mole-killers should be persevered with.

Narcissus fly
Damage is done more by the maggot than the fly, although of course the fly starts it all by laying its egg close to the bulb. A heavy dusting of HCH around the bulb may deter the fly.

The maggot works unseen inside the bulb and damage is not noticed until the plant collapses, or the bulb is dug up and found to be soft or rotting. Harvested bulbs should be examined with care, as should all new bulbs from store. Soft ones should be destroyed.

Red spider mite
If normally green-leaved trees and shrubs develop a bronze leaf color, examine the leaves through a magnifying glass and you are likely to see tiny mites and a little fine silky webbing.

This is the red spider mite. Worst attacks generally occur in early summer and early autumn. Spray thoroughly with dimethoate, fenitrothion, or pirimiphos-methyl.

Rhododendron bug
As it feeds on the undersides of the leaves, this bug causes the surfaces of the leaves to become mottled, the edges to curl downward, and the underneaths to turn rusty brown. First attacks come in early summer; spraying should be carried out immediately, with malathion or HCH, and should be repeated two or three times at three-weekly intervals.

Rose slugworm
Leaves attacked by this pest take on a strange look: the green tissue on the surfaces disappears, leaving only a transparent inner skin. Derris or permethrin, administered immediately, controls it.

Sawflies
There are several species of sawfly which infest various plants, inserting their eggs into plant tissues. The eggs hatch into caterpillars which then feed on the leaves. The leaf-rolling sawfly causes leaves to curl and distort. Pick off infested leaves where possible, and spray the remainder with permethrin or primiphos-methyl.

Slugs and snails
Both these creatures attack almost any plant in the garden and do considerable damage if not kept in check. However, the two best-known

The distinctive skeletal appearance of these leaves (**top**) has been caused by the rose slugworm. The larvae of sawflies (**above center**) are caterpillars that feed on succulent leaves. As mature insects they cause many problems for gardeners; the activities of the leaf-rolling sawfly are all too evident on this rose (**above**). Slugs are notorious garden pests, particularly in moist shady corners.

Holes in leaves (**right**) and slime trails are telltale signs of their presence. Fortunately, excellent deterrents are now available and being improved all the time.

molluscicides — metaldehyde and methiocarb — give reasonable control.

Stones, bricks, boxes, pieces of timber, almost any loose item left lying on the ground can be used by them as a hiding-place and should be cleared away. Rockeries too must be checked regularly or the stones may become nesting-places.

Swift moth

The caterpillar of this moth lives in the soil and attacks the roots of various herbaceous plants, bulbs, corms, and tubers, doing serious damage if not controlled. Sprinkle bromophos wherever the pest is suspected of being active; stir or rake it into the soil.

Thrips

Also known as thunder flies, these small insects damage petals, leaving pale spots. Gladioli seem particularly prone to attack. Spray with permethrin or derris.

Weevils

There are several species of weevil, all of which feed on plants at night, spending the day in the soil or in plant debris. Attention to cleanliness and the incineration of such debris is thus a sound precaution. Where plants have been eaten, HCH dust stirred into the soil close to plants is a further precaution, for weevil larvae feed on roots.

Whitefly

The outdoor species of whitefly is not a major pest and can be controlled by fenitrothion if attacks are severe. The greenhouse whitefly, however, can be a menace, feeding on the undersides of leaves. Spray with permethrin and repeat every three days for three weeks. That makes seven sprays in all, and the three-day interval between each must be adhered to strictly. The reason so many sprays are needed to clear out the infestation is that three stages of the pest are present: eggs, nymphs, and flies (the flies are like mini-moths). There may be survivors at one stage or another after each spray up to the seventh.

Wireworm

This is the larva of the click beetle. It eats the roots of various flowering subjects, and damage can be severe. It is often present in great numbers near where grassland has been recently dug up for cultivation. Bromophos or HCH should be worked into the soil near affected plants.

Woodlouse

Some people suspect this creature of nibbling roots, but it is more generally believed to feed only on decayed wood. About the size of a ladybug, it has a hard gray shell and rolls itself into a ball when scared. Where it is considered a menace, it can be controlled by HCH dust.

Weevils come in all shapes and sizes. Both adults and larva cause problems in the garden. The adults, such as the hazel weevil (**top**) feed at night on the leaves. The evidence of their passing is clearly seen on these rhododendron leaves (**above** and **left**). The U-shaped notches cut into the leaf edges are characteristic of the 12mm (½ in) vine weevils. Most leaf weevils attack at the height of summer.

Control consists of clearing away plant debris where they congregate and incineration of affected leaves. The weevil larvae live in the soil and attack roots, particularly those of ferns and rockery plants.

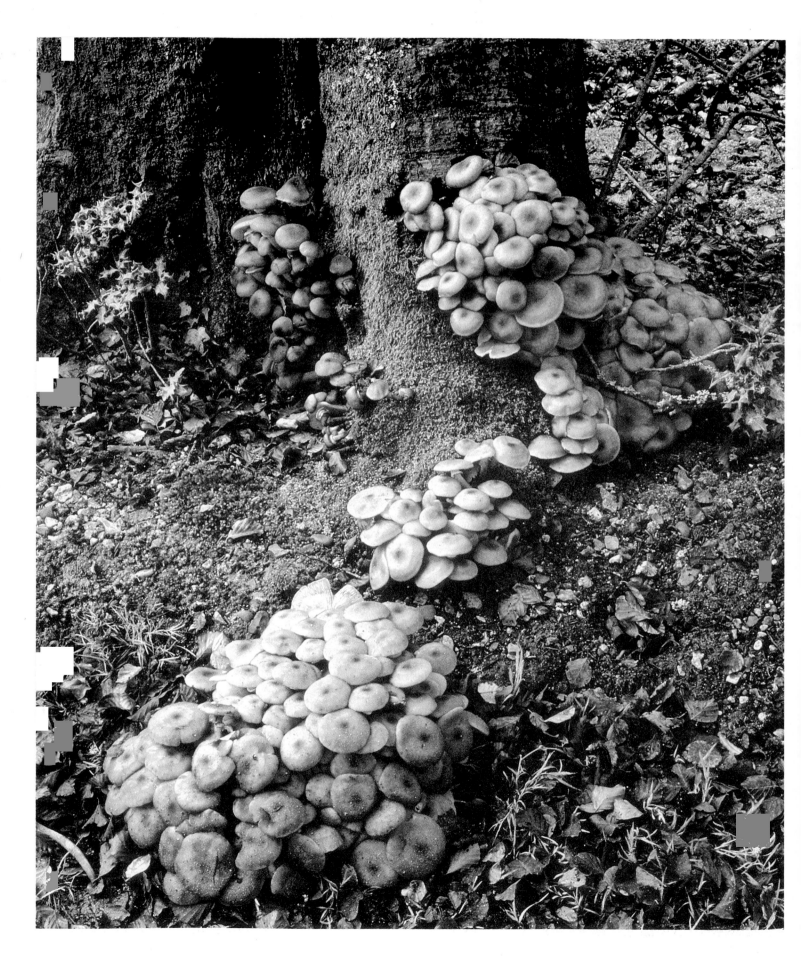

Plant diseases

Armillaria
Armillaria is a fungus which attacks large numbers of trees and shrubs. Honey-colored toadstools appear on the surface under the infected tree or bush, from which follows the alternative name honey fungus. Leaves turn dark brown and die. Black growths like bootlaces appear on the plant's roots, giving rise to an alternative name for it, bootlace fungus.

There is no cure, and the fungus spreads quickly. The only treatment is to dig out and burn every scrap of root, and treat the ground with formaldehyde.

Aster wilt
This form of verticillium wilt is a minute fungus which attacks only asters. All infected plants have to be destroyed.

Anthracnose of willow
A mild form of canker is the first symptom among weeping willows in a wet start to summer. Attacking young foliage as it opens, it is often fatal however.

A liquid copper fungicide applied early enough, and repeated frequently enough, might keep it off.

Bacterial canker
Poplar, ornamental *Prunus*, and some willows are attacked by this bacterial infection. Typical canker wounds characterize it: a small area bare of bark surrounded by rough, swollen bark. It is best to remove infected branches completely. Treat all cut ends with canker paint.

Basal rot
Affecting daffodils and lilies, the rot starts at the base of the bulb and soon spreads. Infected bulbs must be discarded. Protect fresh stocks by dipping in benomyl.

Blackleg
A frequent cause of failure among cuttings of pelargonium, this condition begins on the cut end and may go unnoticed for a while. It can be avoided where fresh sterilized compost is used, and with clean tools and equipment. If

Where bark has become damaged canker (**left**) may set in. Caused by fungi and bacteria, this infection may kill branches that it encircles.

caught in time, the cutting can be trimmed back to clean tissues and rooted in fresh compost.

Black spot
This serious disease of roses was unknown in industrial towns and cities in the days when every chimney belched out smoke and fumes. It is generally accepted that sulphur in those fumes served as an effective fungicide against black spot.

As its name indicates, the disease produces black spots. These appear on the leaves, but the fungus also attacks the shoots. It is a killer, and there is no known cure.

Frequent preventive sprays in infected

areas are necessary. There are several new fungicides which help to control the spread of the disease, including some with systemic action. One sophisticated new spray combines several substances in a cocktail to take care of most rose troubles; it contains triforine, dinocap and sulphur (as fungicides), with permethrin (as insecticide) and a foliar feed.

Botrytis (also known as **grey mold**)
Found on many subjects in periods of heavy humidity, the mold's main victims are chrysanthemums, dahlias and peonies. Both leaves and flowers are attacked. Infected leaves and blooms should be removed and the plants sprayed thoroughly with benomyl.

Bud drop
Buds of various plants may drop unopened for no discernible reason. In fact, it seems commonly to be due to climatic and physical conditions at the time the buds were forming. Perhaps the plants were too dry, or the temperature was fluctuating too severely (too hot by day and too cold by night). No chemical control corrects it. A good mulch of moisture-holding material around the plants, plus watering in dry spells, may help the plants to recover.

Canker
This is a general term to describe infections in open wounds on trees and shrubs. Both bacteria and fungi may be involved. Heavily infected branches should be cut back to clean wood, that is, to the point where the cambium and the bark are seen to be white. Any browning indicates that the canker is still there. Infected wood should be put into the incinerator, and wounds should be treated with a canker paint.

Chlorosis
A large range of plants suffer chlorosis at times; it makes their green leaves turn pale or yellow, or even white, due to a mineral deficiency which in turn is caused by an upset in the acid-alkali balance, 'locking up' a soil constituent.

The toadstools produced by honey fungus (**opposite**) appear at the base of an affected tree or shrub in the autumn. Just beneath the bark a network of fungal filaments spreads throughout the tree as evidence of the infection. The familiar black spot of roses (**left**) is also caused by a fungal infection. Chemical sprays can prevent or contain the infection but not cure it outright. Botrytis is clearly present on this pelargonium leaf (**right**). Rife in humid conditions, this fungus causes leaves, stems and flowers to develop brown patches with a fluffy gray mold.

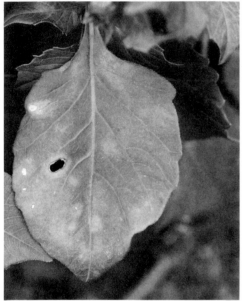

Plants which prefer a somewhat acid soil (rhododendrons, for instance) rapidly become chlorotic in a limy soil. When chlorosis occurs, the soil should be tested; subsequent plantings should be selected with care. In mild cases, sequestrenes (sequestered iron, for example) applied to the soil may be enough to enable plants to recover.

Clematis wilt

This fungal trouble afflicts young specimens of the larger-flowered clematis, such as the 'Jackmaniis'. If the plant is set so that two inches of the base of the stem is below soil level, and if wilted shoots are removed promptly, the young plant usually recovers and fresh shoots spring from the base. Apart from cutting wilted shoots back to clean wood, it is helpful to spray plants with benomyl or a copper fungicide.

Coral spot

Clusters of small, red, raised spots on dead wood are the signs by which to recognize this fungus. But its spores are airborne and they can infect living trees through wounds or cuts. It is important to clear up any dead wood promptly, and to trim off dying branches of all trees before fungus growths appear.

Damping off

The strange name applies to a disease caused by parasitic fungi which afflicts small seedlings, especially if crowded or too damp. It can be avoided by using sterilized seed compost and by sowing thinly. A mild attack caught in

time can be arrested by watering with a mixture called cheshunt compound, made by mixing finely-ground ammonium carbonate (11 parts) and copper sulphate (2 parts). Dissolve three grams to one liter of water (one ounce in two gallons of water) and water the seedlings with it.

Die-back

Die-back is a gradual death from the tip, or cut end, of a shoot back to its junction with a main branch or the trunk. It may be due to a faulty or badly-placed pruning cut or to damage. The remedy is to cut back to clean wood and to treat the cut with a canker paint.

Fairy rings

The lawn toadstool *Marasmius oreades* quickly produces a circular patch of darker green than the rest of the lawn which then spreads in ever-widening circles, finally being made up of two dark green rings with a straw-coloured nearly-bare ring in between them. *Marasmius* is extremely virulent; no matter how much effort is made to remove infected grass and soil, if a tiny spot is left infected it will rapidly take over again. Many people therefore just keep trying to reduce the effect by watering the treble ring with iron sulphate. The dosage rate is 15 grams to 5 liters to 1 sq meter (half an ounce to a gallon of water to each square yard).

Fireblight

Cotoneaster and hawthorn are prone to this bacterial disease which, in some countries, is a notifiable one. The wisest treatment is to grub

Leaf spot is the general name for a host of fungal infections that plague a wide range of plants; ringspot on carnations is one such infection. The very dark spots on these leaves of *Acer* (**top**) are also caused by a kind of leaf spot. The presence of viruses in plants is often difficult to diagnose; many of their symptoms resemble those caused by other disease organisms. The spotted and discoloured appearance of this dahlia leaf (**above**) points to an incurable viral infection. The dusty white symptoms of powdery mildew (**right**) are much easier to identify but not much easier to cure. Spray regularly with a fungicide to ward off the infection.

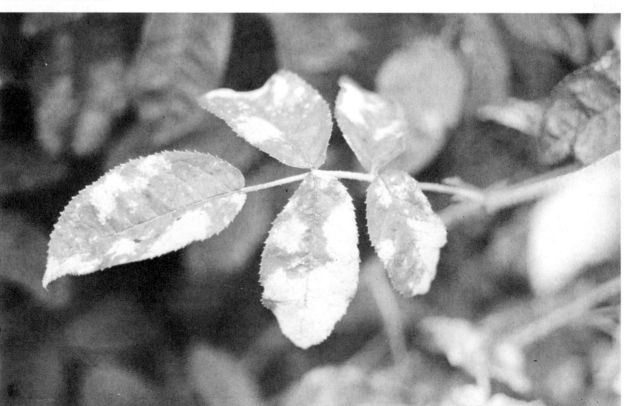

out and burn — although with skilled care, and severe cutting back, experts are sometimes able to save the plant.

Fusarium patch
Also known as snow mold, this fungal disease afflicts lawns. It is encouraged by giving too much nitrogen in autumn lawn treatments, thereby producing soft growth too near the onset of winter. The trouble begins as a small area of yellowing grass which then becomes hay-colored and lifeless. Treat with mercurized lawn sand at 125 grams to the square meter (four ounces to the square yard).

Fusarium wilt
This fungal condition can generally be avoided by clean cultivation. All the same, it also occurs particularly where a susceptible species, such as *Dianthus* is grown for too long on one patch of soil. Affected plants are stunted in growth, with a yellowing of the leaves which then wilt as if lacking moisture. Infected plants should be destroyed and, because the fungus is soil-borne, the soil should be sterilized.

Gray mold See Botrytis

Honey fungus See Armillaria.

Magnesium deficiency
The deficiency shows itself as a bronzing in the spaces between the veins of green leaves. Sometimes an excess of potash 'locks up' the magnesium. To correct the deficiency, magnesium sulphate can be sprinkled lightly on the soil and raked in, or can be dissolved at 20 grams to a liter (3½ ounces to a gallon) of water and poured over the plant. Some of the liquid is absorbed through the leaves, the rest works through the roots.

Manganese deficiency
This deficiency usually goes hand in hand with iron deficiency, which causes a chlorosis and shows as a yellowing of leaves. Sequestrenes, applied in accordance with the makers' directions, correct the deficiency.

Mildew (downy)
Among plants affected by downy mildew are poppy and sweet pea. Leaves turn yellow on the upper side as a grayish mold forms on the underside. Spray thoroughly with mancozeb.

Mildew (powdery)
The powdery condition is more serious than downy mildew and attacks a wide range of plants, coating leaves and stems with its white powder. Nipping off infected tips of shoots can help control it, but it is wise to spray with benomyl or other suitable fungicide.

Rhododendron bud blast
Flower buds attacked by this fungus turn brown, with black bristles of fungal spores, but do not drop off. Indeed, they become tough to remove. Cut them off and burn them. No fungicide appears effective, but since the disease is sometimes carried by leafhoppers, a spray with derris or other aphicide in late summer is a wise precaution.

Ringspot
Carnations seem most affected by this fungus which produces dark rings of spores on their leaves. Infected leaves should be picked off and burned promptly, and the rest of the plants sprayed thoroughly with a copper fungicide like mancozeb.

Rust
Raised spots of reddish brown are seen on many shrubs and trees, caused by fungi and are termed rust. If infected leaves are removed and burned promptly, there should be no need to take any further action. Where attacks are serious, spray with benomyl.

Tulip fire
Symptoms of tulip fire are small fungal growths which appear on bulbs; if these are seen, the bulbs should be discarded immediately. On such bulbs that are planted, scorched areas develop on the leaves and spots on the petals. Dig up and burn infected bulbs, and spray the remaining plants with mancozeb or thiram.

Variegation loss
In plants whose leaves are normally variegated — with yellow or cream streaks or margins — a shoot with plain green leaves may be produced if there is insufficient light. The remedy is to cut the affected shoot clean out and to ensure that the plant gets maximum light thereafter.

Viruses
Virus diseases cause plants to become distorted, or stunted in growth; the infections are carried in microscopic particles which are spread by insects but enter only through wounds. Diagnosis is tricky; there is no cure, and the remedy is prevention. Avoid damaging plants, and keep insects — particularly aphids — well clear.

Witches' brooms
The name given to abnormal growths which appear on some trees, particularly conifers and birch. The growths take the form of a dense bunch of small shoots coming from one spot.

It is doubtful whether they do serious harm, even though they are caused by a fungus. However, it is easy, and perhaps wiser, to cut them off right up to the trunk and treat the wound with a canker paint.

Rust fungus (**far left**) is distinctive for the bright orange powdery residue it produces on the affected plant. Sprays will help to prevent it but destruction of infected parts is the only cure.

The tangled knots of dense branches seen in certain trees may be caused by a fungus. These so-called witches' brooms (**left**) should be cut out if they can be reached. Be sure to paint cut branches against canker.

Propagation

Seed-sowing

Most plant-raising by do-it-yourself gardeners is done by seed-sowing, and most of the subjects are annuals. This reflects the fact that annuals are easy to raise from seed and that they bring quick and highly satisfactory results. Also, sowing usually produces plants more cheaply than other methods.

Where there are failures, they can be traced often to not reading the seedsman's directions printed on the packet, possibly through over-confidence engendered by familiarity with the task.

Hardy annual flower seed can be sown in early to mid-spring in the bed or border where the plants are to flower; it is seldom worth while sowing in an outdoor seedbed for later transplanting.

Half-hardy annuals, more sensitive to frost and low temperatures, are sown no earlier than mid-spring. The first of these sowings should be done under glass, later ones in a sheltered seedbed.

Tender annuals are sown under glass in mid to late spring and subsequently hardened off for planting out when frost risk is finished. Most of these annuals (all classes) present no problems — although sweet pea is an important exception — but there are several points to watch in order to ensure first-class results.

Soil or seed compost should be moist but not wet; seeds must never be overcrowded; the depth of sowing should equal the diameter of the seed; and there should be no drying out between sowing and germination. This latter restriction is easy to ensure indoors by sowing in seed trays and covering each tray with a sheet of glass to lock in moisture, and a sheet of dark paper to keep out light until germination.

Tough seeds

Sweet pea seeds need a little extra care because they have a tough skin. Soak them for 24 hours — those which swell in that time can be sown without further attention; those which fail to swell (probably mostly black seeds) may be classed as too tough for the seed-shoot to break through. Take a razor-blade or sharp knife and nick the skins of these tough ones, and then sow them like the rest. Note, however, that the skins of white, wrinkled, or brown seeds *must not* be nicked. Give these an extra day's soaking if they fail to swell in the first 24 hours. After that, sow them, because there is still a reasonable chance that the shoots will break out.

Not all seeds are quite as simple as the hardy annuals and it pays to examine them and decide which ones need special attention. For example, among trees and shrubs there are seeds even harder than the sweet pea, like those of the peach or the walnut, or of some of

Sow medium-sized seeds indoors or in the greenhouse (**above**) by scattering them thinly on moist seed compost in pots or trays. Cover them with their own depth of compost.

Place the pot or tray in a plastic bag (**above**) to conserve moisture. This will help to ensure germination. A sheet of glass will do the same job. Put the pot in a warm place.

Large or pelleted seeds (**above**) can be spaced out on the seed compost. This will save thinning out later on. Besides covering seed containers with plastic or glass, place dark paper over them until germination occurs.

Many flower seeds are extremely fine. To help ensure an even distribution mix them with sand and sprinkle the mixture across the compost. Such fine seeds hardly need covering at all, just the merest dusting of compost.

the forest trees such as oak; roses are another good example.

These and hard seeds from various shrubs do not respond to soaking. Instead, they require a spell of moist, cold treatment. Mix them with moist peat and put them in a domestic refrigerator at a temperature of about 4°C (just under 40°F) for eight weeks before sowing. They should then be sown in seed compost in a greenhouse at a temperature anywhere between 7°C (45°F) and 15°C (60°F). Another cold method, especially if larger quantities are involved, is to put the seeds in a plant pot containing a mixture comprising half peat and half sand and bury them outdoors in late autumn or early winter. Among horticulturalists this process is described as a form of 'stratification'.

Examine the seeds in early to mid-spring and take out (for sowing) any that have split open. Those that have not split after six months should be buried again and left for another whole year.

Seeds which have undergone this cold treatment should be sown in any recognized seed compost in small pots indoors. Following such chilling, seeds should respond quickly to the greenhouse warmth — anything from 7°C (45°F) to 15°C (60°F) — but not warmer.

Slightly modified forms of these stratification treatments can be given to nearly all seeds of hardy shrubs and trees. They can be sown in small pots of seed compost immediately after gathering in autumn. The pots should then be

Successful germination will produce trays or pots bursting with tiny seedlings. These must be pricked out to another container of compost to enable them to develop into individual plants. This new compost should have more 'body' to it and a trace of fertilizer. Tease out clumps of seedlings (**right**) and carefully remove individual seedlings by holding the leaves (not the stems). Transfer the seedlings to the new container of compost, spacing them out to allow for future growth. Before pricking out it is advisable to spray the seedlings with a suitable fungicide to prevent the development of a fungal disease called 'damping off'; this causes the tiny seedlings to collapse.

plunged outdoors in cool, moist conditions and left till spring, then brought indoors where they normally germinate in a few weeks.

Other types of seed

Besides hard skin, there are other character-istics that differentiate some seeds. They can be like dust (such as begonia), or perhaps oily (like the castor oil plant), or winged (like ash), or plumed (like scabious).

Dust-like seeds should be sown in a seed-tray, on the surface of the compost. They should be lightly pressed into the surface but not covered. Seed of this sort soon loses its viability and ought to be sown as soon after gathering as possible, or stored in a sealed, moisture-proof container.

Oily seeds, perhaps surprisingly, have the same fault as dusty ones in rapidly losing their viability; these too should therefore be sown as soon as possible.

Winged seeds should have their wings removed before sowing.

Plumed seeds should be sown individually, leaving the plume visible above the surface.

Herbaceous perennials form an important group of plant seeds. Although they survive for years — the top growth dying off in autumn and growing again in spring — they vary in length of useful life and tend to deteriorate. The lover of this category of plant has thus continually to be culling and replacing them. Replacements can be raised from cuttings (see below) or from seed.

Sowings can be carried out in spring at the same time as shrubs which have been stratified.

Plants raised in this way can be flowered in the same year. This may be inconvenient where reserve space is limited, in that the plants may be ready for their permanent posi-tions before those positions have been vacated. To avoid such inconvenience, sow herbaceous perennials on a seedbed in early to mid summer. Seedlings from this sowing can be planted in their permanent positions in either autumn or the following spring.

The advice provided here on the sowing of perennials applies equally to the sowing of seeds of alpines and those of rock garden plants.

Seeds and heat

Most seed-sowing routines so far described can be modified by using equipment to raise the temperature at sowing time and for a period immediately after germination. Outdoor sowings, for example, may take place about two weeks earlier if cloches are used before the sowing to get the ground warmed. Even more time can be gained by sowing in cold frames which have brick side-walls. Further time still can be gained by putting soil-warming cables laid below the soil surface in the cold frames.

More warmth is afforded by a greenhouse with sufficient heat to allow for spring sowings of annuals, and stratified shrubs and trees, as already described. In fact, full heating can be provided from mid winter, although it is expensive. It depends on how highly the gardener values the crop.

Where tender plants are wanted from seed for a greenhouse summer display, the cost can be trimmed by using a heated propagating frame — in effect a mini-greenhouse — as a seed-raiser. Propagators are available electrically heated or kerosene heated, and are not expensive either to buy or to run. To the greenhouse enthusiast they are indispensable. Note, however, that seedlings raised in this way need a heated greenhouse when they come out of the propagator.

Other and newer methods of seed-sowing include a practice called fluid sowing, which can stand on its own or can incorporate the technique of pre-germination.

For raising seeds and cuttings a gentle warmth can be a great bonus. Rather than heating the whole room or greenhouse it is more efficient to use electric thermostatically controlled propagators (**top** and **above**).

Modern sowing methods

Fluid sowing involves stirring a quantity of seed into a plastic bag of wallpaper paste, snipping off a corner of the bag, and squeezing ribbons of the mixture into seed drills. The drills are then lightly covered with soil as might be done in normal sowing.

The advantage is that each seed gets a better chance of germinating through having the protection of the paste. Germination should also be fairly even.

A slightly more sophisticated method of following this system is to use a syringe of the type made for icing cakes. Some doubt remains, though, whether these methods actually gain enough normal bare-seed sowing to justify the extra process.

When pre-germination (a useful technique for which is fully described below) is incorporated with the technique, there is definitely a useful bonus. Germination is achieved much more quickly, and is usually near 100 per cent. The secret is in the control of moisture and temperature during the short time the seeds take to sprout.

In other methods of sowing, one aim is to see that the temperature does not drop below a set minimum. Heated propagators are designed to achieve that, but they do not prevent fluctuations. Seeds sown in the open without any help may encounter substantial variations in temperature and moisture, which interrupt the effort to germinate.

The aim of a good pre-germination technique is to avoid both those fluctuations. A shallow box with a secure lid is needed for the first stage. (Suitable types of box are commonly used in home freezers.) A layer or two of soft tissue paper is laid in the bottom, and then a sheet of firm notepaper. Enough water is poured in to get all the paper thoroughly wet, and the surplus is poured off. Seeds are sprinkled onto the paper; care should be taken to ensure that they do not end up touching each other. Finally, the lid is put on securely to prevent moisture loss.

The box must then be placed in a constant temperature: if in doubt aim at between 15° and 18°C (60° and 65°F) — but the seed packet or the seed catalogue usually gives some indication. Avoid going too high, or the seed may be killed. One way of maintaining a constant temperature is to put the box in a closed room that receives no direct sunlight and is kept at a cool, steady temperature, both day and night. Tests with a maximum and minimum thermometer should establish the best position in the room for the required temperature.

If you are using an unheated room, such as a garage, you can use a heated propagator. If its thermostat is set for the minimum required, the fluctuations should be passably small, unless of course the room temperature itself rises above the figure set for the propagator.

Check the box at least once a day. Some of the seed may start sprouting in two or three

Pre-germinate seeds on a moist (but firm) surface in a suitable container (**top**) This usually takes a week.

The sprouted seeds can be sown in a 'carrier medium' of wallpaper paste (**above**) to give them a good start.

days; most of it should within a week. As soon as the seeds have made shoots 5mm (one fifth of an inch) long, put them into wallpaper paste mixed at half the strength normally used for wallpapering. The paste must not contain any fungicide.

A glass jug is useful in which to mix the paste, in that it shows how well the seed is distributed when put in. If the seeds fall straight to the bottom, the paste is too thin; if they float on the surface, it is too stiff. Correct as needed.

Some people wash the sprouted seed out of the box; others prefer to scrape it gently off the sheet of notepaper on which it has sprouted. Either way, it is at this point that it becomes apparent that had the seed been sprouted on the soft tissue it would have been difficult to get out at all.

For sowing outdoors, use the icing syringe or plastic bag in the way described. Temperature at this stage does not have to be normal sowing temperature but only what the plant needs when in growth.

If sowing is being done indoors in a seed tray or pot, the mixture can be poured straight from the jug. Always cover with a sprinkling of soil and keep this moist so that the paste does not set firm, or the seed sprout may not be able to push through.

It may take a week for green growth to appear through the surface.

Cuttings

Although seed-sowing is the only method of sexual propagation, there are various asexual or vegetative methods. Because seed (or the embryo in it) is a product of the union of male pollen and female ovule, illicit mating can occur when insects or winds bring in alien pollen. The progeny of such unions can be very different from what is required by the gardener and so, in seeking to reproduce any plant identically, it is necessary to practice vegetative propagation. Perhaps this is one reason that the rooting of stem cuttings comes second only to seed-sowing in popularity as a means of plant increase.

The three chief classes of stem cuttings are soft, half-ripe, and hard. Cuttings of the soft new shoots of spring quickly go limp when severed. Persuading them to root involves getting the cut to heal (callus) quickly, before the cutting collapses. The essential is to maintain temperature and keep the atmosphere moist to avoid water loss through the leaves. Commercial growers use mist (a constant fog of moisture) plus soil heating. A few keen amateurs do it with cuttings of fuchsia, chrysanthemum, dahlia, pelargonium, and two or three more favorites.

In general, however, amateurs wait for half-ripe cuttings, which are ready from late spring in the greenhouse to summer outdoors, and include both trees and shrubs. A suitable cutting should bend without snapping and straighten itself; 7.5 to 10cm (three or four inches) is a useful length. Trim to just below a node (a leaf-joint); remove leaves from the lower half; dip the end in a rooting powder; and insert the cutting into a pot to half its length in a half-sand half-peat mixture. Put a plastic bag over pot and cuttings, leaving a large volume of air space inside, and secure the bag to the pot with an elastic band. Keep it out of direct sunlight.

Hardwood cuttings are ready from late autumn and can be 15 to 20cm (six to eight inches) long; no pots are required — they can root in a cold frame. Trickle coarse sand into the hole for each cutting. Close the frame tight.

Many hardwood cuttings are taken in winter and set to root in open ground in a sheltered border. Some rose cuttings do extremely well this way if cut 25 to 30cm (10 to 12 inches) long. Make a slit with the spade, put plenty of coarse sand into the slit, and set each cutting two-thirds its own length in the slit. Make firm with your foot. Signs of rooting appear in mid spring, but the cutting should be left undisturbed until autumn.

Soft stem cuttings
Cut a non-flowering shoot just below a leaf-joint (**left**) and remove the lowest leaves. Dip the cut end in hormone rooting powder and plant firmly in a peat and sand cutting mix.

Hardwood cuttings
These need more patience. This hardwood cutting (**left**) has been stripped of most of its leaves before inserting in a cutting mix (**above**) with some sand added to improve drainage.

Heel cuttings
Taking a heel cutting (**left**) is a favorite technique for propagating half-ripe plant material. Pulling a side shoot away from the main stem produces a 'heel' at the base. Trim this slightly, remove the lower leaves and insert the cutting in a suitable mix.

Several cuttings can be taken from the same shoot (**left**). The tip can be used for propagation and the next section can be used to generate a new plant as well. With care it is possible to produce new plants from almost all garden subjects.

Root division

The simplest of all methods of propagating is by root division, which is practiced in every garden. It is not very productive, the object often being not so much to increase stock as to relieve overcrowded growth. On light sandy soil this division is better done in autumn; on heavy soil it is better done in spring.

A well-established herbaceous perennial plant when dug up and examined may be found to have become three or more plants clustered together. These can be pulled apart by hand and replanted separately. Sometimes the old root needs to be cut or chopped.

Iris germanica has thick rhizomatous roots which produce sucker shoots, and is easy to cut into separate plants. This is best done just after flowering finishes in early summer.

The dahlia has a tuberous root normally stored for the winter. Division can be made either at lifting time or at planting time, but must be done carefully. The dahlia root is not actually a tuber like the potato. Any root broken off dies unless it already has a shoot growing from it.

With bulbs and corms, 'dividing' the root, means removing some immature bulbs or corms and growing them on for two or three years until they attain flowering size. In gladioli, the corm dug up at the end of the season has clusters of tiny cormlets (like grains of rice) around the bases. With a tulip, you might find small bulbs around the base of the parent.

The simplest way to propagate dahlias is to cut the tuberous roots (**left**). Do this carefully with a clean sharp knife, ensuring that each divided section has a shoot arising from it. Cut the root either in the autumn before storing for the winter or in the spring just before planting.

Many herbaceous perennials grow from thick rhizomes — underground stems from which shoots arise. It is fairly easy to cut these (**left**) into separate pieces about 7.5cm (3in) long, each with an obvious growing point. Planted separately, these pieces should develop healthy new growth. It is wise to discard any old pieces of rhizome and only replant the youngest sections.

Taking root cuttings (**left**) is a fairly straightforward way of generating new plants for the garden. Herbaceous perennials and woody plants with thick fleshy roots are the best ones to try. Cut sections of root up to 15cm (6in) long and 12mm (½in) in diameter from lifted plants during autumn or winter. Trim the base of each piece with a sloping cut and insert them in a mix of peat, sand and loam with a layer of sand over the top. All being well, new shoots should appear in the spring. Cutting dahlia roots (**right**) needs a steady hand and a sharp clean blade for success.

Layering (**left**) is yet another technique for increasing garden plants. It is especially suitable for shrubby plants with low branches. It involves pegging down a shoot against the soil to encourage roots to develop. This process is aided by partly cutting through the stem at a leaf-joint.

Carnations are ideal subjects for layering. Select a vigorous side shoot and remove the lower leaves. Make a partial cut through the stem (**below**) at a leaf-joint so that a 'tongue' is formed that can be kept open while in contact with the soil. Roots will develop at this point on the stem.

Carefully bend the side shoot down and peg it firmly to the soil (**bottom**) so that the tongue cut in the stem is kept open. Dusting the cut with hormone rooting powder will speed the formation of roots. These should develop in about six weeks, when the new plant can be severed.

Layering

Layering is another easy method suited only to small-scale propagation. It involves pegging a branch to the ground, heaping soil over the pegged spot, and leaving it to form roots there. The new roots support the outer portion of stem, which ultimately can be severed from the parent and planted separately.

Before pegging down, a tongue is cut in the stem, and this cut is kept open with a matchstick to help it callus and make roots. Autumn is a good time for this, on suitable shrubby plants which have branches low enough and flexible enough. It may take between a year and 18 months before the new plant can be moved.

A few herbaceous plants have stems tough enough for layering (carnations, for example), but in the main herbaceous plants are better raised by division, cuttings or seed.

Air layering is a process of making a plant produce roots and shoots from an upright stem. It is not an easy method. A tongue is cut in the stem and part of the stem is encased in damp moss and sealed with polyethylene. The rubber plant *(Ficus robusta)* is a suitable indoor subject for this treatment.

Other methods

Some trees and shrubs send up shoots at points along their outstretched roots. These shoots, called 'suckers', can be dug up with a portion of root and transplanted.

Grafting and budding are popular with commercial growers and nurserymen. The aim is to give the subject a root system that influences its growth. Apples, for instance, may take ten to twenty years to mature and fruit, when grown on their own roots. But an apple stem grafted on to a dwarf subject makes a small tree that begins to fruit in only three or four years.

Budding is a form of grafting, using an eye (dormant growth point) instead of a whole shoot, and is popular with rose tree and apple tree raisers. It is economical because the portion of stem needed for one normal graft may have seven or more eyes, each capable of producing a tree.

GLOSSARY

Acid soil
Soil with little or no LIME, and a pH value of less than 6.5; *see also* ALKALINE/NEUTRAL soil.

Aerial root
Plant that sprouts from the stem of a plant above ground.

Aggregate
Either: sandy, gravelly soil; or: species very similar to the principal.

Alkaline soil
Soil containing chalk or limestone (calcium carbonate) and of a pH value higher than 7.5; *see also* ACID/NEUTRAL soil.

Alternate foliage
Single leaves on both sides of a stem; not OPPOSITE.

Annual
Living for only twelve months or less; *see also* BIENNIAL, PERENNIAL.

Anther
Part of the STAMEN of a flower, a sac bearing (male) pollen.

Bedding plant
Plant — generally a half-hardy annual — HARDENED OFF, then planted out.

Bicolored
Two-colored (of a petal).

Biennial
Growing from seed in one year, flowering — and dying — the next; *see also* ANNUAL, PERENNIAL.

Bloom
Either: coming into flower; or: powdery or waxy surface on plant.

Bract
Small organ comprising modified leaves below the flower; may be one or many.

Bulb
Organ comprising modified leaves that acts as underground food store and repository of embryo shoots; *see also* CORM, TUBER.

Calyx
Ring of SEPALS (either separate or fused into 'cap') around flower bud.

Carpel
Unified female elements of a flower: STIGMA, STYLES and ovary.

Catkins
Long 'tails' of densely-packed FLOWER-SPIKES hanging from a willow, hazel, etc.

Chlorophyll
Green pigment in plants, essential in the process of PHOTOSYNTHESIS.

Clone
Plant derived asexually, i.e., through vegetative propagation (e.g., cuttings).

Columnar tree
Tree shaped cylindrically at its base, then tapering to a narrow cone.

Cordate foliage
Heart-shaped leaves.

Corm
Organ similar to BULB, and with the same functions, but comprising a modified stem.

Corymb
Cluster of flowers on stalks (RACEME) which are progressively longer. so that the outer (or lower) ones open first.

Crown
Junction of a plant's root and stem.

Cultivar
*Culti*vated *var*iety of plant; mutated or hybrid form sustained only by cultivation.

Deciduous
Off which leaves fall in autumn; not evergreen.

Derris
Insecticide made from derris root, active ingredient rotatone; its toxicity is brief — dangerous near ponds.

Dioecious
Having either male or female flowers, but not both; *see also* MONOECIOUS.

Drupe
Fruit containing a seed large enough to be called a 'stone'.

Epicalyx
Secondary CALYX below actual calyx, but not comprising true SEPALS; common in roses.

Epiphyte
Plant growing on, but not feeding on, another plant.

F1 hybrid
First-generation cross-fertilization between two distinct (but related) species.

Fastigiate habit
Of which the branches tend to grow vertically, promoting a COLUMNAR shape.

Floret
Single flower in a flower HEAD.

Flower
The parts of a flower are: petals, SEPALS, STAMENS, STYLES, and occasionally additional organs.

Flowerhead
See HEAD.

Flower-spike
Cylindrical flower HEAD with flowers packed onto a single 'stalk'.

Genus
Group of related species.

Germination
Onset of growth in seed or spore.

Glabrous foliage
Smooth, hairless leaves.

Glaucous foliage
Leaves with a bluish, blue-gray or whitish blue sheen, generally also with powdery or waxy BLOOM.

Globose
Spheroidal

Grafting
Propagative method by which sliced lengths of stem of one species are attached to prepared stock of a related species in order to obtain flowers and fruit of the new plant on the base of the stock.

Habit
General shape of a tree, particularly with reference to the horizontality or verticality of its branches and the quality of its foliage.

Half-hardy
Resistant, but not impervious, to frosts in temperate climates; *see also* HARDY.

Hardening off
Accustoming a not-to-hardy plant to colder temperatures indoors before planting out of doors.

Hardy
Impervious to frosts in temperate climates.

Head
Group of flowers at the top of a single plant-stem.

Hips
False fruit, especially of roses.

Humus
Very rotten organic matter, excellent for improving soil composition.

Hybrid
Resultant species of a cross-fertilization between two (almost always related) species; denoted by *X* in Latin name.

Inflorescence
Flowering parts of a plant.

Lanceolate
Shaped like a spear-blade.

Lateral bud, shoot
Bud or shoot growing out from the side of the main stem.

Layering
Propagative method that makes use of the ability of some plants to root where a branch or trailing stem touches the ground.

Leaf cutting
All or part of a leaf used as a cutting; new

growths may emerge from tiny notches cut in the leaf veins.

Leaf spot
Discoloring fungal or bacterial leaf disease.

Lime
Calcium carbonate (or, rarely, oxide) as an element of ALKALINE soil.

Loam
Soil composition of sand, clay and HUMUS.

Lobe
'Peninsular' area of a leaf that has at least one indentation ('sinus'); *see also* MIDRIB.

Metaldehyde
Slug-killing agent in many preparations; harmful to birds and pets.

Midrib
Prominent vein down the center of a leaf; in a leaf with LOBES it may be branched.

Monoecious
Having both male and female flowers on the one plant; *see also* DIOECIOUS.

Nectar
Sugary secretion of flowers that attracts insects, particularly bees.

Neutral soil
Soil neither ACID nor ALKALINE, with a pH value of between 6.5 and 7.5.

Node
Junction of a plant's stem and leaf, or its stem and a LATERAL bud or shoot.

Opposite foliage
Pairs of leaves on both sides of a stem; not ALTERNATE.

Orbicular foliage
Almost circular leaves.

Osmosis
Liquid filtration process by which water percolates from soil into a root.

Ovate foliage
Egg-shaped leaves, of which the widest diameter is toward the stalk.

Palmate foliage
Leaves with deeply-incised spreading LOBES like the fingers on a hand.

Panicle
Form of INFLORESCENCE in which loose groups of flowers branch from a central stalk; *see also* RACEME.

Peat
Soil composition of non-rotting organic matter; it is almost always ACID.

Peduncle
Stalk of flower or fruit, especially of a single flower; *see also* PETIOLE.

Pendulous
A HABIT of tree, bush or shrub on which branches (and leaves) hang down; the classic example is the weeping willow.

Perennial
Living for more than two years, generally flowering every year; *see also* ANNUAL, and BIENNIAL.

Perfect
Having both male and female parts in a single flower.

Petals
Most colorful part of a flower, at the top above the SEPALS, and generally symmetrical around the sexual organs and the nectar.

Petiole
Stalk of leaf; *see also* PEDUNCLE.

pH value
Measure of whether soil is ACID or ALKALINE; a neutral value is 7; it is usually obtained through the use of a liquid or paper indicator.

Photosynthesis
Process by which a plant derives energy from light, facilitated by the presence of CHLOROPHYLL.

Phototropism
Growing of a plant toward the light; *see also* PHOTOSYNTHESIS.

Pinnate foliage
Leaves comprising leaflets around a single PETIOLE.

Pollarding
Method of inducing vertical growth in trees by cutting off the lower branches.

Potbound
Condition of a potted plant of which the roots are cramped for space.

Pruning
Method of improving shape and condition of plants by careful cutting back at a specific time of the year.

Raceme
Form of INFLORESCENCE in which regular groups of flowers on individual stalks branch from a central stalk; *see also* PANICLE.

Rhizome
Type of CORM that grows horizontally. underground or along the soil surface.

Root ball
Condensed mass of roots seen when a potted plant is unpotted.

Runner
Shoot from the main stem that roots where it touches the ground; this property is utilized in LAYERING.

Sepals
Modified leaves that form a cup-like base for a flower's PETALS.

Serrate foliage
Jagged, toothed leaves.

Sessile
Attached directly. without a stalk.

Species plant
Uncultivated original plant, as opposed to related cultivated species.

Spike
See FLOWER SPIKE.

Sport
Mutant HYBRID appearing unexpectedly.

Stamens
Flower's male organs, comprising fine filaments, an ANTHER on each, usually sited in a ring around the (female) STYLES.

Stigma
Tip of each (female) STYLE that is receptive to (male) pollen.

Stolon
See RUNNER.

Styles
Flower's female organs, comprising fine filaments each extending from an ovary and ending in a STIGMA, usually sited at the center of the flower.

Sucker
Shoot that grows up from a stem or root underground.

Tap root
Plant's main root.

Tomentose foliage
Furred or woolly leaves.

Trifoliate foliage
Leaves comprising three leaflets.

Tuber
Organ comprising swollen part of root that has the same functions as a BULB or CORM; some corms are known as tubers.

Umbel
Cluster of flowers of which the stalks all derive from a single point at the top of a stem.

Variegation
Contrasting coloration on individual leaves or petals, produced by genetic mutation or viral disease.

X
See hybrid.

INDEX

Q

R